TINY TOTS
in Tiaras and Tuxedos

THE LIFE, LOVE, AND
BUSINESS SUCCESS OF KERMIT B. HILL

FRANCENE MARY DIANE HILL

Published by Greater Ville Press

Library of Congress Control Number: 2025920465

Paperback 979-8-9998915-0-1
Hardback 979-8-9998915-1-8
eBook 979-8-9998915-2-5

TABLE OF CONTENTS

DEDICATION

This book is dedicated to my parents, Kermit Bland Hill and Augustus Hugh Hill Sr., whose love story, spanning five years of courtship and forty-two years of marriage, inspired this writing.

My mother served as my first and best role model, her boundless ambitions and irrepressible energy continuing well into her seventies. Through research for this project, I discovered many more of her incredible accomplishments after her passing on August 1, 1995.

My father's easy smile revealed the love he shared for his wife, children, grandchildren, and cousins. His love of family sparked the inspiration for organizing the William A. Thompson Family Reunion, named after his grandfather. Beginning in 1979, the biannual reunion continues today. Despite his leaving this earth in October 1983, I will forever be grateful for his quiet strength that provided me the independence to discover my own path.

FOREWORD

You know the saying "when something is too good to be true, it usually is." Well for me thinking back Tiny Tot Nursery School was "that good" and so much more!

Tiny Tot was the beginning of my educational journey toward academic excellence. Tiny Tot wasn't just a fun and caring pre-school for children but a place of high expectations that motivated you to be your best you. The intentional leadership and vision of Mrs. Kermit Hill helped pave my path and the foundation toward what I have achieved today!

When you're young your parents are your guides to what you do and don't do, most of the time. Since my mother, Mary Montgomery, served as President of Tiny Tot's Parents' Club and at the school all the time, I bene-fitted from what Tiny Tot offered beyond the classroom. My mother credits Mrs. Hill as her catalyst for leadership opportunities and her exact quote was "she had that inside skill to see what you could do and be." So, I remember as a student of Tiny Tot wanting to go to "big kids' school" not just because my mom was always there but being there meant you were going to be smart and learn important things. To a young child that's important to be exposed to what you could be.

Mrs. Hill would be there to greet you and hug you; she was always smiling and laughing. She had a BIG smile and laughed like she was al-ways happy, and I loved that! So, I liked going there to get her hug and see my friends; some of whom I'm close friends with today-personally and professionally.

Her motivation to start the school aligns with what I believe in for kids and learning-start early. Her work as a probation officer motivated her to influence children before they got into trouble. I truly believe and know my career in education and more importantly as a parent of three, it's vital and glaringly valuable to plant the seeds to be your best you as early as you can. Her smile embodied that every day.

The book
Tiny Tots in Tiaras and Tuxedos: The Life, Love, and Business Success of Kermit B. Hill is a true illustration of excellence, love, laughter & legacy and I'm a living testimony of that!

From a forever grateful Tiny Tot Alumnae,
Dr. Stacey Montgomery-Myton

PREFACE

In 1951, when most women are expected to remain homemakers, Kermit Bland Hill makes a decision that challenges both her husband's expectations and society's limitations. What begins as a personal dilemma in a St. Louis home evolves into something far more significant—a story that illuminates an overlooked chapter of American entrepreneurship.

Tiny Tots in Tiaras and Tuxedos reveals how a young African American woman from segregated Little Rock, Arkansas, navigates the complex terrain of marriage, motherhood, and ambition in mid-20th-century America. Born in 1919, Kermit possesses an unusual combination of compassion and business acumen that serves her well as she faces the constraints of her era.

Kermit's early career as a probation officer working with troubled youth sparks insights that prove invaluable in unexpected ways. When circumstances force her to choose between financial security and family expectations, her solution is characteristically innovative—and ultimately impacts thousands of families throughout the baby boom era.

This creative biography, written in Kermit's own voice, draws from her remarkably preserved correspondence spanning 1940 to 1995. Her letters offer historians a rare window into the daily realities of this transformative period, complete with specific dates, cultural references, and personal observations that bring the era to vivid life. Several chapters incorporate Kermit's original writings, capturing not only her strategic thinking but also her interactions with the diverse individuals who shape her journey.

The story unfolds against the backdrop of World War II, the Great Migration, and the emerging Civil Rights movement, offering readers a first-person perspective on African American entrepreneurship during a time when such opportunities are severely limited. Professional photographs document Kermit's innovative approach to building self-confidence in young Black children, while her business records—now permanently archived in the St. Louis Public Library—provide concrete evidence of her remarkable achievements.

How does a woman transform personal constraints into community impact? Kermit's story provides answers that resonate far beyond her era, offering insights into resilience, innovation, and the power of seeing opportunity where others see only obstacles.

ABOUT THE AUTHOR

Francene Mary Diane Hill brings unique qualifications to this biographical work as both Kermit Hill's daughter and a trained researcher with advanced degrees in Psychology (B.A., Smith College) and Human and Family Studies (M.S., Penn State University). After retiring in 2019 from a thirty-year career with Montgomery County Government, Francene has dedicated herself to preserving her mother's entrepreneurial legacy.

As the youngest of four children, Francene grew up immersed in the daily operations of Tiny Tot School, which initially operated from the first floor of their St. Louis home. She and her siblings—Hugh Alan Hill, Dr. Augustus Hugh Hill Jr., and Patrice Smith—worked in every capacity from classroom assistant to camp counselor, eventually serving as board members and directors. This first-hand experience provides Francene with unparalleled insight into both the family dynamics and business operations that shaped her mother's remarkable sixty-year career.

Francene Mary Diane Hill,
Author and daughter of Kermit B. Hill

Tiny Tots in Tiaras and Tuxedos represents Francene's literary debut, though she has since performed at The Moth StorySLAM, contributed freelance articles to AARP, and participated in various writing groups. The book serves as both family tribute and historical documentation of African American women's entrepreneurship before the civil rights era, making it valuable for entrepreneurs, historians, sociologists, and educational professionals.

Francene lives in Silver Spring, Maryland, near her son Keith, with whom she enjoys art, travel, and recreational activities. She continues researching family history while developing her writing career.

ACKNOWLEDGMENTS

This biography would not exist without the generous support of family, friends, and fellow researchers who shared their memories and resources.

My deepest gratitude goes to my son, Keith Hill, who graciously shared his mother's attention with this demanding project. Your patience and encouragement sustained me throughout this journey.

My older brothers, Hugh Alan Hill and Dr. Augustus Hugh Hill Jr.—Tiny Tot School's very first students—provided invaluable perspectives on our family's early years and the business' founding decade. Their memories helped reconstruct the era before my birth and illuminated our parents' pioneering vision.

Two women proved instrumental in capturing my mother's complete story. My mother's first cousin, Cora Mae McCastle, shared childhood memories from their upbringing in Little Rock, Arkansas. My godmother, Geraldine Williams, who first met my mother upon her arrival in St. Louis in 1946, provided a sisterly perspective from their long friendship, which lasted close to fifty years until my mother's passing.

Tiny Tot alumni and staff generously contributed photographs and memorabilia that bring this story to life: Susan Chapman, Vicki Chapman, Rhonda Williams, Cynthia Bosley Head, Stacy Montgomery-Myton, Carla McHaynes Johnson, Jefferalean Nelson, and many others whose contributions appear throughout these pages.

Finally, this research relied heavily on personal and institutional resources: the National Dunbar Alumni Association Historical Collection, the National Dunbar Alumni Association, St. Louis Library Black Family Business archives, Ancestry.com, and numerous other repositories that preserve our community's history. In addition, my newfound God sister and Dunbar alumnae, Linda Moore, shared numerous resources and contacts from Little Rock, Arkansas.

PROLOGUE

November 18, 1962

Kermit Hill unconsciously purses her lips—a habit she developed as a girl whenever deep in thought. This same expression strikes fear in her four children because it usually means their mother is trying to figure out how to punish them for whatever they just did wrong. Today, however, she searches for the source of an odd smell lingering in Turner Middle School's auditorium. *Floor wax? Dusty curtains?* The musty odor persists, but Kermit has no time to worry about it now. In just a few hours, over seventy preschoolers, accompanied by their families and friends, will be swept away by an enchanting performance as the theater magically transforms into a royal courtyard.

Tiny Tot Nursery School's King and Queen Coronation has outgrown its backyard space, so Kermit spends $88 to rent the neighborhood middle school for the annual Parent Teacher Association fundraiser. What began eleven years ago as a small daycare on the first floor of her North St. Louis home with only four neighborhood children and her two- and three-year-old sons has blossomed into something far greater. It was 1951 when her husband, irritated that her salary surpassed his own, insisted she quit her eight-year career with the Federal Government to become a stay-at-home mother. Undaunted, Kermit had the foresight and ingenuity to turn childcare into a thriving business. Over the next decade, Tiny Tot has become a successful solution for busy working mothers during the baby boom.

Now Kermit moves to the front of the stage in a belted, blush-pink dress, her jet-black hair softly framing her almond-colored face. She ticks off her mental checklist, pointing to each teacher to assign tasks.

"Go to the boys' locker room," she directs a petite woman in a white fitted dress. "Make sure seven child-sized tuxedos and bow ties are in place for the king's court." Before the coffee-skinned woman has a chance to move, Kermit adds, "Oh, and check if Mr. Hill's tuxedo and bow tie are there too. They should all be hanging next to the king's royal cloak."

She turns to the two-year-olds' teacher in a yellow print dress. "Take the feathered tiaras and the queen's crown off the stage and into the girls' locker room." The ebony-skinned woman quickly gathers the items and dashes behind the curtains.

Kermit's husband is expected from the florist any minute with bouquets and boutonnières for all the students and teachers. Their two daughters eagerly accompany him to enjoy the intoxicating aroma and colorful floral arrangements in the shop. When they return, their youngest daughter will join eight other flower girls in scattering rose petals before the queen's entrance. Like her brothers before her, their nine-year-old girl will act as herald alongside another boy to officially proclaim the start of the coronation program.

In about an hour, Rosebud Gaines, the local beauty salon owner, will arrive to curl and style all the girls' hair before the show. Kermit hopes the members of the queen's court remember to wear or bring their white dresses, lace ankle socks, and black patent leather shoes.

On stage, Kermit's now thirteen- and fourteen-year-old sons noisily push stacks of child-sized chairs toward the risers while teachers busily arrange them in neat rows.

"Stop dragging those chairs and pick them up," Kermit reprimands, raising her voice to be heard over the screeching furniture. "They'll leave scratch marks on the floor, and I'll lose my deposit. And don't—"

A creaking door and a loud bang echoing through the auditorium interrupt her. A tall man with a thin black mustache on his pale skin ambles in, lugging cameras, flashes, and tripods. Kermit had wisely trusted her instincts ten years ago when she hired a professional photographer to capture Tiny Tot's Tom Thumb Weddings, graduations, and other momentous occasions.

She greets him with a wave. "Good afternoon, Alan." She points to an older woman with cat eyeglasses tethered to a gold chain around her neck. "Miss Oliver, please show Mr. Lane where to set up."

A few hours later, Kermit signals the audio-visual staff, prompting them to dim the house lights. Static from the needle on the vinyl record crackles over the sound system, building anticipation in the crowd. Suddenly, the regal sound of a trumpeter pierces through the ensemble, heralding the beginning of the grand *Pomp and Circumstance Processional*.

In the beam of the spotlight, four-year-old Rhonda Williams gracefully glides down the center aisle in a white full-length ball gown, pausing after every step. Her three-year-old Lady-in-Waiting follows behind, carrying Rhonda's purple train in perfect synchronized step with the new Tiny Tot Queen.

After ascending the stairs, Her Royal Highness faces the audience, glowing in the blue, red, and yellow lights mounted on the stage floor. With a bouquet of white carnations clasped tightly in her hands, she bows her head, extends her arms, and sweeps her right foot behind her. Mesmerized onlookers watch as the child lowers her body until her forehead touches the ground, her stunning ivory gown billowing around her as though she floats on a cloud. With effortless grace, the four-year-old executes a move that would challenge even the most seasoned debutantes—a majestic presentation rehearsed with all the girls before anyone knew who would become queen.

Tiny Tot School Coronation – November 18, 1962
Queen Rhonda Williams

Enthusiastic cheers fill the air as the crowd leaps from their wooden stadium seats to applaud the queen's grand introduction. She pivots to approach last year's king and queen seated on the risers and elegantly repeats her ceremonial bow. The reigning queen takes the crown jewels from her head and carefully places them atop Rhonda's freshly curled hair, indicating the transfer of power. Tiny Tot's new queen ascends the throne next to recently crowned King Elvis Merrill, poised to preside over the midday festivities.

The audience is swept away by the extraordinary performance showcasing Black children in prestigious positions of nobility. Kermit watches from the wings, her heart swelling with pride and purpose. She reflects on the journey that brought her to this moment. It began in 1934, when she was a determined young woman navigating the halls of Paul Dunbar High School in Little Rock, Arkansas, with dreams bigger than anyone expected. She faced trials that tested her resolve and made choices that shaped not only her own destiny but also the lives of countless children who would one day find their voices on this very stage.

How did a teenage girl who grew up in the segregated South, facing limitations at every turn, create a world where young Black children could be kings and queens? The answer lies in the decades between then and now, in the small acts of defiance and large leaps of faith that transformed not just her life, but an entire community's vision of what was possible.

For six decades, generations of Tiny Tot children will carry out Kermit Hill's vision, gaining confidence by participating in a royal fairytale come true. But first, her story must be told—from the beginning.

High School Sweethearts

June 17, 1932 – Little Rock, Arkansas

With visible sweat stains darkening her yellow floral dress, Kermit rushes out of Gibbs Elementary as afternoon temperatures soar to ninety degrees. Even when she applies so much baby powder, with white dust showing through her slip and clothes, she no longer feels fresh by lunchtime. As she completes eighth grade, the changes in her body become impossible to ignore, especially in Arkansas' oppressive humidity.

Growing increasingly self-conscious, Kermit wonders, *Do I stink too?* After turning onto her block, she discreetly sticks her right hand into her damp armpit, takes a sniff, and then repeats the action with her other hand. Looking up with her left hand still at her nose, Kermit spots a boy from her class, staring right at her and grinning. Her heart sinks as she watches him mockingly stick his hand in his armpit, sniff it, then burst out laughing while pointing at her. Her face flushes as she runs away from the growing laughter behind her.

***

As the September sunrise filters through the kitchen curtains, the aroma of frying bacon fills Kermit's home at 3805 W. 18th Street. Her mother, Arvolin, arranges sizzling strips onto two plates, then scoops steaming scrambled eggs alongside them. She weaves through the chattering breakfast customers crowded onto her front porch and slides the dishes in front of a pair of uniformed workers.

***

Before opening her own place, Arvolin works as a laundress, washing and ironing clothes for white families. In 1929, she convinces her customers, Frances and Marion Lay, to hire her as an assistant cook at their restaurant, Lay's Café. The couple immigrated from Ireland before opening the café where Frances waitresses, and Marion struggles as both cook and manager. Within a year, Arvolin gets promoted to head cook, gaining valuable insights into the restaurant business. Two years ago, Arvolin transformed her front porch into a diner, catering to working-class Blacks who were banned from Little Rock's segregated establishments, including Lay's.

***

When Arvolin returns to the kitchen, she finds Kermit still washing the same oatmeal bowl in the sink. "Hurry up, it's time to go," she says, gently nudging her daughter.

Thirteen-year-old Kermit snaps out of her thoughts about starting high school. "Yes, Momma," she replies, quickly drying the dishes. After kissing her mother goodbye, she exchanges "Good morning" with the diners as she heads out the door.

With temperatures climbing into the eighties, Kermit walks a little over a mile, arriving at Little Rock High School with a tiny bead of sweat trailing down her back. After that embarrassing day in eighth grade, she convinced her mother she needed deodorant, and since then no longer worries as much about sweating. She stops to gaze at the two-block, six-story grand structure with its bell tower stretching toward the cloudless blue sky. Four cast stone statues are carved above three arched doorways, fitted with glass paneling.

Teenage boys in suits and ties and girls wearing dresses and pearls barely notice Kermit as they greet each other along the walkway. Though her outfit may not be as expensive as theirs, she feels pleased with her appearance as she smooths her white blouse and pleated navy skirt. The excited students file past the sparkling reflecting pool and ascend the symmetrical set of stairs into the brick building.

Just then, the clanging bell startles Kermit, signaling the start of the school day. With one more pat to her clothes, she gets to steppin', knowing the facility is for whites only, and she has another mile to go before reaching her high school for Negroes. She hurries down South Park Street, unable to imagine that in her lifetime, a handful of students who look like her will integrate in that same building. Twenty-four years later, the National Guard will escort The Little Rock Nine through an angry crowd of white residents as they yell, spit, and throw objects at the teenagers, in protest.

Paul Laurence Dunbar High School, named after the first African American poet, novelist, and playwright to gain worldwide recognition, was built three years before Kermit's arrival. Though the School Board funded Little Rock High School with $1.5 million, it contributed only $30,000 to Dunbar's $400,000 separate but equal construction. The Rosenwald Fund donated $67,000, while a whopping $303,000 was raised by the local community.

Kermit approaches the three-story building, keeping pace with her fellow students, similarly dressed to their white counterparts at Little Rock High School. In addition to offering general education, trade classes, and college preparatory courses, the facility houses Dunbar Junior College, where high school graduates can continue their higher education on-site.

Before classes begin, Kermit catches up with her cousin Kermit Jewel, who goes by "Jewel" to avoid confusion. Born just five months apart, the two grew up more like sisters than cousins, spending time together frequently at family gatherings since Kermit's mother and Jewel's father are siblings. Both girls' parents insist their freshman year at Dunbar is strictly devoted to their studies, delaying any extracurricular activities until the following year.

Once Kermit becomes a sophomore, she signs up for Dunbar's Monitor Club, patrolling the halls to maintain order between classes. As a junior, she meets Elihu Moore, who goes by Jimmy, while serving on the Monitor Club and Usher Board. That same year, Kermit and Jewel qualify for the Pep Squad, cheering the Dunbar Bearcats all the way to the state championship, while wearing waist-length purple and gold capes with matching hats.

Over the Christmas break, Arvolin reiterates her standard message about the importance of education. "You know our people have to work twice as hard to get half as far," she reminds her daughter. "Our family is counting on you to get that diploma, not be in every club out there."

To reassure her mother she can keep up with her schedule, Kermit stays up late after basketball games and rises early before Usher Board meetings to complete her outstanding Latin and Algebra lessons and Biology projects. Following Jewel's suggestion, she begins drinking strong black coffee to help her stay awake longer. However, in her junior year, Kermit discovers a new distraction: a handsome country boy who recently transferred to Dunbar High School.

***

As someone who grew up in Arkansas' largest city, Kermit is fascinated that Augustus was raised on an actual farm in Conway, Arkansas. Despite both having lost contact with their birth fathers, Augustus now lives with his mother and stepfather, Della and Elmer Woods, who married when he was twelve. Although Augustus turns eighteen in March, he transfers into Dunbar's junior class with Kermit.

The summer before their senior year, Arvolin finally allows Augustus to court Kermit when her daughter turns sixteen in July. On Saturday evenings after closing the café, Arvolin chaperones the couple in her living room. While the three listen to *Your Hit Parade* on the radio, Arvolin studies a Bible lesson, seated between Kermit and Augustus on the sofa. For several uncomfortable minutes, they silently sip sweet tea as the sun sinks toward the horizon.

Leaning forward to look past her mother, Kermit asks Augustus, "What song do you think will make number one this week?"

He tilts to meet her gaze. "Cheek to Cheek," he replies with a wink.

Kermit's cheeks flush as she responds, "I like that song. It won last week, too." Glancing at his black, wavy hair, she asks, "Do you get your hair conked?"

Augustus looks annoyed, replying, "No! Everyone thinks that. I have Indian blood on my mother's side."

"Oh," Kermit says, stroking her black shoulder-length curls. "I wish I had your good hair. It takes forever to have mine pressed and styled."

As their conversation lapses, Arvolin hums along to Guy Lombardo's orchestra playing in the background. Embarrassed by her mother, Kermit searches the room, desperate to keep Augustus entertained.

"Do you want to play Chinese checkers?" she asks, crossing to the closet.

"Okay," Augustus responds, joining her.

Kermit sets up the marbles on the star-shaped board while Augustus takes a seat across from her. They talk late into the night over their competitive game. During each lull in conversation, Kermit thinks of a new topic to break the silence.

"Last Saturday, I ran into Rosemary and Hershell shopping for shoes together."

"Did you hear Hardaway Peake is visiting California this summer?"

"I heard he's going with Helen Hogan."

When Arvolin nods off, Augustus quietly sits next to Kermit to sneak a kiss. The radio host announces the week's winning song with a loud flourish, startling Arvolin awake. "It's getting late, Augustus; time for you to go home."

***

When Kermit launches into her senior year, she revs up her extra-curricular activities, now singing with Jimmy in the Glee Club, while expertly juggling her homework, Pep Squad, Usher Board, and Monitor schedules. Augustus, uninterested in social groups, grows increasingly frustrated about constantly competing for her time.

On a rare Saturday evening when Kermit's calendar allows for a date, Augustus asks, "Why do you have to run around so much?" and "Why can't you just stay home sometimes?"

Thirty years later, Augustus still asks these same questions when Kermit serves on the National Boards of Jack and Jill of America, Annie Malone Children's Home, Top Ladies of Distinction, and Church of Christ Women's Auxiliary, while running her own business and raising four children.

In January 1936, Augustus graduates while Kermit finishes her senior year. He continues his education at Dunbar Junior College, allowing the couple to continue seeing one another on campus.

Two weeks before graduation, Jewel shares an advance copy of *The Bearcat* with her cousin and their friend Elsie May Whitlow. Kermit eagerly flips through the Senior Edition of the school's paper until she finds her senior picture and list of social clubs. Glancing at Jewel, they chuckle as they read aloud the passage they both selected for their senior quote: "Smile, and the world smiles with you; Weep and you weep alone." Elsie May searches the paper until she locates their names in the Class Roll under their motto "Out of the Past our Heritage; Into the Future Our Gift."

Jewel retrieves *The Bearcat* and turns to the "Class Will." The friends laugh as she reads what the student editors wrote about them:

"Know all men by these presents that I, the celebrated Senior Class of Dunbar High School, do hereby make my last will and testament.

Kermit leaves her talkativeness to Addie Pelton,

Elsie leaves her Unconcerned Ways to George Pennywitt, and

I leave my Filibustering to Bernice Whitmore."

***

On Thursday evening, May 28th, Dunbar's Class of 1936 parades into the auditorium in caps and gowns while the school band performs "God of Our Fathers." The graduates' muffled footsteps mingle with the ceremonial music filling the packed hall. Following the Invocation, Kermit and Jimmy join the Glee Club in their rendition of "De Gospel Train," their voices blending in celebration. Seniors then present historical skits and recite "The Achievements of the Negro in Arkansas," each presentation met with vigorous applause from proud families. With anxious anticipation, Kermit and her 107 classmates rise to receive their hard-earned diplomas from the School Board president. The commencement concludes as the seniors join the Glee Club one final time for a performance of "Nightfall in Granada," their voices carrying both triumph and farewell.

Paul Laurence Dunbar High School Class of 1936

After the ceremony, Kermit and Augustus celebrate at the graduation party sponsored by the High School Alumni Association. They enthusiastically join the gathering at Mount Temple, Lindy Hopping to the syncopated rhythms of Bill Holloway and his orchestra. The dance floor vibrates with energy as couples swing and spin beneath the overhead lights. As the band transitions to a romantic song, the couple embraces in a slow dance, the music enveloping them.

"I love you," Augustus whispers in Kermit's ear. Her face lights up as she holds him tighter, elated by his tender words. "Now that you've graduated, are you finally ready to get married?"

She squeezes his hand and leads him to a quiet spot away from the other dancers. Ever since his graduation in January, he has wanted to marry her. "You know how much I love you and want to be your wife," she begins, her voice full of emotion. "But we're not ready yet. I'm only sixteen and want to go to nursing school first. And you need your college degree to get a good job to take care of me and our family." Augustus kisses Kermit softly and agrees to wait until they are in a better position to marry.

***

That fall, Kermit joins Augustus at Paul Dunbar Junior College as he begins his second term. She studies Psychology, Biology, Public Speaking, and French—pursuing her dreams despite the barriers of segregation. Augustus graduates in January 1938, and Kermit earns her Social Sciences diploma that May.

She spends the summer working as a private secretary at the Y.M.C.A., then begins substitute teaching during the school year. Her strong secretarial skills soon lead to a position with Judge Scipio Jones, where she works as a stenographer—taking dictation and composing business letters. Impressed by her dedication and professionalism, the judge writes a glowing recommendation that helps her secure a role with the Colored Juvenile Court. In November, she becomes a Pulaski County Probation Officer. This work—shepherding young lives through a system stacked against them—marks the beginning of a lifelong commitment to children who have no one else to speak for them.

Meanwhile, Augustus enrolls at Prairie View State College in Texas to pursue a degree in Industrial Printing. His classes begin in January 1939, giving the high school sweethearts just one more month together before they face the challenges of a long-distance relationship.

Johnson's Juke Joint

December 28, 1939

K ermit and Augustus bridge the distance between Arkansas and Texas through frequent letters, exchanging news from their now separate lives. Augustus, deeply homesick, writes of the familiar faces and places he longs for in Little Rock. Kermit, restless from seeing the same people in the same town where she has lived all her life, expresses her yearning to be anywhere but the place Augustus wishes to return to. They reunite over the summer when he comes home after his first semester, but the time passes quickly. Soon, Augustus is back on the train to Prairie View, leaving Kermit lonely once again.

Three days after Christmas, daytime temperatures struggle to rise above freezing, hovering in the mid-thirties beneath overcast skies. With New Year's Eve approaching, Kermit's festive mood fades when Augustus writes that he cannot afford the train fare home for the holidays. An unexpected telegram from Hot Springs lifts her spirits. Her friend, Willie Irvin Stephenson, is passing through Little Rock that evening on her way back to college at Tennessee State. Eager to show Willie Irvin a good time, Kermit telephones her friend Velma Bright and her cousin Harold Courter to join them for a night of dancing at Johnson's Place.

As the friends head out for the evening, winter's frosty conditions worsen, dipping into the twenties. Bundled up in fur-collared coats, leather gloves, and wool hats, they dash inside the warmth of the juke joint. The stagnant air greets them, carrying the stench of cigarette smoke and stale beer. The sudden rush of frigid air escaping through the open door causes the red, green, and silver Christmas decorations to sway from the ceiling.

Peeling and faded tin signs advertising Regal Whiskey and Nehi beverages are nailed to the wood-paneled walls. Only a few patrons drink at the bar, leaving most of the wooden tables and cushioned booths empty.

Harold collects the three women's coats and hangs them by the door alongside his fedora. His wool navy suit accentuates his broad shoulders, while his red tie and pocket square reveal his attention to style. After taking their drink orders, he crosses the deserted wooden dance floor to summon the bartender, who appears to have abandoned his post on this slow night. Kermit's burgundy dress features a sweetheart neckline that complements her warm brown complexion. She scans the dimly lit establishment, waiting for her eyes to adjust. Shoulder-length chestnut waves brush against the white collar of statuesque Velma's black fitted dress, which is cinched at the waist with a white belt.

Glancing at her friends, Willie Irvin tugs at her black sweater vest over her white blouse and plaid skirt. "Am I dressed okay?" she whispers to Kermit.

"You're fine," Kermit reassures her. "People come here dressed all kinds of ways." As the women decide where to sit, she points out how much the place has changed since her last visit with Augustus. "They really have it fixed cute in here now!" she says, scooting across the red vinyl cushion. "Each booth has a box with a list of the records on the vendor!" Willie Irvin and Velma sit across the booth from Kermit as she continues, "We can sit right here and play whatever you want to hear without moving." Kermit fishes in her coin purse and retrieves a nickel, dropping it into the perfectly sized slot. "The first song's on me."

Willie Irvin eagerly flips through the plastic music pages, her delicate fingers moving quickly through the selections. Harold returns with a drink in each hand, his complexion matching the dark caramel color of the colas. After placing them in front of Kermit and Velma, he says, "I'm going back for the other two." Turning to leave, he adds, "Willie Irvin, pick out a good song so we can dance."

As if by magic, "Flying Home" starts playing from the jukebox next to the bar while Harold retrieves the remaining drinks. The brassy notes fill the room with energy; their upbeat tempo makes feet tap and shoulders sway. As the song continues, the four friends take turns picking popular tunes. Over the next hour, they dance and catch up with some former Dunbar classmates who drift in, exchanging news about their college life and families. Unfortunately, not many people are out on Thursday nights. Kermit sees her friends becoming restless from their frequent glances toward the nearly empty dance floor.

As more patrons abandon the club, she suggests, "How about we go play Bid Whist? We can borrow W.C.'s cards and folding table and play at my house."

An hour later, the four friends hunch around the card table in Kermit's living room. Occasional snores drift down the hall from her mother, Arvolin's bedroom. Fierce winds rattle the windowpanes and doors, whistling through the smallest cracks. Burning wood crackles from the fireplace, filling the home with a rich hickory aroma. Harold drapes his suit jacket across the back of his chair while the women discard their shoes under the table. When Harold and Velma win a round, Velma deals as Kermit eyes her disappointing hand. Sinking into her chair, Kermit raises her eyebrows at her partner, Willie Irvin, trying to signal not to overbid.

Following Kermit's gaze, Harold chuckles, "Girl, you ain't slick. I see you!"

Kermit rolls her eyes and sighs as Willie Irvin once again bids for more books than they can score. After winning another round, Velma deftly shuffles the deck, each card snapping into place and fluttering rhythmically between her red-polished fingernails. She tries to stifle a yawn, blinking her heavy eyelids to stay awake. "My goodness, it's one o'clock!" she exclaims, squinting at her watch. "I've got to go to work in the morning."

"Me too!" Harold and Kermit chuckle in unison.

"But we're not ready for bed yet," Harold adds as Kermit and Willie Irvin nod in agreement.

After putting away the cards and folding up the table, the women slip on their shoes as Harold buttons his jacket. They brace for the below-freezing temperatures of the early morning, tightly wrapping themselves in their winter attire. Harold carries the table to his trunk as the women pile into his car, shivering until the engine warms enough to provide heat. They drop Velma off at home before stopping at W.C.'s to return his playing cards and table. When they arrive, W.C. pulls in behind their car and gets out to greet them, his coat collar turned up to block the cold. Harold rolls down the driver's side window a crack to keep in the heat.

"I just got off work," W.C. says, his warm breath forming clouds in the frosty air. "Let's go to Johnson's."

Kermit looks at Willie Irvin and Harold, who merely shrug. "Why not?" she chuckles.

W.C. squeezes into the back, his long legs cramping against the driver's seat. Throughout the entire car ride, W.C. captivates them with funny stories of impossible situations, his booming voice resonating throughout the vehicle. He shamelessly flirts with the women, even though he knows Kermit's devotion to Augustus. As they approach Johnson's, W.C. insists that Harold let them out at the entrance. He rushes out to politely open the women's doors. While Harold parks, W.C. escorts them inside, with Kermit and Willie Irvin on each arm.

When they enter, the place pulses with life, the festive atmosphere a stark contrast to the deserted club they left a few hours ago. Swing music reverberates across the dance floor as bodies move freely in unbridled joy. Jubilant laughter and lively conversation abound at the packed bar and booths. W.C. directs them to the juke joint's private dining room, pausing as the bartender and regulars enthusiastically welcome the charismatic man's return.

Sensual blues notes filter into the smoke-filled back room, as couples slow drag in the center of the worn hardwood floor. Tastefully arranged tables line the walls. Spectators gather around a boisterous game of cards, its burgundy tablecloth splattered with money, filled ashtrays, flasks, and glasses of whisky. The four players' suit jackets hang haphazardly behind their chairs, their suspenders visible with shirt sleeves rolled to their elbows. With a cigar tightly gripped between his teeth, W.C. gracefully works the crowd in his gold zoot suit. When Kermit sees Harold arrive, she waves him over to their table, decorated with a red imitation rose in a bud vase.

After the bartender takes their orders, W.C. grins slyly, watching Kermit for a reaction. "I got a letter from Augustus last week," he says smoothly.

Kermit turns her attention to him, her heart skipping with excitement. "Oh? What did he say?"

"He said you write him twice a week. Said he doesn't have time to be bothered with answering all those letters."

Kermit feels her cheeks flush with anger and averts her gaze. Her hands clench in her lap as she tries to regain composure. She responds in a slow singsong, "Really?" eliciting laughter from the group. Inside, though, she seethes. *Wait until I write Augustus! He has some nerve saying I write him too much!* "Let's dance!" she blurts out to divert attention away from her embarrassment.

Everyone gets up and swings to the blaring music on the jukebox, their bodies moving in rhythm with the jazz beat. When they return, Willie Irvin spots her ex-boyfriend Carl Elston across the room, his lean frame easily recognizable even in the dim light. The two dated at Tennessee State until their lovers' quarrel before the winter break. When Carl sees her, he grins broadly and heads their way, dodging wildly gesturing dancers. Willie Irvin gets up quickly to cut him off before he can embarrass her in front of her friends.

"Hi sweetheart," Carl purrs sweetly, but loud enough for everyone at the table to overhear. "I didn't know you'd be here! I'm sorry, baby, I really miss you. Please take me back."

Willie Irvin goes silent, her expression guarded as she simply shakes her head before turning away. She returns to her seat, her eyes darting occasionally to where Carl stands watching her. Finally, she nudges Kermit. "What do you think?" she whispers. "Should I give Carl another chance?"

Kermit hesitates to give relationship advice to her young friend, who may blame her if things end poorly. "I'd rather you find out for yourself since you'll be away at school together," she offers, trying to stay neutral. Then, after giving it more thought, she cautions, "But please don't get too serious with him."

Willie Irvin nods as she considers her friend's advice. Then she remembers some gossip about another romance brewing at her college. "Remember Walter Reddick?" she asks, then charges ahead, not waiting for a response. "Well, he went to Tennessee State over Thanksgiving to visit his girlfriend, Bessie Irene. Even though she knew he was coming that evening, Bessie Irene went out with a guy she'd been dating at school. When they got back, Walter was sitting there waiting for her. That's when she told him she'd changed her mind about marrying him! Can you believe that?"

"Oh, poor Walter!" Kermit moans, thinking about how hurt and humiliated Walter must feel. She wonders if the same thing could happen if she visits Augustus at Prairie View. *Is it possible Gus has found someone else at college and changed his mind about marrying me?*

Cab Calloway's Orchestra's "(Hep-Hep) The Jumpin' Jive" blares from the jukebox, momentarily distracting Kermit from her thoughts. The vibrant rhythm draws everyone from their tables as they scramble to find space to jitterbug across the dance floor. W.C. twirls her in dizzying spins, his feet moving in perfect step with hers. Harold and Willie Irvin join them, and soon all four are swept up in the joyful celebration of the holidays. Their energetic dancing continues well past two-thirty in the morning. The rising body heat fogs the juke joint's tiny windows with condensation.

As the song winds down, Willie Irvin glances at her wristwatch. "I've got to get to the station," she gasps with widening eyes. "My train leaves in twenty minutes." The five friends swiftly gather their belongings, exchanging "Happy New Year" wishes as they dash into the biting cold. Slipping on the icy sidewalk, they pile into the car.

With merely minutes to spare, Harold pulls into the Union Station lot on Markham Street as hues of violet and navy blend along the eastern horizon. Quickly stepping out of the car in the brisk, twenty-degree temperature, Kermit tightly hugs her friend goodbye while Harold retrieves her luggage from the trunk. Willie Irvin grabs her bags and rushes to the "Coloreds Only" platform, where she sees Carl waiting for her and grinning. He takes her belongings and graciously offers his hand. She boards the train and the two return to Tennessee State together.

Driving along the deserted Little Rock streets, Harold peers through the snowflake-shaped frost stretching across his windshield. Kermit and her cousin chuckle at W.C.'s snores, breaking the peaceful silence of the early morning. When Harold drops her at home, she thanks him and bounds up the stairs, quickly rushing inside.

By the time Kermit finally crawls into bed, she tosses restlessly, her mind paralyzed with doubts. She replays the troubled college romances Willie Irvin shared, comparing them to her own. *Maybe I should take my own advice and not get too serious with Gus while he's away at Prairie View. If I had only agreed to marry him when he asked, I wouldn't be in this situation.*

As dawn peeks around her window curtain, a wide-awake Kermit decides to make some New Year's Resolutions: one, stop moping around missing Gus; two, spend more time having fun; and three, be open to new possibilities in 1940.

Kermit winces as the shrill of her alarm echoes off the walls. She opens her bloodshot eyes before reluctantly throwing back the warm covers to start a new day at the Pulaski County Probation Office.

ICE BREAK

January 19, 1940

Little Rock's cold spell blasts daytime temperatures into the twenties for the second day in a row, and predictions indicate the mercury will dip even lower after sundown. Kermit bursts through the doors of Lena Jordan Hospital from the crisp, frigid air. The sterile smell of antiseptic mixed with harsh bleach greets her, bringing back memories of previous visits. As a member of her church's hospitality committee, she regularly volunteers to see hospitalized members on the sick and shut-in list. However, no matter how many times Kermit visits, she can never decipher the hospital's layout and always ends up asking for directions. Now, in her current state of shock, she feels even more disoriented as she stands in the entryway facing the chaos of the twenty-bed medical facility.

Fighting back tears, Kermit approaches a passing nurse dressed completely in white, from her starched hat to her stockings and Oxford lace-ups. "Excuse me, I am looking for my mother, Arvolin Bland," she says, hearing the panic rising in her voice. "She fell on the ice, and they told me they brought her here."

In silent footsteps, the nurse leads Kermit down a corridor lined with moaning and coughing children and adults. Several are wrapped in makeshift bandages, while others slump forward with their heads between their legs. A few offer the nurse eager glances, hoping she is there to assist them. When she passes by, the patients collapse back into their melancholy positions and resume their cries of distress.

Kermit and her escort arrive in another section of the facility, stationed by a nurse with a red cross sewn on her starched white hat. After the two nurses confer, the second one rises and waves Kermit over.

"I'm so sorry, honey," she begins, lightly touching Kermit's shoulder. "Mrs. Bland, your mother, had quite a bad spill today. She's suffered a broken leg and can't walk – right now anyway. It's going to take a while for her bones to heal."

Kermit feels tears falling down her cheeks and starts searching for a handkerchief in her purse. The nurse instinctively hands her the industrial-sized blue and white Kleenex box from her desk before continuing. Kermit yanks three white tissues in rapid succession, holding them to her eyes to absorb the flow of tears before they reach her cheeks.

"Your mother also contracted influenza, the flu, while she was out there in this freezing weather, unable to get up. You know how cold it's been today, and just imagine, she was out there in just a dress! Poor thing could've froze to death."

"Can I see her?" she sobs, covering her mouth to muffle the sound.

"Yes, of course, dear. She's been asking about you," the nurse says. "This way." She leads Kermit down a different hallway. "Just know, dear, she's in pretty bad shape."

Even with the nurse's warning, Kermit is stunned when she sees her mother's frail and diminished body, crumpled in the hospital bed. Suspended by a sling and encased in plaster, Arvolin's right leg awkwardly hangs above the mattress while the left is draped by a white blanket. Loose strands of her graying braids stray over her ashen face as she props against two thin pillows. Kermit rushes to her mother's bedside and gives her an awkward hug, careful not to disturb the tubes and wires connected to her arms.

"Oh, baby. Don't cry," Arvolin soothes, her hoarse voice competing with the loud rhythmic sounds from the medical devices.

"Momma, what happened?" Kermit asks, delicately caressing Arvolin's cheek. She scans her mother's injuries, trying to interpret the medical leads and whirling equipment surrounding her.

"Was taking out the trash from the café, same as every day." Arvolin clears her throat, attempting to increase her voice's volume. "Must've been some ice out there 'cause my feet just slid from under me."

"I'm so sorry." Kermit dabs fresh tears filling the corners of her eyes.

"I hit the ground and heard my bone break. Hurt something awful. Couldn't get up so just laid there, no coat, no nothing," Arvolin croaks softly. "Thank God Mr. Craig came looking for me."

"You must've caught your death of cold! It's freezing out there!" Kermit sobs, her words catching in her throat. "Are you hurting?"

"Oh, you know, it's not so bad now," Arvolin responds meekly. She starts to adjust her position, then winces in pain, tightly gripping the blanket.

The nurse crosses to the foot of the bed and reviews Arvolin's medical chart. "Your mother is going to need to stay in the hospital for at least a week. She's going to need antibiotics for the influenza. Plus, we need to monitor her broken leg." She glances between Arvolin and Kermit, pausing for questions before proceeding. "Mrs. Bland has been talking about getting back to her café, but that's just not going to be possible in her condition. How's she going to work when she can't even walk right now? I'm sorry, dear."

Kermit stands at her mother's bedside, too stunned to speak. She nods blankly as the nurse describes her mother's bleak condition. The nurse, noticing Kermit's lack of response, leaves to get the doctor, who predicts an even bleaker diagnosis.

"Your mother is fifty-one years old, and it is very difficult for an elderly woman to recover from a broken leg," the doctor states flatly, pushing his spectacles back up the bridge of his nose. "She also contracted a bad case of influenza, which puts a strain on her lungs and may even develop into more serious complications. She is going to require a lot of help if she survives and is able to be released from the hospital. You need to prepare for all possible outcomes."

Kermit nods at the doctor as he turns and leaves without waiting for a response. She glances down at her now sleeping mother as her mind races. *What am I going to do? How am I going to work and take care of Momma?* She stays at Arvolin's bedside, adjusting pillows, getting her water, and assisting the nurses as she suffers through a painful evening. At the end of visiting hours, the nurse ushers a numb and exhausted Kermit out of her mother's room.

In frigid, below-zero temperatures, Kermit arrives home for the first time without her mother to greet her. The unsettling quiet overwhelms her as she moves through the empty rooms, pausing at the back door to see where her mother fell. Grabbing the salt box from the kitchen cabinet, she steps outside and sprinkles salt on the icy pathway, quickly returning inside to escape the bitter cold. Before going to sleep, she kneels next to the bed she shares with Arvolin and prays for God's guidance and protection over her mother in her time of need.

***

Little Rock's cold spell holds steady in the twenties, and Kermit stands vigil at her mother's bedside after work. She prays vigorously for God's mercy as Arvolin drifts in and out of consciousness. To cope with mounting medical and household expenses, she takes on extra clerical work at an insurance office in the same building as her night shift job as an elevator operator. Even while running back and forth between the probation office and two part-time jobs, Kermit always finds time to stop by the hospital to check on her mother's progress.

Five days after being admitted, Arvolin's condition worsens, and Kermit arrives at the hospital to find a new protocol in place. Now encased in a plastic tent and connected to an additional monitor, her mother lies comatose while the hospital workers wear protective facial masks and gloves. The inconsolable daughter rushes to her mother as the constant beeping of the monitors surrounds her.

"Momma!" an exasperated Kermit shrieks as she sees her mother's unresponsive body. "What happened? Is she dying?" she asks the worker on duty.

When the nurse turns to Kermit, her face briefly reveals a flash of panic before quickly recovering to a neutral expression. She retrieves the tissues from the bedside stand and offers them to Kermit, who takes them to wipe her tears. "I know it's difficult to see your mother like this," the worker begins, gently placing her hand on Kermit's shoulder. "Unfortunately, the influenza developed into pleurisy and pneumonia, which is highly contagious and caused her to go into a coma."

Kermit tosses the used tissues in the trash can before removing her gloves and shaking out of her tweed coat. Peering through the tent at her mother's motionless frame, she whispers, "Oh, Momma, open your eyes." She turns to the nurse and asks softly, "When will she wake back up?"

The worker glances at Arvolin, then clears her throat before responding. "We cannot predict when or... if she will come out of her coma. Right now, we're closely monitoring her condition and doing all we can."

Kermit releases a heavy breath, then pulls more tissues to dry her fresh tears.

"I'm sorry, dearie," the worker says. "It's in God's hands now."

Two days later, a miracle indeed does occur, and Arvolin awakens from her coma. Although still extremely weak and bedridden, her mother improves enough for the doctors to consider her discharge, provided she has sufficient assistance at home. Ten days after Arvolin's accident, Kermit arranges for the Women's Auxiliary to care for her disabled mother during the day but must find other arrangements in the evening. To avoid becoming infected herself, Kermit vacates their shared bedroom and moves to an uncomfortable chair bed in the only other room in the house.

As Kermit removes her clothes from the bedroom closet, she spots the nurse's uniform she bought as a Christmas present for herself. She spent the last three years carefully saving her money to pay for nursing school in the Fall. With Arvolin unable to bring in money from her café, the 20-year-old realizes she is now responsible for not only paying her mother's health expenses, but the mortgage and other household bills as well. Her dreams of becoming a nurse are now unattainable. With her clothes draped across her arm, Kermit closes the closet door, leaving the white uniform hanging on the rack. She slumps in her chair bed without bothering to hang up her clothes, feeling extremely despondent at the sudden change in her future.

Examinations and Expectations

February 5, 1940

I n the sterile examination room, Kermit sits mortified on the vinyl table, scarcely covered by a thin hospital gown that barely reaches her waist. The sharp scent of antiseptic stings her nostrils while overhead lights cast harsh shadows across white cabinets lined with gleaming medical instruments. Her dress lies neatly folded on the oak Windsor chair, her undergarments discreetly hidden beneath the fabric. Goosebumps rise on her exposed skin as she contemplates bolting for the door, but she forces herself to remain still, remembering why she must endure this humiliation.

The events leading to this moment began three nights ago when Arvolin's health took a dangerous turn. Kermit and the caregiver maintained a sleepless vigil, monitoring her mother's precarious condition. During a routine visit to collect clerical work from the district manager at Universal Life Insurance, Kermit finds herself confiding in Mr. Johnson about her mother's illness and her exhausting schedule juggling three jobs.

"It's admirable that you're working so hard to care for your mother," he remarks after listening to her describe her hectic schedule. "Have you ever considered how she would manage if, God forbid, something happened to you?"

The question strikes Kermit silent. Consumed by the demands of her multiple jobs, she has never considered what would happen if she could no longer support her mother.

Mr. Johnson continues, "Most twenty-year-olds don't think they need life insurance, but you're in a unique situation because you care for your mother. Life insurance provides you with peace of mind, knowing that your mother will receive financial support if, and again I say God forbid, you are no longer able to provide for her." The insurance agent sweetens the deal with a special discount as a favor to her, convincing the anxious daughter that she will easily qualify as a young, healthy candidate. Once Kermit completes a physical exam, she only needs to pay small monthly installments for the reassurance of covering her mother's future living expenses. Her boss schedules the appointment and even offers to take her after her shift at the Probation Office.

Now she waits, half-naked and uncertain, while someone on the other side of the door dictates a prescription to the nurse who escorted her to the room. A man with chestnut skin, black-rimmed glasses, a tweed gray suit, and a maroon bow tie enters, carrying a manila file.

"Good evening, I'm Dr. Oba White," he says, extending his hand. "You must be Miss Bland."

"Yes," Kermit says, self-consciously pulling the gown tighter.

"Oh, don't worry," he says, noticing her discomfort. "I won't bite," he chuckles. "You know why? Because you're too tough. When people get to your age, they get tough." He laughs harder, and Kermit joins him, feeling slightly more at ease. "Now let's see how you're doing." He removes the stethoscope from around his neck and inserts the tips in his ears. "This may be a little cold," the physician warns before placing the metal bell over Kermit's chest.

"Oh, it certainly is," Kermit squeals, recoiling slightly. The physician proceeds methodically, selecting different instruments to inspect her ears, probe inside her mouth, thump around her back, and tap her knees until her shins reflexively swing forward. He measures her height at 64¼ inches and records her weight at 123 pounds. Finally, he reaches for a glass container from the cabinet and looks at her apologetically.

"Ok, now the bad part is coming," Dr. White says, reaching for a glass beaker inside the cabinet. "You have to give me a urine sample."

Kermit's mouth drops open. "What? But I can't wet!"

The doctor's head falls back slightly as he releases a deep baritone laugh. "Well, I'm not going to need that much," he smiles, handing her the container. "Go on to the bathroom down the hall and give it a try."

At the conclusion of Kermit's physical examination, Dr. White assures her that she has successfully completed all the tests he administers, mentioning that her urinalysis results will be available in a few weeks. As Kermit gets dressed, he makes a brief stop by the now vacant waiting room to inform Mr. Johnson that she is in good health and eligible to purchase insurance.

Outside the medical facility, the waning crescent moon casts a faint glow over Mr. Johnson's royal blue Chrysler parked on the deserted street. Excited about the prospect of a substantial commission, he hands Kermit his car keys. "Here, in honor of your successful doctor's exam, I'm going to let you drive us back."

Eager to practice driving, Kermit jumps behind the wheel. Despite being her first time driving at night, she confidently starts the engine. During the ride home, she recounts every poke and prod, privately praying she never needs another physical exam again.

***

On days Kermit expects a letter from Augustus, she makes a beeline to the mailman the moment he sets foot inside the Colored Probation Office. By this point, she memorizes his usual arrival time and the sound of his black Postman Oxford shoes echoing down the basement stairs. She hopes Augustus remembers to send her letters to her work address, as she has reminded him repeatedly that the mail arrives much earlier at the Pulaski County Courthouse than the evening deliveries at her house. Last week, Kermit ended up empty-handed when she greeted the mailman. Today, however, he personally delivers an envelope with a Texas postmark in Augustus' familiar handwriting to her desk. Kermit is so engrossed in transcribing her juvenile court case that she completely loses track of time.

After thanking the courier, Kermit slides her stenographer pen under the envelope seal to open it. The letter reveals a homesick Augustus adjusting to his new life as a Prairie View freshman far away from home. Without wasting a moment, she begins her reply on a pale sheet of Pulaski County Juvenile Court stationery.

J. G. Burlingame, Judge   Lillian McDermott, Referee

JUVENILE COURT
PULASKI COUNTY
Little Rock, Arkansas

Old Court House
492 N. 2nd Street
Little Rock, Ark.

Darling:

Was so glad & relieved to hear from you. I expected another letter Friday or Saturday and was very much disappointed when I did not receive it. You have not missed me half as much as I have missed you. I have been blue ever since you left. I have not been anywhere all last week and stayed at home all day Saturday. Mother is really worse. Her influenza has developed into pleurisy & pneumonia and she is really having a bad time of it. We have had to set up at night for the last 3 nites. She was better yesterday but not much.

I really don't know how to advise you about staying down there because I will put too much of my personal feelings into it. Maybe after you have been there two or three weeks you will like it better. For your mother's sake I would advise you to stay there because it would disappoint her for you to return so quickly. I received a letter from Jewell Saturday and she ask about you. Your mother has called me twice to ask about you.

26

-4-

After he had examined me thoroughly he said the bad part was coming and I had to give a specimen of my urine. I told him I could not wet & he just fell out. but I finally managed to give him some of it. It was really funny since I had not had an examination like that in my life. Mr. Johnson let me to the driving on the way back & I really enjoyed it.

Write to me soon & be sweet, please think of me often and I am really lonesome for you.

I thought I would loose mother the latter part of last week but she is some better now. thank the Lord.

Be a sweet boy.

Love + ⌣ (Kisses) again

Yours forever
Kermit

2-5-1940 Kermit Bland letter to Augustus Hill

Two weeks later, Kermit is furious when February fourteenth comes and goes without receiving a Valentine's Day card from Augustus. Already insecure about competing with college girls, this fuels her suspicion that he has found someone new. On Sunday, Kermit spends the day feeding and caring for her mother as she continues to show positive signs of being on the mend. By five o'clock, loneliness drives her to visit her friend Jake and cousin Jewell.

After a few hours of chatting, Kermit suggests, "Hey, how about we go see that new film, *Honeymoon in Bali*? They're showing the Joe Louis/Arturo Godoy fight too."

"Girl, are you crazy?" Jewell laughs. "Do you know how cold it is outside?"

Jake agrees, "Plus it's even colder now that it's dark."

Three hours after arriving at her cousin's house, an undeterred Kermit ventures alone into the freezing sleet toward Lee Theatre. Navigating slippery sidewalks, she thinks that freezing outdoors beats the boredom of staying home with her mother. After purchasing a ticket to the evening feature, she climbs to the segregated balcony, stepping carefully over the sticky floor littered with spilled refreshments. She finds a seat with the best view of the screen, avoiding columns, speakers, and light fixtures that block most of the seats in the separate balcony.

When the house lights brighten the balcony at the end of the motion picture, Kermit recognizes former Dunbar classmates, Addie Muriel and Wesley, seated in the row behind her. The three friends discuss the romantic comedy that they just watched.

"I knew right away when Madeleine Carroll ran into Fred MacMurray, they were going to fall in love," Addie gushes dreamily.

"Oh, me too," Kermit and Wesley agree. The friends descend the narrow staircase into the lobby, jostling with other patrons exiting the theatre. Kermit shifts the conversation to the Joe Louis boxing match that preceded the feature. "What about that fight? Last week I listened to it on the radio with Lois Marie, Helen, and Stanley. But seeing them sparring on the screen was ridiculous! Godoy pawed and hugged Louis all 15 rounds."

"I know," Wesley moans. "Godoy wasn't even boxing!"

When the lobby lights dim, the three friends part ways. In no hurry to return to her monotonous home routine, Kermit walks slowly through the freezing rain. Arriving around ten-thirty, she finds her mother, whom she left in good spirits, crying inconsolably.

"What's wrong? Why are you crying?" Kermit asks, rushing to console her mother. "Are you hurting?"

Arvolin shakes her head, sobbing into her daughter's arms. "Where were you? I was so afraid something happened to you in this cold weather. It's so late, I was so worried about you."

Kermit's brow furrows as she tries to understand her mother's reaction. Arvolin has never worried about her going out late, whether alone or with friends.

"I'm fine, Mother," Kermit repeats, trying to calm her. "I just went to the motion pictures and saw Jewell. I'm okay." She holds her mother tightly as Arvolin continues sobbing, appearing frail and helpless. In that moment, Kermit fears she will remain trapped forever, unable to have a life of her own.

Rat Race and Rewards

March 1, 1940

On her way home from work at the Probation Office, Kermit boards a streetcar crowded with white high school students. Despite available seats in the white section of the trolley, two white boys occupy the last available bench in the cramped Colored section. Kermit recognizes Maggie Wells and another woman, who struggle to maintain their balance as the trolley jerks to the next stop. To prevent themselves from falling, the two women instinctively brace themselves against the back seat, both pressed uncomfortably close to the boys. Despite the open windows, the smell of sweat fills the narrow space.

"Lean on your own breakfast," one of the teens barks at them, meaning they should move over.

"Shut up!" Kermit reflexively yells, her voice cutting through the trolley's rumble.

Both boys' eyes widen in shock, their faces and necks revealing a reddish tint from embarrassment and rage. Quickly, their eyes narrow into slits, glaring at Kermit until the car reaches their stop. Tension heightens inside the streetcar as other passengers shift uncomfortably, anticipating a confrontation.

When the boys exit the trolley, Kermit quickly claims their window seat. As the streetcar lurches forward, one boy reaches through the open window, attempting to strike her. Kermit spits directly in his face before his hand can make contact. Gasps ripple through the car, followed by nervous laughter from other passengers. Despite a pang of guilt, she cannot deny her satisfaction.

The following Saturday, Kermit is due at work by seven-thirty to meet Mrs. Smith for a field visit. Eager for a chance to drive, she takes an earlier trolley, hoping to convince her supervisor to let her be the chauffeur. When she arrives at half-past seven, she sees Mrs. Smith already behind the wheel with the engine running, impatiently blowing the horn. Kermit slides quietly into the passenger seat as they drive five miles to College Station to collect a Pulaski County vehicle. Once again, Mrs. Smith claims the driver's seat before Kermit can object.

They travel north for twenty miles along unpaved roads that send dust clouds billowing in the streaks of early sunlight. The small farmhouse in Jacksonville sits weathered and isolated, its gray paint peeling from years of Arkansas weather. Kermit follows Mrs. Smith up the porch stairs as a woman in a green, flowered dress opens the screen door. An infant with warm caramel-toned skin sucks contentedly on a bottle in her arms.

"Y'all must be from the County," the woman says, adjusting the seven-month-old in her arms. "I'm gonna miss taking care of my niece's precious little one here. But I guess it's time his Momma take him now that she's out of Detention."

Kermit gingerly accepts the infant from the aunt, ensuring the bottle remains securely in his mouth. Carefully climbing into the passenger seat, she inhales the aroma of fresh talcum powder radiating from his tiny body. Mrs. Smith places his small bag of diapers, bottles, and blankets in the back seat before returning to her spot behind the wheel. During the forty-five-minute return trip to Little Rock, Kermit marvels at his miniature fingers and angelic features, her heart swelling with unexpected tenderness.

"You doing okay?" Mrs. Smith asks every few miles, glancing across the seat.

Kermit nods, fascinated by the tiny person content in her embrace.

"You're a natural with that baby, you know that?"

Kermit nods again, her thoughts spinning toward possibilities she rarely allows herself to consider. *Maybe Gus and I will have children of our own someday.*

By the time they deliver the infant to his mother and return the county car, evening shadows stretch across Little Rock's skyline. Around five o'clock, Mrs. Smith drops her off at home, where an exhausted Kermit goes straight to work – preparing dinner, eating with her mother, bathing Arvolin, and tucking her into bed. Finally alone in her chair bed, the memory of the sweet baby fills her with longing. Before sleep claims her, one thought echoes through her mind: *If only I'd said yes to Gus when he wanted to get married, we could've had our own babies by now!*

The following day, Sunday morning temperatures drop twenty degrees into the fifties as the outside conditions turn cold and dreary. Kermit wakes feeling as miserable as the weather, sliding under the covers to linger in bed a little longer. Eventually, she draws the curtains as the staccato rhythm of the rain and snow mixture taps against her window. Between caring for her mother and missing Augustus, her emotions constantly swing between crushing boredom and hopelessness. She moves to her desk, rolls paper into the typewriter, and begins striking keys with determination.

3-2-40
Dear Gus:

Was glad to receive your letter yesterday and was be-ginning to wonder why you did not write sooner. It seems to be you could answer my letters as soon as you receive them if you expect me to answer yours when I get them.

I am getting a little bit lonesome, and I don't go any-where, and no one comes to see me at all. I have been feeling bad for the last week or two. I really wish I could go to school next year because it is too lonesome staying here and you are gone away. I feel lonesome every day and night. I got so blue for a while mother thought I was pregnant, but I told her not to worry about anything like that right now anyway.

Write soon, There it is
Kermit

She applies fresh lipstick and presses her lips firmly against the paper to leave a red imprint. Augustus was thrilled when she randomly sealed her previous letter with a lipstick kiss, requesting she continue the practice. After waving the paper to dry the impression, she carefully folds it into an envelope for tomorrow's mail.

***

After putting away the dinner dishes on Tuesday evening, Kermit tunes in to the NBC Network for Fibber McGee and Molly, her weekly escape from Little Rock's suffocating routine. The real-life married couple, Jim and Marian Jordan, bring their vaudeville experience to the situation comedy, which never fails to lighten her spirits. She and her mother listen intently as Fibber describes opening his closet and an avalanche of junk tumbles out, emphasized by chaotic sounds of circus horns, metal springs, and loud crashes. Once the dust settles, a tiny bell rings, followed by Molly's signature quip, "Tain't funny, McGee!" Kermit and her mother roar with laughter along with the studio audience at the familiar punchline.

***

The following week, Kermit treats a group of children from the Detention Center to a special outing at the circus performing in the new auditorium. Afterwards, she stops by the Lee Theatre to catch another motion picture. Climbing the familiar stairs to the Colored section, she discovers a renovated balcony with carpeted floors and cushioned chairs. Despite the pleasant surprise, her mood remains unchanged. A wave of melancholy, tinged with anger, washes over her as she sits alone in the new seat. She loses herself in Cary Grant's performance in *His Girl Friday*, grateful for the distraction from her monotonous routine.

Caught up in her routine, the month of March flies by in a blur, *going out like a lamb* in warm eighty-four degrees, staying true to the adage. The following month passes just as quickly, with scattered showers promising May flowers. On the last day of April, spring storms arrive with fury, matching Kermit's increasingly turbulent mood. Lightning illuminates the rain-soaked courthouse courtyard as she peers through the Probation Office doorway after work. Four consecutive days of rain leave flooded streets and her patience tested. Thunder rolls overhead while she contemplates waiting out the storm at work or braving the deluge to go home. Approaching footsteps shuffle down the hall, announcing the security guard's arrival. He stops in the doorway beside her, launching into his predictable weather commentary.

"You know what?" he begins, never pausing for response. "My bad knee always aches when it's going to rain, but this time it was a lot worse, so I'm thinking the storm will be worse too."

"Uh-huh," she mumbles, desperately trying to mask her irritation. She tightly secures the black ties of her hair bonnet under her chin, then fastens the top buttons of her tan raincoat. "Well, I better head out. I need to get home to my mother."

Kermit's small white lie catches in her throat—the truth is too painful to admit. Ever since the night she returned home to find her mother sobbing uncontrollably, she has dreaded spending time in the house. Although she is approaching her twenty-first birthday, Arvolin continues to treat her like a child. Yet remaining any longer, listening to the security guard drone on, feels equally unbearable. She opens her umbrella and steps headfirst into the storm.

At the streetcar stop, Kermit quickly realizes that her rain gear is no match for the sheets of water hurled sideways by the intensifying wind. Flash flooding creates a winding river along the curb, overflowing the gutters. Cars speeding through foot-deep puddles splash her with great waves of water as they pass. When the trolley finally arrives, she climbs aboard with a deep sense of relief.

She greets the driver, breathless. "Am I glad to see you! Thought I was going to blow away!"

Her rubber boots squeak across the wooden floorboards, leaving a trail of water as she walks toward the back of the segregated car. Wind gusts rock the trolley, and rain hammers the windows with increasing violence.

"It's getting worse," Kermit says to the woman seated across from her, offering a faint smile. "I'm scared the trolley might not hold up."

The passenger only nods, eyes wide, nervously watching as tree branches and debris sail past the windows. As the streetcar nears her stop, Kermit purses her lips in a silent prayer for safe passage.

Her umbrella surrenders instantly to the wind, flipping inside out and vanishing into the darkness. She abandons all pretense, stumbling through ankle-deep puddles and over fallen limbs as the storm lashes against her. A bolt of lightning strikes a tree behind her, followed by a thunderous crack as she reaches the porch. Shivering, she rummages through her purse for her keys, her soaked clothing clinging to her skin.

Inside, she finds her mother crying once again in the living room.

"Praise the Lord! I was so worried about you," her mother sobs. "The radio bulletin just announced a tornado. I tried to call your office to warn you, but nobody answered."

"It was really scary on the streetcar," Kermit admits, trying to suppress her own rising panic. "But God protected me. I'm safe now." She crosses the room and embraces her mother. "So you can stop worrying, Momma. Please stop crying."

"I'm thankful too," her mother says through her tears. "Now get out of those wet clothes before you catch cold."

"Yes, Momma, that's what I'm about to do," she snaps, hearing the agitation in her voice.

She retreats to the solitude of her room to change, hoping to avoid another argument. A few moments later, she returns to the kitchen to prepare dinner, while the violent thunderstorm continues to rage around them. Once Kermit settles her mother into bed, she returns to her room and begins another letter to Augustus.

4-30-40
Dear Gus:

    Here I am blue again with nothing in the world to do. I wish you were here with me now, but I guess it will be better for you to stay in Prairie View this summer because we both may profit from it later on. I think it will be a wonderful idea for you to stay there this summer and let me come there and visit you when I get my vacation. I know your mother is going to throw a fit when she finds out you are thinking about staying there for the summer but coming here won't benefit her in the least because you will be an added expense on her.

Exhaustion overtakes her at the typewriter. The next morning at work, she continues her post. As she finishes her letter, an ominous thought takes hold: *I wonder if I am going to make any more out of my life than I already have.*

5-1-40

Well, I guess I am off on a spree again. I stay mad around here these days. I have to stay in this dry old office all day long every day and make a measly little sum of $40.00 per month. It is simply disgusting to me. I wish I could hit jackpot, I would really leave town and right away too.

I guess I would come down there first and stay awhile and then I would go on to Chicago and stay with Jewell for a while.

Is it that you don't want to come back and see me, or do you really want to work? You know it would not be wise for us to marry right away because you have to repay your mother for some of the things, she has sacrificed to give you.

I have really become disgusted with life in general.

I wonder if I am going to make any more out of my life than I already have. Guess you think this is the craziest letter you have ever read.

I have so much work to do and I simply don't see how I am going to finish it, but I just had to write this letter to you because I was feeling so low in spirit.

Boy I am so blue, I am singing the Good Morning Blues (smile). Wish you were here to pacify me.

You know you had better bring all your troubles to me. If I thought you were taking your troubles to someone else, I would have a fit.

Well be a sweet boy and write me soon.

Kermit

Summer Reunion

June 22, 1940

The first Saturday of summer arrives under partly sunny skies with temperatures reaching a balmy ninety degrees. At the train station, Kermit waits with Della and Elmer on the platform, her heart racing with anticipation. Augustus' train approaches, engulfing them in a billowing cloud of smoke, brakes squealing and steam hissing as it comes to rest. A rush of adrenaline surges through Kermit, who waves frantically and blows kisses, hoping to catch his attention.

Della pushes past her when Augustus appears in the doorway, determined to reach her son first. But Kermit wraps her arms around him from behind, planting a firm kiss on his cheek before he can escape.

"Hey, hey, I'm glad to see you too," Augustus says, slightly embarrassed at the public display of affection. He extends his hand toward his stepfather, who stands a few feet away from the women.

"Okay, you two, let him get some air," Elmer chuckles, taking a step closer to shake hands. "Good to see you made it home safely, son."

"I'm so glad you decided not to go to Tulsa this summer," Kermit says, unable to contain her relief. "Because I was going to have to find me another boyfriend if you did! I miss you too much."

"I missed you, too," Augustus grins, melting months of Kermit's accumulated loneliness.

Summer unfolds like one of Kermit's romantic motion pictures. Outside of work, the reunited couple spends every possible moment together. Because Arvolin loves listening to Augustus' college life adventures, he comes over daily to help Kermit care for her. They attend The Auditorium's formal dances, dressing their best and enjoying the evening's featured big band ensemble. For the first time in almost a year, Kermit no longer attends Lee

Theatre alone. She loses herself in the feature film, smooching and holding hands with her high school sweetheart. On weekends, the two play competitive cards late into the night, laughing and catching up with Dunbar classmates as a couple.

At Johnson's Place one evening, Kermit snuggles against Augustus' chest in their regular booth, watching couples jitterbug to the melodic riffs from the jukebox. She lovingly takes his hand, tracing his fingers before enclosing it between her palms.

"I'm so happy you're here with me," she says, her face radiating in a warm glow. "Little Rock is so dull and miserable without you." She squeezes his hand, then kisses his cheek, her lips brushing against the bristle of his prickly whiskers. "I can't wait until we get married."

Augustus studies her face, searching her eyes for sincerity. "Are you sure, Kermit?" he asks, his surprise evident. "I've wanted to get married since we graduated Dunbar."

"I know," Kermit responds clearly, her previous doubts gone. "I just wanted to make sure we have enough money to raise a family. That's why I want you to take that Civil Service Postal Exam, and I'm going to take the one for stenographer. I am getting pretty good at shorthand now."

"But you know I'm going to Prairie View for printing," Augustus objects. "I like it too, so why would I take an exam for the Post Office?"

"It doesn't hurt to put more than one iron in the fire," Kermit suggests, her practical nature coming through. "Even though you want to be a printer, you could still work as a mail carrier until you get on good footing and can establish a shop of your own."

Augustus raises his eyebrows at the suggestion, his lips part to speak, but only "huh" comes out. Before speaking, he scratches the itchy hairs sprouting on his cheek. "Huh, I'll think about it," he says. "But I still am getting my degree in printing."

Their remaining weeks together pass with the lightning speed of a summer storm. Too soon, the couple whispers their somber goodbyes on the departure platform, his parents hovering nearby. The chimes from the elevated clock tower ring majestically through Union Station, signaling Augustus to board. With one final kiss, Kermit fights back tears, waiting until the train disappears along the tracks to release them. As she climbs the exit stairs, Della catches a glimpse of her face in the parking lot.

"Now, Kermit, here I am trying to keep from crying, and your crying is making me cry too," she says. She fishes a handkerchief from her purse to dab her eyes. "Well, it's a good thing Augusta didn't see you crying, because he would've felt bad about leaving."

Following a whirlwind summer with Augustus in town, the thought of enduring an unknown amount of time without him crushes her spirit. Kermit removes her glove, using the back of her hand to wipe her flowing tears. Her attempt to compose herself fails as she bawls uncontrollably behind the wheel, as Della and Elmer exchange nervous glances. After composing herself, she starts the engine and takes Augustus' parents home.

Magnolia Runaways

January 30, 1941

As soon as Kermit spots the police car in front of the Pulaski County Juvenile Court building, her heart sinks. "Oh, what now?" she thinks. "The day hasn't even started yet!" Her plans of enjoying a slow workday to write Augustus slip away. Anytime law enforcement shows up first thing in the morning, it is a sure sign of trouble. After flashing her round picture ID pin to the security guard, she spots Mrs. Smith with a middle-aged white officer. His arms flail animatedly as he speaks, gesturing toward three boys piled on the hallway bench. When Mrs. Smith sees Kermit, she raises her hand, signaling him to pause his story.

"Excuse me," Mrs. Smith interrupts, waiting for Kermit to join them. "This is our Probation Officer, Miss Bland. Kermit, this is Patrol Officer Sanders from the North Little Rock Police."

After the two briefly shake hands, Officer Sanders continues his verbal report. "As I was telling Mrs. Smith, me and my partner picked up these three Negro boys at 0200 hours, walking unaccompanied down North Main Street. Following our interrogation at the station, they confessed to running away from home." He leans in conspiratorially, his pungent breath smelling of stale coffee and musky tobacco. "Now get this: they claim to live in Magnolia, Arkansas! Do you know how far they had to walk to get here?"

Kermit glances between Mrs. Smith and the patrol officer, then shakes her head.

Mrs. Smith's face conveys her exhaustion with his rambling story as she cuts in. "A hundred and fifty-one miles," she interrupts, redirecting her attention back to her staff. "Look, Kermit, I already told Officer Sanders we need to bring this to Mr. Mass for his take on how we should handle them."

She turns back to the patrol officer, "Please take these boys to our Detention Center next door while we meet with our C.P.O."

Quickly dropping off her jacket and purse in the office, Kermit catches up with her supervisor as she heads down the hall. They climb the stairs to a wooden-framed door with Chief Probation Officer stenciled on the glass. After two knocks from Mrs. Smith, a gruff voice instructs them to come in.

Smoke escapes into the hall as they enter the office, cluttered with letters, reports, and manila case files piled on the desk. Mr. Mass waves them in with a burning cigarette between his white, tobacco-stained fingers. To avoid the buildup of stale smoke, Kermit lingers by the open door while Mrs. Smith recounts the case of the runaway brothers from Magnolia. The C.P.O. listens intently, flicking his ashes into the overflowing trash pail. Taking another drag, he exhales a long stream of pale smoke before speaking.

"Why did they run away in the first place?" Mr. Mass asks, shifting his gaze between the two women.

"According to the patrol officer, the two oldest boys claim their father is mean to them," Mrs. Smith replies, passing him the police report. "Making them work on the farm instead of going to school, sometimes beating them when they talk back."

"He has the right to raise his kids however he wants," Mr. Mass declares, his words trailing with faint traces of smoke. "Lots of kids drop out to help on the farm, so that's not something we can get involved with either." He scans the report, flipping it to read the back page. "Although they're minors, they haven't committed any crime. We have no reason to keep them here," he continues, returning the report to Mrs. Smith. "You need to take them home today." The two women turn to leave as Mr. Mass adds, "And take Mrs. Tidwell with you in case these boys cause any trouble on the way."

Mrs. Smith nods and closes the door behind them. On their way downstairs, she studies the police report, silently reviewing its details. When they reach their office, she glances at Kermit. "Do you think Harold would mind driving us to Magnolia this afternoon?" she asks. "Could you call and see?"

"Okay, I'll check," Kermit says, moving behind her desk. "I don't think he works today, so it may work out."

"Make sure to tell him how much we appreciated him driving us week before last to take that pregnant girl to Prescott."

The switchboard operator patches Kermit through to her younger cousin, who frequently lets her drive his car. With no plans for the afternoon, Harold eagerly accepts the chance to explore the Arkansas countryside on a long car ride, especially since he has never visited Magnolia. As the temperature climbs to fifty-nine degrees, Harold arrives in his vineyard green Ford sedan, its chrome accents and V8 hood ornament sparkling in the midday sun. When he gets out to open the doors, Kermit immediately slides behind the banjo steering wheel, thrilled for another opportunity to drive.

"Let the two oldest boys get in between me and Mrs. Tidwell in the back," Mrs. Smith instructs. "That way, we'll be by the doors in case they try to run away again. The other brother can sit up front next to Kermit." As they pile onto the camel-toned cloth bench, Harold lets the boy in on the passenger side before getting in.

At one o'clock, Kermit expertly presses her left foot on the clutch and right foot on the brake before moving the floor-mounted shifter to drive out of the parking lot. She navigates the cramped vehicle through the afternoon traffic of commuters, weaving past streetcars and buses in the bustling downtown area. Heading southwest out of downtown Little Rock, the city noises slowly fade, giving way to the peaceful quiet of the countryside.

"But we don't want to go back," the oldest brother protests from the back, his voice cracking with emotion.

"Yeah, we walked all night to get here!" the boy between Kermit and Harold whines, his small arms crossed in anger. "You can't take us back now!"

Kermit's chest tightens with sympathy for the boys, wishing she could take them home with her. In the year since becoming a juvenile probation officer, her attachment to the children grows stronger every day. She smiles at the boy beside her. "Sorry, sweetheart, we have to take you back to your parents." The three brothers moan and slump in their seats, their shoulders sagging in defeat.

As they continue southwest past Fourche Creek, the motion of the car rocks the boys to sleep. Mrs. Tidwell leans forward and taps Harold's shoulder.

"We've been talking all week about how much fun we had at the Twenty-One Nighthawk's Dance," she says, her eyes brightening at the memory. "I've never seen anything that fancy in my life."

"And so many people all dressed up!" Mrs. Smith adds.

"Except for that man who wasn't wearing a full suit and got escorted to the balcony," Harold laughs.

"Oh, I forgot about that," Mrs. Smith chuckles. "Well, every dog and his day were at the Auditorium Friday night." She nudges Kermit playfully. "Even Kermit stopped worrying about Augustus long enough to enjoy herself."

"I did have a good time dancing," Kermit admits, a hint of a blush coloring her cheeks. "Even later on at Johnson's Place with Novelle, after we dropped you two at home. Thanks, Harold, for taking us."

"And for letting us use your car today," Mrs. Smith adds.

Following her seventy-mile trek, Kermit pulls into a gas station in Fordyce, Arkansas, and lets Harold take the wheel. While the service attendant cleans the windshield and checks the tire pressure, the weary passengers stretch their legs as Harold climbs into the driver's seat. Thirty miles past endless rows of dormant crops with sporadic faded red barns, they pass through Camden and turn off the paved road. Harold slows to forty-five miles per hour as the sedan's body lurches and rattles along the bumpy dirt terrain.

Around four o'clock, they pass through the small country town of Stephens, with another thirty miles to go. While the older women nap in the back, Kermit casually chats with the boys about their favorite subjects in school. The late afternoon sun casts long shadows across the rutted road, glinting off the car's polished gunmetal dashboard.

"Uh oh!" Harold shouts, sharply jerking the wheel.

"What?" Kermit asks, turning to see the dirt road ahead disappearing into a deep rut. She gasps, then shields the boy next to her with a protective arm.

Startled awake by the sudden movement, Mrs. Smith and Mrs. Tidwell shout in unison, "What's happening?"

The frightened passengers brace for impact as the front tire hits the road's shoulder, sending the vehicle hurtling into the air. In a horrifying instant, everyone screams as the car flips three times, spinning in a dizzying blur before landing upside down in a desolate cotton field. The car settles as the dazed occupants find themselves in a tangle of bodies, shattered glass, and twisted metal, their stray purses, hats, and shoes tossed aside.

Immediately after the car comes to a halt, only the sputtering engine breaks the stunned silence of the passengers. Clouds of dust particles float around them, masking visibility on the otherwise clear winter day. Then, terrified cries of the three brothers mingle with the moans of the two older women, the sounds piercing through the deserted stretch of backcountry. The two brothers in the rear move first, disentangling their arms and legs from those of the two women.

"Oh, Lord Jesus!" Mrs. Smith gasps, her voice tight with pain. "Ow! My chest." She tries to move her arm out of a cramped position but stops abruptly in agony. "And it hurts to move my arm!" She collapses onto her back, sobbing inconsolably.

When Kermit turns to check on her supervisor, sharp pain shoots through her neck. She gently massages the spot, then notices blood trickling from the head of the crying boy, thrown across her chest.

"I want my mommy," the youngest brother shrieks, seeing his blood splattered on his brown jacket. "Mommy, I want my mommy," he sobs louder, his voice trembling with fear.

Kermit twists upright to comfort him with an embrace, ignoring the protest of her own muscles. With trembling fingers, she applies pressure on his open wound, whispering soothing words against his thick black hair.

"My neck is killing me," Mrs. Tidwell exclaims. Her torn tweed coat rips at the sleeve as she struggles to sit up. "What in Jesus' name happened, Harold?" Before he responds, she adds, "Thank you, Lord, for letting us live."

"I was trying to avoid a ditch!" Harold replies, his navy suit caked with dust and grime. He repositions himself to kneel on the vehicle's tan interior roof and starts shoving the shattered front windshield. "I'm so sorry, everyone. Let me try to get us out."

"Are you hurt, Harold?" Kermit asks, trying to reach him with her free hand, the vehicle's mechanical fumes filling her nostrils.

Harold breaks off the bent sun visor and uses it to knock through the remaining shards of glass. After crawling through the opening, he pauses under the shadow of the crumpled hood. "I just cut my hand on the glass," he says, wiping his bloody palm on his pants leg. "But otherwise, I'm okay." He shakes out of his jacket and yanks off his tie, tossing them on the ground. Kneeling beside the driver's side, he grabs the suspended seat release lever and jerks it forward to reach the wounded passengers trapped in the back.

"I want to go home," the middle son cries, his eyes wildly searching the disheveled passengers tossed around the wrecked car. Clawing past his back seat mates, he shoves a purse and stray black pump aside to get out of the car. His older brother crawls out behind him into the field of dead brown stalks.

Kermit stiffly turns to watch Harold and the oldest boy gingerly drag Mrs. Smith from the mangled vehicle. "Be careful," she cautions, wincing at the cries from her supervisor at the slightest movement. As Kermit presses the cut on the youngest brother's forehead, blood flows faster, leaving streaks of dark red stains on his jacket and her sleeves. Searching the glove box above her head, she finds a polishing flannel cloth to stop his bleeding.

"I just can't believe this!" Harold says weakly, his voice barely audible over the hissing engine. Steam rises from the crushed hood, leaking engine fluid onto the dirt field in dark, oily pools. Behind them, a rattling truck screeches to a halt.

"What happened?" a man yells from the road. "Are y'all alright?"

From her vantage point, Kermit only sees his worn shoes draped by the hem of his frayed overalls. She tries to push open the passenger door, but the impact jams it shut. As Harold and the boy struggle to remove Mrs. Tidwell from the back, the Good Samaritan rescues Kermit and the injured boy from the same shattered windshield where Harold escaped earlier. The farmer quickly retrieves a horse blanket from his truck to cover the women before speeding away to summon help.

Temperatures plunge to the mid-thirties, sending shivers through their numbed bodies. Kermit huddles along the side of the road with her fellow crash survivors, pulling the youngest boy closer to share the warmth of her jacket. Comforting a moaning Mrs. Smith with a gentle embrace, she fears her supervisor may not survive her critical injuries. The older woman's face is ashen, her breathing shallow and labored. Closing her eyes, she silently prays for God's protection and thanks Him for surviving such a horrendous accident.

As dusk's light fades, Kermit mournfully watches her cousin survey the twisted heap of green metal and silver chrome that was once his prized Ford Sedan. A gusty wind spins the three crushed green spoke wheels suspended atop the wrecked car. The bent fourth wheel, broken side mirrors, shattered headlight, and crumpled fender create a trail of destruction from the road's shoulder to where the upturned vehicle now rests.

As nightfall covers the accident site, the wail of an ambulance siren grows louder, its rotating beacon light flashes red on the wounded travelers.

In the dim glow of their kerosene lanterns, the staff administer first aid, triaging the most critically injured passengers. They transport Mrs. Smith, Mrs. Tidwell, and the youngest boy to Magnolia City Hospital, while the others stay behind to wait for the tow truck.

When the ambulance arrives at the hospital, the physicians treat Mrs. Smith's broken arm, cracked ribs, and sprained knee. They work quickly to suture the gash on the injured boy's forehead, then dress the wound with gauze. Mrs. Tidwell's exam reveals a severely sprained neck, prompting the medical staff to stabilize her spine with a metal brace to restrict movement and prevent further damage.

While they wait under the moonlight, Kermit, Harold, and the older brothers salvage what they can of the possessions scattered across the frost-covered field. When the truck arrives, Harold and the driver hoist the wrecked car upright, the metal groaning in protest. While the driver hitches the vehicle to the truck, Kermit climbs into the truck's cab with the brothers, holding them in her lap to stay warm. Harold and the driver squeeze in beside them as they ride in silence to the only repair garage in town. After dropping off the demolished sedan, the four passengers get a ride down the main road to the hospital, passing through the small town's darkened buildings.

Kermit checks on her two coworkers, sharing a hospital room in matching sea green medical gowns. Mrs. Smith is unable to move her arm, torso, and knee because they are bound by casts and bandages. Mrs. Tidwell, confined by her metal brace, sleeps fitfully beside her. After their nurse notices Kermit stiffly holding her neck, she takes her to an examination room for treatment. She gives her painkillers, then carefully wraps her neck with an ace bandage and metal straps.

Taking the brothers into the restroom, Kermit cleans caked dirt and dried blood from their faces and arms, the water in the basin turning rust-colored. She scrounges sandwiches and apple juice that the nurses donate from their lunches, which the boys devour with relish. Kermit finally reaches their anxious parents, who are ecstatic to learn their sons are safe. When they arrive to collect their children, their mother showers them with kisses and hugs while their father scolds them for running away.

"Your mother was sick with worry," he says, his weathered hands gripping his oldest son's shoulders. "You boys were almost killed out there."

Before the tension can escalate, Kermit pulls the parents aside to a quiet corner of the waiting room. In hushed tones, she shares what she learned during their journey—the boys' favorite school subjects, their classmate friendships, and their love of family. "They really like going to school and don't want to fall behind," she explains gently. "You should be proud. You've raised some good kids."

As the parents listen, the father's face softens, his defenses slowly melting away. His wife gently squeezes his hand, her eyes welling with tears. They glance at their weary sons, the oldest protectively embracing his brothers on either side. The youngest sleeps in a fetal position on his brother's lap, while the middle boy rests his head on his sibling's shoulder. The parents return to their sons, gathering them into a family circle.

"Listen, you boys can't be running away like that," the father starts softly. "You got responsibilities at the farm and to your parents." He pauses, feeling his wife's fingers tightly gripping his hand. "But if you boys get your chores done on time, maybe we can figure out a way to get y'all to school on the regular."

The boys exchange glances before breaking into sleepy smiles. "We promise, Daddy," they agree, the two youngest rubbing their eyes. As midnight approaches, the family departs for home, the father carrying his youngest son whose head rests on his shoulder. Kermit repeats her apology for their frightening ordeal and embraces each exhausted brother, whispering goodbye in their ears.

When Kermit locates Harold, he is wandering the hospital reception area in a hapless daze. His once stylish suit hangs crumpled and stained, his tie hangs loosely around his collar, and a stark white bandage covers the jagged cut on his palm.

"What happened to your neck?" He eyes her wrapped neck, his voice hoarse with exhaustion.

"It's sprained, but I'm fine," she replies, comforting her cousin with a gentle embrace. "We all survived. Everyone will be alright."

"How are we going to get back home?" He asks, his shoulders slumping weakly.

"I've been thinking," Kermit begins. "W.C.'s family owns Brothers Funeral Home. Maybe he can use their ambulance to come get us."

They reach W.C. just as he is returning home from a night out with friends. After they explain their dilemma, he agrees to drive his family's ambulance down to Magnolia and give Harold and Kermit a ride back to Little Rock for forty dollars. Around four o'clock early Friday morning, the three weary travelers ride into town under the hush of the dark indigo sky.

***

Nearly two weeks later, the events of that dreadful day still haunt Kermit. Her body stiffens at the memory of the flipping car, her fingers clenching involuntarily. She often cries out in terror at random moments, the crash replaying in her mind without warning—the screams, the shattering glass, the sickening sensation of weightlessness as the car tumbles through the air. In her February 12, 1941, letter to Augustus, she confesses:

Darling, I almost lose my mind every time I think about that wreck. It was the most miserable thing I have ever witnessed.

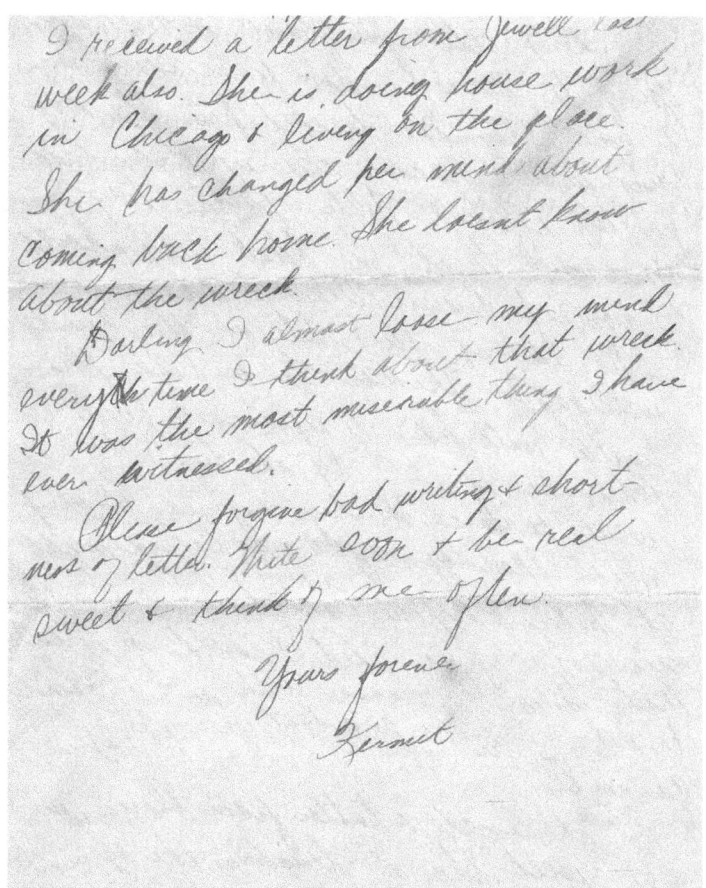

2-12-1941 Kermit Bland Letter to Augustus Hill

After Mrs. Smith's discharge, Kermit visits her at home. She finds her supervisor confined to bed, struggling to sit up and wincing in pain with every breath. Mrs. Smith's normally commanding presence is replaced by a frail, cowering shell of her former self. Mrs. Tidwell's physical injuries are less severe. However, the traumatic experience shatters her confidence. When Kermit visits Mrs. Tidwell, she admits the accident left her with such an emotional toll that she is unable to return to work. Their absence at the juvenile court is keenly felt, and Kermit finds herself shouldering additional responsibilities despite her own lingering trauma.

If you have a dime to spare, Kermit continues in her letter to Augustus, *please send Mrs. Smith a get-well quick card. She would really appreciate it. She and Mrs. Tidwell, both of them are in bed.*

Sadly, Harold learns the hard way that "no good deed goes unpunished" when both Pulaski County and the Arkansas State government refuse to cover the damages to his vehicle. They place the entire financial burden on Mrs. Smith, citing her request for the ride to Magnolia and Harold's agreement. While Mrs. Smith struggles with recovery and lost wages, she must also find a way to pay for his car repairs. Despite losing his cherished Ford Sedan and facing significant expense, Harold maintains his generous spirit, concerned only with Mrs. Smith's recovery rather than material loss.

Momma's Baby Boy

March 3, 1941

When Kermit gets her hands on the application for the clerk carrier exam, she panics—it is due in less than a week. She must first mail the form to Augustus in Prairie View, Texas, where he needs to complete it before sending it to the Ninth U.S. Civil Service District in St. Louis, Missouri. Grabbing a fresh sheet of Juvenile Court letterhead, she quickly jots a note to Augustus with explicit instructions on how to fill out the application and where to send it before the March tenth deadline. She adds, "If you think you can't get it right, mail it back to me, and I will mail it to St. Louis."

Kermit leaves early from her Colored Probation Office to mail the form before the post office closes. She asks the mail clerk about the fastest delivery option to Texas, paying for the extra postage. Carefully, she licks a purple "Special Delivery" ten-cent stamp and three red two-cent stamps, positioning each in the top right corner of the envelope. After Kermit writes "Air-Mail Special" under the postage, the mail clerk stamps the postmark and "Via Air Mail" on the envelope.

A few days later, Kermit feels relieved when Augustus' letter arrives confirming he received the application. However, her relief turns to fury as he shares his mother's doubts about their upcoming June wedding, suggesting he should wait to make sure Kermit is the right person to marry. She feels enraged, especially after all the favors she has done for Della while Augustus was away in college – assisting his mother with her bills, mailing her packages, driving her and Mr. Woods seventy miles round-trip to Conway. Seething, she rolls a clean sheet of Juvenile Court letterhead into the black typewriter and starts rapidly striking the keys.

March 6, 1941
Dear Augustus:

Received yours a few minutes ago and was very glad to hear from you. Also, glad to hear that you had received papers from me and your mother. Hope by this late date, you have filled out same and sent them to St. Louis. I am filing applications also for the Stenographer-Typist examination.

About our little affair: Your mother is not the one I am marrying, and I am not going to be looking to her for support and if we wait four years longer, there is a possibility that we won't have any more than we do now to marry on. When you hit the ground coming home, I intend to lead you to the County Clerk's office where they sell marriage licenses.

Another thing, neither of us is getting any younger and I do want some children before I get too old to raise them myself, so I am making plans toward marrying whenever you come to Little Rock. If these are not your plans, kindly inform me immediately (smile).

Darling I cannot see why you say the entire plan is left up to me because I would very much hate to see you marry me when you don't want me and not find it out until after we were married, however, I know that I want you and will be perfectly satisfied with you for the balance of my life. I know we are the ones who should decide this question, and I am positively not going to let anyone run my business and I hope you won't let anyone run yours.

Honey, don't you think I have had enough time to make up my mind what I wanted, from September to March. I had my mind made up in September what I was going to do when you returned to Little Rock, and that was to marry you before you could get back here good. I wish we were already married. One thing is certain and sure if you have to go to Military Training this summer, I am going to marry you before you go, if you come thru here and still want to

> *marry me. And if you don't go to take Military training,*
> *I am going to marry you right on, whether you return to*
> *school or what now. After all we only live once, and I intend*
> *to do some of the things I would like in this short lifetime of*
> *mine and one of them is to marry you.*

Kermit types furiously, unaware of her new supervisor standing behind her.

"Are you typing another letter to Augustus when you're supposed to be getting your work done?" The Chief Probation Officer's voice breaks Kermit's concentration.

She quickly removes the letter from her typewriter and inserts a court document in its place. Once she completes the files, she slyly slips the letter back in position. Kermit writes about a scuffle at Saturday's Philander Smith basketball game and the electric Victrola Oliver brought to the post-game social. But anger consumes her, and her thoughts inevitably return to Della's comments.

> *Darling, I would not marry you for spite work, and I hope you*
> *won't ever marry me for spite work. I am going to marry you because I*
> *really want you and hope you want me too, and if you ever stop want-*
> *ing me, please please let me know and I will do the same about you.*
>
> *I feel like this about it, your mother has lived her life, as well as*
> *mine, neither of them can live our lives for us. They lived theirs just as*
> *they chose, and I am going to do the same and hope you will likewise,*
> *however, I wanted to get your views on the matter because I have told*
> *practically everyone in Little Rock I was going to marry you when you*
> *returned to Little Rock and I would hate very much to be putting out*
> *the wrong tale.*
>
> *As ever,*
> *Kermit Bland*

Dressed in a crimson jacket, black muskrat fur hat, and tan riding gloves, Gary Cooper rides through a Canadian town on horseback, portraying a North-West Mounted Police officer in a film of the same name. From the segregated balcony of the darkened Lee Theatre three weeks later, Kermit is captivated as Cooper's character, Texas Ranger Dusty Rivers, pursues an outlaw named Jacques Corbeau into Canada. Throughout the two-hour film, Dusty prevents an ambush on the Mounties, becomes entangled in a love triangle, and captures Corbeau, who faces murder charges in Texas.

The next evening at The Gem Theatre, Kermit laughs along with her fellow audience members as Hattie McDaniel exchanges witty banter with her on-screen husband in *Maryland*. McDaniel had made history the previous year as the first African American to win an Oscar for her supporting role as Mammy in *Gone with the Wind*. In this film, she and other African American actors provide comic relief as maids, butlers, stable hands, bookies, and church members. Unlike the Lee Theatre, The Gem serves as a *Colored* theater on West 9th Street, showing films with predominantly Black casts, though never in leading roles.

As the motion picture ends, Kermit wipes away tears of laughter. Reaching into her pocketbook for another tissue, her mood changes when she spots Augustus' unopened letter. Since sending her heated response to his mother's objections about their upcoming wedding, Kermit has regretted allowing her emotions to get the better of her. For the past 19 days, she has tried to distract herself with work and films, but the wait has been nerve-wracking, particularly since his letters usually come within a week. Now that his letter finally arrived this morning, she cannot bring herself to open it.

Oh well, Kermit thinks, still seated in The Gem auditorium. *No time like the present*. With pursed lips, she holds her breath as she opens the envelope and unfolds its contents.

Dear Sweet Darling:

I'm sorry I haven't written sooner, but I don't have much time now with studying for exams and completing my printing work.

Kermit, if I had known my mother's words would upset you so, I never would've mentioned them to you. I'm not going to let any of her worries stop me from marrying you. Know that I have loved you since we were at Dunbar.

Do you remember all the fun times we've had since being together? I can't wait for us to be together as man and wife. Darling, I have been true to you and no one at Prairie View or anywhere else can hold a candle to you,

I love you with all my heart and always will.

Love,
Gus

Fresh tears roll down Kermit's face as she rereads Augustus' words, relieved that she has not ruined her chance of marrying him.

"Excuse me, young lady." An usher in a royal blue and red uniform with a matching pillbox hat approaches her from the next aisle. "We're closed now," he says, gesturing with the broom in his hand.

Kermit glances around the once-crowded theater, realizing she and the cleanup crew are the only ones left.

"Oh, of course," she says, stuffing the letter back into her bag and standing. "I really enjoyed the motion picture."

At the exit, Kermit smells and hears the rain before opening the door. Without an umbrella, she takes an empty red and white popcorn box from the deserted concession stand, tears it along the seam, and holds the flattened container above her head. Feeling ridiculous with her makeshift umbrella, she hopes no one sees her as she dashes into the downpour, trying to protect her pressed hair.

Lightning flashes as Kermit splashes through two blocks of heavy rain before reaching her car with drenched hair, a soaked dress, and hosiery clinging to her legs. Despite her wet appearance, she laughs, wiping away tears now mixed with raindrops. After learning that Augustus still loves her and wants to marry her, a little rain will not bring her down. She is over the moon and will wait for him until the end of time.

Driving home in the storm, Kermit begins singing Lil Green's "Romance in the Dark."

In the dark, it's just you and I
Not a sound and not one sigh
Just the beat of my poor heart
In the dark
Now, in the dark, I get such a thrill
When he presses his fingertips upon my lips
And he begs me to please keep still
In the dark

As Kermit sings, she reflects on Augustus' question about the fun times they shared. She remembers walking home together from the Dunbar Social after missing the last streetcar, her playful protests at his endless kisses, and their slow dances at Johnson's. Lost in these memories, she drives five blocks past her street. She cannot wait to tell Augustus how much "Romance in the Dark" reminds her of their own love story.

Happy Spring

April 26, 1941

Two weeks later, Saturday morning sunlight streams through Kermit's kitchen window as she quickly secures an apron over her dress. Mumbling recipe ingredients to herself, she arranges cans and baking items from the icebox and pantry along the counter. The sweet aroma of butter fills the kitchen as a low flame flickers beneath the pan, making it sizzle and pop.

She rubs butter on the bottom of a round pan, sprinkles it with sugar, and then adds a layer of canned pineapple slices. After washing a bowl of bright red cherries, she picks one up and places it in her mouth, pulling the stem between her teeth. The tart fruit bursts with flavor as she chews. She removes the stems from the others, placing them inside each yellow ring and along the edge of the pan.

"What time does Augustus get in?" Arvolin asks, reading the paper from her usual chair in the living room.

Kermit concentrates on the recipe and carefully measures flour, sugar, and vegetable oil in a large bowl. "His train should be here any minute." She cracks two eggs into the bowl and adds, "His stepdaddy's taking him straight to the civil service postal exam. Then he's coming here."

She stirs the ingredients with a large spatula, then pours the mixture over the pineapple and cherries. Golden bubbles form around the fruit edges as the batter settles. She lights the oven with a match as her mother's footsteps approach from behind.

"You should've had the oven heating up while you were making the cake."

Kermit turns to see her mother peering over her shoulder. "Well, it's too late now, Momma." Following her judgmental gaze to the spilled flour, batter-covered utensils, and sticky measuring cups, she adds, "And don't worry, I'm about to clean up the kitchen too."

The scent of baked pineapple and vanilla fills the house as Kermit straightens the living room and sweeps the oak floors. After cleaning the kitchen, she goes to the bathroom to reapply her makeup while the cake cools on the counter.

The distinctive whine of Mr. Woods' car motor reverberates outside, propelling Kermit to the front door to greet her guests. Augustus emerges from the back seat wearing a white long-sleeved shirt and gray pants, his shoulders sagging with exhaustion. Della waves from the passenger side while waiting for her husband to open her door. Kermit hurries down the steps to greet Augustus at the car with a long kiss and tight embrace.

"How was the exam?" she whispers, trying not to let his parents overhear.

Augustus shrugs, fatigue evident in his voice. "I don't know. I think it went okay."

"Hope so. I've been praying that you'd pass and get one of those good jobs at the post office." Kermit pivots to greet his parents, who wait alongside the car.

"Good to see you!" she says while giving each a brief hug.

"Is Arvolin home?" Della asks, looking past Kermit toward the house.

"Yes. Come on in," Kermit answers, rushing up the steps to open the screen door. "I made a pineapple upside-down cake."

"You did?" Augustus asks, a weary smile appearing for the first time since arriving. "I can't wait to try it!"

"Augusta, help your mother up these steps," Della says, removing her arm from her husband's grasp and extending her hand to her son. He obediently goes to his mother's side and takes her arm.

As many times as she's been here while Augustus was away, Kermit thinks, trying not to roll her eyes, *she's never needed help getting up these stairs before.*

Holding her arm, he takes a step and pauses while Della painstakingly follows, leaning heavily on his arm. When she finally enters the doorway, he reaches back to take Kermit's hand before they enter the house together.

They all enjoy the dessert, savoring the sweet tanginess of the caramelized fruit. As Kermit clears the dishes, her mother asks Augustus' parents for a ride to her church meeting.

"You two behave now," Arvolin teases as she gets in the back seat. Mr. Woods closes the door behind her and settles behind the wheel, finally leaving the reunited couple alone.

Augustus wastes no time kissing Kermit after their parents leave. For once, she resists the urge to pull away, no longer worrying about appearances. After desperately missing him all this time, she feels grateful for his unexpected visit. When they stop kissing, she chuckles and gently wipes her lipstick from his lips.

"Baby, you have no idea how much I've missed you," Augustus says, holding her in an embrace. "I really hate that I have to go back tomorrow."

"Are you sure you can't stay over a little longer?" she pleads. "The Ink Spots are performing here Wednesday." She caresses his face, her fingers gently brushing the growing stubble on his cheeks. "We could go – my treat, of course."

"No, baby, I have to get back to school," he replies, kissing her hand. "You know I'd love to stay and go with you if I could."

"Look, Gus, I have a surprise for you, but we have to leave now to get there on time."

"Oh, Kermit, you know I'd rather just stay home with you."

Taking his hands, she rises and begins pulling him off the sofa. "It won't take long, I promise, but we have to go now."

Augustus reluctantly follows Kermit to borrow her neighbor's car but takes the keys when she heads toward the driver's side.

"What kind of man would I look like letting a woman drive me around?" he asks, offended. He crosses to the passenger side, opening the door so Kermit can climb inside.

"Okay, where are we going?" he asks, pulling onto the street.

"Head over to West 9th Street by Dreamland," Kermit instructs, using her compact to reapply the lipstick Augustus kissed off earlier. "Did I tell you they remodeled it and held their grand opening the same night Count Basie was in town?"

"We're going dancing?" Augustus asks. "Honey, that test wore me out! I don't feel like dancing tonight."

"No, we're not going dancing," Kermit assures him. "But I'm still not telling you where we're going."

Once they park, Kermit and Augustus stroll hand in hand past Dreamland nightclub and The Gem Theatre. After turning on South Gaines Street, she leads him into a glass storefront studio. Framed photographs cover the display window and walls. The acrid smell of developing chemicals mingles with the warm glow of studio lights. The place is packed with grandmothers holding squirming children, parents fussing over infants, and loving couples embracing.

Still holding hands, Kermit leads Augustus toward a man with a warm bronze complexion. He wears a white dress shirt, black suspenders, and baggy pants while squinting at a family of three through a camera lens. Four studio lights surround the family, casting a warm glow on their faces and clothes, making them appear like mannequins. The sharp click of the camera's mechanisms punctuates the hushed conversations.

Augustus speaks in a low whisper, "We're getting our picture done?"

Kermit nods.

"I thought…"

"Can I help you two?" the photographer interrupts, still looking through the lens.

"Yes, I was in here the other day," Kermit answers. "You told me we could come get our portrait taken this afternoon at four o'clock."

The photographer nods, checking his watch. "Okay, y'all will be next."

"Next?" the infant's father jumps up, startling his child, who starts to cry. "We were here first!" Others murmur in agreement, frowning at the newly arrived couple.

Putting his hands up, he replies, "Look, they have an appointment. Y'all just showed up this afternoon." Turning back to the family still posed stiffly in front of the marble backdrop curtain, he assures the waiting customers, "Don't worry, I'll get to all y'all this afternoon."

When their turn arrives, the photographer removes the wooden bench and waves them to the portrait area. He raises the stage lights and positions Kermit on Augustus' left side, unclasping their hands and placing them at their sides.

Seeing no rings, he asks, "You two married?"

"We will be in June," Augustus beams, looking at Kermit grinning back.

"Congratulations," he says, shaking Augustus' hand and patting him on the shoulder. "You're a lucky young man," he says, gesturing at Kermit.

The couple smiles, allowing the photographer to adjust their shoulders, faces, hands, and feet until he is satisfied.

"Now, stay just like that." He holds up both hands and slowly walks backward, stepping over the tangle of electric cords until he reaches the camera. "Don't look at me. Don't look at the camera. Just look over here at this light stand." He points over his right shoulder while crouching to consider the couple through his viewfinder.

Suddenly, Kermit starts giggling, causing both Augustus and the photographer to look at her curiously.

"What's so funny?" Augustus asks, chuckling slightly.

"Don't move!" the photographer bellows, exasperated.

"I'm sorry," she says, covering her mouth and struggling to keep her composure. "I'm ready now," she says, resuming her position.

Augustus glances at her for another second before returning to his pose. The photographer covers his head with the dark cloth attached to the camera, holds up the bulb flash with his right hand, and clicks the shutter to capture the picture.

Leaving the photographer's studio, they admire the sepia proofs of their portrait in the fading daylight.

"We look pretty good!" Augustus jokes. "Seriously, I'm glad you set this up. Our first portrait together."

"See this?" Kermit asks, pointing to their photograph. "I got so tickled in there when I realized that's how we'll be standing when we get married."

"Oh. I was wondering what had gotten into you," Augustus laughs.

As they return to the car, Kermit takes his arm. "On our wedding day, I want to have another one like this made for us to keep forever."

The spring evening settles around them, carrying the promise of their June wedding and the hope that Augustus' exam results will secure their future together. In just two months, they will stand in that same pose – but as husband and wife, ready to face whatever challenges and opportunities await them in their new life together.

CLUB ARISTOCRAT

April 28, 1941

B ehind the wheel of the Pulaski County vehicle, harsh afternoon sunlight streams through the windshield directly into Kermit's eyes. For the second time today, she navigates winding dirt roads along the edge of the Pinnacle Mountains. Beside her, Mrs. Smith anxiously clutches the dashboard, while an eight-year-old boy slides from side to side in the back seat.

Kermit usually uses the drive to get to know their young charge, but this time, she remains silent. She stares straight ahead, focused on negotiating the treacherous mountain path before the setting sun plunges them into darkness.

Filling the silence, the boy talks nonstop, his eyes wide as he takes in the colorful beauty of the mountainous terrain. Jagged rocks line both sides of the road, with blooming trees scattered across the hillsides. The road curves between the clear, glassy waters of Lake Maumelle on one side and the flowing Arkansas River on the other. As they ascend the River Mountain, the boy offers enthusiastic commentary on the landscape, noting wildlife hidden among the forestry.

Kermit steals fleeting glances at him in the rearview mirror, stunned that this excited, typical eight-year-old is the same boy accused of theft, arson, and truancy back in Roland. After several unproductive visits to the local sheriff's office, he becomes a ward of the county. Feeling defeated and ill-equipped to manage him, his parents watch helplessly as Mrs. Smith and Kermit leave with their son. Later this week, they are scheduled to attend his hearing before the Pulaski County Juvenile Judge in Little Rock.

Thankfully, the sun still hangs above the horizon when Kermit checks the boy into the detention center and drops Mrs. Smith at home. She arrives at her own house before six o'clock and collapses into bed, her shoulders and calves tight from the nerve-wracking trip through the hillsides and valleys. She lets her eyes close, planning a short nap before choir rehearsal that evening.

When she opens them again, the clock reads nine-thirty—long past rehearsal. She rises slowly, massaging tight neck muscles, slips into her nightgown, and returns to bed for the night.

After work the following evening, a thunderstorm rages outside the Mount Zion Baptist Church while Kermit attends the B.E.T. Club meeting. When the deacon adjourns with the benediction, she spots Velma and W.C., who cross the floor to meet her.

"Hey, Kermit!" W.C. greets, an unlit cigar dangling from his mouth. "Lloyd's grand opening is tonight. Do you want to walk over there with us?"

"He's supposed to have done it up really nice, too," Velma adds, practically bouncing with anticipation.

"I don't really care for Lloyd's," Kermit states flatly. Then, recognizing the disappointment flashing over her friends' faces, she offers, "But I guess I could go see what he's done with the place. Is it still raining?"

"No, I think the storm's passed over," W.C. answers. "After you, ladies," he says, gesturing toward the door.

When they arrive, a crowd mills around the front of the building. A handwritten sign taped to the door announces: "Grand Opening Postponed."

"What happened?" W.C. asks.

"Lloyd said it wasn't finished yet," one of the bystanders responds.

"You're kidding?" Kermit says. "We came all the way over here for nothing?"

"Upstairs is open," the man suggests, pointing to the side entrance.

"Dreamland?" Kermit asks excitedly. "I've never been up there before."

"Yes," W.C. answers, holding the door open for Kermit and Velma. "But it's now called *Club Aristocrat* since the remodel."

Ascending the shiny new hardwood steps, Kermit stops at the landing. She scans the elegant layout of the immense bar, pink tablecloths, and alternating pink and white painted diamonds lining the balcony. The scent of cigarettes and perfume mingles in the warm air, while the soft glow of table lamps creates intimate pools of light throughout the room.

"It's really solid up here!" she says in awe.

Several couples swing across the hardwood floor, dancing the jitterbug to a five-piece orchestra outfitted in pale pink dress jackets. Onlookers snap their fingers to the beat while smoking or talking with friends. Every stool around the bar is occupied by women in brightly colored dresses. They sip cocktails and laugh at the men surrounding them, vying for their attention. The band's brass instruments gleam under the stage lights, and the rhythm section keeps perfect time, filling the space with infectious energy.

"Look, there's a place to sit," Velma points to a table with four empty seats.

"You two go ahead, and I'll get us something to drink," W.C. says. "Ginger ale as usual?"

They both nod and head to the table. By the time W.C. arrives with their sodas, the band ends their set, and the dancers return to their seats. A tall, brown-skinned man in a black tuxedo steps up to the microphone in the center of the stage.

"Ladies and gentlemen," he announces with a broad smile and bass voice. "Thank you for coming out to the new and improved Club Aristocrat!" He pulls out a white handkerchief and wipes the sweat from his forehead before continuing with an even bigger smile. "Make sure you come back and bring your friends tomorrow night to see The Ink Spots perform right here on this very stage!" The audience applauds enthusiastically as Kermit leans over to Velma.

"I wanted to bring Gus to see them, but he had to get back to school," she says as the nightclub owner continues making announcements. "I also heard they're going to be in a new motion picture called *The Great American Broadcast* as singing Pullman porters. I can't wait to see that."

The club musicians and a shapely woman singer in a tight pink sequin gown return to their places on the stage as the owner finishes speaking. Under the direction of the band leader, they start a new jazz song as patrons fill the dance floor. W.C. and Velma join the dancers, and by the next song, Kermit follows with an old high school classmate. The lively atmosphere carries them well past midnight, finally leaving the club after two in the morning.

The late night leaves Kermit struggling the following morning as she prepares for Wednesday's workday. At the Colored Juvenile Courthouse, she tries to focus on the trial hearing for three teenagers arrested for stealing, but her mind keeps returning to Augustus. Only a few pen strokes fill her mostly blank stenographer pad as the attorneys debate the young boys' fate. Judge Newton taps his gavel several times, ending the arguments and bringing her attention back to the proceedings in time to record his decision.

Back in her office, the familiar routine of legal documents and court reports feels strangely distant after the previous night's excitement. Kermit makes a little yelp when she spots a letter on her desk with familiar handwriting. Not bothering to find scissors to cut open the envelope neatly, she loosens the sealed flap with her pen and begins devouring Augustus' letter. Taking a sheet of Pulaski County stationery off her desk, she is about to start writing when she hears her supervisor's voice.

"I know you're about to write the judge's ruling on that paper."

Kermit's cheeks flush as she sees Mrs. Smith smirking at her from the doorway with a hand on her hip. "Uh, yes, okay," she says while placing the letterhead in the typewriter and rolling it in front of the keys.

Between her paltry notes and multiple typing errors, Kermit struggles to complete the court report. The shrill ring from the black rotary telephone on her desk interrupts her progress, causing her to stop and turn on her professional voice.

"Good morning, Colored Probation Office. Kermit Bland speaking."

"Hi Kermit, how are you?" Not recognizing her friend's voice distorted through the receiver, she continues in her business tone.

"I'm fine, thank you," she responds. "Who's calling, please?"

"It's Juanita! Girl, don't you know my voice by now?"

"Oh, sorry, I wasn't sure," she answers, more relaxed. "What's going on?"

"Has Augustus left yet?" Juanita sounds slightly annoyed.

"Yes, he left Sunday," Kermit answers, untangling the tightly wound telephone cord from the mouthpiece. "Why?"

Laughing, she says, "Well, tell him I have a beating in store for him."

"What?" she asks, concerned. "What did he do?"

"Saturday afternoon, I was on the streetcar and thought I saw him, I guess on his way to your house. I waved, and Augustus looked straight at me and wouldn't wave back," Juanita relays, annoyed again.

Kermit smiles. "Oh, Juanita, he just didn't see you."

"Well, it made me feel like a penny with a hole in it!" Juanita laughs again.

Kermit laughs, too. "Okay, I'll let him know, but I'm sure he just didn't see you." Looking at the office clock, she says, "Look, Juanita, I have to go back to work. I'll call you later."

"Alright, bye girl," she hears from the receiver before placing it back on the telephone base.

By the time she hands the completed file to Mrs. Smith, most of her coworkers have left the office for lunch.

"Thank you," Mrs. Smith says while taking the report. "Going to lunch?"

Checking her watch, Kermit answers, "No. I don't have enough time to eat at home, so I'll just stay here and write Gus."

"Okay, well, tell him I said hello," Mrs. Smith replies, reviewing the case report.

"I will," she says, picking up a pen and another sheet of stationery from her desk.

April 30, 1941
Dearest Augustus

Received your sweet letter this A.M. & was so glad to get it. Darling, I really do believe we really love each other & always will. I almost cried when I received your letter this morning.

I really did hate to see you leave Sunday night. I went home & just boo-hoo-ed. Darling those few days were heaven to me. I really hope we have lots more days like those days. You know I am going to keep my picture we had made. Darling, I hope you will always love me because I know I am going to love you always. You know I can't forget that we are already married. I feel that way now & have felt that way since you first arrived. Darling these few lines are music to my ears. I hope, trust & pray we will always feel the way we do about each other.

I am certainly glad you enjoyed the cake. If you let me know the exact date of your return, I will have you another one waiting for you. (Smile).

Well dear, I want you to study hard & make good these next few weeks & always remember my heart is in yours whatever you do because I will always love you & you alone. Mrs. Smith told me to tell you hello for her, Mrs. Tidwell & mother send love.

I received your card yesterday & was really happy to get it. I almost shouted when I received your letter in this morning's mail.

Write me as soon as you possibly can & pray that these three weeks fly by so we can be together again.

Forever yours,
Kermit
Please forgive bad writing.

On Sunday, Kermit stares absently through the windshield on the passenger's side of Harold's car as the wipers try to keep pace with the pouring rain. Sometime during the morning's church service, dark overcast skies release a drenching rainstorm, leaving unavoidable puddles along the sidewalk.

"Is it still okay for me to come for dinner?" Harold asks, glancing at his unusually quiet cousin.

"Huh?" Kermit looks over to meet his gaze as tires splash across the streets.

His eyebrows furrow as he looks back at his cousin. "Do you want me to just drop you off at home, or is it still okay for me to come to dinner?" he repeats.

"No, of course you're still invited," she answers. "Mother's been cooking all day for her favorite nephew."

"That's good because I'm really hungry," Harold chuckles, slowing as the rain picks up. Turning to face the road, he narrows his eyes to focus on steering through the sudden downpour. "I can barely see in all this rain."

"I know, be careful," Kermit cautions, glancing back through the windshield. "I'd hate if you had another accident in your new car."

They ride in silence as Harold concentrates on guiding his car through the partially flooded streets. After a few blocks of maneuvering around other cars and pedestrians in the storm, he feels comfortable enough to pick up the conversation.

"So, you and Augustus really getting married next month?" he says with a grin, his dimples showing.

Kermit's face brightens. "Yes! He comes home May 21st, and we get married in June."

"Wow, he must really love you," he laughs. "Out of all those other girls, you're the one who finally got him to the altar."

"What other girls?" Kermit scans his face to see if he is joking.

"Oh come on, Kermit," Harold teases. "You know Augustus went out with Charlotte Perry for a while. He'd go see her when you stayed over at Mrs. Swayze's." Kermit falls silent and returns to staring at the rain pummeling the windshield as he continues. "And what about those times he visited those college girls at Philander Smith?" He pulls into the space across the street from her house.

"I do remember that," Kermit says, squirming uncomfortably on the beige mohair upholstery. Trying to cut off any further discussion about Augustus' other women in front of her mother, she says with finality, "Anyway, it doesn't matter since we'll be married in June."

But Harold's casual words have planted seeds of doubt that grow stronger with each passing day. Three straight days of spring rainstorms contribute to Kermit's foul mood as Harold's comments continue to ring in her ears. In her dimly lit basement office, she feels some comfort when Augustus' letter arrives in the morning mail. After reading it, she wastes no time writing him back, her questions now demanding answers that she hopes will quiet her restless heart.

May 6th, 1941
Dearest Augustus:

Darling, was really glad to receive your sweet missive of love. It found me blue & lonesome for you and counting the days until your return.

We don't have but 15 more days to wait now & those 15 days cannot pass too swiftly for me.

I hope you can get your notebooks, term papers, drawings & everything else in O.K. because I really want to see you make a good grade.

In the matter we were talking about what do you want the 3rd party to be (girl or boy)? (Smile)

I paid on a set of dishes yesterday (Smile) I think they are pretty too. Don't worry, I will be there when the train pulls in waiting for you & whatever your plans are for the rest of the night I am right with you. I will really be a happy soul when I get into your arms to stay.

You did too see some other girls because you saw Margaret Bryant with her sister Bessie Bryant & all the girls on Philander Smith's campus.

Listen Augustus I want to ask you something & I want you to really tell me the truth. Did you ever go with Charlotte Perry & did you ever go to see her? Be sure & answer both these questions in your next letter.

If you don't have to take that training, dear, are we going to live together this summer after we marry? I only hope you can find a good job when you come back from school.

Listen dear, have you heard from your examination yet? Be sure & let me know when you do because I am going to Mrs. Robinson, Post Mistress about giving you a tryout as substitute carrier.

You said you were going to tell me whether you were planning to work in Prairie View this summer or not. Also about the vacancies in Tuskegee.

Listen dear, if you don't have to take the military training are you planning to finish that ½ year in school?

You say you love me but you don't ever discuss your plans with me. I am always the last one to find out what you are thinking about doing.

Darling, I really wish we were already married then maybe I would not be so terribly jealous of you.

Well, darling, guess I will close. I have a slight headache & don't feel so well.

Wish you were here to cheer me up because I feel like I need it now.

Write soon & be real sweet for me because remember we are the same as married (Smile).

Forever yours,
Kermit

C. P. Newton, Judge

A. J. Moss, Referee

JUVENILE COURT
PULASKI COUNTY

LITTLE ROCK, ARKANSAS

May 6th 1941.

Dearest Augustus:

Darling, was really glad to receive your sweet missive of love. It found me blue & lonsome for you & counting the days until your return. We don't have but 15 more days to wait now. & those 15 " cannot pass to swiftly for me. I hope you can get your note book, term paper, drawings & everything else in O. K. because I really want to see you make a good grade.

In the matter we were talking about what do you want the 3rd party to be (girl or boy) (Smile)

5-6-1941 Kermit Bland Letter to Augustus Hill

Making Moves in May

May 13, 1941

The following weeks blur together as Kermit juggles her professional duties with wedding preparations. Her work takes her throughout Pulaski County, each case requiring careful attention and compassion. One morning, as she drives down a dirt driveway, the sharp stench of manure and farm animals drifts through the open car windows. Dust dances in the sunlight as her county vehicle disturbs the quiet rural road. Kermit waves at a man steering a mule-driven plow through the corn fields, but he only eyes her with suspicion. A screen door bangs shut as her Pulaski County vehicle approaches the farmhouse. Squinting against the morning sun, a brown-skinned woman stands on the porch, her hands firmly planted on her hips.

Kermit takes a deep breath as she gets out of the car with her case file under her arm. Chickens scatter across the yard, clucking indignantly as they rush out of her path.

"Good morning! I'm Probation Officer Bland," she greets with her warmest smile. "Are you Mrs. Lancaster?"

"This here's private property," the woman says, not budging from her stance. "What do you want?"

"I'm from the Juvenile Court in Little Rock," she holds up the round photo ID button hung on a chain around her neck. "I believe your daughter is being held at our Detention Center."

"Erma Mae?" she asks, her voice rising as she relaxes her arms. "Are you sure?"

"I'm afraid so, ma'am," Kermit answers, opening her olive-green folder. "She was caught stealing from the Walgreens."

"Lord Jesus!" she exclaims. "Just what did she steal?"

"Do you mind if we sit?" Kermit gestures toward the weathered rocking chairs on the porch. "I have to go over a few things since Erma Mae is a minor."

"What's going on here?" The man from the fields now stands a few feet behind Kermit, sweat staining his work shirt.

"This woman says Erma Mae stole something!" the woman replies.

"That can't be right!" he snorts. "Erma Mae's in Little Rock for the summer with my mother!"

"Yes, I'm sorry to be the bearer of bad news," Kermit interjects. "But as I was telling your... *wife?*" she pauses for either of them to correct her assumption. Hearing none, she continues, "She was picked up for stealing at the Little Rock Walgreens. I'm Kermit Bland, a Pulaski County Probation Officer," once again showing her ID. "I was sent here by the Juvenile Court to let you know what your responsibilities are as her parents, and what's going to happen to your daughter."

While there, Kermit mediates tearful phone calls with their daughter and contacts the grandmother in Little Rock, who remains unaware of the arrest. She schedules their visit to the Detention Center, advises them of Erma Mae's possible sentences, and provides the telephone number for a court-appointed attorney.

Ninety minutes later, she drives back to Little Rock with signed legal documents indicating the father's cooperation with the court's orders. At the office, she places the case folder in the outgoing bin and draws a sharp breath when she sees Augustus' letter in the mail tray. She removes the envelope, purses her lips, and anxiously reads his latest correspondence. Taking a pen and stationery, she settles into her desk chair in the waning afternoon light.

May 13, 1941
Dearest Augustus:

Ten more days before your arrival & boy will I be glad when that day arrives.

Harold may have been teasing when he said you used to go to see Carolyn when I was staying with Mrs. Swayze. Which reminds me that Mrs. Swayze had a stroke recently. This is her second one & she is in bed now. Yes Carolyn is the same one that used to go with James.

I want you to take that Military training & I don't want you to take it. We have been apart so long I really would like to be with you awhile now. I feel the same way. I really fear if we don't marry this summer our chances will be slim for getting married.

I am hoping, trusting & praying that you will be able to find a good job here. How are you getting along with your class? Have you completed your notebooks, term papers, drawings & etc. or are you still behind with everything?

Darling, I really will be glad when you come back. "Lil Green" the woman who made "In the Dark" famous will be here on the 15th of this month. I really wish you were here to go with me but I don't think I will go if I have to go alone.

Little Rock is still quite dull. Graduation is going off with a bang. Hope you will be here to take part in some of it.
Write soon & be sweet & always remember that I love you with all my heart.

Yours forever,
Kermit Bland

As May progresses into the following week, Kermit finds herself caught between anticipation and anxiety. Augustus' homecoming approaches, bringing with it the promise of their long-awaited wedding while clashing with the looming threat of the draft. Summer arrives early with rising temperatures reaching the nineties every day that week. Kermit dreads venturing outside in the sticky humidity but has too much on her plate before his arrival.

On Monday, the midday sun bakes the trolley like an oven as Kermit travels to meet the postmistress on her lunch break. Although Augustus still awaits the results of his civil service exam, she persuades the supervisor to let him intern as a substitute mail carrier. With their nuptials set for next month, she hopes Uncle Sam will not call him for military training anytime soon.

The following afternoon, Kermit boards another packed streetcar after work. Even with the windows open, the stifling air provides little relief as passengers jerk along the tracks. She steps off the trolley on Main Street downtown and bypasses the department store's glass front doors. Rounding the corner, she heads to the back entrance under the "Negroes Only" sign hanging above the frame. The stench of nearby garbage fermenting in the sweltering heat creates a sharp contrast to the perfume salesperson spritzing white customers at the front. Covering her nose with her handkerchief, she rushes into the building and waits for the separate elevator to arrive.

Standing a few feet from the register on the third floor, Kermit retrieves her receipt, cash, and Pulaski County employee identification from her handbag. Adjusting her facial muscles into a friendly, non-threatening expression, she waits as the salesman waits on all the white customers in the housewares section. As more white shoppers arrive, he makes sure to assist them before begrudgingly acknowledging Kermit.

"Yes?"

"I'm here to pick up the dishes I put on layaway," she answers, proudly offering the store receipt listing her previous payments. The clerk takes it and opens the cash drawer, removing the department's brown eleven-by-seventeen-inch ledger. After flipping through its pages, he locates her information and jots down a note. He counts, then recounts her money three times before placing it in the drawer, slamming it shut with unnecessary force.

"Do you have any identification?" he asks, refusing to look at her as he studies the register.

Kermit hands the salesperson her employment card, who meticulously inspects both sides before recording her name, address, and social security number. Afterwards, he stamps PAID on the ledger and Kermit's receipt, returning it to her. Still holding her county identification, the clerk leaves without a word, stashing the store's record book under his arm.

For twenty minutes, she watches while he confers with his manager, the two sending fleeting glances her way from across the floor. The manager eventually crosses to Kermit as the salesperson returns to helping customers. After he repeats the same verification process as the clerk, he finally retrieves the dishes from the storeroom. When she leaves with her boxed plates, she struggles to balance the large, bulky container with her handbag.

On the trolley ride home, the weight of the dishes strains her arm muscles as the streetcar lurches through the afternoon heat. Finally arriving on her doorstep, Kermit's clothing clings uncomfortably to the moist perspiration covering her glistening body. Inside the cool living room, she gently deposits the box on the wooden floor, admiring it from the sofa. Despite her exhausted state, she feels giddy knowing she and Augustus will have their own dinnerware to start their life together as man and wife. Each completed task brings Kermit closer to the moment she has waited for so long.

Mrs. Smith invites Kermit to dinner on Wednesday, giving her a well-needed respite from her endless errands. She catches a ride with her supervisor after work, grateful to escape another trolley ride in the compounding heat. Fanning herself on the stoop, she waits while Mrs. Smith fumbles with her keys to unlock the door. Inside, a chorus of *Surprise* greets Kermit as she crosses the threshold. She stares blankly as grinning friends, coworkers, Mrs. Tidwell, Arvolin, and soon-to-be mother-in-law gather around her.

Noticing her uncertainty, her mother squeezes her in an embrace, saying, "It's your bridal shower, baby."

"But how did you...?" Kermit glances past her mother at Mrs. Smith. "Oh, thank you so much," she says, wiping away the tears welling up in her eyes. "Y'all are so sweet."

Following dinner, Mrs. Smith serves vanilla cake with chocolate icing while Kermit opens gifts. Married women advise the bride-to-be on having a happy marriage and what to expect on the wedding night. Ensuring everyone has a slice, the hostess slips into the hall, returning with a large bag.

"This is from me." Mrs. Smith presents Kermit with a folded pink and blue blanket.

"Oh, this is beautiful," she gushes, smoothing the soft fabric with her hand. "Did you crochet this yourself?"

"Sure did," her supervisor quips. "It can go in the nursery, whether you have a girl or a boy."

Everyone laughs as Kermit's complexion takes on a reddish glow from embarrassment. "Well, thank you so much. It's lovely."

"How soon do you think you'll have a baby?" Mrs. Tidwell asks, sparking whispers from other guests.

With every eye on her, Kermit blushes again, glancing awkwardly at Augustus' mother. "We've only talked about it once, so we're still deciding on the matter," she stammers, then attempts to steer the conversation in another direction. "I can't thank you all enough, especially Mrs. Smith, Momma, and everyone. This has really been the nicest shower."

The warmth of friendship and community support fills Kermit with gratitude as she realizes how many people care about her happiness and future with Augustus.

Thursday morning's sunlight glints through the dusty windows of the stone and brick train depot as Kermit paces nervously, her heels clicking rhythmically along the floor. A few feet away, Augustus' parents talk quietly on the wooden benches of the musty *Colored* waiting area. Elmer fans himself with his brown fedora while his wife, Della, uses a white plastic accordion fan. In her new navy and white pinstriped dress and white hat, Kermit waves a flimsy train schedule in her face in a futile attempt to cool off.

So far, Augustus' train is already twenty minutes late. After repeated attempts to retrieve updates on the train's arrival from the white man at the counter, Kermit realizes he does not know or care to find out. As usual, her mind races with worst-case scenarios—*What if the train crashed? What if it ran off the tracks? What if the engine caught on fire? What if the conductor got sick or even died? What if the conductor got lost and took the wrong route? What if Augustus missed the train?*

"Kermit, why don't you sit down?" Della asks, patting the space beside her. "Walking back and forth won't make Agusta get here any faster."

Kermit settles in the space between Della and a man with a brown leather duffel bag, who kicks it away to give her more room. She methodically yanks each fingertip of her white gloves before staring at her slender fingers. *If Augustus is being true with me, I will have a wedding ring on my finger by this time next month*, she thinks. Inhaling deeply to calm her nerves, she closes her eyes to pray that Augustus will arrive safely.

An hour later, the screeching train whistle answers her prayers as Augustus' train enters the station. He emerges among a cloud of steam and smoke, lugging his bag over his shoulder with a weary grin. The young couple's building anticipation now culminates in these final moments of waiting. Soon, their separate lives will finally come together as one.

ARVOLIN'S ROSES

June 14, 1941

Beneath the intense midday sun, Augustus steers Mrs. Smith's 1940 Chevrolet Sedan past fields of Black-eyed Susans sprouting along State Road 30. Beside him, Kermit silently stares through the window, watching the countryside rush past in a blur of green and gold. The sweet floral aroma of blooming wildflowers mingles with the leather upholstery, carried on the humid June breeze.

For the third time since they left Little Rock twenty minutes ago, Kermit unclasps her purse to open a small tan envelope, confirming two dollars and fifty cents remain safely inside.

Seated behind her, Mrs. Smith leans forward to tap her shoulder. "You okay, Kermit?" she teases. "I don't think I've ever seen you so quiet."

Amused laughter rises from the three women in the back seat.

Augustus glances at Kermit, furrowing his brow with concern.

"Having second thoughts?" Della chimes in from her position between Mrs. Smith and Arvolin. "You know it's not too late to call it off if you're not ready."

"Not at all, Mrs. Woods, I've *been* ready!" Kermit exclaims. She turns to the back to face her mother. "Isn't that right, Momma?"

"Oh, my goodness, yes," Arvolin confirms with a chuckle. "That's all she's talked about nonstop for a year now."

Augustus slows down as they approach the *Welcome to Saline County* sign. "Look, we're here!"

Kermit checks the map and responds, "Almost." She directs him to Market Street, where they travel five blocks into the town of Benton. He turns at the next stop sign and parks on Main Street.

Starting behind him, Augustus opens each car door and extends his right hand to assist first Arvolin, then his mother, and finally Mrs. Smith out safely. He repeats the process on the passenger side, kissing Kermit after helping her out.

"You look beautiful, honey," he says, taking her hand as Kermit beams.

"I don't understand why we had to come all the way out here in the first place," Della grumbles, her pale cheeks flushed with red blotches from the heat. "Why couldn't y'all just get the wedding license in Little Rock?" She wipes the beads of perspiration dotting her hairline with her handkerchief.

Kermit glances at Augustus, nudging him to respond. "Remember when I said it would take longer?" he asks, slowing his pace for her to catch up to them. "Saline County is faster and less hassle. Plus, I hear they don't make Negroes jump through as many unnecessary hoops like in Little Rock."

They ascend the walkway of the buff-yellow brick courthouse, anchored by a four-story clock tower. Crossing under the rounded arch entrance, they escape the 84-degree heat and enter the cooler, wood-paneled interior. The sharp echo of footsteps on marble floors mingles with the murmur of voices in the bustling foyer. Saturday afternoon, visitors rush in all directions, creating a tangle of bodies in the hallways.

Following the signs to the Office of the County Clerk, they navigate the crowd and join the line of waiting customers extending out the door.

Kermit removes the tan envelope and her birth certificate from her purse, then whispers to Augustus, "Remember to get your draft card out."

Retrieving his wallet from his black trousers, he removes the card and returns the wallet to his back pocket. Every few minutes, excited couples leave the room, clasping their legal document as the steady rhythm of typewriter keys fills the air. When the line moves further inside the clerk's office, Augustus slips his hand through Kermit's arm, and she steps closer to him.

"One last stop to make it official," he says, his eyes crinkling as he smiles.

"I feel like we're already married," she whispers, kissing him on the cheek.

"Okay, you lovebirds," Mrs. Smith says playfully. "Save some of that for the wedding."

Kermit grins as her face flushes, then covers her mouth to stifle a laugh. Turning to Mrs. Smith, she says, "Thanks again for coming to back us with our marriage bond. Your support means so much to us."

"Of course," Mrs. Smith says. "No disrespect to your mother, but I think of you more like a daughter, after all this time."

"None taken," Arvolin interjects.

"I wish nothing but the best for both you and Augustus. I know you'll have many happy years together."

When they arrive at the front desk, they present the clerk with their identification and money. She rolls the legal-size Bond for Marriage License document into the typewriter and enters Augustus' name as principal and surety for the penal sum of one hundred dollars. In the blank spaces for who is obligated for a license authorizing the solemnization of the Rite of Matrimony between the said, she types: "Augustus Hill (Colored) and Miss Kermit Bland (Colored)."

Under the space to faithfully comply with the marriage within sixty days, Augustus signs as Principal, Kermit signs beneath his signature, and Mrs. Smith signs as Surety.

The deputy clerk completes the next sections of the Marriage Affidavit and Marriage License, commanding both parties to solemnize the Rite and publish the Banns of Matrimony between them. Following Augustus' name, she enters his age as 24, then Kermit's as 21. She completes the final sections for the Certificate of Marriage and Certificate of Record by typing Rev. Fred T. Guy as the minister responsible for certifying the license once the wedding ceremony is complete.

The district clerk signs the form in three places, then hands it to Augustus, along with a Marriage License coupon to be filed with the State Register of Vital Statistics.

"Congratulations," she says. "Your Arkansas marriage license registration is complete."

On the morning of June 15, the sun emerges from the horizon, painting soft gradient colors of apricot and indigo across the sky. Scattered wispy clouds reflect the first hues of golden sunlight, creating a vibrant canvas above. Kermit stirs in bed, trying to grasp the fragments of a dream slipping away. As she gradually awakens, a few beats pass before the realization hits her: today is her wedding day.

Rising too quickly, she stumbles to the dresser to check her pocket calendar, a grin spreading across her face. Then she pushes back the curtains, revealing a typical Sunday morning with children playing and an occasional vehicle passing by.

Still giddy, Kermit charges into the kitchen where her mother finishes breakfast.

"Well, look who's up," Arvolin greets her with a smile. "You'd think this was just another Sunday the way you're sleeping." She rises to embrace her daughter.

"So it's really today?" Kermit stammers, her waking voice sounding raspy. "I'm not still dreaming?"

"After all this time?" Arvolin chuckles, shaking her head in disbelief. "Yes, baby, you're marrying Augustus today. Now hurry up and take your bath so we can get you all dolled up."

Half an hour later, Kermit emerges from the bathroom, where her Maid of Honor, Juanita Long, waits for her in the living room.

"I know you didn't think I was going to let you get ready by yourself," she chuckles.

All three women head to the bedroom to prepare Kermit for her bridal debut. Leaning back on her walnut chair, she gratefully accepts their assistance while trying to calm the swarm of butterflies fluttering around her nervous stomach.

Juanita artistically applies her friend's makeup, the soft brush tickling her cheeks as she blends face powder and outlines her lips with color. Arvolin carefully sweeps her daughter's soft black curls away from her face as she lets the ringlets flow gracefully down her back.

Careful not to disturb her makeup and hair, Kermit slips into a white dress adorned with a contrasting blue floral print on the bodice and skirt. The crisp cotton fabric rustles softly as she adjusts the outfit, which accentuates her figure with a scoop neckline that cinches at the waist and is topped with cap sleeves. Indicating the daytime semi-formal attire, her white gloves extend past her slender wrist, landing in the middle of her forearm.

Arvolin slips out of the room while Juanita applies the finishing touches, pinning Kermit's white netted veil to her hair. When Kermit admires her transformation in the mirror, her mother reappears, clutching a bouquet of white roses freshly pruned from her garden, their sweet fragrance filling the small room.

"Oh, Momma, they're beautiful," her eyes brim with tears as she embraces first her mother, then her maid of honor. "Thank you both for making me feel so special."

Juanita rushes to grab a tissue and dabs the edges of her friend's eyes. "Uh-uh, no crying allowed," she chuckles. "You're going to mess up all my hard work."

"I know, I'll try," Kermit smiles. "But keep those tissues handy." She slips into her black leather kiltie pumps, decorated with a panel that curls over the toes. When she turns around, she finds both her mother and friend now crying. "Oh no. If you two start, how do you expect me not to cry?"

Laughing, Juanita quickly grabs more tissues for Arvolin and herself, then dries Kermit's face and reapplies her makeup.

Juanita drives them to Mount Zion Baptist Church, where she finds a spot on South Cross Street under the shade of a maple tree. "I'm going inside to make sure everything's ready," she says, exiting the car. She climbs the concrete stairs, passing morning worshipers departing the tan brick building framed with stained-glass windows.

Although Kermit and her mother are members here, she wants a small ceremony to save her mother money. Juanita enters the middle-arched doorway below a row of five arched windows.

"Do you think Gus is here?" Kermit asks nervously, scanning the street. "I don't see his stepdaddy's car."

"Stop worrying, baby," Arvolin reassures her daughter, leaning forward to pat her shoulder. "You know it's bad luck for the bride and groom to see each other before the wedding. So stop looking around before you accidentally see him."

Kermit diverts her eyes, turning her attention inside the car. Reaching for her black oversized purse, she starts rummaging through its contents to distract herself. "I honestly didn't think this day would ever come," she says, reorganizing the items in her bag, "but I'm so happy it's finally here."

Juanita returns with Mrs. Smith, and they walk together to the passenger side. Opening the door, her supervisor gushes, "Oh, Kermit, you are the perfect picture of a glowing bride."

"Thank you so much," she replies, her cheeks flushing slightly. "It's all thanks to these two."

"Everything's ready," Juanita says, taking Kermit's hand. "How are you feeling?"

"I'm a little nervous," she admits, "but I'm ready to get married to Gus. Is he here?"

"Yes. Reverend Guy is talking with him now in his office," Juanita says. "So we can go into the choir room until the service starts." While Mrs. Smith assists Kermit, Juanita takes the roses from Arvolin and helps her out of the back.

Arvolin, Mrs. Smith, and Juanita circle Kermit to shield her from a possible sighting by Augustus. Beneath the golden sunlight, they ascend the stairs, chatting animatedly and laughing. When they arrive at the landing, Kermit pauses to glance over her shoulder.

"I'm going inside the church as a single woman and coming out married," she says in disbelief.

The women murmur in excitement as they cross through the arched entrance.

Tucked away in the choir room, Kermit twiddles her gloved thumbs while she paces the wooden floor, ignoring her mother's pleas to sit beside her. Juanita trails behind the bride-to-be, borrowing a church fan to cool her friend. Next to Arvolin, Mrs. Smith searches her purse until she locates a square white cloth.

"Kermit, I made this for your wedding day," Mrs. Smith rises to present her with a laced handkerchief, embroidered with a yellow *K* and blue flower in one corner.

"Mrs. Smith, this is beautiful," she stops pacing to examine the gift, carefully running her gloved fingers across the delicate stitching.

After the two women embrace, Mrs. Smith says, "It can qualify for your 'something blue.' Do you have one already?"

Kermit furrows her brows. "Why, no," she stammers, turning to her mother whose expression reveals a revelation.

"We've been so busy, I forgot," Arvolin gasps, reciting the adage in unison with Mrs. Smith. "Something old, something new, something borrowed, something blue, and a sixpence in her shoe."

"Oh no, I remember that now," Kermit groans. "Those are things the bride's supposed to have for good luck."

"That's right," Juanita says, joining the search of the room stocked with hymnals and Bibles. "Here," she says, thrusting her white beaded handbag at Kermit. "You can borrow this for the ceremony."

"Okay, that's something borrowed and something blue," Mrs. Smith counts on her fingers. "What about old and new?"

"My dress is new," Kermit says, grasping the fabric outward along the skirt.

"Perfect," Juanita says, still searching the room for other tokens in the rhyme. Briefly reclaiming her bag from Kermit, she retrieves a coin purse and removes a penny. "Take off your shoe," she instructs.

Kermit slips off one shoe, dropping a few inches shorter as she stands on her stocking foot. Juanita places the coin inside the toe box, then slides her friend's foot back into her pumps. Kermit shifts uncomfortably from side to side, feeling the penny move around the ball of her foot.

"She still needs something old," Arvolin says, shuffling the papers discarded on the upright piano in the corner.

A knock at the door interrupts their search as Augustus' mother peeks inside. "It's time," she says. "Augusta, his best man, and the pastor are all waiting at the altar."

Arvolin rushes to her side, asking, "Della, do you have something old that Kermit can use for good luck?"

The mother of the groom slips inside, closing the door behind her. "I don't think so," she mumbles, rummaging through her dress pockets. "Well, this sachet is kind of old." Della offers, presenting a cloth pouch with a faint scent of cloves and cinnamon.

"Oh, Mrs. Woods, may I borrow it, just for the wedding?" Kermit asks.

Tightly gripping the pouch, Della assesses Kermit, then notices the other women watching her expectantly. "Of course, dear," she says, finally releasing her grip and depositing the scented sachet in her hand.

Kermit thanks her with an embrace, then hugs the other women surrounding her. She repeats the rhyme, ensuring she has collected all the items. "Something old," she holds up the sachet, "something new," she glances at her dress. "Something borrowed," she lifts the purse in her hands, then the handkerchief, "something blue." Kicking up her foot, she ends the poem, laughing, "and a sixpence in my shoe."

The women cheer and applaud, their gloved hands muffling the sound.

Before taking their seats in the sanctuary, Arvolin, Mrs. Smith, and Della each take turns kissing Kermit on the cheek and complimenting her radiant appearance. Juanita powders the bride's face one last time as the wedding processional plays on the sanctuary organ.

"It's time," Juanita singsongs in a high-pitched tone, squeezing Kermit's hands in giddy excitement. She hands her the bouquet of white roses, fluffing her veil and straightening any stray hairs.

Together, they walk down the hallway leading to the sanctuary, where Augustus' father waits, standing in for her own father during the ceremony. Juanita slowly starts down the gently sloping aisle, keeping pace with the uplifting tempo of the processional march.

Kermit exhales a brief prayer before joining Mr. Woods, who slips his hand through her right arm. At the altar, her groom grins at her, sporting a white formal jacket, white dress shirt, black bow tie, and black formal pants. His eyes never leave her face as she approaches, his body swaying slightly in nervous excitement.

W.C., the best man, wears a black suit and tie and gently nudges Augustus. Both men's polished shoes glint in the pale light of the copper chandelier suspended from the pressed-metal ceiling. Reverend Frederick Guy stands clasping a Bible, wearing a white clergy robe with black panels embroidered in gold crosses. When the maid of honor arrives in front of the pulpit, she takes her position across from the best man and beside the officiating minister.

The organist begins the familiar melody of the Bridal Chorus, signaling the intimate gathering to rise as "Here Comes the Bride" rings through the vestibule. Kermit nods at Mr. Woods, indicating she is ready for her escorted promenade down the aisle.

As she steps outside the vestibule, her white dress reflects a kaleidoscope of colors from the sunlight filtering through the stained glass of the elliptical skylight. During the entirety of the bridal procession, the intendants lock eyes, unaware of any other guests there to witness their wedding ceremony.

Before going to sit next to his wife, Mr. Woods pats Kermit's hand and transfers it to Augustus' arm. As the guests return to their pews, Reverend Guy begins the ceremony.

"Dearly beloved, we are gathered here today in the sight of God and these witnesses to join together Kermit Bland and Augustus Hill in holy matrimony. Marriage is a gift from God, a sacred covenant, and a beautiful expression of love, commitment, and faith. It is not to be entered into lightly, but reverently, soberly, and in the fear of God."

In the presence of their closest family and friends, Kermit and Augustus become husband and wife, pledging their love to one another in sickness and in health. After exchanging their wedding bands, Reverend Guy concludes the ceremony by declaring, "By the authority vested in me by God and the State of Arkansas, I now pronounce you husband and wife. Augustus, you may kiss your bride."

The newly married couple embraces in an extended kiss as their guests respond with an enthusiastic standing ovation.

Following years of waiting and months of planning, Mr. and Mrs. Augustus Hill depart Mount Zion Church, marking the passage into their new life as one. The white roses from Arvolin's garden, now carried by her daughter as a married woman, seemed to bloom brighter in the afternoon sun—a symbol of love carefully tended and finally allowed to flourish.

PART II

ALTRUSA CLUB

September 19, 1941

Driving to work with Mrs. Smith in the autumn storm, Kermit counts her blessings as they pass a crowd of passengers huddled under umbrellas waiting for the streetcar. In May, Mrs. Smith's boarder was drafted, leaving her desperate for a new tenant to supplement her income. Kermit quickly offered to rent the room with Augustus once they married, as they decided to postpone their honeymoon until after the war. It is the perfect solution because they will be staying with her dear friend, who loves Augustus almost as much as she does.

On Friday after work, Kermit counts the hodgepodge of plates and cups scattered across the kitchen counter while Augustus eats dinner behind her. The rose-pattern set she bought in May for their new household only came with four salad plates, four dinner plates, and four coffee cups—about half what she needs for the meeting she is hosting tonight. She picks out the best-looking ones to borrow from Mrs. Smith's collection and returns the rest to the cupboard. Stacking a half dozen plates, she carries them into the dining room with Augustus watching.

"How many are coming?" he calls above the clanking dishes. He pushes the remaining peas together on his plate and scoops them into his mouth.

"Not really sure," she returns and retrieves another load. "Could be anywhere from 10 to 15." Augustus rises and slides his dirty dishes into the newly vacated spot on the counter next to the enameled apron sink.

"Oh, Gus, not there!" she whines.

"What? I was going to wash them," he says, startled. "I didn't want to be in your way while you were getting ready."

"Oh, sorry," she says, placing a hand on his arm. "I'm just so worried about tonight. I want everything to be perfect." She swivels and continues arranging the dishes in the next room. As the sunlight fades into the evening sky, Kermit sweeps through the living room, switching on lamps, dusting tables, fluffing sofa cushions, and pulling the curtains shut. She uses the back of her hand to wipe the tiny beads of sweat forming along her hairline.

"I don't understand why you always need to get involved with these things," he says, leaning against the doorway.

"But I want to, honey; it's my idea." Back in the kitchen, she loops her fingers around the cup handles and smiles when Augustus picks up the remaining saucers. "I've worked with troubled kids at the Juvenile Court for two years now. I want to help them before they end up at the Detention Center or County Farm like that girl I told you about."

"Okay, Kermit," he sighs, following her into the dining room. "I just don't like to see you so worked up."

"Thanks, I'm just a little nervous." After finishing the table, they position the yellow-mustard couch and striped velvet chairs in a circle in the living room before returning to the kitchen. After washing her hands in the sink, Kermit removes a platter of egg salad sandwiches from the icebox and begins cutting them diagonally.

"What's it called again?" Augustus asks, rolling up his sleeves and turning on the faucet.

"Al-TROO-sa," Kermit sounds the word out. "It's spelled A-L-T-R-U-S-A. It's a women's group that does charity work, and this will be the first one in Little Rock." Augustus nods, washing his dishes and stacking them on the counter to dry. After checking her list, she arranges green grapes and orange slices decoratively around the sandwiches and returns the tray to the fridge. "What are you doing tonight?"

"I don't know. Probably right here, drinking my coffee and reading the paper."

"Oh," Kermit says, trying to think of something to keep him busy and out of their way. "Why don't you see if you can fix that broken drawer in our room?" Before he can answer, she sees the first guests arrive through the kitchen window. "Okay, honey," she gives him a quick peck. "They're here. I'll talk with you when we're done."

Kermit opens her front door, letting in a cool evening breeze carrying the perfume scents of four women wearing colorful dresses and cotton sweaters. "Come in, ladies!" As she waves in her visitors, Mrs. Smith trails behind them, carrying a dish with an aluminum cake cover.

"Sorry, I'm late," Mrs. Smith apologizes. "I got to talking to your mother when I picked up her pound cake and lost track of time." She places the cake on the empty stand on the dining room table. "The table looks pretty, Kermit! You did a great job decorating."

"Thanks," she says, smoothing the white tablecloth around the cake stand. Two rapid knocks rattle the wooden door, and Mrs. Smith crosses the paneled floor to answer it. "Have a seat, everyone," Kermit gestures to the arranged chairs as members from her church's benevolence committee join the gathering. Shortly after they are seated, Kermit's fellow volunteers at the Young Women's Christian Association (YWCA) arrive, and she initiates introductions.

While the women are chatting, Kermit steps into the kitchen to review her notes from the Public Speaking Class she took at Dunbar Junior College. Strolling back into the center of the room, she projects her voice to command attention. "Good evening, everyone," she smiles and makes eye contact as she speaks. "I'm so glad you all could join me tonight for the inaugural Altrusa Club meeting of Little Rock." The women applaud enthusiastically as Kermit continues. "As I was telling my husband tonight, our club's mission is near and dear to my heart. Most of you know I work at the Pulaski County Juvenile Court, where a lot of troubled children end up in the Detention Center or County Farm. We can help some of these families in need before they get to my office."

"We see some of those same families at our food and clothing donations," a parishioner comments. "You wouldn't believe how many needy people there are around here."

"At the YWCA too," a member adds. "We do Christian work for women and children, and many are poor."

"That's why I invited you tonight. I've seen each one of you in action and know you are committed to serving our community," Kermit observes, distributing pamphlets to the gathering. "So, to become an official Altrusa Club, we'll need to elect officers—president, treasurer, secretary—collect membership dues and have charitable priorities." Kermit anxiously waits while the women look over the club materials. "Any questions?"

A church member glances around the room before raising her hand tentatively. "Yes?"

"How will we know who to help?"

"We'll collect recommendations from our churches and civic groups and vote as a group," Kermit answers.

Another woman raises her hand, and Kermit nods to her. "I know someone who would be great in this group. Can we invite other members?"

"As long as they are committed to Altrusa's goals and have a kind heart," Kermit replies.

"This is a wonderful idea, Kermit," a YWCA volunteer says. "Let's do it." Murmurs of agreement spread through the room.

"And I think Kermit should be our president," Mrs. Smith declares, followed by "I second it" from another person.

By the end of the meeting, the 14 women at 1515 W. 17th Street have formed the first Altrusa Club of Little Rock, Arkansas, with elected officers, program committees, and a quarterly agenda. After the business is conducted, Kermit serves the refreshments while Mrs. Smith serves cake and coffee. When the last guest departs, Kermit finds Augustus sound asleep in their room. She tiptoes to the dresser to get her nightgown and is tickled to see that the drawer is fixed.

DAY OF INFAMY

December 8, 1941

O n a chilly Monday morning, sunlight casts shadows across the marble floors as Pulaski County employees hurry through the corridors, all on edge about the bombing of a Hawaiian island 4,000 miles away. When Kermit arrives bundled up in her wool navy coat, she finds her coworkers jockeying for position around the desk of a clerk who is reading aloud from the Arkansas Gazette. In the background, radio announcers interrupt the morning variety show with urgent news bulletins. Kermit angles for a spot around the crowded desk, making out the headline, "Hundreds Killed as Japs Attack U.S.," as the woman begins the next article.

December 7. War struck without warning from the sky and sea today at the Hawaiian Islands. Japanese bombs took a heavy toll in American lives. Wave after wave of planes streaked over Oahu in an attack which the army said started at 8:10 am Honolulu time and which ended around 9:25, an hour and 15 minutes later.

"Why hit Honolulu?" a woman Kermit recognizes from the Detention Center asks above the growing murmurs.

"I don't know," the clerk answers, gliding her finger over the newspaper. "Says they attacked a lot of islands in the Pacific."

"Does it say anything about us joining the war?" Kermit asks, wondering how soon Augustus will need to report for duty.

"Let's see," the clerk scans the paper for more information. "Here, it says,

Congress Vote on War May be Sought Tonight. President Roosevelt announced he would deliver today a special message to Congress. Whether Mr. Roosevelt will ask for a declaration of war by this country was left uncertain after a hurriedly summoned meeting of his cabinet and Congressional leaders of both parties tonight at the White House.

I guess we'll find out sometime today after he meets with Congress," the clerk concludes.

No one speaks as a sense of dread spreads across the room, and they slowly disperse to their workstations. Kermit feels a nervous tinge tightening in her stomach as she returns to her desk and sees the framed picture she took with Augustus before they married. She desperately wants to talk to him now, but remembers his boss reprimanded him the last time she called him at work. Since Mrs. Smith is tied up in court all morning, she picks up the phone and asks the switchboard operator to connect her to her old home number.

"Hello," Arvolin answers.

"It's me, Momma," Kermit whispers, turning away from her eavesdropping coworker at the adjoining desk. "Have you heard about them bombing Hawaii?"

"Lord yes, it's all they're talking about on the radio," Arvolin says anxiously. "It's just awful!"

"I know. It's got me worried about what this means for Gus," Kermit says, glancing back at their photograph. "Do you think Uncle Sam will call him before Christmas?"

"I sure hope not, baby," Arvolin answers.

"Me too. I'm so scared, Momma," Kermit turns and sees her coworker is still listening and tries to lower her voice. "What am I going to do?"

"Listen, Kermit, you're gonna worry yourself to death," Arvolin warns. "It does you no good."

"But you worry all the time," Kermit reminds her, her voice louder than intended. "Probably where I get it from."

"Well, that's different. I'm your mother and supposed to worry about you," Arvolin chuckles. "But lately I've been trying to follow that Serenity Prayer we learned at bible study. Do you remember?"

"Yes, Momma," Kermit closes her eyes to help her recall the words. "*God, grant me the serenity to accept the things I cannot change, courage to change the things I can, and wisdom to know the difference.*"

"That's right," Arvolin says. "Now look, Kermit, even though Christmas falls on December twenty-fifth, you can celebrate early if it turns out Augustus has to go off to war. You've got a little more than two weeks before Christmas, so start making the house look festive now. You can trim the tree together and surprise him with an early Christmas gift just in case."

"That's a good idea," Kermit agrees and flips the pages of her desk calendar to count the days.

"Just focus on the time you have together," Arvolin says. "And give your worries to the Lord in prayer."

"Thanks, Momma. I will."

"Now go on and get into the Christmas Spirit for Augustus," Arvolin encourages.

***

Shortly after Kermit hangs up from Arvolin, Mrs. Smith returns from court, and Kermit excitedly shares her mother's suggestion to decorate the house early for the holidays. While they discuss their plans, staff from neighboring offices begin to reassemble around the black metal radio for President Roosevelt's address to Congress, announced to take place around noon. Over the next 30 minutes, radio correspondents offer theories on what the American people can expect from the speech as they wait for him to appear.

At 12:30 p.m., the employee lunch bell echoes in the deserted corridor, but no one moves to leave their spot in the packed office. A few moments later, the Speaker of the House introduces the president of the United States to the senators and representatives, who respond with enthusiastic applause and cheers. Once the ovation dies down, Franklin Roosevelt's voice breaks through the broadcasting static.

Mr. Vice President, Mr. Speaker, members of the Senate and the House of Representatives: Yesterday, December 7, 1941 – a date which will live in infamy – the United States of America was suddenly and deliberately attacked by naval and air forces of the Empire of Japan.

As Roosevelt's voice resonates throughout the office, the rapid clicking of typewriter keys and shuffling papers slows to a halt as workers stop to listen. At her desk, Kermit purses her lips as she surveys the worried faces of her colleagues.

The attack yesterday on the Hawaiian Islands has caused severe damage to American naval and military forces. I regret to tell you that very many American lives have been lost.

A gust of wind rattles the windows, causing a few to look pensively at the swaying trees while President Roosevelt continues to lay out his case to

Congress. Emphasizing the extent of the Pearl Harbor tragedy, he methodically lists six additional territories hit with surprise strikes over the last 24 hours.

No matter how long it may take us to overcome this premeditated invasion, the American people in their righteous might will win through to absolute victory.

"That's right!" the courtroom bailiff yells, pumping his fist as members of Congress applaud. Kermit and a few others shush him as the president continues.

With confidence in our armed forces, with the unbounding determination of our people, we will gain the inevitable triumph, so help us God.

I ask that the Congress declare that, since the unprovoked and dastardly attack by Japan on Sunday, December 7, 1941, a state of war has existed between the United States and the Japanese Empire.

Congress immediately delivers another thunderous ovation, accentuated by whistles and more cheers. A probation officer leaning on Kermit's desk asks, "Is that it?" Kermit shrugs and places a finger to her lips, intently listening to the radio broadcast. Reporters quickly summarize the speech and begin debating the probability of Congress approving a war declaration.

As the cramped occupants file out of the small space, the close air holds the smell of wool coats and nervous perspiration. Falling behind the crowd, Mrs. Smith looks at Kermit, still sitting at her desk. "Aren't you going to lunch?"

"No. I couldn't eat right now even if I tried," she says, holding her abdomen. "My stomach's still tied up in knots." Kermit stares wearily at the stack of assignments overflowing from her inbox that she usually clears immediately. Recalling her conversation with her mother, she removes her notepad from the drawer and starts jotting down ideas for an early Christmas with Augustus. When the bell signals the end of lunch, Kermit's holiday plans are complete, and her coworkers return to their desks.

Prioritizing her inbox projects, Kermit starts rapidly typing case reports for the two o'clock in the afternoon docket. Before she leaves for court, a news anchor announces that Congress has approved President Roosevelt's request to declare war on Japan. Two hours later, she returns to a packed office again gathered around the radio. Kermit squeezes past the crowd to her desk while the reporter describes the president, now in the Oval Office and wearing a black armband to honor the lives lost at Pearl Harbor. At

4:10 p.m., Kermit's worst fears are realized as President Roosevelt signs the declaration of war, followed by the applause of those present in the office and on the radio.

Suddenly, a voice from outside the building shouts, "We're at war! We're at war!" Kermit and several of her coworkers rush to the window and see crowds of people running through the streets, their faces filled with fear and uncertainty.

***

Just three days after the surprise attack on Pearl Harbor, Germany and Italy declare war on the United States. In response, the U.S. officially joins World War II by declaring war on these countries.

On December 25, 1941, Augustus and Kermit spend their first Christmas together as husband and wife, surrounded by family and friends. Five more years will pass before the couple will celebrate Christmas together again.

CIVIL VALENTINE'S DAY

February 14, 1942

Winter's chill breaks in February as the midday sun pushes temperatures into the low sixties. Shifting uncomfortably in her heels, Kermit waits in a line that wraps around the Little Rock Post Office and Courthouse Building. By her last count, she is twelfth out of forty-three women and four men spending their Valentine's Day in the most unromantic location. At least Augustus is taking her to the Sweethearts' Dance tonight so she can blow off some steam after her Civil Service Exam. She finds herself studying the faces of the other applicants to determine who can type faster or take dictation better than she can.

Returning the friendly smile of the Black woman behind her, Kermit decides to size up her competition. "Hello, my name is Kermit," she starts, removing one glove to shake her hand.

"Hi, I'm Melinda," the woman in a brown wool jacket responds.

"Nice to meet you," Kermit pulls her glove back over her bare hand. "I was wondering, when did you send in your application for today's test?"

"Um, it was around Thanksgiving. I saw the ad in the newspaper hiring typists and stenographers in Washington, DC. Why?"

"Because I applied at the end of March -- almost a year ago," Kermit responds irritably. "I had no idea it would take so long for them to schedule my exam."

"Me either," the petite woman behind Melinda chimes in. "I'm her cousin, Lela, by the way." She pushes her eyeglasses up the bridge of her thin nose before shaking Kermit's gloved hand. "I've been waiting over a year and a half, but I'm not complaining. I'm so ready to get out of Little Rock and nab one of those secretary jobs up North."

"You took the words right out of my mouth," Kermit chuckles. "My husband's going in the military any day now, and I plan to follow him out of this dull, dusty town the minute he leaves."

"It's about time," someone in front of Kermit mumbles sarcastically. She turns, thinking the person is commenting on their conversation, but notices the line crawling up the stairs and into the five-story limestone structure with Greek columns above the entrance. Leaving the fresh air, Kermit recognizes the stale smell of the grand postal lobby where she used to mail packages to Augustus when he attended college in Texas. She trails past the bank of elevators for the courtrooms upstairs and lands in the newly renovated east wing.

Outside a room brightened by harsh ceiling lights, a white woman in a pinstriped skirt suit stands erect, gesturing like a traffic cop. "Please hang your belongings on the coat racks, then find your name organized in alphabetical order on the desks." She repeats her instructions as more people file into the room of secretary desks arranged in five rows of ten, each supplied with a black typewriter, blank sheets of paper, a stenographer pad, two pens, and two pencils.

When Kermit passes the instructor, she catches the sweet scent of the red carnation adorned with a tiny white baby's breath pinned to her lapel. Once she locates her assigned seat, she familiarizes herself with the Remington typewriter's carriage, roller, ribbon, and knobs for spacing and margin release. To warm up, she lightly places her eight fingers in the starting position on the third row of white keys, gliding her fingers along the tops without pushing down. Although her office uses Underwoods, she hopes the similarities between the models will be an advantage to her performance.

When the clock strikes one o'clock, the woman takes her place behind the podium and flips past the first few pages of her black binder. "Good afternoon and Happy Valentine's Day!" Kermit and her fellow candidates echo her greeting. "Thank you for your application for the Civil Service Exam for stenographer, typist, clerk, and office machine operator. Some of you may have been waiting a long time for this day." Kermit looks at Melinda and Lela and nods in agreement. "Well, the United States Civil Service Commission, which I represent, recently received permission from President Franklin Roosevelt to expand state quotas for National Defense. The salaries start at $1,440 a year, even for Negroes, with a good chance for advancement for those who have the ability." Excited murmurs sweep across the room as the applicants imagine earning that much money. Kermit squirms in her seat as she calculates a potential pay increase that would more than double her current annual salary of $600.

The Commission representative removes her silver stopwatch hung on a chain around her neck and holds it with her thumb poised above the start button. "So, let's get started. The first part of the exam is typing, and the second will be dictation. To pass, you will need to type at a moderate speed with minimal errors and transcribe dictation at 96 words per minute." Kermit and the other participants exchange worried glances as they consider how they will perform under such strict pressure. "When I say *go*, you flip over the first page on your desk and start typing. Ready? Set? Go!"

For the next fifteen minutes, a commotion of fluttering papers, tapping typewriter keys, ringing margin bells, and carriage returns fills the area. Remembering the County's clerical training film, Kermit focuses on hitting the keys accurately rather than worrying about her speed. Before she knows it, the representative shouts, "Time!" The typists release a collective sigh of relief, some slump in their chairs, while others rub their eyes.

After a ten-minute stretch break, the applicants record the instructor's dialogue on the notepads provided. When they are dismissed, Kermit joins Melinda and Lela in the corridor below a mural depicting a farm scene.

"How do you think you did?" Kermit asks, smiling at other participants shuffling past the trio.

"I don't know," Lela sighs, cleaning her glasses with a handkerchief. "It was a lot harder than I expected."

Melinda nods, "I had the most trouble with the dictation. My shorthand needs work. What about you?"

"I feel pretty good about the dictation. I did a lot of shorthand when I worked for a judge and an insurance company," Kermit responds, putting on her coat and gloves. "My downfall is usually typing errors, but today I tried to do better."

Lela latches onto her cousin's arm. "Oh, but wouldn't it be something if we got one of those high-paying jobs?"

"Yes indeed," Kermit agrees as they move toward the door. "Maybe we'll even be working in the same place."

"That would be something," Melinda says, buttoning her jacket. "Then we could room together too."

"Best of luck to you both," Kermit says as they leave the warmth of the building into a much colder afternoon.

"You too," the cousins say simultaneously.

On the Post Office steps, Kermit shields her eyes against the sharp sunlight streaming through the shadows cast by the downtown buildings. A crisp breeze cuts through the late afternoon air, carrying a hint of the evening chill. Her heart leaps when she spots Augustus, dashing in a black-and-white houndstooth coat, tipping his gray fedora with a subtle bow. Cradled in the crook of his arm are a small box of chocolates and a single red rose, ready to begin their Valentine's Day evening.

Uncle Sam Wants You

May 26, 1942

O n the last Tuesday in May, temperatures drop to the low seventies, falling from the afternoon high of eighty-four degrees. Holding the black handle with a damp washcloth, Kermit presses the hot cast iron along the olive-green shirt collar to form a crisp crease. Steam rises as she rearranges the garment on the board, meticulously ironing the sleeves, front pockets, and body to eliminate stubborn wrinkles in the herringbone cotton material. To examine her handiwork, she lifts the shirt by the lapels and notices the detail on the brass buttons—each adorned with the coat of arms eagle clutching an olive branch and thirteen arrows in its talons. She squints, trying to read the banner in the eagle's beak, but cannot decipher the words. With careful hands, she folds the shirt next to the matching uniform pants in Augustus' suitcase.

For the third time in the last half hour, Kermit picks up the May 14th Order to Report for Induction letter Augustus received from the president. Once more, she scrutinizes it for any loophole that might excuse him from reporting tomorrow for military training. She reads the section that always sends chills down her spine:

Willful failure to report promptly to this Local Board at the hour and on the day named in this notice is a violation of the Selective Service and Training Act of 1940 and subjects the violator to fine and imprisonment.

Prepare in Triplicate

May 14, 1942

(Date of mailing)

(STAMP OF LOCAL BOARD)

ORDER TO REPORT FOR INDUCTION

The President of the United States,

To _____ Augustus _____ Hugh _____ Hill _____
(First name)   (Middle name)   (Last name)

Order No. _____ 476 _____

GREETING:

Having submitted yourself to a Local Board composed of your neighbors for the purpose of determining your availability for training and service in the armed forces of the United States, you are hereby

notified that you have now been selected for training and service in the _____ Army _____
(Army, Navy, Marine Corps)

You will, therefore, report to the Local Board named above at _____ 902 Boyle Building _____
(Place of reporting)

at _____ 7:30 A _____ m., on the _____ 27 _____ day of _____ May _____, 19 _____ 42 _____
(Hour of reporting)

This Local Board will furnish transportation to an induction station of the service for which you have been selected. You will there be examined and if accepted for training and service, you will then be inducted into the stated branch of the service.

Persons reporting to the induction station in some instances may be rejected for physical or other reasons. It is well to keep this in mind in arranging your affairs, to prevent any undue hardship if you are rejected at the induction station. If you are employed, you should advise your employer of this notice and of the possibility that you may not be accepted at the induction station. Your employer can then be prepared to replace you if you are accepted, or to continue your employment if you are rejected.

If you are not accepted, you will be furnished transportation to the place where you were living when ordered to report for induction by this Local Board.

Willful failure to report promptly to this Local Board at the hour and on the day named in this notice is a violation of the Selective Training and Service Act of 1940 and subjects the violator to fine and imprisonment. Bring with you sufficient clothing for 3 days.

You must keep this form and bring it with you when you report to the Local Board.

If you are so far removed from your own Local Board that reporting in compliance with this Order will be a serious hardship and you desire to report to a Local Board in the area of which you are now located, go immediately to that Local Board and make written request for transfer of your delivery for induction, taking this Order with you.

Member of Local Board.

D. S. S. Form 150
(Revised 5/2/41)

5-14-1942 Augustus Hill's Order to Report for Induction

With a deep sigh, she folds the notice and slips it back into the envelope. Glancing around the room for anything she has forgotten, Kermit spots their framed wedding picture and places it on top of his packed belongings, snapping the luggage clasp shut with finality. On her way out, she secures the letter underneath the suitcase handle and turns off the bedroom light.

In the kitchen, she finds Mrs. Smith bustling between boiling pots and the pantry, retrieving seasonings and canned goods. The sound of bubbling water mingles with the sizzle of dishes cooking in the oven.

"What can I help you with?" Kermit asks, tying an apron over her canary yellow dress.

"Finish setting the table and put napkins out," Mrs. Smith responds, wiping her hands on her floral apron. "Did you finish packing?"

"I wish I could pack myself up in that suitcase," Kermit says, taking six glasses off the shelf.

"I'm sure you do." Mrs. Smith laughs, opening the oven door and releasing the golden aroma of baked chicken into the air. Poking the breast with a fork, she nods with satisfaction. "I can't believe Augustus leaves for Camp Robinson in the morning."

"Me either! I've been going over his induction letter with a fine-tooth comb, trying to find any reason for him not to go."

"Any luck?" Mrs. Smith wipes the counter with a dishcloth, collecting food scraps in her palm.

"Not really," Kermit sighs. "The only thing I found is that he could be rejected for physical or other reasons, so I guess there's a slight chance they could find something tomorrow."

"Didn't Gus already pass his physical a couple of weeks ago?"

"Yes, I know, but it also says *other reasons*," Kermit offers, hope threading through her voice. "So I'm still holding out a little."

"Oh, Kermit," Mrs. Smith pats her shoulder with a sad smile. "Don't hold your breath on that one."

"I know," Kermit concedes, her voice small.

"At least Camp Robinson is right up the road in North Little Rock," Mrs. Smith says, brightening. "He won't be as far as Texas this time!"

Kermit admires Mrs. Smith's positive outlook. "You're right. He won't have to catch a train back home, and I can visit too."

As she circles the table, arranging forks and knives beside each plate, she hears the front door creak open. Her mother and in-laws enter through the threshold, followed by Augustus. In the afternoon sunlight streaming through the windows, Kermit exchanges kisses with their dinner guests and reaches toward Mrs. Woods with a warm smile.

"Let me take that sweet potato pie off your hands."

"This pie is just for my baby," Della says, swiftly turning away. "He won't have his Momma's cooking over at that army base."

Kermit flashes Augustus a quick look as he jumps in to intervene.

"Now, Momma, you know there's enough pie for everyone," he says, giving Kermit a hug and a kiss.

Kermit forces a brittle smile and turns to Mr. Woods. "I'll put your hat in the closet for you," she says, taking his navy fedora from his hands.

"Hello everyone," Mrs. Smith enters the room holding a steaming casserole dish of macaroni and cheese, protecting her hands with a dishtowel. "Dinner's almost ready, so take a seat." She trails off, returning to the kitchen for another dish.

"Let me help you," Kermit follows her, feeling tears threatening.

When Mrs. Smith turns and sees Kermit's face, she offers a brief hug. "Don't let her get to you today," she whispers. "You don't want to spoil the little time you have left with Augustus."

"Thanks," Kermit says, squeezing her back. "I've been trying to keep it together all day, but it's so hard, especially when she starts up."

"Try and put yourself in her position. In her eyes, you've taken away her only child," Mrs. Smith explains, her voice gentle but firm. "But you're married now—you have to learn to get along." She turns off the oven and transfers the golden chicken to the counter. "Oh, and don't forget your apron."

Kermit nods, dabbing her eyes with the apron's ruffled hem before pulling it over her head. With a potholder, she picks up the hot dish of string beans and slides it onto the iron trivet in the center of the table. Mrs. Smith carries in the roasted chicken and places it at the head of the table for Mr. Woods to carve. Before sitting next to Augustus, Kermit brings a wicker basket of rolls wrapped in a checkered towel.

"Augustus, we sure are going to miss you around here," Mrs. Smith says, leaning over to hug him at his place across from his stepfather. She settles in the empty chair between him and Della, releasing a sigh of relief.

"We sure are," Arvolin echoes, patting her daughter's shoulder. "I know Kermit sure will."

"You can say that again," Kermit agrees, her voice thick with emotion.

"I'll miss you all too," Augustus replies warmly. "And thanks for coming tonight to see me off."

"Yes indeed. We're sorry to see you go, son, but we're very proud of you." Mr. Woods clears his throat. "You know I may be drafted soon, too. They made me register two weeks after my birthday in February." Elmer takes a sip of punch and wipes his mouth with his napkin.

"Elmer, no! I didn't know that," Arvolin says, looking back and forth between him and Della in disbelief.

"Can you believe it?" Della shakes her head. "It's bad enough they want to take my only child, but they want to take my husband too." She removes the napkin from her plate and wipes her eyes.

"I hope they know a broken-down forty-one-year-old like me can't help them win this war," Elmer chuckles. "I'm praying it was only a formality. Now let's bow our heads and thank God for this wonderful-smelling feast before it gets cold."

Following dinner, Della serves her sweet potato pie, cutting everyone except Augustus a sliver of a piece. Handing a slice to Kermit, she asks, "Am I going to be a grandmother soon?"

Kermit catches herself before responding, trying to think of something appropriate.

"Oh, Della," Mrs. Smith interjects. "Give them a little time to be newlyweds for a while. It'll happen in God's time." Kermit gives her a slight nod and smiles in appreciation.

"I just think she's working too hard to make me some grandbabies," Della continues. "Augusta's going into the Army tomorrow, so time's slipping by."

Augustus leans over and kisses Kermit on the cheek. "Don't worry, Momma. It'll happen before you know it."

Arvolin chimes in, "Are you with child now? I wouldn't mind spoiling a few grandbabies myself!"

"No, Momma, I don't think so," Kermit says, quickly breaking off a piece of pie with her fork. "You really outdid yourself with this sweet potato pie, Mrs. Woods," she gushes, stuffing the sweet pastry in her mouth. "It's so moist and delicious!" Thankfully, everyone joins in praising Della's dessert and moves off the topic of her possible pregnancy for the remainder of the evening.

The following morning at daybreak, Kermit sits next to Augustus as he slowly navigates the car down West 14th Street, shielding his eyes from the rising sun. Cool air seeps through the slightly open window, carrying the scent of dirt moistened by the morning dew.

"Can you see okay?" She flips down the driver's sun visor, but it fails to block the sun peeking over the horizon. "Oh, sorry, that doesn't help."

"It's fine," Augustus squints at the street, his knuckles tightly gripping the steering wheel. "I'll be turning on Broadway in a few blocks anyway."

She returns the visor to its original position. "Did you remember to bring your induction letter?"

"You already asked me a hundred times," Augustus chuckles, though tension edges his voice. "It's right here in my shirt pocket." The envelope rustles softly as he pats the chest of his cotton jacket.

"Okay, I'm just making sure because the instructions said you're supposed to bring it with you." Kermit fidgets with her wedding ring, twisting it around her left finger as they pass familiar houses from her route to work. "Do you know how the Local Board's supposed to get you to Camp Robinson after you report to the Boyle Building?"

"No. Probably a bus or something," Augustus replies, turning onto West Capitol Street.

"Well, if they find some reason you aren't able to take the training, call me right away and I'll come pick you up first thing."

"Okay, I will," Augustus says, slowing down to find a parking spot along the street packed with recruits reporting for military training. Finding a space behind six other cars on Main Street, he turns off the engine, glancing hesitantly at his wife. "Well, we're here."

Nerves and dread overwhelm Kermit as she gazes at the twelve-story marble skyscraper glowing in the golden sunrise. "It sure is a beautiful building," she marvels. "Even taller than the Pyramid where I used to work the elevators."

"Kermit," Augustus gently touches her cheek, guiding her face toward him. "You know I have to go now." He searches her eyes and takes her hands in his. "There's already a line out there, and I still need to get to the ninth floor and find room 902 by seven-thirty."

"I know," Kermit says, wrapping her arms around him. "I just can't believe it's time already." They kiss and hold each other, neither wanting to break the moment.

"I love you so much," Augustus whispers in her ear.

"I love you too," Kermit says, slowly releasing him. "Be careful for me, and please, please come back safe." With those words, her fear of possibly losing her husband triggers tears rolling down her cheeks.

"Oh, honey, please don't cry," he soothes, wiping her tears with his thumb. "You know I can't take it when you cry."

"I'm sorry. I'm trying not to," Kermit says, reaching into her purse to retrieve her handkerchief. "You better go. I don't want to make you late and get you in trouble with the Local Board."

Augustus gets out of the car and removes his suitcase from the trunk as Kermit dabs her eyes and runny nose. He opens the passenger door and extends his hand to help her onto the sidewalk. They embrace and kiss once more while passersby look on with understanding smiles.

"Remember to call me as soon as you can," Kermit says as he escorts her to the driver's side, and she slides behind the wheel.

"Okay, I will," Augustus says, shutting the door with a gentle thud. "Miss you already."

Kermit turns on the engine and grips the steering wheel as Augustus joins twenty other men waiting to enter the Local Board. At the entrance, a white officer holds a clipboard and checks off their names before directing them inside. When Augustus approaches the uniformed man, Kermit holds her breath, praying this is all a huge mistake and he will be sent home right then. She exhales as the officer locates his name, and Augustus disappears through the door. Still grasping the wheel, Kermit watches until the last recruit is cleared for entry. She shifts the car into drive, facing an uncertain future without her husband.

STENOGRAPHERS FOR NATIONAL DEFENSE

May 29, 1942

Two days after Augustus starts military training, Kermit and Mrs. Smith drive home as another stifling ninety-degree day slides into the more comfortable seventies. With the car windows rolled down, they pass oak-lined streets where bright green leaves sway in the evening breeze. When they arrive home, the red carrier flag on their mailbox stands raised, indicating a delivery. After Kermit parks next to the curb, Mrs. Smith gets out to retrieve the letters from the black metal box.

Before Kermit can open the front door, Mrs. Smith calls, "Kermit! Look what came today!" She waves a thick tan envelope in the golden afternoon light.

Kermit cuts across the patchy lawn, her heels sinking into the soft ground. Seeing the U.S. Civil Service Commission return address, she gasps and slides her finger under the sealed flap. After scanning the cover letter, she shows Mrs. Smith. "I passed! I passed my Civil Service exam!" They hug and scream with excitement.

UNCLE SAM NEEDS STENOGRAPHERS

The government needs stenographers for National Defense. One is prone to think of National Defense in terms of soldiers, sailors and marines. But there are many types of defense work behind the lines.

It is estimated that the government has approximately 85,000 stenographers, typists and secretaries on the payroll. Many young men and women are responding to the call. Thousands more are needed.

Aside from the present emergency, the opportunities for stenographers in the government service are favorable. Good stenographers are always in demand. The positions pay $1,440 a year to start, with a good chance for advancement in positions of greater responsibility, such as secretarial positions, in the cases of those who have the ability.

The examination announced by the Civil Service Commission for stenographers is open until further notice. The examination consists solely of a dictation test at 96 words a minute and transcription of notes. All persons who can qualify are urged to apply now.

1942 "Uncle Sam Needs Stenographers" Newspaper Ad

"I knew you would," Mrs. Smith says, beaming with pride.

Kermit shuffles through the papers. "They want me to start next month at the Washington Defense Department!"

"That soon?" Mrs. Smith asks, noticing her nosy next-door neighbor approaching from the chain-link fence.

"What you two carrying on about?" The neighbor's black eyebrows furrow beneath loose gray strands of hair as she peers at the documents in Kermit's hand.

"Oh, nothing really," Kermit replies, folding the papers and cramming them back into the envelope. "Didn't mean to disturb you." She slides the envelope into her black patent leather purse before the neighbor can read it.

"You have a good evening now," Mrs. Smith calls as she and Kermit trail into the house, leaving the neighbor gaping at the curb. Once inside,

Mrs. Smith closes the door and draws the living room curtains. "Your new job will be splashed all over the Arkansas Gazette if she gets wind of it," she laughs. They hang their sweaters and pocketbooks in the closet before crossing into the kitchen.

"You got that right," Kermit chuckles, removing the envelope and spreading its contents across the table. She switches on the light as Mrs. Smith takes a seat. "I need to pass a medical exam and send in this green application with job references."

"Well, I can be one of your references," Mrs. Smith offers.

"I'm counting on it," Kermit smiles. Her heels click as she starts pacing across the linoleum floor. "I need to tell Gus and Momma." She stops pacing in front of the phone on the enamel counter.

"I had no doubt you'd get one of those secretary jobs up North," Mrs. Smith says, reading the notice.

"I can't believe I'm finally leaving Little Rock." Kermit looks at her watch. "I'm not sure I could even get through to Gus now." She places her hand on the phone, tapping it with her fingers. "This should qualify as a special circumstance, right?"

"I think so," Mrs. Smith agrees. "It doesn't hurt to try."

Kermit picks up the earpiece, listening for the operator to answer. "Camp Robinson, please." She covers the mouthpiece with her hand. "Should I say it's an emergency?"

"Yes," Mrs. Smith nods.

Kermit leaves an urgent message for Augustus at the military base, then calls her mother with the news. After reading her the entire offer letter over the phone, Arvolin responds with a series of questions.

"How are you going to get there? Where will you live? What did Augustus say about it?"

"They sent a travel voucher for a train to Washington," Kermit picks up the voucher and studies it. "It doesn't say if I have to pay it back or not." She flips through the papers and picks up another document. "They have a place in DC on Bryant Street where I can rent a room if I need to. Do we have any relatives living in Washington where I could stay?"

"No, not that I can recall," Arvolin says. "But you still haven't told me what Augustus said. What does he think about you being so far away and living by yourself while he's off in the military?"

"I haven't had a chance to talk to Gus yet," Kermit states. "But I left a message for him to call me as soon as he can." She looks at her watch again, then checks it against the clock hanging above the table. "But he knows I applied for these National Defense jobs in DC. I told you too." She glances through the kitchen window as a couple passes under the streetlight. "There's no point in me staying around here when he's gone for who knows how long."

Mrs. Smith gets up, takes a pot from the stove, and fills it with water. Kermit collects her papers from the counter and table and returns them to the envelope. "Okay, Momma, I'll talk with you more tomorrow. We're about to get dinner started."

"What did she say?" Mrs. Smith washes three potatoes in the sink, then slices them into cubes.

"She's worried about what Gus will say," Kermit responds, putting on an apron.

"Are you?" Mrs. Smith turns to gauge her response.

"Maybe a little," Kermit admits. "But he knows how lonesome I got when he was in Texas. If he's gone, I'm getting out of here on the first thing smoking."

"I believe that," Mrs. Smith chuckles. She puts the cut potatoes into the pot and lights the stove with a match. "First Gus, now you," she shakes her head. "I guess I'm going to have to start looking for a new tenant and fast." She hugs Kermit. "I am going to miss you so much."

Kermit squeezes her back. "I'll miss you too. But you know I'll be back to visit you and Momma."

"You know your mother's probably hoping Augustus will talk you into staying because she doesn't want you to go," Mrs. Smith says.

"Hmm. I didn't think about that," Kermit says. "You know that reminds me of something she told me." She puts the envelope in her apron pocket and leans against the counter. "When I was little, my father went to Michigan to find work. A while later, he sent for me and Momma to join him. After we were packed up to go, her mother got sick. Momma stayed to nurse her back to health. When we got ready to move a second time, my grandmother got sick again. That kept happening until we eventually lost track of my father."

"I didn't know that," Mrs. Smith says. "So you think her mother was pretending to be sick to keep her nearby?"

"Yes, that's right," Kermit says. "I need to make sure Momma knows I'm going to be back or find a way to bring her with me." Kermit washes her hands in the sink and wipes them on a dish towel. "Here I am supposed to be helping you with dinner, and I've done nothing but rattle on about me and my new job."

"Don't worry about that," Mrs. Smith says. "I'll make dinner tonight. You go and get started on that application."

***

Wrapped in Augustus' arms, Kermit feels like the Guest House at Camp Robinson is spinning. On the last day of May, they stand surrounded by the animated chatter of soldiers visiting their families at bench-style tables in the smoke-filled area. Signs posted on the concrete walls instruct recruits and their guests on proper conduct during visits.

"It feels like I'm dreaming." Kermit caresses his face while planting a kiss on his mouth and both cheeks.

"You're a sight for sore eyes." Augustus takes a step back to admire her navy and white dress.

"On Wednesday, I didn't know when I'd see you again. And here we are, together just four days later."

"I know." Augustus picks up his olive duffel bag and flings it over his shoulder. "But let's get out of here before they change their minds." He leads her down the stuffy corridor and into the cool morning breeze. When he opens the passenger door, a group of officers passes, triggering him to drop his bag and salute at attention. Not sure what to do, Kermit stands stiffly until the men disappear into the building. She slides into the seat as Augustus tosses his bag into the trunk.

When he gets behind the wheel, Kermit asks, "Do you have to salute every time?"

"Pretty much, but not if we're inside, but it depends," Augustus stammers. "They gave us a handbook to keep it all straight." He reaches inside his jacket pocket and pulls out a beige booklet titled *Handbook of Information Camp Joseph T. Robinson*. "I haven't gone through it all, but it has a lot of information. You can look through it while I'm on leave."

Kermit opens the handbook and begins flipping through the pages. "I meant to tell you how handsome you look in your uniform," she says, touching his shirt sleeve.

"Thank you, baby," Augustus smiles. He pulls between the two imposing stone pillars that rise twenty feet above the military base entrance. The same uniformed man who greeted Kermit earlier remains stationed under a red-roofed awning that matches the red-roofed stone guard booths in front of each pillar. Augustus exchanges salutes with the white soldier and presents him with his orders. After reviewing the paperwork, the guard waves them off the base.

Once they turn onto Military Road, Kermit turns to face him. "So, tell me, what happened? Your telegram didn't say how you got a furlough so soon."

"First, tell me where we're going," Augustus says, loosening his tie. "I really want to get out of this uniform."

"I just need to stop by the Probation Office to pick up a few things, and then we can go home," Kermit says. "Now tell me!"

"Oh, it's been crazy since you called me. I've talked to so many people—first my Company Commander, then his Commander, and a lot of other officers after that. All asking about your job in Washington." Augustus wipes the sweat from his temple and rolls down the window to let in some air.

"Really? What did they want to know?"

"Pretty much everything. Where you'll be working, what you'll be doing when you start. They seemed to be taken by surprise that a Colored woman wanted to contribute to the war or serve the country. Like we shouldn't want to do things like that."

"Maybe they don't think Negroes deserve to get these jobs," Kermit adds.

"Probably," Augustus says. "Honestly, until they started making such a fuss, I hadn't even thought about how a secretary could help in the war."

"Huh," Kermit chuckles. "Now you know I'm defending my country just like you. Only with a typewriter and stenographer pad!" They laugh as Augustus travels south onto MacArthur Drive, passing small shops in the harsh morning light. "But you still haven't told me how you got the furlough."

"Well, I'm getting to that," Augustus says. "Like I was saying, I told them you'd be starting your job with the War Service next month." He glances at Kermit before continuing. "I haven't had a chance to tell you yet, but I'm about to leave Arkansas, too. I'm being transferred on June tenth."

"What?" Kermit shakes her head in disbelief. "Where?"

"Fort Sill. It's in Lawton, Oklahoma."

"But your training won't be finished by then, will it?"

"No, I'll continue training there," Augustus responds. "But that's how I got the furlough. They made a special concession for us to spend this week together before we go our separate ways. My Company Commander kept saying furloughs are never given to recruits still in training." He points to the handbook Kermit has already discarded on the seat. "I looked it up in the handbook. It says if soldiers are still in training, they are only granted furloughs for something serious, like a death in the family."

Kermit sighs and stares out the window as they pass a neighborhood of white houses and maple trees sprouting bright burgundy-red leaves. "I guess it was meant to be then. But Oklahoma? We'll be even farther away."

"I know. I don't think I know anyone there either. Maybe some friends from college or cousins. I'll have to ask Momma if we have any family there."

"She's going to have a fit," Kermit chuckles.

"I'm sure. I'm going to wait to tell her on the day before I get back to base."

As the car winds through town, the couple cherishes these fleeting moments together, acutely aware that time is slipping away. The unexpected furlough has offered them a rare gift—one final reunion before duty pulls them in opposite directions. With Augustus bound for Fort Sill and Kermit preparing for her new post in Washington, they face an uncertain future separated by even greater distances. Not yet a year into their marriage, they must now learn to serve both their country and each other from afar, preserving the bond that unites them as husband and wife across the miles.

Keeping Secrets

June 20, 1942 - Washington, DC

Clutching her purse and suitcase, Kermit steps outside Union Station into the muggy afternoon. The oppressive humidity causes her butterscotch dress to cling to her moist skin like a damp rag, and the edges of her pressed hair begin to coil. Following her friends' advice, she forces herself to stay awake for most of her two-day journey to ensure that no one on the train tries to steal her money or belongings. Now, as she readies to embark on her new life in the Nation's Capital, her adrenaline kicks in.

While thousands of travelers push past her, Kermit stops in her tracks, gaping at the marble buildings towering against the hazy summer sky. At the center of the station's semicircular driveway stands a fifteen-foot statue of Christopher Columbus at a ship's prow, flanked by a globe and two lions. A constant whirlwind of black Fords and Chevrolets drives past the memorial to pick up or drop off commuters.

Kermit spots a traffic cop on the corner of Massachusetts Avenue, giving directions to a group of uniformed soldiers. When the men leave, she approaches him, a flutter of excitement and nervousness in her stomach. "Excuse me, officer," Kermit says. "Would you please tell me how to get to the US Civil Service Commission?"

"Hold on." He searches the bustling sidewalk, then points up North Capitol Street. "See that woman in the green dress? Follow her. She's headed there, too. Just let the trolley conductor know where you're going, and he'll drop you off at the right stop."

Thirty minutes later, Kermit and the woman in the green dress join the line outside the War Department at 20th and B Streets, Northeast. When she finally escapes the sweltering afternoon air, she enters a stuffy office where a black oscillating fan merely pushes hot air over its twenty-five occupants.

Stashing her suitcase against the wall, Kermit sinks into an empty desk chair in the two back rows assigned to Negroes. A few more people file into the remaining four seats, followed by a white man in a pressed black business suit, starched white shirt, and thin black tie.

"Good afternoon," he announces, his voice commanding attention.

Kermit and her colleagues echo his greeting in unison.

"You are about to embark on a mission from President Roosevelt to serve your country in the War Department." His booming voice resonates throughout the room as he paces deliberately up and down the five rows of desks. He pauses in front of each person, holding eye contact before moving to the next. "You may not be an enlisted soldier in the military, but your work is vital to winning our war effort." He locks eyes with Kermit, his gaze penetrating enough to make her straighten her posture. "Today you will take an oath of office, swearing to support and defend the Constitution of the United States against all enemies, foreign and domestic." He continues up the next aisle, the leather of his polished oxfords creaking with each step. "You will sign an affidavit affirming that you will not discuss anything learned from your connection with the War Department." At the end of the last row, he reverses and retraces his steps. "That includes your family, your friends, your neighbors, your pastor—anyone."

When a red-haired woman in a black swing skirt and a pale canary blouse hesitantly raises her hand, his thick eyebrows furrow in a mix of confusion and annoyance. He quickly regains his composure and offers her a curt nod of acknowledgment.

"I'm sorry to interrupt, but I have a question." As everyone watches, her freckled face and neck flush scarlet with embarrassment. "Are you saying I can't even tell my husband?" A few chuckles and low murmurs ripple around the room, but Kermit is thinking the same thing.

With a stern look, the director strides across the room and stands squarely in front of her. "Yes. That includes your husband, your mother, your father, your brother, and your sister."

"I don't know if I can do that," her voice quivers slightly, almost a whimper.

"You need to be sure, or you shouldn't accept the job offer." His steely gray eyes hold her gaze for an extra three seconds before moving down the aisle. "That goes for all of you," he strides to the adjoining row and passes Kermit again. "You also need to be cautious when discussing politics or the military." No one dares ask another question or look away from his intense gaze. "Violating any of these requirements is considered a criminal offense, and the individual will be prosecuted to the highest extent of the law." He stands at the front of the room facing them with his feet shoulder-length apart and hands clasped behind his back. "If you are unable to swear or affirm all of the items I discussed, do not go any further and leave now."

Kermit stiffens in her chair, her mind racing with worry. *What did I get myself into? Will I be a spy? Can I keep secrets from Gus? What about Momma? Could I really get arrested if I tell them?*

As the weight of the commitment sinks in, the room falls into uncomfortable silence. The only sound is the steady hum of the fan motor and the soft whirring of its blades spinning inside their metal cage. Suddenly, the red-haired woman avoids eye contact and bolts out the door, the click of her heels echoing in the tense atmosphere.

"Anyone else?" the director asks, his tone challenging.

The silence continues for another beat before five more applicants collect their belongings and leave. With a deep, steadying breath that fills her lungs with the stale office air, Kermit accepts her duty to maintain the confidentiality of the War Department and her country.

"Okay, for those who are still with us," he says, taking a stack of papers and distributing them around the room. "This is the Oath of Office and Personnel Affidavit. Please stand and raise your right hand." Kermit and the remaining applicants follow his command. "Now, repeat after me."

Following an afternoon of endless paperwork and orientations, Kermit leaves the Civil Service building, proudly clutching her new assignment as a junior typist. Until she sees it for herself, she would never believe they would pay a Negro this much money—let alone a Negro woman. But here it is on her official civilian secretarial pool assignment in black and white. In a matter of days, her salary jumps from a meager $50 a month at the Pulaski County Juvenile Court to a whopping $120 a month at the Office of the Secretary of War. It feels almost too good to be true.

"Thank you, Jesus," Kermit whispers in prayer. She lugs her suitcase to the trolley stop, then checks the address of her assigned housing. When the train arrives, she waits for the white passengers to board before getting on herself. "166 Bryant Street," she tells the operator.

"Is that Northwest or Northeast?" he asks impatiently, drumming his fingers on the fare box.

"Oh, I didn't know there was more than one Bryant Street," she responds, confused.

"Pay your fare and board at the back door," he says, handing her a ticket. "When you figure out which one you're going to, let me know."

Kermit drops her nickel and three pennies in the fare box and exits the car. She hurries along the curb to the trolley's back entrance and finds a seat behind the "Coloreds Only" sign. She pulls out her Civil Service documents and frantically rifles through them. *Where did I put that paper?* she thinks. *I just had it!* The streetcar jerks along H Street N.E. for five blocks before Kermit finally locates her address. At the next stop, she drags her suitcase out the rear door and quickly reenters through the front.

"It's Northwest. I'm going to 166 Bryant Street, Northwest," she says, panting slightly.

The operator looks at her blankly, his weathered face showing no recognition. "Okay. That'll be eight cents."

"No, I already paid," Kermit shows him her paid fare ticket. "I got on at the Civil Service Building, but didn't know if I was going to Bryant Street Northwest or Northeast. Remember?"

He examines her ticket and returns it. "Okay, this looks like it's from today. I'll let you know when we get to your stop."

"Thank you," Kermit says, realizing he clearly does not remember her or their encounter just a few minutes ago. She exits the car and returns to her seat from the rear.

By the time Kermit is dropped off at the intersection of Second and Bryant Streets, Northwest, the sun hovers above the horizon, casting long shadows across the brick facades. At first glance, the block of two-level brick houses seems cramped and tightly packed. Upon closer inspection, she realizes they are connected row houses, sharing roofs and walls with their adjacent neighbors. As she drags herself up the four steps, exhaustion catches up with her. Pausing on the landing to catch her breath, she peeks inside the home's bay window into a neatly decorated sunroom. Her gaze meets a tan-skinned woman perched on a wicker chair, who immediately jumps up and greets her at the front door.

"Kermit, is that you?" Her perfectly shaped eyebrows lift above her hazel eyes expectantly.

"Yes, ma'am," Kermit answers, matching the woman's warm smile. "You must be Mrs. Richardson."

"Call me Gina, sugar," she ushers her into the foyer and closes the door with a gentle click. "Did you get lost? I've been looking out for you all day."

"I'm so sorry. My train was late coming in, so I went straight to the War Department from the station." Kermit detects a hint of lavender as she enters. Beyond the sunroom, a white crocheted runner and two taper candles adorn the dining room table, which is flanked by six oak press-back chairs.

"That's no problem, honey," she takes Kermit's suitcase and heads up the banister stairs with white railings. "Come on, your room is up here."

"Oh, I can take that," Kermit reaches for her bag, but Gina is already halfway to the next level, moving with the grace of someone half her age. As she reaches the second floor, she turns right and disappears. When Kermit reaches the furnished room, her luggage is already set at the foot of the bed. "Thank you so much."

"No, thank you," Gina stands next to the oak dresser and mirror, smoothing her floral-print dress. "I usually rent to Howard University professors, but they go back home over the summer. You coming to town did me a big favor." She crosses the carpet and unlocks a door that leads to the balcony. "You can sit out here whenever you like, just remember to keep the door locked."

As Kermit steps out onto the balcony, the cool evening air brushes against her skin, bringing welcome relief from the day's heat. The balcony overlooks the back of the row houses across the courtyard, where laundry flutters on clotheslines and the distant sounds of children playing fill the air. "This is so nice."

"There's a porch underneath, too, that leads to a small backyard." They enter the room, and Gina leads her back into the hall. "Your bathroom is here, and I'm right across the hall." She turns to face Kermit. "The kitchen is downstairs, but you can figure all that out later. You go ahead and settle in. I'll check on you in a bit."

"Thanks so much," Kermit says, standing at her doorway. "Your home is lovely. I'm sure I'll love it here."

"You're so welcome, sweetie." In a flash, Gina descends the stairs, her footsteps fading into the quiet house.

Filled with excitement, Kermit explores her new room, opening drawers and stepping into the walk-in closet. She runs her fingers along the smooth wood of the dresser and tests the softness of the quilted bedspread. For the first time in her life, she has a space of her own in a city filled with promise.

Ten days later, Kermit secures a permanent position in the War Department's Allocation and Allotment Branch. Under the newly enacted Servicemen's Dependents Act of 1942, she tirelessly processes requests from Army, Navy, Marine Corps, and Coast Guard personnel seeking financial support for their families. Her colleagues quickly take note of her efficiency and precision, often turning to her for help with their own cases.

She has finally left Little Rock behind. Now, in the heart of Washington, D.C., Kermit stands on her own—confident, capable, and ready for whatever comes next.

Bombing New York

September 2, 1942 – Harlem, New York

A s an employee of the War Department with top-secret clearance, Kermit has access to a wealth of confidential information on World War II, several continents away. She also becomes susceptible to the rampant gossip that sweeps across the country about possible global conflicts. Over the summer, rumors intensify about enemy forces planning to drop an atomic bomb on New York City to disrupt Wall Street, national landmarks, and densely populated areas.

On the first Wednesday in September, the scorching midday sun turns Kermit's government building into an oven, surpassing the eighty-six-degree temperatures outside. Half past noon, she and two coworkers eat lunch at a four-top table anchored to the tile floor of their office cafeteria. Oscillating fans hang from the ceiling, blowing the stifling air around the hall packed with federal employees.

"Did you hear they're talking about bombing New York?" Kermit asks her tablemates. She bites into her egg salad sandwich, then brushes away traces of breadcrumbs from her lips.

Alice, a petite woman in a gold linen dress, replies, "Yes, it's awful!" She tastes the mashed potatoes on her fork and frowns. Picking up the salt-shaker, she sprinkles it liberally over the white creamy dish.

"I heard on the news that place is crawling with German spies," adds Mavis, an office clerk with her brunette hair pinned back in a tight bun.

"That's scary," Kermit says, setting down her sandwich. "I've always wanted to see New York, but haven't had a chance yet." She blows on the steaming black coffee in her cup before gingerly sipping it, the bitter liquid warming her throat.

"I said the same thing to my mother last week," Alice says. "Kermit, why don't we go before they bomb the city?"

"You think?" Kermit's black eyebrows furrow on her almond-colored face as she considers Alice's suggestion.

"Yes," Alice's voice rises slightly in excitement. "We have Monday off for Labor Day, so we should make a weekend out of it!"

"Where would we stay?" Kermit returns her sandwich to the plate. "I don't know anyone there, do you?"

"I have a cousin who lives up there in Brooklyn. Paul can find us a hotel because he knows the area."

"Really?" Kermit's excitement grows at the thought of visiting the big city, a thrill running through her. "Oh, but the hotel won't take the reservation unless it's from a man. Can your cousin make it for us?"

"I'm sure he can. I'll call him tonight and let you know."

Kermit turns to Mavis. "Do you want to come up with us?"

"No. You won't catch me up there," she says, vigorously shaking her head, her pearl earrings swinging with the motion. "New York is dangerous with lots of hoodlums who take advantage of people from out of town." Kermit purses her lips and nervously glances at Alice. "If you end up going, make sure you don't talk to anyone or get hooked up with any strangers while you're there," Mavis cautions, her brown eyes widening for emphasis.

"Okay, we won't," Alice replies. Kermit nods in agreement.

On Saturday afternoon, Kermit and Alice reach Manhattan's Penn Station as hundreds of travelers hurry to their weekend destinations. They gawk at the sculpted eagles along the arched windows, tilting their heads back to capture the majestic murals adorning the vaulted ceiling. The marble walls amplify the loud voices echoing throughout the spacious concourse, creating a symphony of bustling humanity. Setting their suitcases in front of a gift shop, they stop to get their bearings.

"I can't believe we're actually here," Kermit says, peeking at the souvenirs inside the store. She catches her reflection in the glass window and straightens the crochet collar on her chartreuse and white print dress. Reaching inside her black clamshell purse, Kermit reapplies her crimson lipstick, using the glass as a mirror.

"I know! This is so exciting," Alice says, checking her appearance in the window. She reaches for her compact and powders her copper-toned face.

After tucking stray hairs behind her ears, Alice removes a piece of paper from her purse. "Paul said we need to..."

Chimes from the four-foot Roman numeral clock suspended between two steel columns interrupt her. The women marvel as it plays the four tones of the Westminster Quarters, indicating it is a quarter past the hour. Once the ringing stops, Alice continues. "He said we needed to take another train to get to our hotel in Harlem. We should be on 7th Avenue when we get outside." She shows the paper to Kermit, pointing to the directions written in shorthand. "We turn left, walk up one block, and should see a sign that says 'I.R.T.'—short for Interborough Rapid Transit."

"Okay," Kermit nods enthusiastically. "Onward Christian Soldiers," she chuckles, adjusting her grip on her suitcase.

A few minutes later, Kermit and Alice descend the stairs to the underground transit station, clumsily maneuvering their luggage while wearing high heels that click against the concrete steps. At the ticket booth, they count out the coins for the five-cent fare, ensuring they shield their money from any prying eyes. The ticket agent directs them to the correct platform, and they navigate past the crush of commuters along the white-tiled wall lined with advertising posters for everything from cigarettes to war bonds.

When the train arrives with a screech of metal on metal, the momentum from the boarding passengers sweeps them onto the already crowded train. Moving quickly, they grab two seats by the door, storing their bags on their laps.

"I never imagined all these people were under the streets," Kermit says as the train jerks away from the station. Alice's gaze sweeps along the steel car, noting the soot stains along the walls and ceiling. A mix of tourists, locals, and families chat as they sway with the movement of the train. "I wish Gus could see this."

"How's he doing?" Alice asks, watching the lights dim as the car passes through the dark tunnel.

"Okay," Kermit says. "Did I tell you they moved him again?"

"No! He's not in Oklahoma anymore? Since when?"

"Last month," Kermit sighs, shaking her head. "He's in Michigan now. In a French-sounding town near Canada. It's called..." She purses her lips, trying to recall the name. "Sault Sainte Marie."

"Never heard of it," Alice says. "But at least Michigan is a little closer."

"I guess," Kermit shrugs, absentmindedly fingering the gold locket around her neck—Gus' gift before he left for boot camp. "It's definitely better than him being shipped overseas."

"Ain't that the truth," Alice agrees.

As the train approaches the next stop, it jolts to a halt just before many of the commuters rush out of the car. A caramel-toned woman in a blue polka-dot dress sits across the aisle from them and glances at their suitcases. "Hi, I'm Josephine. You girls from out of town?" She smiles broadly, pushing her wire-rimmed glasses up her nose.

Kermit follows the woman's gaze and looks back at Alice. "Yes," she answers curtly and stares straight ahead. She wonders if this woman is one of the city slickers Mavis warned them about.

"You have someplace to stay?" Josephine slides closer to them, and the harsh stench of her perfume—something cheap and overly floral—drifts across the aisle.

"Yes," Alice says, eyeing her suspiciously.

Josephine leans across the aisle. "Are you sure?" She leans in closer and whispers, "Because sometimes these hotels say they don't have your reservation if you're Colored."

"Well, we're sure," Kermit says confidently. "Her cousin Paul made it for us."

"Uh-huh," the woman says doubtfully. "Is your cousin here with you?" She scans the front and back of the mostly empty car to see if a man is nearby.

"No," Alice answers. She tightly clutches the handle of her suitcase and nudges Kermit to do the same.

"Well, tell you what," Josephine's voice gets lower again, conspiratorial. "Why don't I go with you to make sure you have someplace to stay tonight? I wouldn't want you two to be stuck here in New York with nowhere to go."

Kermit and Alice exchange glances but remain silent. As the train reaches their stop, they swiftly disembark with the strange woman trailing closely behind. They depart the station on Lenox Avenue in a vibrant African American community with restaurants, shops, and clubs. The aroma of fried fish and baking bread wafts from nearby establishments, mixing with the scent of automobile exhaust.

"Look, there's the Apollo Theatre," Kermit squeals, pointing to the marquee flickering above the theater's entrance. "I've heard so much about it, and now we're right here!"

"Oh, and the Savoy! It's right next door," Alice points excitedly.

They cross the street to get a closer look at the popular dance hall, joining other onlookers milling outside. A man standing near the entrance approaches them, his zoot suit hanging loosely on his lanky frame. "You ladies look like you came to New York to have a good time," he says, grinning. "I can tell just by looking at you that you can really cut a rug," he chuckles. "While you're in town, you've got to catch tonight's show at the Savoy." He hands all three a leaflet from the stack he's holding. "Bring this here flyer with you tonight, and you can get in for free."

"Thank you!" Kermit says, reading the paper, her heart racing at the prospect. She smiles at Alice. "Dancing at the famous Savoy? I can't wait!"

They stroll past street musicians performing lively jazz tunes, the sound of trumpets and saxophones filling the air. As the women continue up Lenox Avenue, artists call to them, gesturing towards their paintings displayed along the sidewalk. When they arrive at the three-story terracotta hotel, Josephine accompanies them to the mahogany receptionist's desk.

"Good afternoon," an African American man in a chestnut suit and thin tie stands to greet them, the golden buttons on his jacket catching the light. "How may I help you three lovely ladies?"

"Well, it's actually just the two of us," Alice points to Kermit and back to herself. "We have a room reservation for tonight and Sunday."

"Oh, I see," he glances at Josephine curiously, who simply smiles and nods back. "Is it for one room or two?"

"One," Alice replies. "We'll be sharing the room."

"What name is the reservation under?" The clerk opens the hotel's guest book and flips the pages until locating the current date.

"Kermit Hill and Alice Wilson."

His finger slides down one page and then the other until he reaches the bottom of the fourth page. "Sorry, ladies, I don't seem to have your names here."

Kermit shoots her friend a nervous look. "Are you sure Paul made the reservation?" She wipes the beads of sweat forming along her hairline.

"Yes," Alice says. "Please check again."

The clerk nods. "Of course." He repeats his search for the reservation, this time starting from the last page and moving up.

Kermit steps closer to Alice and asks hopefully, "Maybe your cousin put it under his name instead of ours?" She peers over the counter at the clerk. "Could you check if you have a Paul...what's his last name, Alice?"

"It's Wilson, same as mine. He's my uncle's son," she rambles anxiously, her fingers nervously twisting her handkerchief. "That's a good idea. Check for Paul Wilson, too."

While the clerk pores over the hotel's bookings, a sly grin spreads across Josephine's face. She nods at them and whispers, "Uh-huh. What did I tell you?"

"No Paul Wilson either. I'm sorry," he gives them a sympathetic look.

"Well, it's a good thing I came with you," Josephine says, grinning triumphantly.

"This is awful," Kermit tells Alice. "We came all the way up here..." she trails off, her stomach knotting with disappointment.

"I'm sorry," Alice says. "Paul is usually such a stand-up guy."

Kermit looks back at the front desk attendant. "Please, could you check under our names once more? We're positive he made the reservation for us."

"Okay. I'll go through the list again and read each name aloud." He starts with the first name on the list and begins reciting the names. After five names, he says, "Oh, wait. Kermit Hill and Alice Wilson?"

"Yes, that's us," they say in unison, relief washing over their faces.

"My sincere apologies. When I saw Kermit, I was expecting a man."

The two women exchange a glance and burst into laughter, the tension melting away. As the clerk finishes checking them into their room, their unwelcome New York escort leaves the hotel dejected. Once they settle into the room, Kermit says incredulously, "Can you believe that? The hotel was going to put an unmarried man and a woman in the same room!"

REQUEST DENIED

October 22, 1942 – Newark, New Jersey

As neighborhood trees spill their bronze, crimson, and amber leaves along Washington, D.C.'s sidewalks, Kermit settles into the rhythm of her new job and life in the capital. Her increased salary lets her support her mother back in Arkansas and still afford the fashionable dresses and suits for her new professional lifestyle. Weekly letters connect her to Augustus, punctuated by the occasional crackling long-distance call, his voice barely rising above the static. For now, he remains in Sault Sainte Marie, Canada, stationed with the Colored 100th Coast Artillery Regiment.

When the agency offers her a promotion at the New Jersey branch, Kermit fights it tooth and nail. She adores her life in D.C., and rumors of foul-smelling air and rude locals in the Garden State only steel her opposition. She types a formal letter to her supervisor, making her case plain, concluding:

It would be impossible for me to make the transfer with the Allowance and Allotment Division to Newark, New Jersey.

Despite her vigorous objections, Kermit receives a Pennsylvania Coach Railroad ticket and finds herself bound for the Garden State two weeks later.

On a chilly Saturday afternoon in November, she departs the train at Newark Penn Station as temperatures dip below freezing. When she locates her assigned housing at 52 Hartford Street, it is cold and bare, nothing like the cozy and colorful home she left behind in DC. To make matters worse, Kermit's new landlord embodies the stereotype of the mean New Jerseyans that people warned her about. On the bright side, she lives within a short twenty-minute walk of her new workplace. Plus, with her promotion to assistant clerk, Kermit enjoys a $180 bump in her annual salary—now reaching $1,620.

As the sunrise peaks above the skyline on Monday, November 9th, Kermit arrives forty-five minutes early at the impressive brick skyscraper at 213 Washington Street. She stops to gawk at the twenty-one-story structure that encompasses an entire city block. Looking for the separate Colored entrance, she circles the building along Bank Street, University Avenue, and Academy Street. Finding none, she enters the front door and approaches the guard standing inside the foyer. Her heels click against the newly tiled floor, and she detects an overwhelming scent of fresh paint.

"May I help you?" As she comes closer, she guesses the security officer is in his fifties with traces of gray in his black mustache. He wears a dark navy suit and tie with a matching hat that covers his mostly gray hair.

"Good morning, sir," Kermit starts. "Today's my first day at the Office of Dependency Benefits. Is this where I'm supposed to enter the building?"

"Yes, you're in the right place," he answers with a smile. "In fact, I'm expecting a couple hundred new workers today." He turns to look at the wall clock behind him. "But they told me I had another thirty minutes or so before they'd start showing up."

"That's right, I just got here early," Kermit explains. "I wasn't sure how long it would take me to get here on the bus, and I didn't want to be late on my first day."

"I see," he says. "Well, you've got yourself a brand-new workplace. They just finished building it last month."

"It sure is nice," Kermit admires the halls and offices she can view from her stance. "I smelled the new paint when I came in."

"Do you know where you're supposed to report?" He takes a clipboard and starts flipping through the pages.

"Yes, my unit is on the 12th floor." She removes a picture ID hung around her neck. "Here's my work badge." The circular red badge hangs from a metal bead chain, though the back also holds a clasp for pinning to clothing. At the center is her official black-and-white employment photo, with her name printed beneath it. Bold lettering encircles the edge: *O.D.B. – WAR DEPT – NEWARK*, with *GET 'EM PAID* stamped along the bottom—a clear emblem of her duty at the Office of Dependency Benefits.

Kermit Hill's War Department Office of Dependency Benefits ID

"Thank you." The guard lifts the ID to compare the photo to her face. "It's you, alright," he chuckles and returns it to her. "You may be the first one to arrive, but someone will be there soon. Vivian over there will take you up to your floor."

Across the lobby, a petite woman with a cinnamon-brown complexion waves at her. The top and skirt of her gray uniform are neatly pressed as she stands alongside the elevator.

On the ride up, Kermit whispers, "You know, I walked up and down the block looking for a Colored entrance to the building."

Vivian smiles. "It's so nice when they don't have one, isn't it? You'll still see them sometimes, but it's getting better."

"That's good to hear," Kermit says. The doors open to a modern office with new furnishings, typewriters, and windows overlooking downtown. "Will you look at this? I've never worked at such a fancy place before."

"Every floor is just like this," Vivian says. "It's all brand-new stuff."

"I can't believe they let Negroes work in such a fancy new office," Kermit marvels, stepping onto the floor. "It's beautiful."

"It really is," Vivian agrees. "Well, I better be getting back downstairs. Have a good day."

"Thanks, Vivian." Kermit crosses to the window as sunlight fills the room. Maybe New Jersey isn't so bad after all.

In the morning of her first day, Kermit attends orientation, repeating her oath to protect military secrets under the Espionage Act, which carries the penalty of death or long-term imprisonment. After a brief lunch, she weaves past her typing coworkers, hearing the familiar sounds of clicking keys, ringing margin bells, and whirring return carriages. When she knocks on her new supervisor's office door, an Italian American man opens it, gesturing for her to sit.

"Good morning, Kermit." His charcoal gray suit hangs loosely off his thin frame as he stands awkwardly by the entrance. Although her manager is only a couple of years older than she is, his receding hairline causes him to appear much older than his twenty-six years. His dishwater blond eyebrows fade against his pale skin, and his thin hair is combed back with a high side part.

"Good morning, Mr. Ottaviano," Kermit says, sitting in the chair on the opposite side of his desk. She positions her pen on the notepad, poised to take dictation.

He opens his drawer and retrieves an olive-green folder. "Okay, let's get started," he says, clearing his throat. Her supervisor stops to examine the ivory-colored form, then shuffles through the other papers in the file. "Hold on, it looks like you haven't had an Efficiency Rating before. Is that correct?"

"Yes," she nods. "This will be my first."

"Oh," he looks slightly flustered, then quickly regains his composure. "Since you just started your new position this month, this rating will only cover your employment as an assistant clerk. Do you understand?"

"Yes, sir." Kermit's pen scratches shorthand notes across the paper.

"What are you writing?" he asks, looking across the desk curiously.

"Just jotting down what you said about the assistant clerk position and the dates of my review," she stops writing and flips to the next page of her pad.

He clears his throat again, leaning back and causing his chair to squeak. "Well, just so you know, you don't have to take dictation for this. You'll be sent a copy for your records once it's signed by the reviewing official."

"Okay," Kermit says, continuing to take notes.

"Let's get started," Mr. Ottaviano repeats. He straightens his black tie and rakes his fingers through his hair. "It looks like your previous supervisor, Ruth Robinson, thinks very highly of you. She wrote a very favorable recommendation in August."

"Yes, that was very kind of her," Kermit blushes, slightly embarrassed. She nervously taps the end of her pen on her notepad.

"You obviously do good work, or you wouldn't have been promoted so quickly." He studies the rest of Kermit's folder. "In fact, it seems you've been an efficient worker since you started in the department in Washington." He smiles, causing slight wrinkles to form around his eyes and nose. "From these ratings, I can see you're very committed to your job, and your work is outstanding."

"I try to do my best, sir."

"Well, it shows. We really appreciate all you do here, Kermit. I'm going to give you another *Very Good* rating."

"Thank you so much, Mr. Ottaviano."

"I'll send this through to the personnel officer, and you should get your copy within the week." He stands, signaling Kermit to do the same. "And thank you for doing your part by supporting the war effort." He reaches across the desk, and they shake hands.

"I'm happy to." Kermit starts to leave, but turns back. "I'm not sure if you know, but my husband is serving in the Army. He's stationed in Canada now, somewhere close to Michigan."

"You don't say?" He casually leans on his desk, crossing his arms. "I'll be joining the Army myself next September."

"Oh, good luck to you, sir. I'll be praying for you."

Kermit returns to her desk to complete her last case of the day. She verifies the eligibility of a Coast Guard member who applied for financial assistance for his wife and newborn child. While reviewing the supporting documents, her mind wanders to when she and Augustus might have their baby. Maybe she will become pregnant on his next furlough.

"You ready to go?" Standing beside her desk is Mattie, her coworker who transferred from DC one month before she did. Mattie's wool tan coat is already buttoned, and her beige pocketbook dangles from her arm.

"Girl, you scared me," Kermit says, startled. "I didn't even hear you come up." She rises and shimmies into her navy coat. "Let me drop this off and I'll be ready to go." They walk down the hall, and she places the folder into the inbox outside Mr. Ottaviano's now vacant office.

On the bus ride home, Kermit and Mattie travel past the Newark train station and along the Passaic River.

"You know what's crazy?" Kermit stares blankly out the window as the bus maneuvers through the stop-and-go traffic on the downtown streets. "When Gus was away at school, I couldn't wait to get married because I was so lonely in Little Rock. Now I'm married, and I'm still just as lonely as I was before."

Mattie shakes her head sadly and reaches over to give Kermit a side hug. "But you have friends here, like me."

"I know," Kermit turns, hugging her friend. "You know I'm so grateful for you, but it's different. I knew Gus would be going into the Army soon after we got married. But I had no idea how hard it would be living apart."

The bus crosses over the Hackensack River into Jersey City as the setting sun creates an orange glow across the city skyline. It stops at Lincoln Park, where several commuters disembark. As the bus turns onto Duncan Avenue, exhaust fumes drift inside through the cracks of the windows.

"I've been thinking," Kermit continues. "When I moved from Little Rock, I left my mother all alone. Gus' mother is there, but she's married, and she and her husband are pretty involved with their church."

"You're not thinking about moving back, are you?" Mattie says worriedly.

"No," Kermit says, shaking her head. "I could never find a job in Little Rock that would pay enough. But I am thinking about bringing Momma here. My new apartment has plenty of room. Plus, with Momma around, I won't feel so lonely."

"That makes sense," Mattie says. "Having your mother here will help take your mind off things."

"I hope so," Kermit says. "The only issue is my mother is stubborn and may not want to leave home. She's never lived outside Arkansas, and she loves being the Matron at the Juvenile Detention Center, where I used to work. It'll take some convincing to get her here."

"Well, I know if anyone can talk her into it, you can," Mattie chuckles. "I'm sure she'll want to be closer to her only child, too."

Their route continues down Montgomery Street towards the Hudson River with the Statue of Liberty posing majestically in the distance. When the bus reaches Fremont Street, they get off at their Jersey City apartment complex. Children play in the grass courtyard under the watchful eye of their mothers, who sit on their patios. A few neighbors wave as Kermit and Mattie approach the corner of their building.

"Thanks for listening," Kermit says, giving Mattie another hug.

"No problem, girl," Mattie says. "See you tomorrow."

Kermit steps into her first-floor apartment, thinking about all she needs to do before her mother arrives. On the kitchen table are piles of mail, sorted into bills, letters, and work documents. Boxes from her move remain unopened by the closet door. Dishes from this morning's breakfast sit unwashed in the sink.

Kermit sighs: she can already hear her mother's voice nagging her about not keeping her place neat. Truthfully, she feels a little apprehensive about living with her mother again, remembering all the arguments they had before she moved out to get married. She hangs up her coat and purse and begins cleaning the apartment. She knows being together will be better for both of them. Hopefully, they will get along better this time.

Matron Resigns

Mrs. Arvolin Bland, matron of Detention Home for the past two and one half years, resigns her position to join her daughter, Mrs. Kermit B. Hill, Newark, N. J. She will be accompanied by her neice, Miss Ruth Hood Scott.

"Matron Resigns" Arkansas Press Article about Arvolin Bland

ROMANTIC GETAWAY

December 30, 1942 - Bear Mountain, NY

As the evening storm rages outside, raindrops pound against the windowpane while Kermit and five other women wait their turn at Dorothy's kitchen table in her makeshift beauty salon. Since Kermit's move to Jersey City last month, Dorothy is the only one who has perfected a press and curl without burning her ears or scalp. Others know this too, willingly putting aside up to two hours for her stylish results. Against the backdrop of Glenn Miller's swing rhythms crackling from the Philco radio, the women chat about their plans for New Year's Eve and hopes for 1943.

The stench of singed hair fills the cramped apartment, mingling with the subtle nutty aroma of the shea butter ointment Dorothy uses during the hair straightening process. The stove's blue and white gas flames dance hypnotically around the metal teeth of a styling comb and the gleaming clamp of a curling iron. Lined against the wall behind the beauty supplies sits a tin of Crisco shortening and three matching beige containers decorated with bright red cherries for flour, rice, and sugar.

"Your turn, Kermit," Dorothy calls when a woman with freshly pressed curls vacates the chair next to the stove. After shampooing and drying Kermit's hair, the beautician wraps a white terrycloth towel around her neck. Dorothy sections her coal-black strands into four equal parts with a wide-toothed comb, then pins them in place with large gold bobby pins. Dipping her index and middle fingers into a round tin of gel, she applies it to Kermit's scalp and hairline. Grabbing the thick black handle, Dorothy removes the hot comb from the dancing flames and cools it with a damp towel. Guiding Kermit's head forward, she starts at the nape of her neck and carefully pulls the hot comb through her hair. Kermit flinches when the hair oil sizzles from the heat of the styling tool.

"You better stay still, girl, if you don't want me to burn you," Dorothy warns, firmly steadying Kermit's head with her palm.

"I know, I'm sorry," Kermit apologizes meekly. She steels herself for the hot comb, tightly shutting her eyes and grasping the ends of the towel.

"You don't want Augustus' hands to get tangled in this nappy kitchen when he's running his fingers through your hair," Dorothy teases, moving to her next section of hair.

Kermit relaxes her shoulders and opens her eyes. "No, I don't," she chuckles. "I can't wait to see him tomorrow."

"How long has it been?"

"The last time I saw him was June fifth," Kermit answers. "So almost seven months ago."

Dorothy tilts Kermit's head to the side. "Cover your ear," she instructs. Kermit takes the towel from her neck and covers her ear while bending it down. "Is he still in Michigan?"

"I think so. He's right on the Canadian border." Kermit squeezes her eyes shut as she feels the heat of the comb near her skin and hears more sizzling. "I think he goes back and forth."

"Huh. Isn't that something?" Dorothy returns the comb to the flame and picks up the curling iron. She cools it off on the damp towel before wrapping two inches of Kermit's freshly straightened hair around the barrel, then presses down the clamp. "Well, you'll be looking like Lena Horne and Dorothy Dandridge combined when I get through with you."

"You always do," Kermit grins.

"It's still coming down pretty hard out there," Dorothy says, finishing up Kermit's curls. "Be sure to tie your rain bonnet real tight and hold your umbrella close to your head so your hair won't get wet."

"Okay, I will," Kermit says. Reaching inside her navy purse, she removes an envelope containing the money for her hair plus a tip. "Thanks so much and have a happy new year!"

The following morning, Kermit gazes out the train window, content in Augustus' embrace. Sunlight catches his bronze American Campaign Medal—awarded for his service in Ontario, Canada. The striped and round insignia patches on his sleeves stretch against his forearms. The train chugs northward along the Hudson River, its churning water carrying branches and leaves in the opposite direction. Following overnight showers, gray scattered clouds slowly dissipate, revealing patches of blue sky along the winter landscape. As the temperature inside the cabin drops, Kermit transfers her blue wool coat from her lap to her shoulders, using it as a blanket.

"You cold?" Augustus asks, drawing her closer.

"A little," she answers, tucking the coat collar under her chin.

"Well, I know how to warm you up," he grins, kissing her.

"I'm sure you do," she chuckles. "I've missed you so much."

The reunited couple continues to kiss until the train pulls into the next station. As passengers disembark and board, a man in a tan tweed coat settles in the seat across the aisle. He tips his fedora in their direction, then places it on top of his leather bag.

"You in the service?" he asks, the corners of his lips creasing into a smile.

"Yes, Army," Augustus nods, straightening his posture slightly. "Home on furlough from Sault Sainte Marie, Canada."

"We're all very proud of you," the passenger rises to firmly shake Augustus' hand. "You come home safe for that young lady over there. Enjoy your time with her."

"Thank you. I will," Augustus responds, appreciative of the man's recognition.

Kermit beams at Augustus after the passenger returns to his newspaper. "Have I told you how handsome you look in that uniform?" She glides her fingers across his ribbon award bar above his left breast pocket, then admires the Army collar discs pinned to his lapel.

"Maybe once or twice," he chuckles. "You look pretty snazzy yourself." He caresses her neck, brushing against her double strand of pearls. "I like this necklace," he says, rubbing the smooth pearls between his fingers.

"Thanks," Kermit says. "I got it in DC before I moved, along with these matching earrings." She unclasps the pearl earring on her earlobe to show him.

"Well, you look very pretty," Augustus holds her closer.

The brakes screech as the train slows to a stop. The conductor walks down the aisle calling, "Bear Mountain!"

"That's us," Augustus says, rising to help Kermit into her coat. He retrieves her suitcase from the luggage bin, then swings his duffel bag over his shoulder. Once the white passengers disembark the train cars, they are allowed to follow them onto the platform. "Over there," Augustus nods to the shuttle loading tourists for Bear Mountain.

On the bus, Kermit anxiously squeezes Augustus' hand as they ascend the mountainside along a steep, winding roadway. Upon reaching the summit, they discover panoramic views of Hudson Valley. Bathed in the midafternoon sun, they marvel at the breathtaking sights as cotton ball clouds float gracefully across the cobalt sky. The valley stretches before them like a patchwork quilt of emerald forests and silver ribbons of water, all framed by distant purple mountains dissolving into the horizon.

"Oh, Gus, this is beautiful," Kermit gushes, staring off into the rugged terrain dotted with eastern white pines and snow-dusted hemlock trees. "I bet I can see all the way to Jersey City from here," she jokes, her eyes sparkling with delight.

"It's really something to see, alright." He places their luggage under a towering pine tree, then retrieves his Kodak Brownie camera from his bag. "Let's go to the overlook to get a better view." They follow the gravel path around several large rocks with evergreen trees and mountain laurel bushes sprouting from their cracks. When they arrive at the lookout point, they encounter a white couple with their two children, admiring the scene. In the shadow of a moss-covered boulder, they stand aside, waiting until the family departs. Then Augustus takes Kermit's hand, guiding her to the mountainside opening. Kermit removes her coat, draping it elegantly off her shoulders.

He lets out a low whistle. "Will you look at that!" In the distance, the Hudson River flows through moss-colored peaks with jagged sandstone and slate rocks. Augustus snaps a few pictures of Kermit as she playfully poses with one hand behind her head, the other resting on her hip. He embraces her from behind as they admire the view, the crisp mountain air filling their lungs. When another couple comes along, they move to let them take their place.

"Do you want me to take your picture?" The man offers, reaching out his palm. Augustus and Kermit briefly exchange looks, then nod.

"Thank you, that would be nice," Augustus replies.

The two couples search for a picturesque backdrop before deciding on a grassy spot with overgrown bushes dotted with late-season winterberries, their bright red fruits standing out against the winter landscape. Augustus hands the camera to the man and sits on the hill in front of Kermit.

"Ready? One, two, three," he snaps the picture and returns the camera.

12-30-1942 Augustus and Kermit Hill, Bear Mountain, NY

"Thank you so much," Augustus and Kermit say in unison.

"You're welcome," he replies. "Have a good day."

Augustus leads Kermit down the gravel path back to their bags. "We should go check in now," he says, picking up their belongings. They follow the signs to a grand rustic lodge located at the mountain's peak. Three-foot boulders line the driveway and guard the entrance. As they approach, Kermit pauses to survey the massive three-story structure. Large colorful stones construct the foundation, while dark brown logs cover the upper floors. On the second level, a large veranda wraps around the front and side of the building, covered with evergreen climbing ivy, its tendrils reaching toward the sky.

"Are you sure it's okay for us to stay here?" she asks hesitantly, her voice dropping to a whisper.

"You know I would've checked it out before bringing you," Augustus assures her. "One of my Army buddies stayed here over the summer. He said the National Association for the Advancement of Colored People held their meeting up here a year ago."

"No telling! I'm glad times are changing for our people."

"At least in some places," Augustus sighs wearily.

As they get closer, they realize the letters on the inn's sign are made of twisted hickory branches, artfully arranged to spell out the hotel's name. They enter under the emerald-green awning, and the valet opens the heavy wooden door for them. "Welcome to the Grand View Hotel," he greets them with a warm smile.

"Thank you," Augustus gives Kermit a nod of *I told you so.*

"It's such an impressive hotel you have here," Kermit says, stepping into the vestibule and inhaling the scent of pine and wood smoke.

"Did you know it was built out of the mountain's rocks and chestnut trees?"

"No, that's wonderful," Kermit replies, taking in the rustic décor. "I've never seen a fireplace like that."

"Go ahead and take a look," he encourages.

She crosses the lobby to the floor-to-ceiling stone wall with two life-size bronze bear cubs on the hearth. On either side of the roaring fire, the cubs stand on their hind legs holding walking sticks, their metallic surfaces gleaming in the firelight. Her eyes fix on the four majestic stag heads with sixteen-point antlers mounted above the fireplace, their glass eyes seeming to follow her movement. She gingerly reaches out her hand and touches the rock wall, feeling its cool, rough texture beneath her fingertips.

"Just beautiful," Kermit says. She strolls through the expansive room decorated with hand-crafted Adirondack wood furnishings—sturdy chairs with wide armrests and deep-cushioned leather sofas—eventually returning to Augustus' side.

"What can I do for you today?" A receptionist greets them at the inn's front desk, his voice cheerful and welcoming.

"We have reservations for tonight," Augustus removes a folded confirmation letter from his wallet and presents it to the clerk.

"Wonderful. You'll be staying in our cabins," he says, flipping the pages of the leather-bound guest book. "Make sure you come to our special New Year's Eve party tonight. We'll have a live band, dancing, and a champagne toast at midnight."

"Oh, that sounds really nice," Kermit says, her eyes lighting up. "I can't believe it'll be 1943 in a few hours."

"This year has really flown by," agrees the receptionist. "Here's your key. Our hotel offers several activities to keep you busy during your stay. We haven't had enough snow yet for skiing, but you're welcome to go ice skating or learn archery while you're here."

"Thanks again," Augustus says, slipping the key into his pocket.

Later that evening, Augustus escorts Kermit to the dance hall dressed in their finest attire. Wrapped in a soft rabbit fur stole, she wears a beaded cream gown that catches the light with each movement. Atop her black loose curls sits a matching wool bowler hat, topped with an elegant side ribbon bow. Following Kermit's encouragement, Augustus stays in his tan uniform to coordinate with his wife's outfit. Black and white crepe paper streamers cascade from the ceiling while twinkling fairy lights trace the Happy New Year banner on the log cabin wall. Elegant chinaware is arranged on crisp white tablecloths, and white taper candles cast flickering golden shadows around the festive room.

Across the dining hall, the same African American couple who took their picture sits at a four-top table. The man waves them over, and they walk over to join them.

"Well, hello and happy new year," the man says, his voice warm and inviting. "I didn't know you two were staying here, too."

"Yes, we're here for the night," Augustus replies.

"Why don't you join us?" He stands and waves to the two empty wooden cane back chairs at the table. "We didn't get to properly meet earlier. This is my wife, Gracie, and I'm Sturman."

"Nice to meet you," Kermit and Augustus say together as they take turns shaking hands with the couple.

"I'm Augustus, and this is my wife, Kermit," he says, placing a protective hand around her waist. "We'd love to join you." Augustus pulls a chair out for Kermit and then sits beside her.

Following a three-course culinary feast of roast duck, winter vegetables, and chocolate mousse, the musicians take to the stage, performing lively jazz melodies that fill the room. The four-piece band—piano, trumpet, bass, and drums—launches into a rendition of Duke Ellington's "Take the 'A' Train." Hotel party guests of all ages and backgrounds celebrate the last day of the year, kicking up their heels on the chestnut floor. The two couples hesitantly join in, dancing alongside white families and couples for the first time, all seemingly embracing the promise of the new year.

With just fifteen minutes left on the clock, ushers gracefully weave through the crowd, distributing colorful paper party hats and lively silver horns. Excitement grows as waiters move swiftly, pouring effervescent champagne into delicate crystal flutes that catch and scatter the light. As the clock strikes midnight, the crowd erupts with jubilant chants of "Happy New Year" as hotel staff throw handfuls of shimmering confetti in every direction. Surrounded by excited cheers, Kermit and Augustus clink their flutes and toast the New Year with an extended kiss. After sipping the sparkling wine, Kermit rubs her nose from the tickling bubbles.

"Baby, I'm so glad we're going into 1943 together," Augustus whispers, his arms caressing her waist. Kermit nestles her head on his shoulder as they sway to the music, barely heard over the boisterous festivities. Exuberant revelers swirl around them, tooting horns, guzzling champagne, and joyously shouting in celebration of the new year. Amidst the jubilations, Kermit treasures their fleeting moment together, determined not to think about the looming war that will soon take Augustus from her side.

FOR BETTER, FOR WORSE

August 25, 1943

Since being promoted to senior clerk on August 1st, Kermit's stress has increased considerably. Not only has her workload doubled, but colleagues now frequently seek her guidance in unraveling complex military security cases. To qualify for the promotion, she undergoes her second background check since joining the War Department last year. However, the results of her most recent O'Hanlon Loyalty and Character Report from July are still pending, contributing to her anxiety.

Besides the pressures she feels at work, Kermit feels irritated with her husband, who transferred to Camp Stewart in Georgia last month. Two weeks ago, he sent her a telegram indicating he would be on furlough in three days and to meet him in Little Rock. After she miraculously receives approval for the unexpected leave request and arranges for someone to cover her unit, he sends another telegram delaying the trip. In his August 11 letter, he writes:

Dear Sweet Darling,

I just received your letters today. I got three at one time.

Listen, sugar, don't get your leave on the 16th, for I don't know ex-actly what date I will leave yet, but I will either leave somewhere around that time or the last of Aug. You wait until I send you a telegram stating the exact date. I will telegram you the date and won't write.

Understand, baby, and I don't want any fire about you, not sure you can get your leave. You tell those folks I am in the Army, and I can't set no date two weeks ahead, but you will be leaving there sometime between 16th and 1st of September.

I am still deeply in love with you and can't help that. You have been a sweet girl from the start. Please stay sweet for me. I do love you with all my heart and always will.

True Love and you know it.

Love,
Gus

Despite the sweet words in his letter, Kermit still fumes. Augustus seems to think she can just come and go on his whim, with no regard for her job or the responsibilities it entails.

As if that were not enough, she receives a letter from her cousin Maurice in Little Rock, which makes her doubt her husband's loyalty. According to Maurice, Augustus keeps in touch with his old flame, Charlotte Perry. This woman spreads rumors that Augustus continues to have feelings for her, suggesting they will reunite during his leave to Little Rock. If what Maurice says is true, Kermit is being played for a fool. She decides against confronting Augustus immediately, only telling him she has something serious to talk to him about. She grapples with a mix of emotions—anger, confusion, embarrassment, and regret.

Two days ago, Kermit had received another letter from Augustus instructing her to call his base headquarters that evening while he was on duty. When Kermit arrives home from work, her mother stands by the kitchen counter, peeling the skin off three white potatoes. A pan of water heats on the gas stove, and a whole chicken thaws next to the pile of discarded potato skins. The open window circulates humid, stagnant August air throughout the room, carrying the faint smell of approaching rain and the soft sounds of neighbors chatting on their stoops.

"Hi, Momma," Kermit says, crossing the tile floor to peck her on the cheek. Underneath her suit jacket, her blouse clings to her back, damp with perspiration from the walk home.

"Hi, baby. How was your day?" Arvolin asks, chopping potatoes and dropping them into the boiling water. Her weathered hands move with practiced efficiency, despite the arthritic joints from years of running her café.

"Can't complain," Kermit says, collapsing into the kitchen chair, the vinyl squeaking under her sudden weight. "What'd you do today?"

"Washed some clothes," Arvolin starts. She rinses the poultry, then pats it dry with a flour sack cloth. "Went to the store with Barbara next door. It got pretty hot out there today." Using a butcher knife, she cuts the bird's backbone with a sharp crack, separating it into two parts. She chops the bird into pieces, the knife's loud banging punctuating each strike against the wooden cutting board.

Kermit rubs her temples as her mother forcefully hacks off the wings, breasts, thighs, and drumsticks. The raw smell of poultry triggers nausea as Arvolin butchers the remaining carcass, the metallic scent of fresh meat mingling with the starch of potatoes. "I'm getting a slight headache," Kermit says, standing to leave, her chair scraping against the linoleum floor. "I'm going to get some aspirin and lie down for a while."

"You going to eat?" Arvolin asks. She removes the pepper and salt from the cabinet and begins seasoning the chicken pieces, the spices forming small mounds on the pale flesh as her wrinkled fingers work with practiced precision.

Kermit passes through the doorway, responding, "Probably later. I have to call Gus in a little while, so I'll eat then." Her voice trails behind her as she disappears into the hallway, her shoulders slumping in exhaustion.

After Arvolin retires to her bedroom that evening, Kermit sits alone at the kitchen table in front of a plate of fried chicken breast, mashed potatoes, and sliced beets. The food has cooled, losing its appeal as her appetite wanes with anxiety. After a few minutes of idly pushing her fork around her uneaten dinner, she covers her plate with tin foil and places it on a shelf in the icebox. Feeling something in her pocket, she fishes out the aspirin she had forgotten to take earlier. Placing the tablet on her tongue, she washes it down with a gulp of iced tea, the cold liquid offering momentary relief from the oppressive heat as it slides down her throat.

Kermit picks up the black rotary telephone handset on the counter, its surface smooth and cool against her palm. She listens carefully for any background noises that could indicate eavesdroppers on the party line, but hears none. Inserting her finger into the hole for number four, she rotates it clockwise until it reaches the dial stop. After waiting for the circular disc to spin back to its resting position, she dials seven, then five, and listens for the series of clicks indicating that the call has connected. A male voice with a slow southern drawl answers the phone, "Good evening. Camp Stewart Company headquarters."

"May I speak to Private Augustus Hill? He's supposed to be on Charge of Quarters tonight." While she waits, Kermit fidgets with the telephone cord, twisting it absently around her finger. Despite her anger, a lump rises in her throat, and her heart skips when Augustus picks up.

"Hello? Kermit?"

Briefly, the sound of his deep, soothing voice melts her heart, the familiar cadence causing her to doubt her resolve. "Yes, Gus, it's me," she answers, struggling to keep her voice steady.

"Baby, I'm so glad you called," Augustus says, his words rushing forth with noticeable relief. "You don't know how bothered I've been, worrying about what's troubling you." Loud voices of men laughing and joking can be heard in the background, their raucous energy a stark contrast to the tension in his voice.

"I'm not sure where to start," Kermit sighs, her free hand clutching the edge of the counter. "I got news that really upset me." Outside her window, a low rumble of thunder echoes in the distance. She pushes the yellow curtain aside to search the night sky for an approaching storm, the darkness a backdrop to the flickering lightning on the horizon.

"What is it, baby?" Augustus presses. "You seem like you're afraid to tell me." His voice rises slightly with a sense of urgency as heavy thuds and scuffling footsteps intensify in the background. "Don't be that way, Kermit. Tell me your troubles. I always bring mine to you."

Trying to push down the lump still stuck in her throat, Kermit swallows before asking, "Gus, do you still love me?" Her voice sounds small, even to her ears.

"That's what's got you so upset?" Augustus questions, his pitch rising higher as his words tumble out hurriedly. "Of course, baby. I'm yours forever, you know that. Darling, ever since I was large enough to love a girl, it has been you all the way. Not part of the way, but all the way."

Hearing her husband proclaim his love usually eases her doubts, but this time his words fail to convince her. The rehearsed quality of his declaration rings hollow in her ears. After taking another sip of tea, she takes a deep breath before pressing forward. "Are you still talking to Charlotte Perry?" The name feels bitter on her tongue.

"Charlotte Perry?" he repeats, the slight pause before her name speaking volumes. As the background noises become softer, it seems as if the other men are also waiting for his reply, the sudden quiet amplifying the tension. "Why are you asking about her?"

"Huh. I guess I have my answer, then," Kermit says softly as tears well up in her eyes, blurring the kitchen into a watery haze. She snatches the dish towel off the cabinet knob and dabs the corners of her eyes, the fabric rough against her skin.

"Well, yes, okay," Augustus stammers, his cool confidence cracking. "She writes to me, but so do a lot of people. That doesn't mean anything."

Kermit cries inconsolably, pressing the towel against her mouth to stifle any sound that would wake her mother. Hot tears stream down her face as the evening breeze picks up outside. She reaches over to the sink, holding the towel under a stream of cold water. After wringing it out, she applies the damp, cool cloth to her face, attempting to stem the flow of tears while sniffing continuously.

"Listen, baby. It really doesn't mean anything," Augustus soothes, his voice taking on that familiar honeyed tone that typically persuades her. "She doesn't mean anything to me. You're the one I truly love."

Kermit takes another gulp of tea to try to compose herself. She wipes her nose and sniffs before replying, her voice trembling with barely contained hurt. "So why are you planning a little rendezvous together when you get to Little Rock?"

"I'm not. I'm not planning any rendezvous with her," Augustus protests, the defensiveness in his tone heightening her suspicions. "I may have written something like 'I'll see you when I get to town,' but I say that to everyone back home. It doesn't mean I'm planning anything special with her."

"Well, she sure seems to think so," Kermit says, her voice hardening. "Like you're having a little secret affair." She refills her empty glass from the pitcher on the counter and takes another sip, her fingers trembling as she grips it tightly.

"Kermit, what's got into you?" Augustus asks, his voice rising with uncertainty and fear. "I wouldn't, couldn't forsake you for anything in this world or the next one to come. I married you for life, not for a little experience." He strains to speak louder above the growing sounds of men roughhousing around him. "Hold on, baby." She hears his muffled voice, "Hey! Come on! Why don't you go to the other room? I'm trying to talk to my wife in here." He returns to the phone, "Sorry about that. Now, look. You can't be believing everything you hear. I told you that our love couldn't stand no fibbing around like this, and you know that's true. I love you and not Charlotte or anyone else. You get me?"

Kermit nods and mumbles, "Uh-huh," too emotionally drained to argue further.

"I'm going to be with you the whole time I'm in Little Rock, so there's no chance of me going off somewhere anyway," he says, speaking rapidly again as if rushing to seal the matter. "But the point is, I don't want to be with anyone else but you."

Kermit's eyes flicker toward the kitchen window as a flash of lightning briefly illuminates the evening sky, followed by a low rumble of thunder. She ponders how much influence this woman has over her husband and if she can trust his loyalty to their marriage, especially when they are apart. The storm approaches, the air now heavy with electricity and her unspoken doubts.

"Now, I'm going to have to get off the telephone soon because there's a line of fellas waiting to use it," Augustus continues, as the men around him shout their impatience. "So, about my furlough. Put in for your leave for the first of September, but don't leave New Jersey until you hear from me. I'm pretty sure I'll get it then, so you put in for yours now. I'll send a telegram when I know for sure. Get me?"

"Yes, alright," Kermit answers, her voice masking her lingering doubts. She catches her shadowy reflection in the gap between the window curtains, searching for answers from the woman staring back at her. "I'm probably bringing Momma. She misses home and wants to visit her friends."

"That's fine. Look, I gotta go like I said," Augustus repeats, urgency creeping back into his tone. "But always know how much I love you. I want us to be happy again. It means so much to me realizing I have a sweet wife at home waiting for me. It gives me something to be living for."

"Okay. I'll see you then," Kermit replies, wondering if her voice sounds as hollow to him as it does to her.

"I can't wait to hold you tightly in my arms," Augustus adds, causing some men in the background to tell him to hurry up and end the call, their jeers and whistles carrying through the line.

"Me too," Kermit responds mechanically. "Love you." Her words feel shallow, devoid of their usual warmth.

"I love you, too, baby. Don't you ever forget that," Augustus says before hanging up the phone, leaving his words hanging in the air.

Kermit listens to the low-pitched buzz for a few seconds when the line disconnects. Returning the handset to its base, she gazes out the window, splattered with light rain, before going to bed. Throughout the stormy evening, she tosses and turns restlessly as the rumbling thunder intensifies. Finally, around two in the morning, she drifts off to sleep, the steady rain creating a calming rhythm. She dreams about reuniting with Augustus in Little Rock, wondering if her husband's reassurances will prove true when they finally meet face to face, or if their marriage will reach its breaking point.

HOMETOWN REUNION

September 1, 1943 - Little Rock, Arkansas

When Kermit tells Mrs. Smith that she and her husband, Augustus, are returning home for a two-week visit, her dear friend arranges for the couple to stay in the very room they occupied after their wedding. Since Kermit's mother is staying with relatives during their visit and Kermit dislikes Augustus' suggestion to stay with his mother, she quickly accepts Mrs. Smith's offer.

When Kermit and her mother, Arvolin's train, finally screeches to a halt at Little Rock's Union Station, both women are exhausted from their twenty-eight-hour journey. The stagnant air and stifling heat inside their segregated car feel barely distinguishable from the oppressive ninety-eight-degree temperature outside on the platform. Their once freshly laundered cotton dresses cling to the sweat on their bodies as they maneuver through the station with the gracious assistance of an off-duty Red Cap Pullman Porter. Tobacco smoke and diesel fumes hang thick in the humid air. Once outside, they spot Mrs. Smith beside her forest-green Chevrolet sedan, waving enthusiastically in a cranberry and white striped dress.

"Welcome home!" Mrs. Smith greets them, embracing them warmly. "It's so good to see y'all."

"It's good to be home," Arvolin says, returning her embrace. She removes a white plastic accordion fan from her purse and begins rapidly fanning the beads of sweat along her hairline. "My Lord, it's hot out here."

"Thanks for coming to get us," Kermit says. "But don't get too close—I must stink to high heaven after that trip."

"Don't you worry about that," Mrs. Smith chuckles. "I'm glad you could come for a visit." She hands Kermit her car keys. "And you know you're driving," she laughs.

"Just like old times," Kermit chuckles. She moves to the rear of the car to unlock the trunk, then steps aside so the porter can load their leather suitcases.

Mrs. Smith opens the back car door for Arvolin while asking her, "How are you liking New Jersey?"

"Oh, it's all right," Arvolin answers slowly, eyeing her daughter, who she suspects is listening intently for her reply. "It's got a peculiar smell from all those factories, but I suppose you get used to it."

Once all their luggage is packed into the trunk, Kermit attempts to tip the porter for his generosity. He politely declines by gently closing her outstretched hand and giving it a little shake of appreciation. "Thank you so much," Kermit says, smiling broadly. She removes the tissues tucked inside her sleeve and wipes her brow. Then she slides behind the wheel and starts the engine as Mrs. Smith climbs into the passenger seat.

"When is Augustus getting here?" Mrs. Smith asks as they pull away from the station, the car's tires crunching over loose gravel.

"Later tonight. I want to take a bath and freshen up before his train arrives from Georgia," Kermit replies. "I'll drop Momma off at Uncle Sherman's house first, then we can go to your house."

As the orange sun sinks into the hazy horizon, a newly refreshed Kermit returns to the train station in Mrs. Smith's car, accompanied by her in-laws, Elmer and Della Woods. Despite Augustus' reassurances that nothing is happening between him and his ex-girlfriend, Kermit still feels apprehensive about how it will feel to be with him. She had hoped her reunion with her husband would involve just the two of them, but Della insists on being there to greet "her baby" as soon as he sets foot in town. Kermit already senses that her mother-in-law does not think she is good enough for her son, but she feels even more uncomfortable, wondering if Augustus has told Della about their argument.

A sharp, piercing sound of the locomotive whistle breaks into Kermit's thoughts. The blasts grow louder as the train approaches the station, dispersing hot clouds of steam into the already humid air. In her lime dress and wide-brimmed hat, Kermit cranes her neck, hoping to spot Augustus among the swarm of disembarking passengers. A boisterous group of army soldiers passes them, but Augustus is not with the group. Finally, he appears from another side exit, wearing an olive uniform and duffel bag slung over his shoulder.

Della is the first to rush to her son. "Oh, Augusta," she cries, using her pet name for him. She wraps her arms around Augustus' neck as he bends over and kisses her cheek. Her black patent leather purse swings on her arm and bounces off his back as they embrace. "I'm so glad the Lord brought Momma's baby back home safely."

"Me too, Momma." He winks and smiles at Kermit over Della's shoulder. Once Della releases her grip, Augustus kisses and embraces his wife. "Hi, baby," he says softly. "It means so much seeing you here to greet me. I missed you so much."

"I missed you, too," Kermit says, holding him close. Glancing into his eyes, she interprets his expression to mean that he might feel as uneasy as she does.

"Welcome home, son," Mr. Woods says, extending his hand. "How's that Army treating you?"

"It's all right," Augustus says, shaking his stepfather's hand.

"Looks to me like you got darker," Della says, scanning his face. "You been out in that sun, haven't you?"

"Can't help it," Augustus says with a shrug. "We do all our drills outside, even when it's pouring."

"Let's get you home," Kermit says. "Do you want to drive, Gus?" She holds up the car keys, hoping he will agree, as she still feels drained from her long trip.

"What do you think?" He takes the keys and opens the passenger door for her while Elmer does the same for Della.

In the days that follow, whenever Kermit and Augustus are alone in their old room at Mrs. Smith's house, an uneasy tension settles between them—echoing the awkwardness of their early days as newlyweds. When Kermit tries to address the strain, Augustus grows visibly irritated, either cutting off the conversation or snapping, "We've already been over this."

To make matters worse, Kermit spots a familiar figure across the crowded hardwood floor while they dance at Dreamland on Friday night. Charlotte—his former girlfriend and the source of their argument—shows up unexpectedly at the nightclub.

"Did you invite her?" Kermit demands, her face heated with anger.

"Of course not," Augustus sighs. "Let's just go."

They leave the nightclub, but the incident ignites another day of arguments between the couple on Saturday. Noticing the friction between her house guests, Mrs. Smith tries to intervene by proposing a leisurely drive around town in her car. Remarkably, the simple strategy appears to work wonders because they return home reunited, spending the evening together in their room.

The following morning, Kermit and Augustus join their mothers and Mrs. Smith at Christ Temple for the communion service, held every first Sunday of the month. Although they frequented the church while they lived in Little Rock, Reverend Geter directs them to stand and say a few words during the time set aside to welcome visitors. Augustus, dressed in his beige uniform, nods and smiles, saying, "It's good to be home." Being careful not to upstage her husband, Kermit, wearing her blue pinstriped work suit, simply repeats his reply. Afterward, church members respond with *Amens* and applause. Following the pastor's benediction, former Dunbar classmates, neighbors, and friends swarm Kermit and Augustus, welcoming them back to their hometown.

After church, they gather at the Woods' home for Sunday dinner. Seated in their usual chairs in the living room, Augustus and his stepfather silently listen to the radio as the clanking pots, creaking cabinet doors, and rushing footsteps of the women indicate that they are hurriedly preparing the afternoon meal. The scent of brown sugar and ham mingles with the aroma of cooked greens when Elmer pronounces the blessing for the meal. He adds a special prayer of thanksgiving for the safe return home of Augustus, Kermit, and Arvolin. As soon as the grace ends, Della picks up the plate in front of her husband and commences piling it with food.

"Aren't you going to serve your husband, Kermit?" Della asks, looking back and forth between the couple. "He's been working so hard... doing his duty... serving our country..." She trails off.

"Yes, I know," Kermit says. She winces as her chair scrapes across the wooden floor when she stands. Retrieving Augustus' plate, Kermit begins adding a spoonful of food from each of the serving dishes.

"Thank you, baby," Augustus smiles. "But don't put too much on there," he adds, holding his jaw. "My teeth have been bothering me something awful."

"I thought I noticed you favoring your right side when eating," Kermit says, preparing to serve him a spoonful of bright green peas. "What happened?"

"It started hurting about a month ago. When it really got bad, I went to see the dentist at Camp Stewart," Augustus says.

"Is it a cavity?" Mrs. Smith asks, cutting into the thick slice of ham on her plate. "I had one of those, and it hurt every time I ate."

"It started like that, but it's gotten worse," Augustus answers. "Six teeth are so rotten the dentist's going to remove them when I get back on base."

"Six? My goodness!" Kermit exclaims.

"Yes." Augustus points to his left cheek. "He said there are three on the bottom and one on top on this side." He then points to the right side of his face. "Then there's one on top and bottom over here. After he takes them out, he's going to put in a plate."

"You're getting dentures?" Kermit asks, trying to imagine how this new development would change their lives. "I didn't know it was that serious!"

"Well, I'm just getting a plate. It's like dentures, but only for the rotten teeth. Dentures would be if I was getting all my teeth removed."

"That's just awful," Della says. "So it hurts you to eat, Augusta?"

"Yes, but mostly on this side of my mouth." He points to his left cheek. "I try to eat more soft things now that won't bother me so much."

"I wish I had known, Augusta," Della says sadly. "I prepared all this food, and you can't even eat it." She frowns, clasping her hands and dropping them to her lap.

"Don't worry, Momma," Augustus chuckles. "I can eat; I just have to chew on one side."

As Kermit continues to serve Augustus' plate, she becomes more selective, opting for smaller portions of food that are easier to chew. "Here you go, honey," she says, setting the plate before her husband.

Elmer stops eating and studies his stepson from across the table. "The army's paying for it?"

"Yes, sir," Augustus responds. "I don't have to pay a dime."

"Will your bad teeth keep you from going overseas?" Elmer asks.

"That's a good point, Elmer," Arvolin says, turning to Augustus. "Surely you can't fight in the war with your teeth hurting so much."

"No, afraid not," Augustus shakes his head. "That's why they're putting in the bridge before I get shipped off."

"I wish you didn't have to go at all," Kermit says. "But be sure to tell me how it goes. And let me know if you feel any better after you get your new teeth put in."

"I will," Augustus replies, cautiously taking a bite of okra as everyone looks on. Noticing their stares, he says, "Hey, I'm fine, really. Go on and dig in. Everything looks delicious."

By the end of their visit to Little Rock, Kermit and Augustus feel truly reunited. At Union Station, as Kermit embraces her husband goodbye, she no longer doubts his sincerity and commitment to their marriage. Just before she and Arvolin board the train back to New Jersey, she turns to wave at Augustus and Mrs. Smith standing on the platform. As the locomotive gathers steam and lurches forward, she blows him a kiss. He returns the gesture, eyes fixed on her until the train disappears from view.

Inside the crowded, segregated car, Kermit settles beside her mother among the hum of conversation and clatter of luggage. She bites her lip, fighting back another swell of tears. With Augustus' deployment looming, the questions resurface: Would she see him again—and if so, when?

Home of Happy Feet

July 15, 1944 – Harlem, New York

Two days after her twenty-fifth birthday, Kermit steps off the packed Lenox Avenue streetcar at 140th Street, closely followed by her friend Mattie. A late evening breeze flows past them, carrying the savory aromas of Harlem's late-night food joints. Kermit wears her favorite dancing outfit, a black and white print dress that twirls around her when she spins on the dance floor. Her hair is styled in loose waves that frame her almond-toned face, the colorful gems of her black button earrings catching the glow of streetlamps as she passes.

Mattie, a half-head shorter than her coworker, quickly tucks the back of her neatly pressed white blouse into her plaid cobalt skirt before catching up with Kermit, who is already a few steps ahead. A gold necklace hangs from Mattie's neck, and a white silk flower is pinned on the side of her brunette hair. During their ten-minute trolley ride from the train station, Kermit shares the story of her first trip to Harlem.

"That was two years ago when my girlfriend and I had trouble checking into a hotel because the clerk expected me to be a man," Kermit recalls, chuckling at her youthful innocence. "We were so green. We couldn't believe they were going to let an unmarried couple stay in the same room."

On this warm summer evening, the heels of Kermit's black peep-toe shoes click along the brightly lit sidewalk as they maneuver through the Saturday bystanders. The air fills with an aroma of roasted peanuts from street vendors mixed with the pungent odor of gasoline fumes from passing automobiles. As the women hurry to their destination, several men greet them with an enthusiastic, "Good evening, ladies," lifting their hats, nodding, or winking as they pass.

Kermit and Mattie both smile at their greetings, occasionally responding with a casual "Good evening," as they continue down the block. They lock arms and move in sync as they navigate through the growing crowd.

"There it is," Mattie exclaims, pointing to the brick building adorned with a massive flashing marquee that illuminates the street. Bright white bulbs spell out "SAVOY" in capital letters, surrounded by neon musical notes that twinkle against the red background. Close to a hundred patrons—men in dark suits and fedoras and women in colorful dresses and skirts—gather outside the ballroom. Though most of the customers are African American, whites are also present in this uniquely integrated dance hall, a rare phenomenon in segregated America.

To the right of the entrance, some men survey a row of elegant women seated against the wall, each with perfectly coiffed hair and impeccable makeup. The sign above the booth reads, "3 Dances with Hostess – 25 cents – Buy Tickets Here." For the cost of a cocktail, the men can choose one of these "Savoy Hostesses" to be their dance partner for three musical numbers, learning the latest dance steps from her if needed. However, any hostess who dares to meet a customer outside the venue will lose her job instantly—a rule strictly enforced by management.

"Looks like a nice crowd," Kermit observes as she walks under the marquee and joins the main ticket line. "Hopefully, that means we'll get a lot of dancing in tonight. "Silhouettes of couples bounce against the large front windows in rhythm with the lively jazz music that spills onto the street. Saxophone riffs and trumpet blasts punctuate the night air, inviting passersby to join the excitement inside.

"I sure hope so," Mattie agrees, adjusting the flower in her hair. "Sounds like the band is already swinging."

Kermit checks her watch and sucks her teeth, a small frown creasing her brow. "We're too late to get in for thirty cents," she says, disappointed. "Now it'll cost us twice as much." She opens her purse and retrieves six dimes, the coins catching the light as she counts them.

Mattie reaches into her skirt pocket and counts out the money for the admission. "Good thing today's payday," she says, tightly clutching the coins in her palm.

Tickets in hand, the two friends eagerly enter the ballroom, where the beat of the house band pulsates through the floorboards and up into their bodies. A man in a beige pinstriped zoot suit, matching the color of his complexion, greets them with a wide smile beneath his thin mustache. "Welcome to The Savoy, the House of Happy Feet!" As he swings open the door, they are met with a wave of rhythmic swing music, the air thick with stale smoke and body heat. "You two beautiful young ladies enjoy yourselves tonight," he adds, presenting a program featuring a dancing couple sketched on the cover. Listed inside the pamphlet are the evening's performing bands, along with an announcement of the night's Lindy Hop dance contest.

At the corridor's end, Kermit and Mattie see grinning couples swinging across the mahogany dance floor, which spans the length of a city block. Spectators line the floor, cheering energetic dancers with shouts and clapping to the beat, their enthusiasm infectious. In the middle of the dance floor, musicians dressed in white tuxedo jackets, black pants, and ties, perform upbeat swing tunes on the metal clamshell bandstand, their instruments gleaming under the overhead lights.

"This place is really hopping," Kermit remarks, raising her voice to be heard above the music. She bobs in place, a smile spreading across her face as her right foot taps involuntarily. "This is just how I want to celebrate my birthday."

"And we can blow off some steam while having some fun," Mattie responds, also moving to the beat as her shoulders shimmy slightly.

The women find an open spot along the line of bystanders to watch the dancers, clapping in rhythm with the others. Hundreds of dancers effortlessly glide across the floor, spinning away and then coming back in close for a backward dip. With seamless energy, the couples remain in constant motion, smoothly transitioning through an endless number of steps, their bodies seemingly weightless as they fly across the floor.

"They're really good," Kermit remarks, her eyes wide with admiration. "I recognize some of these moves—like the Flying Charleston and Pimp Walk, but what are *they* doing?" She points to a couple kicking their legs around while rocking on the balls of their feet, their movements perfectly synchronized despite the complexity.

"I have no idea," Mattie answers, mouth slightly agape. "Look at them!" They watch as a woman flips over her partner's shoulder, her yellow skirt and white slip briefly revealing her underwear before she lands behind him. Then the woman spins around and flips her partner over her shoulder, her slender arms displaying surprising strength. "Unbelievable! How'd they do that?"

Kermit starts to respond, but is mesmerized by the remarkable display of the dancers' precision and skills. The friends continue to watch until the song ends, and the floor clears briefly. Seeing all the tables are occupied, Kermit spots an empty two-seater lounge chair next to the small bar. "Let's grab that seat before someone else gets it."

The women push past the swarm of people and cross the gold and blue carpet, its plush fibers cushioning their steps. They sink into the velvet chaise, sitting for the first time since departing the streetcar, the soft material a welcome relief after standing.

"It's good to get off my feet for a minute," Mattie sighs, rubbing her hand along the cushion's soft material, her fingertips tracing small circles on the luxurious fabric.

"Sure is," Kermit agrees, stretching her legs slightly. "They've done some renovating since I've been here." She scans the décor, taking in the elegant surroundings. "This carpet is new," she says, looking down. "And the wallpaper is too. I can't remember what color it was before they changed it to copper, but it looks a lot fancier now."

Within minutes, a chocolate-skinned man in a navy pinstriped suit and tie approaches Mattie to ask for a turn on the dance floor. His eyes crinkle at the corners when he smiles, revealing a dimple in his right cheek. Standing next to him is another man with copper-colored skin and a thin black mustache. Taller than his companion, he wears a gray double-breasted suit and black tie and extends a hand to Kermit, his movements smooth and confident. Both women eagerly abandon their shared seat, exchanging a quick grin as they jump up to try out new Lindy Hop moves.

As Kermit steps onto the hardwood floor, she feels the tiles vibrating beneath her feet to the rhythm of the fast-paced dancers and the thrum of the bass. Following her partner's lead, Kermit starts swinging her arms and crossing her legs in the scissors kick, her dress swirling around her knees. Then he twirls her close and pushes her away, their hands clasped firmly. Her lips purse in concentration as she kicks her heels in a circle, then turns into the Sailor step with a thigh slap, the sound sharp against the music. After a few more songs, Kermit relaxes, incorporating the Flying Charleston and Fishtail into her steps as her dress floats around her like a black and white cloud.

After several rounds of swing music, the house band ends their set, allowing the visiting band to immediately start up on the second stage. Exhausted, cheeks flushed and breathing heavily, Kermit and Mattie find an empty table and accept their new friends' offer to buy them ginger ales. Voices and clinking glasses amplify in the nightclub as more dancers leave the floor, the buzz of conversation rising to fill the brief musical interlude.

"Whew, that was fun!" Kermit exclaims, wiping her brow with the cloth table napkin, small beads of perspiration glistening on her forehead.

"Man, the Savoy is my new favorite spot," Mattie replies as she fans herself with her hand, her chest still rising and falling rapidly from exertion.

Kermit and Mattie's dance partners return with their drinks, placing glasses of ice floating in fizzing, golden liquid in front of them. The ice cubes clink against the glass, and bubbles rise to the surface in tiny streams. They thank the men for the drinks, who respond by tilting their glasses in a toasting gesture, the overhead lights catching the amber liquid. With a nod, their partners step back a few paces, hovering within a couple of feet of the table, their presence both attentive and respectful.

Kermit watches the couples dancing, a wistful look crossing her face. "I hope I get to bring Gus here one day," she murmurs, her fingers tracing patterns in the condensation on her glass.

Mattie gulps down her drink before asking, "How's he doing?" She places her empty glass on the table with a soft thud.

"Okay," Kermit answers, her expression sobering. "Still overseas in New Guinea. He doesn't like it one bit. Says it's nothing but a hot, dirty swamp." She fiddles with the small gold band on her finger, twisting it absent-mindedly.

"Sorry to hear," Mattie says, reaching across to briefly touch Kermit's hand. "Praying he comes back safe."

"You and me both," Kermit says, raising her glass to Mattie's with a clink. The sound is lost in the swell of music beginning anew.

"Henry's anxious to get back, too," Mattie says, leaning closer so Kermit can hear her. "Said as soon as he steps foot back in the States, he's taking me down the aisle! I can't wait because I miss him something awful." Her eyes shine with hope despite the unknown length of their separation.

"I completely understand," Kermit says, squeezing Mattie's hand in shared comfort.

Before long, the musicians play "Stompin' at The Savoy," the 1934 jazz standard recorded by Chick Webb's orchestra and Ella Fitzgerald. The familiar opening notes draw appreciative whoops from the crowd. Hearing the popular tune about dancing at The Savoy Ballroom sparks the return of more dancers jamming the floor, their bodies moving as one with the rhythm. Kermit and Mattie's dance partners reappear at their sides, extending their hands, blocking any new prospects heading their way. The girlfriends spend the rest of the evening kicking up their heels to the energetic sounds of the club band, losing themselves in the music, and momentarily forgetting their worries about waiting for their soldiers to return from the war.

At two in the morning, harsh overhead lights brighten the dance hall, signaling closing time. The sudden brightness reveals sweaty faces and disheveled clothing across the previously dimly lit ballroom. Hustling to catch the last train back to New Jersey, Kermit and Mattie make their way toward the exit, their feet aching pleasantly from hours of dancing. They weave past lingering patrons who joke with friends or slyly try to catch a better glimpse of their dance partners in the light. Moments after they step out into the cool morning air, their dance partners dart out the door as the women cross Lenox Avenue.

"Hello," calls Kermit's partner, waving and smiling at the women as they briskly walk down the now deserted sidewalk. The streetlights cast long shadows ahead of them.

"Hello," calls Mattie's partner, slightly louder, his voice echoing in the quiet street.

Neither woman acknowledges the calls, quickening their pace slightly, trying not to mislead them into thinking they are interested in a relationship beyond the evening's dancing.

"That's okay," says Kermit's partner, even louder as the men start to turn back towards the club. "You knew how to speak when you wanted someone to dance with you." His voice revealing a hint of sarcasm and resignation.

Kermit and Mattie shoot each other a side glance and start laughing as they rush down the steps of the train station, their footfalls echoing in the tiled stairwell. The night's memories will sustain them through another week of work and worry, another week of waiting for letters from their men fighting overseas.

VICTORY DAYS

August 14, 1945 – Manhattan, New York

T he day begins like any typical Tuesday in August, with Kermit riding to work on the stifling city bus packed with morning commuters. For the past few days, newspapers and radio broadcasts have been announcing that the president will be making a special statement to reporters at the White House that evening.

Upon entering her office building, the security guard greets Kermit with a question that distracts her and alters the course of her day. "Did you hear? Everyone's saying Japan is supposed to surrender today."

"I've certainly been praying for it," Kermit replies. When Germany surrendered in May, she expected Japan to surrender soon afterward, finally ending the war in the Pacific, where Augustus is deployed. At the time, Kermit joined in the spontaneous celebrations at work upon hearing President Truman announce Victory in Europe Day. She then watched enviously as newsreels showed women reuniting with returning soldiers, while thousands gathered in celebration in Times Square.

As the weeks turned into months, Kermit's hope faded. She threw herself into her work as a supervisor in the Office of Dependency Benefits. Kermit is responsible for keeping her team of twenty Allotment Branch clerks focused on expediting beneficiary payments. She motivates her employees by repeating the "Get 'em Paid" slogan found on their ID badges, frequently reminding staff that military families rely on them for support. However, even Kermit has trouble concentrating today.

By the time Kermit meets her friends Etta and Josephine at lunch, the office rumor mill is at a fever pitch. Excited voices fill the cafeteria, drowning out the muted sounds of clinking dishes and scraping chairs. As Kermit sits before her untouched egg salad sandwich and a lukewarm cup of coffee, she asks her friends, "Do you really think the war could be over tonight?"

Glancing over her shoulder, Etta leans in and whispers, "Don't tell anyone, but Chief Waller said the Japanese surrendered weeks ago. Back when we bombed Hiroshima."

Josephine nods, saying, "I heard that too. Probably had to work out the details with Japan first."

"If that's true, they could've already started sending soldiers back home," Kermit says. "Did you see all those servicemen who just showed up in Times Square on V-E Day?"

"Yes, there sure were a lot of them running around," Etta answers.

"You know what, Kermit," Josephine starts. "I think you may be right. They must've been shipping them back here before President Truman said anything."

"Makes sense," Etta adds. "How else did they all get back so soon?"

"Right, and I bet they'll do the same thing this time," Kermit says. "The president and the military probably want to keep it a secret, so they wouldn't let our husbands tell us they were coming back today." She checks the time on her watch. "If we head over to New York right after work, we'll be there to welcome them back!"

"What?" Josephine asks. "You're thinking our husbands are already in town and just waiting for President Truman to say they can come home?"

"Well, it's possible, isn't it?" Kermit asks. "Why would they keep our troops over there if they're done fighting?"

"But we're not even sure the war's over yet," Josephine counters.

"Come on, Josephine," Etta urges. "Let's go see! We could be with our husbands tonight!"

"Yes, what do we have to lose?" Kermit asks. "And if it doesn't happen today, we just would've had a quick visit to the city."

The shrill clanging of the office bell interrupts the cafeteria conversations, signaling the end of the lunch period. The three women join their coworkers as they stand, collect their dishes and trash from the tables, and dispose of the items on the kitchen trays.

"Okay, I'll go," Josephine says, walking alongside her friends to their desks. "I wouldn't want to miss the chance of being with Earl for one second. We've been apart for nearly three years now."

"Same for me and Jackson," Etta says. "How long has it been since you've seen Gus?"

"It'll be two years next month," Kermit replies. "I can't believe I could see him tonight."

When the three women meet outside their office building after work, the sidewalks are clogged with bystanders milling about in the late afternoon sun. As they maneuver through the crowd to the bus stop, they overhear snippets of conversations about Japan, the war, and President Truman.

"Look at all these people out here," Etta says. "I bet the bus is going to be more crowded than usual."

"Train too," Kermit says. "Let's hurry up and get to the station while we still can."

By 6:10 p.m., the three friends are clinging to the handrails of the packed Main Line train to Manhattan with no room to escape the stench of musty, sweaty passengers at the end of their humid summer workday. However, no one seems to mind as the commuters jostle against each other as the train jerks along the route. A group of sailors starts singing "Anchors Aweigh," prompting others to either laugh or join in. Numerous loud discussions between riders compete with the metallic clanking of wheels on the tracks and the hiss of the steam engine, causing several to shout in a futile attempt to be heard above the deafening sounds.

When the train arrives at Penn Station thirty-five minutes later, the atmosphere onboard has become increasingly eager and frenzied. Caught up in the surge of passengers, Kermit, Etta, and Josephine are pushed onto the platform, then swept up the stairs and out into the chaotic commotion of the street. In the golden sunlight, they find themselves engulfed by a sea of people of all ages, ethnicities, and backgrounds. Car horns blare at pedestrians spilling onto the sidewalk and into the street. At the corner, a man with reddish brown skin hands them a small American flag attached to a wooden stick. After shoving the flag inside her purse, Kermit tries to ask him if there has been any news about Japan, but the flow of exiting passengers propels her further up the sidewalk before she has a chance. She feels a hand grab hers and is relieved to see it is Josephine, who is also holding Etta's hand.

Josephine leans closer to Kermit's ear and says, "Let's move away from the station where it's less crowded." She nods toward an unoccupied spot in the middle of the block. Kermit leads the threesome up West 34th Street until they reach the front of a coffee shop with a "Closed" sign hanging inside the glass door.

"I never would've imagined there'd be so many people down here," Etta shouts above the growing uproar surrounding them.

"Me either," Kermit and Josephine reply simultaneously.

"We need to stick close together, so we don't get lost," Josephine recommends, reluctantly releasing her friends' hands. "How on earth do we find our husbands in all this chaos?"

Kermit purses her lips and scans the excited passersby. She approaches an African American couple coming their way. "Excuse me," she says loudly, waving her hand to get their attention. "Have you heard any news from the president about the war?"

The woman shakes her head. "Nothing yet," the man answers. "But I think we will any minute."

"Okay, thank you," Kermit says, nodding her head in appreciation. She turns to her friends, about to speak, when several women in business attire suddenly rush out of the office building next to the coffee shop. Kermit pivots to avoid a near miss as the workers scamper onto the sidewalk to join the impromptu assembly. "I think we should go to Times Square because that's where everybody went on V-E Day. What do you all think?"

"Okay," Josephine answers.

Etta nods and says, "How do we get there?"

Kermit looks at the street sign and points down the block. "Let's walk over to 7th Avenue," she says. "Then we can go up to Broadway at Times Square." Holding hands again, the trio squeezes through the massive crowd. Interspersed among the revelers are uniformed soldiers representing all branches of the military. Whenever an African American man in an Army uniform passes by, one of the women asks what troop or assignment he is from, hoping to locate their husbands, but to no avail.

After crossing West 41st Street, the multitude of individuals now overwhelming the streets and sidewalks slows the women's progress. Despite the humid and dense environment, the anxious gathering maintains an exuberant spirit as they await news under the stifling summer sun. A group of playing children darts between Etta and Kermit, momentarily separating their clenched hands. Once they join hands again, the friends plow through the celebrants filling 7th Avenue between the long shadows cast by tall buildings.

Suddenly, a thunderous roar erupts ahead of them, continuing past like a crashing wave. Bells ring, car horns blare, and a rush of elated people stream out of buildings, flooding into the already-packed streets. Kermit, Etta, and Josephine stop as the crush of people around them cheer, yell, and hoot in celebration. Spurred by the contagious excitement surrounding them, the women begin to scream and hug one another.

"Japan must've surrendered," Kermit says, laughing and wiping away tears.

"I'm so happy," Etta squeals, also crying. "Look!" she says, pointing to red, white, and blue ticker tape floating like snowflakes from office windows and rooftops. She reaches up to catch the strips of paper before they land on the ground. Kermit and Josephine join in, gleefully twirling amidst the floating streamers.

Josephine points to a group of sailors in crisp white uniforms scaling a lamp post. Upon reaching the top, they unfurl a large American flag and hoist it in the air, letting it flap freely in the wind. Reaching into her bag, Josephine retrieves her flag and yells, "Get your flags!" Kermit and Etta comply, and the trio proudly waves their flags in the air.

Perched above the street, several news cameras capture the festivities as thousands of celebrants wave, jump, and shout enthusiastically. Jubilant revelers share alcohol with friends and strangers, raising their bottles in victory after every swig. Music drifts from nearby windows, sparking some to dance while others clap to the beat. Caught up in the moment, men impulsively grab nearby women, dipping them backward over their arms and kissing them passionately.

Witnessing the euphoric spirit of the diverse crowd of various skin colors, Kermit feels a sense of unity and hope. She taps the shoulder of the white woman next to her and asks, "Is it really over?"

"Yes," she answers, standing on her toes and pointing above the crowd to the New York Times skyscraper on West 43rd Street. "See the headline on the Times Tower?"

Kermit follows her gaze and sees, "Official—Truman Announces Japanese Surrender" on the news zipper scrolling around the building.

Elated, she shakes her friends' shoulders and points to the notice. "Look," she shouts. "It's official!"

Swept up in the whirlwind of emotions, Kermit, Etta, and Josephine embrace tightly, leaping with joy and shedding tears of happiness. The women shout excitedly, vigorously waving and cheering to catch the attention of cameras scanning over the overwhelming crowd. Overjoyed people display newspapers, still fresh with ink, bearing the headline "Japan Surrenders!" practically screaming off the page. With tears uncontrollably streaming down her face, Kermit stands transfixed, unable to believe that the news she has prayed for all this time is true, written in bold, black print.

"I just can't believe it," Kermit says repeatedly. She pulls her handkerchief out of her purse and wipes her eyes. "The war is finally over."

"I know," Etta agrees. "It doesn't feel real."

Shadows briefly engulf the revelers as the sun dips below the skyline. Then Times Square's shimmering billboard lights brighten the festivities, igniting a new round of cheers from the celebrants. Firecrackers sparkle and pop around the street, leaving behind a smoky sulfur scent in the air. Kermit scans the throngs of individuals surrounding them, still searching for a familiar face in an Army uniform. Suddenly, she bursts into laughter, so intense her eyes water.

"Well," she says, still laughing, "if our husbands are here, I don't think we're going to find them." Her friends join in the laughter.

"No, I don't think so," Josephine chimes in. "But I'm so glad we were here to see this."

"Me too," Etta agrees.

"Wouldn't it be funny if they went home to surprise us and we're out here," Kermit says, continuing to laugh.

Etta stops laughing and starts to look concerned. "Oh, Kermit," she says. "What if that's true!"

Now Kermit and Josephine stop laughing, too, and the women exchange worried glances. Josephine exclaims, "Oh no!"

Navigating through knee-high piles of streamers and trash littering the streets, Kermit, Etta, and Josephine anxiously make their way back to Penn Station. Despite multiple delays from an overburdened transit system struggling to accommodate the endless waves of commuters, the women eventually return to New Jersey after midnight.

Key in hand, Kermit hurries around the walkway of her apartment complex and hastily unlocks the door. Instead of finding Augustus, she discovers her mother asleep on the living room sofa under the soft light of the lamp. To confirm her husband has not yet returned from his military service, Kermit strides across the floor to find an empty bedroom. Disappointed, Kermit returns to the living room and helps Arvolin to bed.

The next day, Kermit meets Etta and Josephine for lunch in the cafeteria, which buzzes with excitement about the end of the war. Each woman shares her story of rushing home, hoping to be greeted by her husband, only to face disappointment when he is not there. Although their reunions with their husbands will have to wait a little longer, the women share an unforgettable experience as they join the rest of the country in rejoicing in Times Square at the end of World War II.

CHRISTMAS PRESENT

December 25, 1945 – Jersey City, New Jersey

Awintry mix of rain and sleet taps a staccato rhythm against Kermit's bedroom window, rousing her from a restless sleep. Since it is a holiday, Arvolin attempts to let her daughter sleep in by tiptoeing around the kitchen, quietly preparing breakfast. The savory aroma of frying scrapple drifts into Kermit's bedroom, triggering her mouth to water. Although she tries to resist, her internal clock will not allow her to stay in bed for another minute.

Throwing off the covers, Kermit immediately regrets leaving the warm comfort of her bed. Bracing herself against the chilly air, she slides her feet into her beige slippers stored under the bed ruffle and wraps herself in a faded yellow housecoat hanging in the closet. As Kermit opens the bedroom door, the smooth voice of Nat King Cole singing "The Christmas Song" drifts from the radio. Humming along, she shuffles into the bathroom, then joins her mother in the kitchen.

"Good morning, Momma," Kermit greets Arvolin, hugging her shoulder and kissing her cheek. She grabs a cup from the cabinet and pours steaming coffee from the aluminum kettle boiling on the stove.

"Merry Christmas," Arvolin responds cheerfully as she stirs browning cubes of potatoes in a sizzling pan next to the coffee pot. Golden-brown pieces of steaming scrapple are piled on the corner of a blue and white serving dish on the counter.

"Yes, Merry Christmas to you too," Kermit replies, pulling back the window curtain to watch the freezing rain bounce off the snowdrifts in the apartment courtyard. "At least it's not snowing today," she says, taking a sip of her hot coffee.

"Lord, yes," Arvolin agrees, peeking out the window and gesturing with her spatula. "Those ten inches we got last week still haven't melted yet." She turns back to cooking, then adds, "I've had enough snow to last me all winter."

Kermit chuckles as she sits at the table. "How're you feeling on this fine Christmas morning?"

"Can't complain," Arvolin answers. She shaves off pieces from the butter block and melts them into the potatoes before stirring in salt and pepper. "This rain's got my knees aching, but that's about it." She turns away from the stove to look at her daughter with concern. "How about you? You're up earlier than I expected."

"I tried to stay in bed a little later, but..." Kermit trails off. She bounces out of her chair, briefly startling her mother. "Just three more days, Momma! How can I sleep when Gus will be here on Friday?"

"I know, baby," Arvolin replies, smiling. "I'm so thankful he's coming back in one piece." She turns off the burners under the potatoes and coffee. "So many soldiers got injured in this war, or didn't come home at all."

"Believe me, I stay on my knees thanking God for protecting him while he was overseas," Kermit says. "And I'm still praying because Gus still has to make it across the country from California."

Arvolin spoons sugar into an empty coffee cup before pouring coffee from the kettle. As she stirs the two ingredients together, the spoon clinks against the cup. Arvolin takes a cautious sip of the hot liquid before asking, "How long before he leaves California?"

"He's supposed to leave tomorrow and arrive in New Jersey at Camp Monmouth on Thursday," Kermit says, retrieving her cup from the table to refill it. "Then he'll finally get discharged Friday." Removing two plates from the cabinet, she hands one to her mother, who serves herself breakfast. Kermit scoops up hash browns and scrapple on her dish, then pulls two forks out of the drawer and hands one to Arvolin.

The two women place their food on the kitchen table and sit across from one another. After Arvolin says grace, she asks, "Are you going to pick up Gus from that base?"

"No, he's supposed to be getting a ride with one of his Army buddies," Kermit responds. "Gus said he has to go through a lot of discharge procedures before he's released. He won't get here until sometime Friday evening."

After breakfast, Kermit washes the dishes while Arvolin crosses into the living room. A selection of instrumental Christmas melodies plays on the radio while each woman sings merrily from their separate rooms. Once the kitchen is clean, Kermit joins her mother in the next room, where the refreshing scent of pine greets her. She watches as Arvolin bends over their four-foot balsam fir tree, draping popcorn garlands over the bottom pine branches. Kermit picks up the red ribbons off the coffee table and begins tying them around the dark green tree.

"It's looking pretty good," Kermit says, straightening a red glass pinecone ornament hanging on a branch. She picks up the silver tinsel and separates the strands. "When we put on this tinsel, it will really look Christmassy."

"That's not until last," Arvolin cautions. "I have a few more ornaments to add first. I want the tree to look especially nice for Augustus. He's missed so many Christmases already."

"I was just telling that to Brenda the other day," Kermit says. "Gus and I haven't spent Christmas together since we got married in 1941." She gathers the pine needles scattered on the floor around the tree and discards them in the trash. "We're still not going to be together on Christmas this year either," she continues. "But at least we'll be able to celebrate together three days later."

"That's right," Arvolin agrees. "We'll open presents and have our Christmas dinner then, too. I guess I better finish moving my things into the other bedroom before Gus gets home."

"Don't worry about that. Gus can do it when he gets here," Kermit says. "I'm so grateful you came up here to be with me, Momma. You've been such a big help."

"I was glad to do it," Arvolin says, beaming at her daughter. She arranges the last two gold-painted ornaments on the tree. "Now, you can put on the tinsel."

After work on Friday, Kermit enters her apartment, shivering as snow flurries swirl around her. She removes her black gloves and stuffs them in the pocket of her navy wool coat before hanging them in the closet. As she enters the foyer, the aroma of baked ham mingling with the sweet scent of apple pie greets her. At the kitchen table, Arvolin strings green beans with an apron protecting her teal dress and colorful red scarf. Her gray hair, usually pinned up in braids, is styled in tight finger waves laid flat around her head.

"Hi, Momma," Kermit says. "It's downright freezing out there." She rushes over to peck her mother's cheek, adding, "You look pretty. Very festive."

"Thank you, baby." Arvolin glances up briefly as her adept fingers quickly remove strings and snap the fresh beans in half.

"I've got to hurry up and get dressed before Gus gets home," Kermit says, her heels clicking across the tile floor. Before she disappears out the doorway, she turns back and says, "Sure smells good in here."

In her bedroom, Kermit kicks off her work shoes with a thump and peels off her suit. She dashes into the bathroom, splashing water all over the sink and floor in her rush to quickly freshen up. Kermit reapplies her makeup, combs her hair, and then haphazardly wipes a rag over the spilled water, stray black hairs, and beige foundation powder.

Back in her room, she slips into a forest green belted dress, accented with large sparkling sequined bows sewn on the right shoulder and left hip. After checking her appearance in the dresser mirror, she puts on her black peep-toe shoes, designed with a bow on top. Kermit returns to find her mother adding chopped potatoes and onions to the pot of simmering green beans.

Arvolin surveys her daughter's outfit, saying, "I think Gus is going to like that dress on you."

"I sure hope so," Kermit says, grinning. "He's due here any minute." She takes an apron off the wall hook. "What can I help you with?"

"Oh no, I don't want you to get anything on that dress," Arvolin objects. "Just set the table with the good china. Dinner's almost ready, and I'm sure Gus will be ready to eat when he gets here."

Half an hour later, Kermit and Arvolin rush to the door in response to the rapid, nonstop knocking. When Kermit twists the knob, she finds a laughing Augustus, wearing an olive fur flapper hat and wool coat with a striped Army sleeve insignia. He is still banging on the door as it swings open.

"Oh, Gus," Kermit says, laughing as she leaps into his arms. Her momentum knocks his duffel bag off his shoulder and into a snowbank along the path. They both laugh and embrace in a kiss. "I can't tell you how much I've missed you."

"You don't know how long I've been dreaming about this," Augustus says, holding her waist. Noticing the porch light reflecting off the sequined bows on Kermit's dress, he adds, "Baby, you look so beautiful. That dress makes you look like a Christmas present."

"Get on in here before you two catch a cold," Arvolin fusses from behind the door. Then she adds in a softer tone, "Welcome home, Augustus."

Augustus retrieves his bag from the snow and brushes off the bottom before returning it to his shoulder. He turns to reveal a man standing a few feet behind him with skin the color of molasses. Extending his hand, Augustus introduces the similarly dressed man in Army-issued winter attire. "This is Duncan from my unit," Augustus says, waving his friend closer. "He lives in Newark and was nice enough to give me a ride to Jersey City." Augustus turns to Kermit, "This is my wife, Kermit, and her mother, Mrs. Arvolin Bland." Then he turns to his friend, placing a hand on his shoulder. "This is Duncan."

"Nice to meet you," Kermit says, shaking Duncan's extended hand.

"I'm the one who's glad to finally meet you," Duncan replies. "You're all Gus talks about—day and night," he teases, laughing and slapping Augustus on the shoulder.

Kermit and Augustus exchange glances and blush. Then she slips her arm around Augustus and kisses him on the cheek.

"Now y'all get in here before we all get sick," Arvolin fusses louder.

Kermit, Augustus, and Duncan chuckle as they enter the apartment, and Arvolin quickly slams the door behind them. Augustus drops his bag on the floor, and then he and Duncan remove their hats. Turning to hug Arvolin, Augustus says, "It's good to see you, Momma Bland."

"It's been way too long. Good to see you too, Augustus," Arvolin says, squeezing him tightly. "I'm so glad you made it back home safely." She turns to shake hands with Duncan. "So nice to meet you, Duncan. I hope you're staying for dinner. We've got plenty."

"I appreciate the offer, ma'am," Duncan says. "But my wife's waiting for me at home, and I can't wait to see her."

"Well, don't let us keep you apart another minute," Arvolin says. "Newark's just around the corner, so you and your wife will have to come back for dinner another time soon."

"We'd love to," Duncan says, turning to leave. "It was nice meeting you two young ladies."

Augustus hugs his friend before letting him out the door. Removing his coat, he surveys the apartment, pausing at the tree. "Will you look at that," he says. "That Christmas tree is beautiful!"

"Momma decorated it," Kermit says as she takes Augustus' coat and hat to the closet.

Augustus admires the decorations and then catches a glimpse of something above the tree. "Is that mistletoe?" he asks, grinning.

"Where?" Kermit asks, confused. Following Augustus' gaze, Kermit notices a small plant adorned with oval evergreen leaves and red berries that is securely fastened with a red bow and dangling from the ceiling. "When did that get there?" She looks back and forth between her mother and Augustus, surprised.

Covering her mouth, Arvolin bursts out laughing and says, "I had Mr. Baker from next door put it up for me while you were at work."

Augustus winks at Kermit and guides her beneath the mistletoe, where he plants a lingering kiss on her lips. "Merry Christmas, baby," he says.

"Merry Christmas," Kermit replies, caressing his face. She gently traces a finger over his lips, then across his thin, black mustache. "I've missed you so much." After kissing again, Kermit says, "Let me show you around the place."

Augustus retrieves his duffel bag and follows Kermit through the kitchen. Stopping to smell the aroma coming from the simmering dishes, he says, "I have missed good ol' home cooking being over there in that jungle."

"Well, dinner's ready whenever you are," Arvolin says, stepping in the doorway.

"That's good because I'm hungry," Augustus says. "Let me put my things away and get washed up first."

Guiding Augustus through the apartment, Kermit concludes her tour in their bedroom. With a thud, his bag hits the floor. He quietly pushes the bedroom door closed, eager for some long-awaited alone time with his wife.

Thirty-five minutes later, the reunited couple emerges from the bedroom grinning and holding hands. In the living room, Arvolin looks up from her crocheting as The Jack Benny Show plays on the radio. Wrapping the loose yarn around her crochet needles, Arvolin asks, "Ready to eat now?"

"Ready," Augustus says with a chuckle.

"Well, take a seat," Arvolin says as she gestures to the table. "We postponed having Christmas dinner until you got here."

Kermit hurries into the kitchen, saying, "Momma, come sit at the table. I'll get the food." Moments later, she returns with two plates of steaming green beans, creamy macaroni and cheese, and slices of rosy ham with a brown sugar crust. She places one in front of Augustus and the other in front of her mother. After bringing her dinner plate to the table, Kermit kisses Augustus and then says, "I'm so happy you're home, Gus. I still can't believe you're right here next to me."

"I feel the same way, sugar," Augustus says. "Most days, I wasn't sure I'd ever get out of New Guinea. It still doesn't feel real being here, but I'm so glad I am."

"We are too," Arvolin says, placing her napkin in her lap. "Augustus, can you say the blessing? We haven't had a man around to do the honors in quite some time."

"Yes, of course," Augustus replies. "Let's bow our heads."

After they begin eating, Kermit asks, "So, what's the first thing you want to do now that you're back? Do you have any ideas?"

"Well," Augustus starts, swallowing hard. "I do want to go see Momma."

"In Yakima?" Kermit asks incredulously. "Gus, you just got home," she whines.

"I know, baby," Augustus says, caressing his wife's arm. "But she's been very worried about me."

"I've been worried about you, too!" Kermit protests. "Both of us have," she adds, glancing at her mother.

"I understand, Kermit, but you know Momma," Augustus says. "My commanding officer told me she even wrote President Roosevelt last December, asking him to send me back home. That was a year ago, so she really wants to see me now."

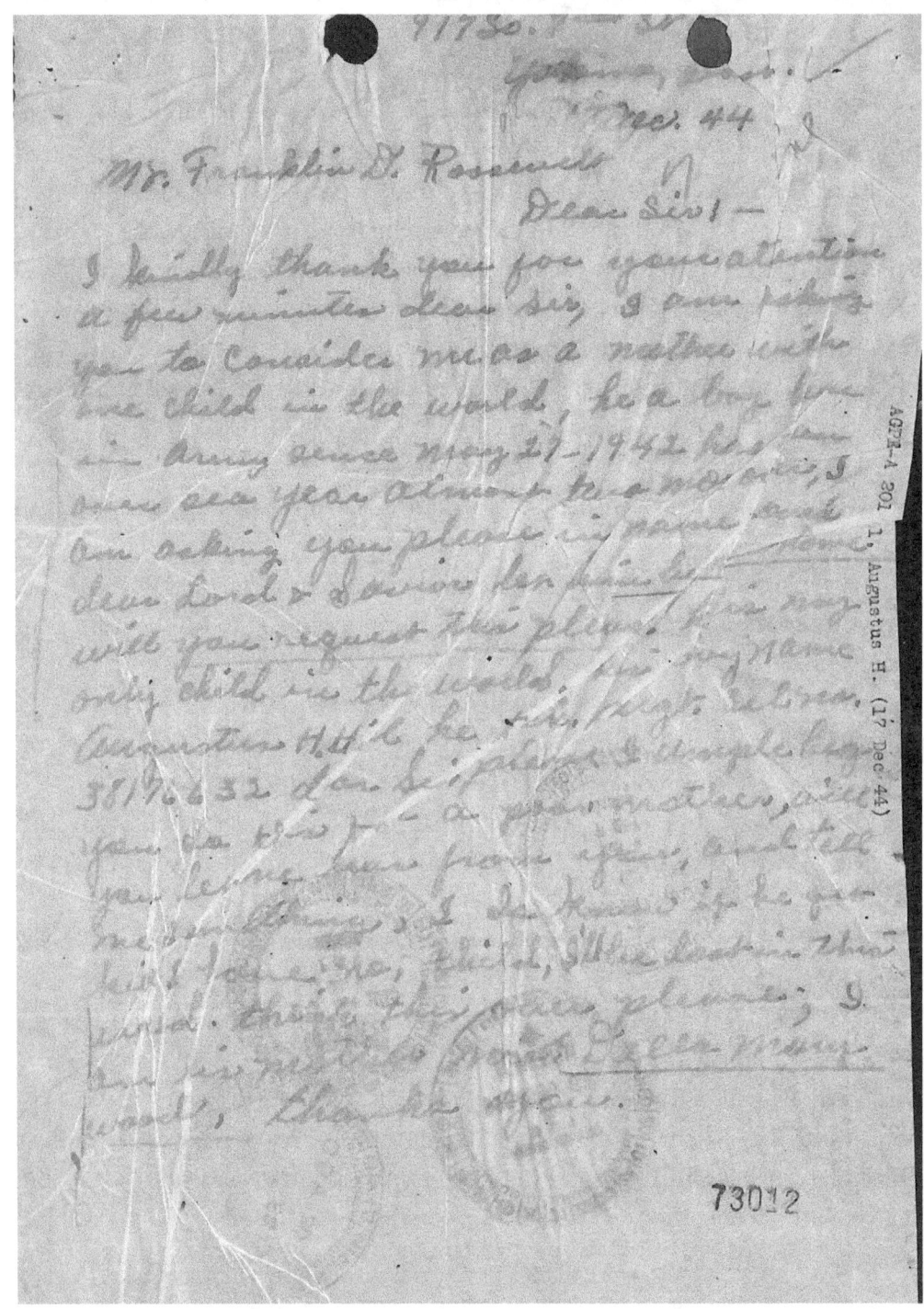

12-17-1944 Della Woods letter to President Franklin D. Roosevelt

Stunned, Kermit feels a lump growing in her throat. "When are you thinking about going?" she croaks.

"In a few days," Augustus says. "I'm only going to stay a week so I can get back here and look for work." He pushes his chair back and pulls Kermit onto his lap. "You can come with me," he encourages. "I know she'd love to see you, Daddy, too."

Kermit purses her lips, saying, "I don't know if I can take time off now. I start a new job in a couple of weeks."

"Look here," Augustus says, gently turning Kermit's face toward his own, "your husband just got back home from fighting in the war. Those folks better let you off work so you can spend time with him—I mean, me, and our family."

"He's right, Kermit," Arvolin agrees. "And you know he has to see his Momma after being overseas all these years."

Hugging Augustus' neck, Kermit says, "Now that you're finally home, I just don't want to let you go."

Augustus wraps his arms around Kermit's waist, who tightens her embrace. "Me either," he says. "That's why you need to come on and go with me to see Momma."

Gently caressing his face, Kermit kisses Augustus, then runs her fingers through his hair. "Alright," she sighs. "Hopefully, it won't be too busy next week since we already have Tuesday off for New Year's. I'll call my supervisor in the morning."

Augustus grins and then kisses Kermit. "I'm so happy you're coming with me, baby," he says, nuzzling her neck.

"I've never been to Washington state before," Kermit adds as she stands. "It'll be good to see what it's like on that side of the country."

Arvolin begins clearing the table. "We better hurry up and open the Christmas presents before you two leave for Yakima," she says, putting the platters on the counter.

Kermit and Augustus bring their dishes into the kitchen while Arvolin puts away the food. Kermit turns the dial on the radio until she finds a station playing jazz. Meanwhile, Augustus slips into the bedroom where he retrieves two boxes wrapped in red ribbons from his bag. In the kitchen, Arvolin cuts the apple pie, transferring three slices onto dessert plates. For the first time in four years, the trio exchanges Christmas gifts and shares memories of past holidays spent apart.

As the apartment quiets and the last gift is stashed away, Kermit leans against Augustus, treasuring this Christmas memory. A tremor of excitement courses through her—her husband is finally home, and their life together is about to begin anew. During his military service, she has lived independently, working full-time, managing bills, and making decisions alone. Now she must learn to relinquish these responsibilities to her husband once more. Watching him, she senses something has changed in his manner since his time overseas. In the coming months, their reunion will also include a period of rediscovery. She tightens her grip on his hand, steadying herself for their future of reunion and renewal, determined that they will face whatever awaits them together.

PART III

POUNDING THE PAVEMENT

March 14, 1946

hree months after reuniting with her husband, Kermit starts to worry
about Augustus. Since their return from visiting his mother in Yakima,
Washington, in early January, Augustus has been looking for work, and
Kermit can sense his growing frustration. He trusted the Army's promises
that after serving his country for five years, he would have no trouble finding a job. However, no employment opportunities have materialized in the
six weeks since he applied for veterans' preference, giving him a five-point
priority on the Federal Employment application. While Kermit expected
some challenges with Augustus transitioning from military to civilian
life, even she is surprised by the obstacles he has encountered in securing
employment.

Adding to Augustus' stress, three days ago, he turned twenty-nine,
intensifying the pressure he feels to financially support his family. Not
wanting to pile on further stress, Kermit decides to postpone telling him
that over the past three months, she has been in heated meetings debating
the future of the War Department in the post-World War II era. Every day,
she fields questions from anxious staff worrying whether their jobs at the
Office of Dependency Benefits will be needed now that the servicemen have
returned home. As Kermit rides down the elevator after work, she ponders
how she and Augustus will support themselves and their mothers if they
both become unemployed.

Exiting the building, Kermit barely notices the mid-March sun has
driven the temperatures to seventy-eight degrees. Lost in thought, she climbs
aboard the city bus, finds a seat, and stares out the window, determined to
discuss her concerns with Augustus that evening. Walking through her

garden apartment complex, she spots landscape workers planting buttercup daffodils, grape hyacinths, and crimson tulips in the courtyard.

"Hello," Kermit greets the workers, stopping to admire their work. "The flowers are very pretty."

"Thanks, ma'am," they answer in unison as they continue digging in the dirt.

As the floral scent reaches Kermit's nostrils, she takes in the signs of spring surrounding her. Birds are chirping in the distance, and the previously bare tree branches are now sprouting white and pink buds. One of the gardeners looks up at Kermit, then lifts a tulip in her direction as the others watch curiously.

"Go ahead," he says, still holding the red flower with the bulb hanging off the green stem. "You can plant it in a pot and spruce up your apartment."

"Oh, that's so nice. Thank you so much," Kermit says as she holds the tulip gingerly in her hand, its powerful aroma engulfing her. She follows the path to her apartment and unlocks her door, carefully holding the plant by the flower's bud. "Hello," she calls as she swings the door open.

"Hi," Augustus greets as he rises from the kitchen table. He kisses her, then sees the tulip. "Where'd you get the flower?"

"One of the apartment workers gave it to me," Kermit answers. "They're planting them in the garden outside. Isn't it pretty?"

"Yes," Arvolin answers from the kitchen. "It needs to be put in water or dirt to grow." She reaches into the top cabinet and removes a glass tumbler with vertical ribs. "Here, you can use this for now."

Kermit places the bulb in the glass and fills it with water from the sink faucet. She then places the tumbler on the windowsill, leaning the stem and bud against the glass pane.

Augustus crosses the tile floor and picks up a letter from the stack of opened mail on the kitchen table. "Baby, look what came today," he says, handing the tri-folded paper to his wife. "It's from the New York Post Office. They want me to come in to apply for a substitute clerk position."

"Oh, that's wonderful, Gus," Kermit says as she hugs him in relief. Then she reads the letter, and a frown forms across her face. "It's only temporary?"

"I know," Augustus says wearily. "I guess it would be on a trial basis until they decide if they want to hire me permanently. I'd also just work as an alternate for the full-time clerks."

"At least it's a start," Kermit says, still reading the document.

"They aren't paying that much either," Augustus adds. "I could wait and see if something better comes through. The Army said..."

"No," Kermit interrupts. "We need to grab this while it's still available." She takes Augustus' hand. "I've been wanting to tell you something," she starts. "I'm not sure how much longer I'll have a job." Kermit slides into the kitchen chair and then absently starts flipping through the opened envelopes.

"Why?" Augustus asks. "I thought you were doing so well there. What reason would they have to fire you?"

"No, not fire me," Kermit says. "I work at the War Department, and there's no longer a war. My job may no longer exist."

Augustus stands silently beside his wife for a few seconds. "So, how long will you have a job?"

"Not sure. They're still discussing it right now," Kermit says. "I may still have a job, but we need to be prepared in case I don't. I won't know for sure until maybe summertime. So that's why you need to take this job, because it may be our only income if my department is eliminated."

"I see," Augustus sighs, retrieving a small cardboard box from his shirt pocket. The box displays "Camel" in baby blue letters arched above a reddish-brown camel in a desert, accompanied by three palm trees and a pyramid. He takes a cigarette from the pack and places it in his mouth, lighting it with a match. "Well, I'm going to need at least two letters of recommendation," he says, exhaling a wisp of smoke. "I was thinking of someone from my unit or perhaps from the ordnance plant where I used to work back home," Augustus suggests.

"No, that would take too long. Plus, you need to get down there tomorrow before they offer it to someone else," Kermit says hurriedly. "I can ask Mr. Baker, who lives in the unit next door," she says, picking up a pen and writing shorthand notes on the back of the envelope. "And Carol, who's over at the next apartment building? They'd be happy to write recommendations for you. We can go over tonight so you can take them with you Friday."

"Okay," Augustus says as he picks up the letter. "It also says I'm supposed to pay the post office sixty-five cents for a surety bond," he adds, shaking his head in disbelief. "I haven't even gotten the job yet, and they want me to pay them!" He takes another drag from his cigarette, then blows smoke from the side of his mouth.

"Looks like we have a lot of work to do tonight," Kermit says, scribbling more notes. "Tomorrow, you can wear the new shirt and tie I got you for your birthday."

By the following Tuesday, Augustus has started working at the New York Post Office. Kermit, whose office is closer to their apartment, arrives home before him after work. Anxiously awaiting his return, she sorts through the mail at the kitchen table until she can hear about his day. Amongst the monthly bills and correspondence, there is a letter addressed to Augustus from the Veterans Administration, which she sets aside for him.

The moment Kermit hears the key unlocking their front door, she is on her feet, asking, "How'd it go?"

Augustus chuckles slightly, saying, "It was fine." He removes his gray fedora and black coat and places them in the closet. He kisses Kermit, then crosses into the kitchen where he greets Arvolin, who is stirring a simmering pot of cabbage on the stove. "Let me go hang up my jacket, and I'll tell you when I come back."

When Augustus returns to the kitchen a few minutes later, he has removed his tan tweed jacket and printed black tie with sand-colored clamshells. His white dress shirt is tucked neatly into his tweed trousers, the sleeves rolled up to his elbows. Augustus sits at the kitchen table across from his wife, who glances up from writing a check.

"So, how was your first day?" Kermit asks as she stuffs the check into a stamped envelope.

"It was fine," Augustus repeats. "I got my photo taken for my ID card." He reaches inside his shirt pocket and pulls out the badge to show her.

"Your picture turned out nice," Kermit says, rising to show Arvolin. "Doesn't Gus look good here, Momma?"

"Uh-huh," Arvolin says, smiling. "You took a good picture."

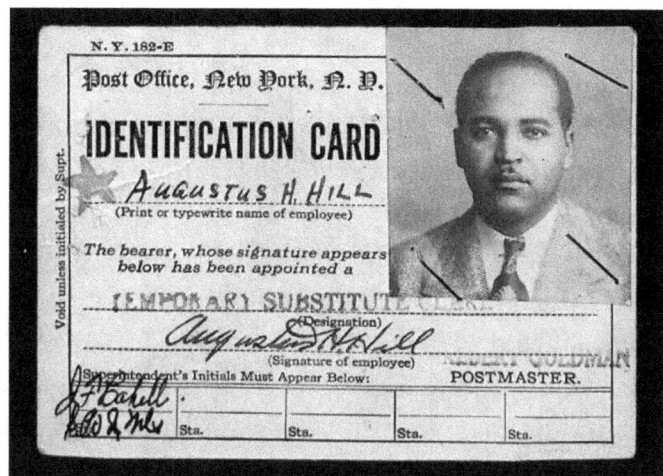

3-19-1946 Augustus Hill NY Post Office ID

Kermit clears her throat and reads the card aloud in an authoritative voice. "Post Office, New York, NY. Identification Card. Augustus H. Hill. The bearer, whose signature appears below, has been appointed a temporary substitute clerk. Albert Goldman, Postmaster." Laughing, she returns the ID to Augustus, saying, "That's great. What else did you do?"

"Not much, mostly just filled out a lot of paperwork," Augustus says, slipping the card back into his pocket. "They went over the job duties of a substitute clerk, and how it's illegal to steal or tamper with the mail."

"Do you think you'll like it there?" Kermit asks.

"I guess," Augustus answers, shrugging slightly. "It sounds similar to what I was doing in the Army." He reaches over to the envelope addressed to him on the table, which is slightly buried under the day's mail. "What's this?"

"Oh, I forgot to show that to you earlier," Kermit says. "It came today from the Veterans Administration. Probably something about your military benefits."

Augustus slides his finger under the seal to open the envelope. As he reads the letter, he says, "Kermit, this is a job offer!"

"A job?" Kermit asks, walking over to read the letter over his shoulder. "What's it for?"

"A detail clerk," Augustus says, flipping to the next page. "They want me to come in tomorrow for a physical and start Friday."

"What a blessing," Arvolin says, chuckling.

"Sure is," Kermit adds. "Last week you got a job at the New York Post Office, and now you have another at the Veterans office. When it rains, it pours!"

"This one pays a lot more, though," Augustus says. "The salary is $1,704 a year." He looks up at Kermit, who is standing behind him. "What am I going to do? I just started at the post office today."

Kermit takes the offer letter and returns to her seat to review it. "This one's much better," she says, pushing the stack of opened envelopes aside and spreading the four pages of the Veterans Administration letter across the table. "I think you have to tell the post office you got a better offer. That was just a substitute, a temporary position anyway. This one's permanent and pays more, too. They'll understand."

"You think so?" Augustus asks, rubbing the sprouting whiskers that are irritating his face. "Everyone was so nice and welcoming today."

"Even so," Kermit says. "Just go in there and be polite and apologetic. You don't want to burn any bridges, but this job is just a better offer. Tell them you just got the letter when you got home—which is true. Plus, you need the extra money to support your family."

Augustus scoots his chair next to Kermit so they can review the details together. He points to the second page and says, "This says I'm supposed to go in for a physical at the Veterans Center at 500 Park Avenue in the city, then report to their offices on Broadway."

Kermit rises and goes to her bedroom, returning with a street map of New York City and a Manhattan transit schedule. Turning from preparing dinner, Arvolin stands behind Kermit, curiously watching over her daughter's shoulder to see what she is doing. After Kermit opens the map and the transportation schedule, she asks Augustus, "What's the address of the New York Post Office?"

"Umm," Augustus stammers. He fishes inside his pants pocket, initially removing coins that clink on the table. He then retrieves a folded piece of paper, which he reads aloud. "421 8th Avenue."

Kermit searches the map until she locates the address, placing her right index finger on the spot. "Okay," she begins. "You go here to the post office first thing in the morning and tell them you need to resign. You'll need to put it in writing, so I'll help you write the resignation letter tonight." She checks the correspondence, then surveys the map, placing her left index finger on the next location. "Then you take a bus here to 500 Park Avenue for your physical." Kermit keeps her left finger on the map, then moves her right finger down the map and stops close to the bottom of Manhattan. "After you're done, you'll have to take a train down here to 346 Broadway to report to the Veterans Administration office."

"That's a lot of traveling," Arvolin comments. "You think you can do all that in one day, Augustus?"

Augustus sighs. "I think so," he says, then he looks at Kermit. "You'll have to write all this down for me."

"I will," Kermit says. "You'll also need extra bus and train fare for to-morrow." She crosses the kitchen and removes two clean pieces of paper from the drawer. Returning to her seat, she writes Augustus' itinerary for the next day on one sheet. Then she hands the other one and her pen to her husband. "Here. Use this to write your letter of resignation," Kermit says. "I think you're really going to like working for the Veterans office. This is an answer to our prayers."

CROSS COUNTRY

January 13, 1947 – St. Louis, Missouri

With the end of the war, Kermit's position at the War Department becomes increasingly uncertain. Her department undergoes prompt reorganization, and all employees face downgrades to lower pay scales. She attends weekly managers' meetings to discuss new restrictions, shifting responsibilities, and shrinking workloads. Her staff look to her for assurance, but she fears both her position and theirs may vanish by the following year.

Meanwhile, Augustus' first cousin, Vernessa Bennet, urges them to join her in Bakersfield, California. His mother and her father are siblings, and the two families spent most of their childhood together on the same farm in Conway, Arkansas. Vernessa moved to Bakersfield five years ago with her husband and often praises the area's ideal weather and progressive outlook. She believes California offers greater opportunities for Negroes. A further incentive for Augustus is that they would be living closer to his mother and stepfather in Yakima, Washington.

To prepare for the move, Kermit consults with her personnel director about positions available for her and Augustus on the West Coast. Unfortunately, no transfer opportunities exist at the moment, though several vacancies remain open in St. Louis, Missouri. After considering their options, Kermit and Augustus decide to take a leap of faith—temporarily relocating to the Midwest to save money and secure employment before making their way to California.

After packing up all their belongings, Kermit, Augustus, and Arvolin arrive in St. Louis over the Christmas holidays. The married couple begins work in the same federal complex, though Kermit's years with the government earn her a higher grade in a different department. They report to their respective offices in January 1947.

After completing an exhaustive eight-hour orientation on Friday, Kermit returns early Monday morning to the Army Finance Center to begin her new role as a claims examiner. Though she is new to the St. Louis office, most of the civil service procedures mirror those she followed in New Jersey. She easily falls back into familiar duties and feels grateful that both she and Augustus have secured employment at the same agency. Augustus begins as a temporary file clerk in the Files and Search Branch of the Administration Center, while Kermit joins the Determination and Correspondence Branch.

As they drive through the guarded entrance at 4300 Goodfellow Boulevard, they marvel at the sheer scale of their new workplace. The federal complex spans 62.5 acres and includes twenty-three two-story brick buildings, several stretching over two city blocks in length. The morning sun casts long shadows between the uniform structures, creating geometric patterns across the frost-covered grounds. Augustus finds a spot in the parking lot next to their building. They follow the crowd of employees hurrying inside to escape the crisp morning air.

Kermit and Augustus stand close to the white concrete wall, trying not to block the rush of staff in the hallway. The corridor echoes with the sound of hurried footsteps and muffled conversations. Pulling off her gloves, Kermit asks, "Do you know where you're going?"

Augustus removes his hat and checks his paperwork. "Room 1240 for a medical exam with Dr. Duncan." He takes off his tweed coat and drapes it over his arm. "Meet you here at the end of the day?"

"Okay. I should be done around 5:30. Good luck."

After giving her a quick kiss on the cheek, Augustus heads down the hallway, checking office numbers as he passes. Kermit turns the opposite direction and climbs to the second floor, locating the Family Allowance Division. The large workplace contains ten rows of four oak desks fully stocked with modern office equipment. Bulletin boards line the walls, and the only window overlooks the parking lot. She hangs up her coat and hat, then approaches a white man seated at the front of the room and introduces herself.

"Yes, Kermit, I've been expecting you. I'm Mr. Wallace. Have a seat." He gestures toward a wooden chair beside his desk. "I've reviewed your personnel file from New Jersey's Office of Dependency Benefits. You come highly recommended."

"Thank you." A group of women enters, casting brief glances her way before settling at their desks. Within minutes, the room fills with the familiar rhythm of typewriters, telephones, and office chatter, reminding her of her previous positions.

"Now, you were originally scheduled to work here as a claims reviewer," Mr. Wallace begins. "But after discussing your background with my supervisor, we believe you'd be better suited for a claims recorder position at the Waiver Board."

"Oh, okay. What's the difference between the two?"

"Well, the claims recorder is a grade six, compared to the grade five reviewer. It also comes with more responsibility—you'd be supervising examiners and assessing claims from soldiers who received erroneous payments. You'd determine whether the claims were false and if the soldiers are responsible for repayment."

"So, this would be a promotion?" Kermit asks, unable to hide her surprise.

"That's right. Are you willing to accept the position?"

"Yes, of course. I appreciate the offer."

"Good." He opens a drawer and pulls out a form. "Personnel will need to update your transfer and promotion paperwork first." Taking a black and gold fountain pen from its holder, he begins filling out the form. "If all goes smoothly, you'll start the new position next Monday."

"Monday? So what do I do until then?"

"Don't worry, you'll still be getting paid." He chuckles. "You'll work here this week and report to the Waiver Board next Monday."

That evening, during their twenty-minute drive home, Kermit excitedly tells Augustus about her promotion. As they turn onto Natural Bridge Avenue, she compares the sprawling St. Louis Administration Center—home to over fifteen thousand employees—to her sleek skyscraper office in Newark. While passing Sherman Park on Kingshighway Boulevard, she lists the former New Jersey colleagues she encountered on her first day. By the time they reach their small walk-up apartment on Enright Avenue, Kermit realizes Augustus has hardly spoken.

"How was your day?" she asks as they climb the first set of concrete steps. "How did the physical go?"

"I passed," Augustus responds, unlocking the door. As the sun dips below the horizon, painting the sky in shades of orange and purple, he ushers her in and locks up. They ascend to the second floor, pass the shared bathroom, and enter their rented unit, where Arvolin prepares dinner in the kitchenette. The aroma of pot roast and vegetables fills the small space.

"How was your first day?" she greets, holding a wooden spoon.

"Good," they respond in unison, each greeting her with an embrace.

"Dinner's almost ready." Arvolin returns to the stove.

Kermit switches on the table lamp in the living room while Augustus opens the valve on the radiator, releasing a hiss of steam. He sits on the bench by the bay window, continuing their conversation in low tones.

"The doctor said I got jungle rot from that New Guinea swamp," he reveals quietly.

"Gus, why didn't you tell me sooner?" Kermit removes her heels and joins him on the bench. "Is that what's causing the sores and corns on your feet?"

"Uh-huh. I didn't have this pain or swelling before the Army." He unties his shoes and gently removes them, rubbing his feet.

"Did the doctor say what you can do for it?"

"He gave me a prescription ointment and told me to soak my feet in the tub with Epsom salt. He also said I might qualify for disability."

"Really? From the Army?" Kermit asks.

"It's possible. He's starting the paperwork, and I'll file a claim next week."

"Oh, Gus, that extra money could really help us with the move to California."

"I know. It's not guaranteed, but it's worth a try."

"Definitely. But you still qualified for the file clerk job, right?"

"Uh-huh. After the physical, I completed my paperwork and got sworn in."

"Good." She pats his shoulder, then disappears into the bedroom. She returns wearing slippers and a housecoat. "We need to get that prescription filled and pick up some Epsom salt."

A month later, the couple schedules a meeting with the human resources manager during their lunch break. While waiting outside the personnel office, Kermit brushes lint from her khaki wool dress as Augustus smokes a cigarette. The smell of meatloaf with tomato sauce—Thursday's cafeteria special—wafts through the corridor, making their stomachs rumble. They watch workers stream past, hurrying toward the lunchroom with the urgency of people who know their time is limited.

An older Black man with graying temples exits the office. Moments later, a white man with dishwater-blond hair and a mustache appears at the doorway.

"Mr. and Mrs. Hill?" he asks, adjusting his blue-and-white bowtie.

"Yes," they reply in unison, shaking his hand.

"I'm Mr. Russell. Come on in."

They enter the windowless office, which contains three four-drawer black file cabinets towering against the walls like metal sentinels. Overhead lighting casts a yellow glow on the wooden desk, stacked with brown folders that seem to multiply daily. Once they sit, Mr. Russell joins them behind the desk.

"How can I help you today?" he asks, removing two folders from the pile.

"Thank you for seeing us," Kermit begins. "We moved here from New Jersey last month—"

"Yes, I reviewed your files before you came in," Mr. Russell interrupts.

"Well, we're hoping to find work in California or Washington state to be near family. Do you know of any openings in those areas?"

"You're already planning to leave St. Louis?" Mr. Russell chuckles. "That snowstorm yesterday didn't scare you off, did it?"

"No. We just want to be closer to family. My mother and stepfather are in Yakima, and I have a cousin in Bakersfield," Augustus explains.

"I'm only teasing." Mr. Russell chuckles, flipping through the paperwork. "Augustus, before working for the Veterans office, you were in the service, correct?"

"Yes, sir. Army from '42 to '45—honorably discharged."

"Kermit, you started at the War Department in D.C. in 1942 and then moved to New Jersey?"

"That's right."

"I recommend you both take the civil service exam for grades one through four and see what comes up." Mr. Russell stands to retrieve a folder. "This is Form 57—Application for Federal Employment. List your preferred work locations under section 15-c on the first page." He hands them the forms. "With your experience, you're strong candidates. West Coast jobs are competitive, but you never know when something might become available."

"Thank you," Augustus responds as they rise to leave.

The couple applies for clerk positions in Yakima, Washington, and Los Angeles, California. As a backup, they include St. Louis. After turning in their forms, they spend the last ten minutes of their lunch break enjoying a quick bite of meatloaf before heading back to work, their hopes for California burning brighter with each completed application.

In Sickness and In Health

March 27, 1947

Deep inside their windowless offices, Kermit and Augustus focus on their work, oblivious to the storm gathering outside. When they leave the building, nearly six inches of snow greets them, blanketing every surface in pristine white. Augustus briskly brushes off their car, and they merge into the slow procession of vehicles inching through the snow-covered parking lot toward Goodfellow Avenue.

Heavy flakes swirl around the vehicle, quickly accumulating on the windshield and hampering Augustus' visibility. He grips the steering wheel, squinting through the snow while aligning his tires with the dark tracks left by other drivers. Kermit nervously surveys the white haze around them for any sign of approaching traffic. When Augustus turns the corner, their car fishtails, losing traction on the slippery asphalt.

"Be careful, honey," Kermit shrieks, bracing herself against the dashboard as they slide off course.

"I'm trying," Augustus responds, wrestling with the steering wheel. As they crawl further down the snowy path, he sneezes, involuntarily swerving the car a second time.

"Gus!" Kermit shouts. "Watch out!"

Augustus slams on the brakes, locking the wheels as their vehicle skids into a snow embankment on the curb. "Sorry, I couldn't stop." His voice carries exhaustion. "Are you okay?"

"Yes. Do you want me to drive?"

"No, I'm fine." Augustus coughs and rubs his nose with the back of his gloved hand. "We're almost home now anyway." Looking through the rearview mirror, he waits for the drivers behind him to pass before backing out of the snowdrift and continuing down the street.

As they arrive in their neighborhood, Augustus struggles to find a clear spot along the unplowed streets. He eventually gives up, parking in the snowbank as their car tires spin to gain traction. When Kermit and Augustus gingerly climb over the mounds of snow, icy winds sting their faces. Their footprints sink deep into the snow-covered path leading up to their duplex. Once inside, Augustus sneezes again, triggering a coughing fit as they ascend the staircase.

"You need to gargle with salt water as soon as we get in the door," Kermit announces, brushing snow off his coat. "Is there any Vicks VapoRub left?"

"Yes." Augustus stammers between coughs. "There should be about half a jar left."

At the end of the dimly lit hall, Arvolin stands in their doorway. "I could hear you coming a mile away with all that coughing." She shakes her head, her forehead creasing with concern. "I'll make you some tea with honey, and you go gargle with some salt water."

"I already told him," Kermit notes as they cross the wooden threshold into their apartment.

"Thanks." Augustus' voice emerges thick with congestion. "I thought I was getting over this cold."

"It's all this up-and-down weather we're having," Arvolin observes. "Just on Sunday it was warm and sunny, and look at all this snow we're getting today."

"Yes, that's probably it." Kermit hangs up her coat and hat. "I'm actually not feeling well myself. I'm going to lie down for a while."

Arvolin feels Kermit's forehead with the back of her hand. "Are you coming down with something too?"

"I don't know. Maybe."

"Huh, you don't feel warm." Arvolin examines her daughter with experienced eyes. "Do you think some tea will help?"

"Not right now." Kermit heads toward her room. "I'm just really tired."

"Well, you both need to take off those wet clothes. I'll make some chicken soup." Arvolin moves toward the kitchenette, her slippers shuffling against the wooden floor.

While the couple changes clothes in their bedroom, Kermit locates the navy jar with the green Vicks VapoRub label on the nightstand. "Here, Gus. Let me rub this on your chest before you put on a shirt." When she twists open the lid, the pungent menthol scent immediately turns her stomach. She tries to fight the stomach-churning feeling but quickly replaces the lid to avoid nausea. "Eww, has this gone bad? It smells awful."

Augustus takes the jar and opens it. "Smells the same to me." He takes a whiff. "It's always had a strong odor, though."

"Well, it's making me sick." Kermit holds her stomach, her face pale. "I can't stand the smell of it now." She covers her nose and moves across the room. "Take it with you when you go gargle in the bathroom. You'll have to put it on yourself this time."

As Augustus departs, Kermit crawls into bed, pulling the quilts over her head. When he returns later that evening, she lies sound asleep. Gently shaking Kermit awake, he whispers, "Hey, do you want some soup?"

"No, I can't eat right now," Kermit mumbles with her eyes still closed. "Just want sleep."

Early the following morning, Augustus shaves in their shared bathroom with the other tenants down the hall. Kermit, clad in her wool forest green pantsuit, sits by the bay window, sipping coffee as the morning sun reflects off the fallen snow. Although six inches of snow clings to the grass and trees, patches of the roadways and sidewalks peek through the white blanket.

Wrapped in her mint green terry housecoat, Arvolin joins her daughter. "How are you feeling today?"

"About the same." Kermit takes another sip of coffee, then grimaces at her cup.

"There's some oatmeal in there if you want." Arvolin nods toward the kitchenette.

"No, thank you." Kermit crosses to the sink and pours the coffee down the drain. "I don't have much of an appetite. Nothing tastes the same lately."

Arvolin follows her daughter, lowering her voice. "Baby, do you think you could be with child?"

Kermit frowns at her mother. "No. What makes you say that?"

"Come sit down a minute." Arvolin guides Kermit to the table, pulling her chair closer. "Last night you said you weren't feeling well, but you didn't have a fever. Then Augustus told me how you couldn't stand the smell of VapoRub. And you went to bed so early. That's not like you at all."

"That doesn't mean—" Kermit protests.

"Are you still having your monthlies?" Arvolin interrupts.

"Of course." Kermit asserts, then pauses, trying to remember. "Right after we moved here in January."

Arvolin points at the wall calendar. "And on Tuesday it'll be April, baby."

Before Kermit can respond, Augustus enters, wearing a white undershirt and blue flannel pajama trousers. "Good morning." He shuffles past, clearing his throat before adding, "I'll be ready to go in a few minutes."

"Okay," Kermit stares at her mother as she responds to him. "Your cold seems a little better."

"Yes, I think so." He slips into the bedroom. "That tea and soup Momma Bland made really seemed to help clear me up."

After Augustus closes the door behind him, Kermit gently caresses her stomach. "Do you really think so?"

"Sounds like it to me." Arvolin smiles, tears escaping her eyes as she embraces her daughter.

Stunned into silence, Kermit considers the possibility of her pregnancy. She unconsciously purses her lips, her thoughts racing in a million directions at once.

"Are you going to tell Augustus?" Arvolin chuckles softly. "Well, you'll have to eventually."

"I don't know." Kermit stammers. "Shouldn't I wait until I'm sure? Until I can see a doctor? But I don't even know any doctors in St. Louis yet. What kind of doctor does the test for that anyway?"

"Kermit, slow down." Arvolin scoots her chair next to her daughter and rubs her back gently. "If you haven't bled since January, you're probably already two months along by now. I think you should go talk to Augustus and go from there."

"All right," Kermit speaks softly. "Thanks, Momma." She embraces her mother, then stands to push in her chair. After checking her watch, she adds, "But Gus and I need to get to the office. Oh, what am I going to do about work with a baby?"

Arvolin clasps her daughter's hands. "I'm right here, Kermit. And I would love to help out with my grandchild whenever you need me."

"Oh, you're such a blessing." Kermit leans down to hug Arvolin. "That means so much to me." As the doorknob of their bedroom door rattles, she whispers, "Okay, I'll tell Gus in the car."

Wearing a tweed beige suit and chestnut tie, Augustus quickly crosses the room. He puts on his coat and hat before asking, "You ready? We better get going." Retrieving Kermit's coat, he holds it up for her to slip on. Kermit nods, smoothly inserting her arms into the coat sleeves and then removing her gloves from the pocket. She carefully positions her hat so as not to disturb her hairstyle, then grabs her purse from the coat stand.

"Ready." Kermit glances at her teary-eyed mother. "See you tonight," she calls before following Augustus out. After descending the staircase, they discover the shoveled pathway, making their trip to the car less treacherous. Augustus opens the passenger door and helps Kermit over the melting snow pile.

Squirming in her seat, Kermit watches Augustus start the engine and clear the accumulated snow off the car. She searches her mind for how to begin as he cautiously steers the car onto Enright Avenue. Pursing her lips, she begins, "Gus."

Staring straight ahead at the grayish slush of melting snow, Augustus crawls down the road. "Uh-huh?" he murmurs when they reach the next block.

"I think—no, I do have something to tell you." Kermit continues, carefully choosing her words, "but I'm not really sure yet."

Augustus slowly rolls to a stop sign and glances her way. "What is it?"

Kermit inhales a deep breath to calm her nerves. "Well, I was talking to Momma this morning and she thinks—" she stutters. "Well, she doesn't know really," Kermit inhales again, "but she thinks I may, or we may be having a baby."

"Kermit!" Augustus bellows, glancing at her stomach. "A baby? Really?"

She nods and starts tearing up. "What do you think?"

"What do I think?" Augustus repeats incredulously. "I don't know. I... I wasn't expecting this." He stammers, eyes widening. "But it's good. I think it's good, great." His voice grows excited. "What about you? Do you feel all right?" He reaches across the seat and grabs her hand.

"I'm okay. Momma thinks that's why I've been so tired and feeling sick lately."

Glancing in the rearview mirror, Augustus notices a line of cars behind him. He continues through the intersection and pulls over in the next block. Sliding across the seat, he wraps his arms around Kermit as they kiss. "Why on earth would you tell me something like this when I'm driving?" he chuckles.

"I don't know." Kermit laughs through tears. "I didn't know how to tell you." She takes her handkerchief out of her purse and dabs her eyes. "Gus, if I'm truly having a baby, you know what that means."

Augustus looks at her questioningly. "No, what?"

"Our apartment. Remember? The landlord said, when we moved in, he doesn't allow any children."

"Oh boy." Augustus rubs his forehead. "I didn't even think about that. I guess we'll have to find a new place before the baby comes." After another kiss, he slides behind the steering wheel. "That's okay." He starts to laugh. "A baby." He chuckles, joining the line of traffic. "I'm thirty years old and about to be a father."

Baby Makes Four

December 20, 1947

K ermit's pregnancy forces the couple to abandon their adults-only rental and delay their California dreams. In April, Augustus purchases their first home at 3212 North Newstead Avenue using funds from the GI Bill's low-mortgage program for veterans. The three-story brick structure rises from its white stone foundation in the diverse Greater Ville neighborhood, where German and Irish immigrants populate tree-lined streets. The vacant unit upstairs offers an unexpected advantage—Arvolin can live nearby while maintaining her independence.

Kermit settles at the kitchen table of their new home, nursing her six-week-old son while writing thank-you notes for the cascade of baby gifts they have received. When discussing names for their little boy, Augustus surprisingly chooses Hugh, the name of his birth father, whom he has never met. Kermit finds the choice odd since Della rarely discusses the father of her only child, and Kermit remains uncertain whether he is still alive. Sensing her mother-in-law is keeping a secret about the elder Hugh, Kermit decides not to pry.

While Augustus shops at the hardware store, Arvolin comes down to visit her grandson and help Kermit with household chores. After removing the diapers, underwear, and shirts flapping on the backyard clothesline, she rushes inside out of the chilly winter air. Carrying the wooden splint laundry basket full of clothes into the kitchen, Arvolin sits next to Kermit and begins neatly folding them.

"Do you want me to hold Hugh?" Arvolin asks, playfully covering her face with the diaper from the basket in a game of peek-a-boo with the newborn.

Kermit chuckles. "Weren't you the one who told me that holding him too much would spoil him?"

"That doesn't apply to me," Arvolin teases. "Grandmothers are supposed to spoil their grandchildren."

"Okay," Kermit laughs. "When I'm done feeding him, you can put him down for his nap." With her free hand, she slides a notecard into an envelope, then licks and seals it. After flipping through her address book, she writes the recipient's address on the envelope. "We've received such nice gifts," she gushes. She rips a stamp from the postage sheet, presses it on a damp sea sponge, then sticks it on the top right corner of the envelope. "Remind me to show you the cute outfit Gus' cousin, Vernessa, sent all the way from California. She's so disappointed we're not relocating there this year."

Arvolin peeks around the diaper at Hugh. "Is he done eating yet?" she asks.

"Oh yes, he's done," Kermit says, rebuttoning her nightgown. "Here you go, but don't forget to burp him."

"Did you forget who raised you, young lady?" Arvolin huffs as she carefully cradles Hugh. She tightly wraps the infant in a white blanket decorated with blue teddy bears and a powder blue silk border. Kermit drapes a white burping pad over Arvolin's shoulder and helps her mother position Hugh onto the pad. Gently rubbing her grandson's back, Arvolin coos to him in a sing-song tone. "How's my little Hughey doing?" As she carries him to the wooden oak cradle, Hugh burps. "Oh my," Arvolin exclaims with a laugh. "You're not ready to go to sleep, are you? You want to stay in Grandma's arms a little while longer, don't you, sweetie?"

"Momma," Kermit scolds. "You know Hugh gets cranky if he doesn't get his nap."

Arvolin rocks her grandson, who tightly grips her index finger. She gently lowers the infant onto the mattress covered with a fitted blue and white sheet. As she tucks him under the blanket, she sighs, "I guess mother knows best."

As the cradle gently rocks with Hugh's movements, Kermit lowers the white roller blinds to shade the afternoon sun. She joins her mother as they watch him suck his fist and drift off to sleep. "Come on," Kermit says quietly. "Let me show you all the gifts we received while he's napping." She leads her mother into the nursery, filled with packages haphazardly stacked on the dresser and floor. Sorting through the boxes, Kermit locates a navy suspender shorts outfit with gold buttons. The white shirt features blue stripes on the cuffs and shawl collar with an embroidered nautical emblem on the short sleeves. The matching navy-brimmed white hat also displays an embroidered nautical emblem in the center. Kermit assembles the pieces of the outfit, topping them with the matching navy tie. "Isn't this adorable?" she asks.

"Aww, what a cute sailor suit," Arvolin says. "But where in the world would he wear such a thing?"

"I have no idea," Kermit chuckles. "It's too big for him now anyway. I have some time to think of someplace special while he grows into it. But it's just so cute!"

While Kermit shows Arvolin the rest of the gifts, Augustus enters through the back porch, carrying a shopping bag from Straub Hardware. "Anyone home?" he calls, placing the brown paper bag on a kitchen chair.

Kermit rushes to meet him. "Shh," she hushes, gesturing toward the front room. "The baby's sleeping."

"Oh," Augustus whispers, attempting to suppress a laugh and placing a finger to his lips. After kissing Kermit, he tiptoes to the cradle as the hardwood floor creaks under his footsteps. When Augustus reaches his son, Hugh remains undisturbed, snuggled under his blanket. Kermit and Arvolin join Augustus, and the threesome admires the napping newborn. "Isn't he something?" Augustus whispers.

"Well, I certainly think so," Kermit replies. "But I may be a bit biased."

"Sure is a handsome young man," Arvolin agrees.

"Let's go so he can finish his nap," Kermit says, guiding them out of the room. When they reach the kitchen, she removes the bag from the chair and peeks inside. "How'd you do at the hardware store?" she asks, handing the bag to Augustus. "Did you find something to fix the bathroom leak?"

Reaching inside the bag, Augustus removes a P-Trap sink pipe, plumbers' putty, and washers. "The man at the store told me to try these," he says, presenting the items. "I'm going to work on it this afternoon, so if you need to use the sink, do it before I get started."

"Okay, good," Kermit says, settling into a chair. "Before you got here, I was showing Momma all the nice gifts Hugh received." She shuffles through the thank-you cards, checking off her list of gifts in the notebook. "He won't need Santa to bring him anything for his first Christmas."

"Y'all are truly blessed to get all those nice things," Arvolin says as she resumes folding the laundry. "Your father and I didn't have half of those when you were coming up."

Kermit nods. "I sure miss Daddy. I wish he could've seen his grandchild."

"Me too," Arvolin agrees, affectionately squeezing her daughter's hand. "I miss him every day." She swipes away a tear rolling down her cheek. "I don't regret staying in Little Rock to take care of your grandmother. But I should've taken you and joined him in Michigan when he found work."

When Hugh stirs in his sleep, the cradle gently rocks. All three turn, collectively holding their breath to see if he wakes. When they only hear the infant cooing, they resume their conversation.

"You know," Augustus says, still gazing at his son, "My mother can't wait to see her grandson. She's thinking about coming in the spring when it gets a little warmer."

"That would be nice," Arvolin says. "I haven't seen Della in a while now. It'd be good to see her again."

"But she wants us to send her the money for her train fare," Kermit interjects, exchanging glances with her husband. "So, we have to save the money first."

"Oh. Well, tell her I'm looking forward to seeing her when she comes," Arvolin says. Holding a dress shirt, she flicks her wrist to shake out the wrinkles, then aligns the seams. In one smooth motion, she tucks the sleeves inside before folding the shirt in crisp creases. "I forgot to ask you, Augustus, how's your new job at the post office?"

"It's been fine so far," he replies. "I spent my first week matching postal codes with locations to sort letters faster. You wouldn't believe how much mail goes through that place."

"That's really something," Arvolin says. "I guess if Kermit goes back to work, you two won't be at the same place anymore."

"If?" Kermit interrupts. "What do you mean, 'if'?"

"Well, now that you have Hugh..." Arvolin trails off.

"That's why I need to hurry up and get back to work," Kermit responds. "A baby is so expensive with diapers, clothes, and other baby stuff. We're going to need both our paychecks—especially as Hugh gets older." Kermit secures the thank-you notes with a rubber band and drops them in the wall-mounted letter rack. "In fact, my paid leave runs out this week, so we're only going to be on Gus' salary until I can start bringing in money again." She slips the notebook and pen into the drawer, then cleans off the kitchen table with a wet dishcloth. "They already dropped me to a lower grade and made me take a Fit for Duty exam when I got pregnant. When I return, I'll have to fight even harder to prove I can still do my job and hopefully get my old salary back."

"Well, with Gus' new job, I thought..." Arvolin freezes when she catches Kermit glaring at her. "Hmm, let me go put the laundry away," she recovers, rising to leave.

Once Arvolin is out of earshot, Augustus states, "Well, I agree with your mother. I don't think you should go back to work. Just stay home and take care of Hugh."

"Gus," Kermit sighs. "You know we need both of our salaries just to afford the mortgage on this place alone." She noisily removes pots from the cabinet to prepare lunch. "That doesn't even include the cost of a growing boy. Plus, we need to pay for your mother's visit too."

"I'm making more at the post office than I did at the Army Finance Center," Augustus counters. "My cousin Preston has worked there for five years, and he says they have a lot of opportunities for Negroes."

"Maybe so," Kermit says. "But right now, keeping my job is for the best." Opening the refrigerator, she removes a stalk of celery, carrots, and an onion, then places them on the counter. She hastily grabs a paring knife from the utensil drawer and begins peeling the ruddy orange outer skin off the carrots. Next, she picks at the base of the celery stalk with her finger and yanks off the green strings. Removing a butcher's knife from the knife block, she adds, "And my mother can watch Hugh while I'm at work." She slices the onion, then chops the remaining vegetables into bite-sized cubes.

Augustus drops the hardware items back in the bag. "For now," he concedes. "I'm supposed to be the breadwinner of this family, not my wife." He carries the bag into the front room to watch Hugh as he wakes from his nap. "So, when I move up the ranks at the post office, I want you to be the one raising our child, not your mother."

Guess Who's Coming to Dinner

April 6, 1948

In the month since Kermit returned from maternity leave, she feels constantly scrutinized by her new supervisor. Before becoming a mother, her previous supervisor raved in a glowing review, "Ms. Hill is an unusually intelligent person, and her decisions are extraordinarily accurate." Now, everything Kermit does is questioned, and she sees no path to regaining her previous salary. To review her options, Kermit meets with the personnel manager, who suggests a risky strategy: transfer from her current Board Member position to a fiscal accounting clerk position where she can compete for promotions and higher pay. However, the transfer will cost her a twenty-three percent decrease in her current salary and a twenty-eight percent decrease from what she was making last year. After discussing the proposal with Augustus, Kermit decides to accept the reassignment.

In light of their tighter finances, Kermit hopes Augustus will convince his mother to delay her trip to visit her new grandson. Scrambling to cover Della's travel costs is bad enough, but her stay also coincides with Kermit's first week in her new job. Truthfully, Kermit wants to delay the scrutiny of her judgmental mother-in-law for as long as possible. But Augustus buckles under Della's guilt-inducing pleas, so his mother is due in town that evening as scheduled.

The Class E Allotment Division, where Kermit now works, occupies a different building on the other side of the St. Louis Administration Center. However, by the end of her first day, she realizes the layout of the building is virtually identical to where she previously worked.

On Tuesday, Kermit and the other fiscal accounting clerks file into the Army Finance Center office. Overhead, ceiling fixtures cast a pale light across rows of metal desks, while typewriter bells ring and adding machines clatter in the background. She retrieves a black binder labeled "Allotment Audits" from her drawer. Flipping through the pages, she finds the section on duplicate payments and begins reviewing the unresolved cases. As she works through her assignments, her thoughts drift to her mother-in-law's imminent visit, already bracing for potential tension or sharp remarks. She plans to get home in time to dust and clear any clutter before her arrival.

After work, drizzling rain sprays Kermit's cheeks as she rushes across the slick pavement to the bus stop. Twenty-five minutes later, she steps off the bus at Newstead and Ashland Avenues, shielding her face with her rain bonnet. Dodging puddles along the block, Kermit darts through the rain shower to her home's walkway. As she approaches her front porch, she hears Hugh's piercing wails and quickly unlocks the door. Bustling through the foyer, she spots Arvolin, her flushed face damp with perspiration, bouncing a weeping Hugh.

Dropping her purse and keys, Kermit rushes to her son. "What's wrong?" she asks, reaching for her infant. At the sound of his mother's voice, Hugh squirms and sobs louder. She retrieves her son, caressing him against her drenched trench coat. "There, there, Mommy's here," she soothes, rubbing his back gently.

"I can't get him to eat," Arvolin sighs. She gestures toward the table strewn with an upturned baby bottle, a pacifier, milk jug, and an open can of Carnation Evaporated Milk, its red and white label accented with three pink flowers. "I've tried everything—but nothing's working today. He may be teething or just wants his mommy."

"Okay," Kermit says as Hugh continues screaming. With her mother's help, she slips out of her coat and drops into the burgundy upholstered arm-chair. Unbuttoning her blouse, she starts to nurse her crying child. "Ouch," she cries when he latches on. "Somebody's teeth are coming in, alright."

Arvolin dabs her brow with the burping pad on her shoulder, then returns the milk jug and Carnation can to the refrigerator. "What time does Della's train get in?" she asks, wiping off the table with a dish towel. She opens the oven door and checks on the bubbling chicken and dumplings casserole.

"It should be in by now," Kermit says. She winces, tightly shutting her eyes at the sensation of nursing a teething infant. "Gus is going to pick her up after he gets off work. The station's downtown, just a few blocks away from him at the post office." Turning towards Hugh, Kermit kisses his forehead and smooths the black wisps of curls on his head. "I see you're feeling better."

Arvolin shakes her head. "He wasn't having that bottle today."

"Thanks, Momma," Kermit says. "I was just telling someone today, I don't know what I would do without you."

"Thanks, baby," Arvolin smiles as she fans herself with a dish towel.

"Go on upstairs and take a little rest before Gus gets back," Kermit encourages. "We'll probably eat in about an hour, so come down around six-thirty."

Arvolin caresses the top of Hugh's head. "Okay. See you soon," she calls, slipping out the back door.

Cradling her infant, Kermit enters the bathroom and removes his sea-green sleeper and soiled diaper. After rinsing a washcloth under the sink faucet, she gently washes his tear-stained face. As Hugh squirms in the sink, Kermit lathers the damp cloth with the white bar of Ivory soap and bathes him. She responds to Hugh's babbling in a high-pitched sing-song voice. "That's right, my little baby's getting nice and clean, isn't he?"

Kermit wraps the writhing baby in a towel and carries him into the nursery. After dusting his mahogany-colored body with white talcum powder, she struggles to dress him in a shorts outfit as his chubby arms and legs alternately punch the air. As she slips on his socks, she hears her husband and mother-in-law enter the house.

"We're home!" Augustus calls.

"Coming!" replies Kermit, steeling herself for her houseguest. Placing her child into the cradle of her arm, she whispers, "Okay, your other grandma's here. I need you to help Mommy get through this visit." She listens as Augustus hangs Della's coat in the foyer and starts a tour of the house. Hearing their footsteps approaching, Kermit meets them in the hallway. "Momma Woods! It's so good to see you. How was your trip?"

Della's wavy black hair, pinned in a low bun, parts slightly off-center. Her round, wire-rimmed glasses rest against a pale, parchment-toned complexion that could easily be mistaken for white. She often talks about relatives she visits in Texas who are passing.

"Oh my," exclaims Della, talking over Kermit's greeting. "Look at my chocolate little grandbaby." She takes the infant from Kermit's grasp, and

Hugh starts to cry. "Oh, you're alright," Della assures, placing Hugh on her shoulder against the embroidered collar of her taupe dress. "I'm your grandma. Grandma Woods," she says, hoisting him on her shoulder.

"Hi there," Augustus greets, kissing his wife. He hauls Della's cream hard-case travel bag and purse into the nursery. "You'll be in here, Momma," he says as he loosens his brick and cream tie. "The baby will sleep in our room while you're here." When Hugh's cries intensify, Augustus pats his son's head and chuckles. "What's the matter, Hugh?" Moving behind Della, he makes animated faces at Hugh and grasps his son's flailing arms.

Resisting the urge to rescue her son, Kermit folds her arms while pursing her lips. When her eyes meet Della's, Kermit plasters a strained smile across her face. "So, are you hungry?" she asks under gritted teeth. "Momma's coming down in a bit to join us for dinner." To escape her six-month-old's distressing, high-pitched screams, Kermit moves into the kitchen to set the table.

"Are you still fussing?" Della scolds, rocking her grandson back and forth. "Oh, your mommy and daddy must be spoiling you."

"Here we go," Kermit whispers under her breath. She glances over her shoulder to see if Augustus will respond to his mother's remark. Hearing none, she does. "Hugh's not spoiled. He just needs some time to get used to you."

Disregarding Kermit's comments, Della asks Hugh, "Is my grandbaby hungry? Maybe you need something to eat."

"He just ate," Kermit retorts, working hard to keep a light tone in her voice. She hears a rapid tapping on the back door and sees her mother stepping inside.

"Hello! Anybody home?" Arvolin greets, shutting the door behind her. Hearing Hugh's sobs, she adds, "Oh no! I thought you got him to settle down."

Kermit gives Arvolin a weary smile. "Gus' mother has him," she says, moving closer to her mother. "Why don't you see if you can give her a hand?"

Arvolin passes through the living room to find Della and Augustus attempting to calm the wailing infant in the hall. "Well, look who's here," Arvolin chuckles. She kisses Della and Augustus on the cheek. "It's so good to see you, Della."

"You too, Arvolin," Della replies. "How have you been?" She shifts the agitated baby between her shoulders and arms as Augustus slips into the kitchen.

"Good," Arvolin replies as she gently rubs her grandson's head. "Hugh's been cranky lately. He's got new teeth coming in." Arvolin positions herself closer to the infant. "Why don't you let me take him so you can get freshened up for dinner?"

"Oh, thank you, dear," Della says, passing Hugh to her. "I do need to visit the little girls' room before we eat," she whispers, slipping into the bathroom.

Listening to her exhausted son's whimpering and colicky cries becomes unbearable for the young mother. Kermit rushes through the living room, retrieves Hugh from Arvolin, and comforts him. "It's okay, baby," she soothes as she glares at her husband.

"I know, I know, but what do you want me to do?" Augustus asks quietly. "She's excited to see her grandson. Give her some time."

Shaking her head, Kermit says, "Can you take the bassinet out of the nursery and put it in our room, please?" Lifting the infant onto her shoulder, she gently rubs his back as he coos. "Hugh's so worked up; he just needs to go to sleep." Cradling Hugh with one hand, Kermit pours sweet tea into four glasses. As Arvolin removes the casserole from the oven, the kitchen fills with the savory aromas of melted cheese, chicken, and succotash simmering on the stove.

When Augustus retrieves the bassinet from the nursery, Della emerges from the bathroom. "What's wrong, baby?" she asks her son. "You look upset."

"I'm fine, Momma," he replies. "Just moving the baby's bed out of your room so he can sleep."

"Already?" Della whines. "I just got here. Does he have to go to bed so soon?"

"Well, it's past his bedtime, and he's really tired," Augustus replies. "You'll get to spend more time with him during your visit." As he moves the bedding into the next room, Della follows closely behind.

"You didn't show me your bedroom," Della remarks, surveying the layout. "Is this new furniture?" She runs her index finger along the top of the oak dresser, checking for dust.

"Some of it is," Augustus replies, setting up the infant bed. Guiding his mother out of the room, he adds, "Let's go eat. Dinner's ready."

Kermit smoothly slips past them as she takes Hugh to bed. She dresses him in a cotton sleeper and tucks him under the blanket. Watching as he drifts off to sleep, she whispers, "This is going to be a long week." Pausing to glance at her reflection in the standing mirror, she takes in a deep breath before joining her family for dinner.

While Kermit works during the day, she appreciates her mother taking on the task of entertaining Della. Most days, the weather is warm enough for the women to visit on the front porch while Hugh plays in his crib. Occasionally, their stout, ebony-skinned neighbor, Lulu Scott, joins them, bringing her twins who are the same age as Hugh.

However, in the evenings and on weekends, Kermit's mother-in-law remains constantly underfoot. On Saturday, Della refuses to eat lunch until her son returns from his shift at the post office. That evening, she bursts into their bedroom, interrupting an intimate moment between the couple. "My baby, my baby," Della cries, throwing her arms around her son. Kermit shrieks at the intrusion, yanking the blanket over her shoulders in disbelief.

Following an extremely trying week with Della, Kermit eagerly awaits her mother-in-law's departure back to Yakima on Sunday. She silently counts the remaining minutes until Augustus' mother steps aboard the train that afternoon. After church, the family gathers at the Scotts' house next door, joining Lulu, her husband, Milton, and their six-month-old twins for dinner.

Once they finish, Augustus loads Della's luggage into the car while Kermit retrieves their camera to capture the moment. In the front yard, Arvolin holds a sleeping Hugh, dressed in a white shorts suit, matching socks, and Stride Rite shoes. Della and Lulu come outside to join Arvolin as the three women chat in the afternoon sun.

Holding the camera, Kermit descends the porch stairs to the sidewalk. "Okay," she calls, waving them to stand together. "Y'all get in line for a picture."

"Here, you take Hugh," Arvolin says as she transfers her grandson to Augustus. The shuffling around wakes Hugh, who begins fussing. Augustus stiffly holds his son, trying to prevent him from spitting up on his navy pin-striped suit. Della, wearing a belted white long-sleeved button-down dress, saddles up next to her son, and Arvolin and Lulu fall in line.

While Kermit focuses on the group, Arvolin stops her. "Wait," she says. "You should be in the picture. I'll take it."

Skeptically, Kermit asks, "Do you even know how to use the camera?"

"Oh, go on. I've seen you and Augustus take enough pictures to figure it out," her mother replies. She steps out of line to join her daughter and retrieves the camera. "Go ahead and get next to Augustus and Hugh."

"Alright, Momma," Kermit acquiesces. Pointing to the shutter button, she adds, "Here's where you push to take the picture."

As Kermit climbs the steps, Arvolin fumbles with the camera, awkwardly squinting through the viewfinder. Della shifts closer to her son, denying her daughter-in-law space to stand beside Augustus. Ignoring the deliberate slight, Kermit smooths the pleats of her blue suit skirt and adjusts the blouse bow before positioning herself behind her husband's shoulder with an undaunted smile.

Arvolin tilts the camera diagonally to fit everyone in the lens' frame. "Okay. Here I go. I'm about to take the picture. Everyone smile," she directs and snaps the photo.

4-11-1948 Baby Hugh Hill, Augustus Hill, Kermit Hill, Della Woods, Lulu Scott

Cutest Baby

July 4, 1948

Scattered showers move the annual Fourth of July picnic indoors, crowding the congregation into the humid church basement after service. Enticing aromas drift from the kitchen where Kermit's mother, Arvolin, and the picnic committee put finishing touches on the barbecued chicken, macaroni salad, and sweet watermelon balls. While waiting to be served, Augustus chats with fellow members as Kermit feeds their son. In honor of the holiday, she wears a patriotic navy and white dress, matching hat, and peep-toe shoes with a red bow. Her husband sits beside her in a navy suit, a red pocket square adding a festive touch. Hugh loudly sucks on a bottle of apple juice, sporting a navy pinstriped shorts set, his thick black curls tucked under his sailor hat.

Bishop Mitchell mingles with the picnickers, highlighting points from his earlier sermon promising independence for God's people. The white stole against his black robe creates a stark contrast, mirroring the pale skin against his black pompadour. When he approaches Kermit and Augustus, he asks, "How old is this handsome young man?"

Swiftly removing Hugh's bottle, Kermit positions her son to face the minister. "He'll be eight months in a couple days," she replies.

As Hugh begins to fuss, Bishop Mitchell chuckles. "Looks like someone wants his juice back." Kermit returns the bottle to quiet her wailing son. "By the way," he adds, "did you hear we're holding a baby contest this summer?"

Kermit glances at her husband, who shakes his head. "No, we didn't," she replies.

"Well, I suggest you get this little man in the running. It's open to babies under a year old," the bishop continues. "It's a fundraiser for our building fund, and the baby who raises the most money wins a new piano."

"Oh, I always wanted to play the piano," Kermit says, turning to her husband. "And we could start Hugh on piano lessons when he gets older."

"Sister Johnson is in charge of the contest. She's around here somewhere," Bishop Mitchell says, scanning the room. "Go find her and she'll give you all the information."

"I sure will," Kermit says. "Thanks so much."

Bishop Mitchell playfully shakes Hugh's brown leather shoe before moving to the next table. "Enjoy the rest of your holiday."

The following Saturday, Kermit strolls around Sister Johnson's backyard, chatting with other mothers participating in the church's baby contest. To prevent comparisons among contestants, the women are instructed to leave their infants at home, so Arvolin volunteers to babysit Hugh for the afternoon. A canary yellow umbrella accented with white fringe shades them from the midday sun, while a comfortable breeze keeps temperatures in the low eighties. The hostess greets her guests, directing them to complete entry forms for the competition. A middle-aged woman whom Kermit does not recognize assists Sister Johnson with the gathering. Her smoky brown skin glistens with perspiration as she busily arranges platters of diagonally sliced egg salad sandwiches, fruit salad, and lemonade.

"Please have a seat," Sister Johnson begins, pouring herself a glass. "What a blessing to have this nice weather. This week's been so hot, I was afraid we'd have to meet indoors." With murmurs of agreement, the ladies settle onto the thick yellow cushions of the patio furniture.

"After we eat, I'll go over the contest rules. Go on and get to know one another. We're all church folk here, so we're going to have a friendly competition."

As they start eating, Kermit searches the faces of the mothers. She recognizes about half of those in attendance, but only a few by name. She catches the eye of the woman beside her, outfitted in a blue floral dress. A white straw hat adorned with colorful flowers sits atop her shoulder-length black curls. "Hello," she begins. "My name is Kermit Hill."

"Nice to meet you," the woman says in an elongated southern drawl. "I'm Geraldine Williams."

"How long have you been a member of Christ Temple?" Kermit asks.

"Oh, I'd say it's been a couple years now," Geraldine replies. "I joined after me and Leonard got married in '46. It's his family's church."

"That's what happened to me, too. I grew up Baptist, but joined Gus' church after we married in '41 in Little Rock. We just moved to St. Louis from New Jersey last year."

"Well, isn't that something," Geraldine exclaims. "That's a lot of moving around."

"It sure is!" Kermit chuckles. "Spent some time in Washington, D.C., too, before moving to Jersey City."

"Grass sure doesn't have time to grow under your feet," Geraldine chuckles. "Besides here, I've only been in Mississippi, where I grew up in a little town called Prentiss."

Following an awkward silence, they sip their drinks and scan the yard. When the woman helping Sister Johnson returns with a lemon cake, Geraldine nods in her direction. "That there is my husband's mother. The other Mrs. Williams," she chuckles. "She and Sister Johnson are longtime friends."

"Oh, nice," Kermit smiles at the elder Mrs. Williams, who begins cutting the cake. When she offers them slices, Geraldine makes introductions.

As the women finish their desserts, Sister Johnson kicks off the meeting. She begins by having everyone introduce themselves, sharing their husband's name, and then their baby's name and age. Geraldine stands up when her turn comes. "Sister Geraldine Williams," she announces. "My husband is Leonard, who also happens to be Sister Williams' son." She waves to her mother-in-law as laughter erupts among the women. "My son's name is Ronald and he's five months old." After a brief round of applause, Kermit follows suit.

Once the introductions are complete, Sister Johnson outlines the rules of the competition, which will run through the end of July. "Whoever raises the most money will be crowned the cutest baby and get a brand-new piano," she explains. "The winner's photo will be featured in the church bulletin on August 1st." The women smile at each other as another round of applause erupts. "If you want your baby to win, you should ask everyone you know to donate. That includes your relatives, friends, neighbors—even the mailman!" Sister Johnson chuckles. "Just make sure all checks are made out to Christ Temple. Bishop Mitchell has pledged to donate to all the babies in the contest, so be sure to go to him with your hand out and tell him I sent you." The women laugh and applaud while Sister Johnson takes another sip. "Now, go on and get your baby that piano!" As the women disperse, Kermit and Geraldine exchange numbers, promising to get their families together soon.

Following Sister Johnson's advice, Kermit spends the next three weeks working all her networks to win the church's baby contest. She creatively decorates a used coffee can with baby-themed wrapping paper and cuts a slit on the lid to collect donations. At work, she positions it prominently beside Hugh's photograph on her desk. If a coworker passes without depositing money, she rattles the can, hoping the metallic jingle of coins will inspire generosity. During lunch, Kermit canvases the cafeteria, interrupting diners' midday meals to solicit spare change.

On weekends, she traverses the neighborhood streets, pushing Hugh's stroller along sidewalks underneath the oppressive July sun. Knocking on doors and smiling at sympathetic residents, she props up Hugh, outfitted in adorable short sets, to request donations towards her cause.

During this same period, Kermit and Geraldine grow closer as their families spend more time together. Just a week after their initial meeting, the two families join for Sunday dinner hosted by the Hills. While Kermit, Geraldine, and the grandmothers dote over the babies inside, their husbands smoke in the cool shadows in the backyard.

The following Saturday, Geraldine returns the favor, inviting Kermit and Hugh to the Williams' home for lunch. They enjoy a satisfying meal of fried chicken and apple pie. Afterward, the two women bond while their infants get acquainted on a crochet blanket nearby.

When August 1st finally arrives, Kermit and Geraldine's families sit next to each other on the church's wooden pews. As the congregation fills the sanctuary, ushers move through the aisles, distributing fans to relieve the summer humidity. When anxious members ask for a bulletin with the winning baby's announcement, they receive assurances that it will come after the scripture reading. Anticipation mounts as Bishop Mitchell majestically approaches the podium and scans the packed pews. He clears his throat and takes a sip of water before speaking.

"Well, looks like we have a full house," he chuckles, his baritone voice resonating through the sanctuary. "Anything special happening today?" Polite laughter spreads across the assembly, as some members shift in their pews. "I understand there is some sort of contest going on. People been worrying the ushers for the church bulletin like never before," he remarks, his words eliciting another wave of laughter. "Alright, I won't make you wait any longer." He rips open an envelope and dramatically removes an index card. "Without further ado, the winner of the Christ Temple Cutest Baby is..." He pauses for a moment, savoring the anticipation, before announcing with a chuckle. "Little Ronald Williams."

Kermit gasps, along with other stunned members in the assembly. Recovering quickly, she joins the congregation in applause and smiles at Geraldine. With a gentle nudge, she prompts Geraldine to rise and turn in a circle, showing her infant to the filled sanctuary. Leonard escorts his family to the altar, where they proudly accept the piano certificate from Bishop Mitchell and Sister Johnson.

While ushers swiftly distribute the Sunday bulletin among the congregants, Augustus wraps his arm around Kermit, squeezing her shoulder in comfort. As an oblivious Hugh naps on his father's lap, she quickly dabs her eyes before Geraldine and her family return. Smiling through watery eyes, Kermit mouths, "Thank you," to her husband. With slight hesitation, she opens the program, confirming Ronald Williams won Christ Temple's Cutest Baby Contest, his image grinning back at her.

After the service, a woman Kermit remembers from Sister Johnson's house pulls her aside. "You know how Geraldine won, don't you?" she whispers.

"Of course, she raised the most money," Kermit sighs. "Although I was sure I had it in the bag."

The woman's chestnut eyes dart around the bustling corridor before leaning closer to Kermit. "I heard Bishop Mitchell donated more money to Geraldine to make sure she won," she says in a husky voice. "Sister Johnson and Geraldine's mother-in-law are real tight friends, so she pushed the bishop to put in something extra for her." She rolls her eyes, then tilts her head to the side. "Isn't that some mess?"

"No. That can't be true," Kermit says, her words catching in her throat. Before she can continue, the Williams family catches up with them.

"Well, that sure was an unexpected surprise," Geraldine beams. After seeing their frozen expressions, she adds, "Look, Kermit. Sorry you didn't win, but as soon as we get the piano installed, y'all can come over whenever you want to play on it."

Kermit plasters a grin across her face. "Sure will," she responds dryly.

In the days that follow, Kermit thwarts every invitation Geraldine makes to get together. When Kermit finds another place for her family to sit that Sunday, Geraldine catches up with her while they are leaving the sanctuary. "Kermit!" she calls as the Hill family descends the church stairs. "What's happened? Something's changed between us. If I've done something to hurt you, I'm sorry. But I can't for the life of me figure out what it is."

Cradling her infant, Kermit purses her lips as she glares at Geraldine in the harsh summer sunshine. "You stole that baby contest," she hisses, her eyes welling with tears. "I know you used your mother-in-law's friendship with Sister Johnson to get Bishop Mitchell to give you more money."

Geraldine frowns, her forehead creasing with genuine confusion. "That's a lie," she snaps, shaking her head in denial. "I mean, that's just not true at all," she recovers more calmly. "I raised all that money, fair and square. I used my savings and donations I got from Leonard's job and my family reunion in July."

Kermit eyes her skeptically, doubt covering her face. Geraldine places a reassuring hand on her friend's arm. "Let's go and ask the bishop himself," she suggests. "You know he'll tell the truth, especially here at church and on a Sunday."

When her son begins to fuss, Kermit transfers him to her shoulder, rubbing his back until he quiets against her neck. "Okay," she concedes. She glances at her husband, who is chatting with another member a few steps below them. "I'll be right back," she says to him before following Geraldine up the stairs. As the women reach the landing, they encounter the confused stares of Leonard, his mother, and their son, still giddy over winning the baby competition.

"We need to see Bishop Mitchell real quick," Geraldine explains before they can voice their questions. Pointing towards the sidewalk, she adds, "Y'all can go visit with Augustus for a while until we get back."

They return to the solace of the sanctuary, where the hushed conversations of the remaining members float across the room. The bishop stands just inside his office doorway, one arm out of his black robe. "Bishop Mitchell," Geraldine calls, her voice echoing in the open space. "If you wouldn't mind, could you spare us a moment?"

As the two women cross the hardwood floor, Bishop Mitchell shrugs back into his robe. "Of course, I always have time for you two lovely young ladies," he says with a warm smile. Gesturing towards two cane-backed oak chairs, he settles into his high-backed leather chair behind the mahogany desk. Positioned on the back wall hangs a framed rendering of Jesus, glowing in radiant light as he gazes upward, hands folded in prayer.

Geraldine takes the lead, explaining the rumor circulating that he has tipped the contest in her favor. As she continues, creases deepen across the minister's beige brow, his black eyes dart between the two women.

Kermit listens in silence; a burning sensation builds in her throat as she struggles to tame her raw emotions of fury and betrayal. She stares blankly at a gold-plated figure of Christ draped in a loincloth, hanging on a wooden cross.

Geraldine concludes by saying, "And she's been acting funny towards me ever since." She crosses her arms and leans back in her chair, staring straight at him.

Bishop Mitchell scans the women's faces, pausing for any additional comments. "Look at you two," he sighs, shaking his head in disappointment. "I think that contest has caused more trouble than it's worth." He rises and ambles around the desk, leaning his thin frame against the polished edge. "Now, Sister Hill, I'm surprised at you, listening to that idle gossip," he scolds in a paternal tone. Gesturing towards a sleeping Hugh, he asks, "How much did I contribute to that little boy's contest?"

"Ten dollars," Kermit replies, gently stroking her son's back.

"And how about you, Sister Williams. How much did I give to your son?"

"It was the same—ten dollars," she confirms, her voice rising slightly.

"There, you see? Ask any one of those mothers in the contest out there and they'll tell you the same thing," he says, gesturing toward the door. "How would it look for the bishop to favor one child over another? You remember what happened to Jacob when he favored Joseph over his other eleven sons?" They both nod. "We can't have that kind of jealousy among our church members." He rises to his feet, outstretching his arms around them. "Go on and hug one another."

Initially, the two women exchange uncertain glances, tears glistening in their eyes. Kermit rises, placing her napping infant on her shoulder. "I'm sorry," she says, searching her friend's eyes for forgiveness. She extends her free arm, welcoming Geraldine in an embrace that envelops Hugh.

Bishop Mitchell gently pats each woman's back, saying, "And don't let small talk separate you two again."

As they pull apart, Kermit feels a burden lifting from her shoulders. The bitterness that clouded her judgment over the past week dissipates as she sees forgiveness in her friend's warm expression. She resolves not to allow suspicion to poison their budding friendship again. Geraldine's smile reflects a similar relief, the tension between them melting away in the bishop's paneled office.

"Why don't we get the boys together next weekend?" Kermit suggests, her voice thick with emotion. "Hugh's been missing his time with Ronald."

"I'd like that," Geraldine says, her elongated Mississippi drawl evident. "And don't forget, that piano is just as much yours as it is mine."

As they walk back into the sunshine to rejoin their families, Kermit realizes that while she hasn't won the contest, she has gained something far more valuable—a lesson in trust and a friendship worth preserving.

CHANGING SEASONS

October 15, 1948

Around Labor Day, Kermit notices familiar signs hinting that she might be pregnant. She feels nauseous in the morning from her husband's burnt toast, and later when she encounters her coworker's rose perfume. Then, her body temperature swings drastically, shifting from freezing cold to unbearably hot within minutes. By the first week of October, the absence of her period erases any doubt—she is expecting another baby.

Although Kermit has not shared the news with her supervisor, her frequent bathroom trips prove difficult for him to ignore. The unusually warm October weather leaves her feeling like a chicken roasting in the oven. Despite her husband and mother pleading with her to eat, she cannot stomach the sight of food, fearing she will not keep it down. After working through another lunch period without eating, exhaustion and weakness overcome her as she struggles to focus on her final projects before the weekend.

Observing Kermit's unusually subdued demeanor, a coworker leans closer and whispers, "How you doing there?"

Heat surges through Kermit's body, flushing her cheeks with a deep purple glow. Unable to respond, she shakes her head quickly, her eyes wide with panic. In a desperate attempt to steady herself, she slams both hands on her desktop as her vision blurs. Squinting, Kermit tries to focus on Pearl, who spins with the rest of the office fixtures around her. Her eyes close as she collapses onto her desk, unconscious.

"Kermit!" Her coworker shrieks, rushing to cradle her limp body. Other clerks jump into action, fanning her, gathering wet towels, and contacting the on-site medical unit.

Hours later, Kermit awakens to the overwhelming stench of antiseptic stinging her nostrils. Her eyes slowly focus, revealing a dimly lit hospital room cast in unfamiliar shadows and shapes. Outside the window, the orange globe against the purple-tinted sky indicates late afternoon. When she tries to move, she feels a prick on her left arm from the intravenous needle connected to the fluid bag suspended from a metal pole. A white hospital gown replaces her work clothes, and her lower body lies practically immobile between a cotton blanket and starched linen sheets tucked tightly beneath the mattress. A thin white privacy curtain separates Kermit from the patient loudly snoring beside her.

Muffled footsteps approach as a healthcare worker appears at her bedside, a crisp white uniform displaying "Homer G. Phillips Hospital" embroidered above the left breast pocket. The woman twists the lamp knob, casting harsh light across her almond-colored face. "Mrs. Hill, I'm happy to see you're awake," she greets. The stiff wings of her domed white nurse cap hold firmly onto her gray, tight curls with the assistance of large black bobby pins. "How are you feeling?" she asks, scratching the clipboard with a pen clasped in her left hand.

"I'm okay," Kermit croaks, clearing her throat. "What happened? Why am I here?"

The activity awakens Kermit's roommate, who wakes coughing. The bed frame creaks in protest as she rolls over and moans in pain.

"According to your workplace, you passed out and they couldn't revive you," the nurse explains, pouring water into a short huck glass with rippled sides. She holds the glass to Kermit's lips as she sips. "The doctor ordered several tests, but you may be anemic. We won't know for sure until the tests come in." After Kermit finishes drinking, the medical aide crosses to the other side of her bed to examine the intravenous bag's content level, noting it on her chart. "We're giving you some fluids here to help you regain your strength. Your husband said you haven't been eating?"

Kermit attempts to sit up to see past the curtain into the hallway. "Is Gus here?"

The nurse steadies Kermit with a firm hand. "Please, don't try to get up, Mrs. Hill. You're much too weak," she instructs sternly. "Your husband is in the waiting room. He can come back in once I've finished examining you." Taking a thermometer from her breast pocket protector, she flicks her wrist to shake down the mercury and sticks it inside Kermit's mouth. The nurse gently places two fingers on the inside of Kermit's wrist, checking her pulse. After positioning the stethoscope's earpieces, she listens to Kermit's heartbeat by placing the bell on her chest. "Take a deep breath." Carefully guiding Kermit's torso off the mattress, the worker zigzags the stethoscope bell across her back.

The examination continues as a blood pressure cuff secures above Kermit's right elbow, and the stethoscope's horn slides underneath. After rapidly squeezing the pump, the cuff inflates tightly around Kermit's arm, allowing the pressure reading to be calculated on the sphygmomanometer. As the air in the cuff releases, the nurse shakes her head, "Mrs. Hill, your blood pressure is quite high. I'll inform the doctor and check it again tonight." The hospital worker removes the thermometer and frowns. "And your temperature's high too," she adds, shaking the thermometer before disposing of it in a tube of alcohol on the shelf.

Kermit touches her forehead with her right palm. "I have been feeling hot lately, but I thought it was the warm weather or," she trails off, glancing at her stomach.

Following her gaze, the nurse asks, "Do you think you might be pregnant?"

Glancing at the divider curtain toward her roommate, Kermit whispers, "Well, I haven't had my monthlies since August, and I've been throwing up like I did with my first baby."

After scribbling more notes on the medical chart, the health worker says, "Well, we'll see what your blood test shows when they come in next week. After you get more fluids in you, I'll come back to draw some blood and get a urine sample. I'll retake your blood pressure and temperature then, too." The nurse refills the glass and holds it for Kermit. "Drink as much water as you can so you don't get dehydrated. We'll try to see if you can eat any solid foods at breakfast."

Kermit stops drinking and struggles unsuccessfully to push herself up. "Breakfast? I can't stay overnight," she objects. "I have to get home and take care of my baby."

Applying gentle pressure on Kermit's shoulder to keep her still, the nurse replies, "I'm so sorry, Mrs. Hill. I'm afraid you're not ready to leave the hospital yet. We want to make sure you're healthy enough to take good care of your little baby and the one that might be on the way." With a firm hand, she fluffs Kermit's pillows, the dull thud echoing in the room, then tightly tucks the disturbed blanket beneath the mattress corners. "The doctor will come by tomorrow morning to see how you're doing. In a few days, we'll have your lab work in." Crossing to the window, she lowers the blinds and closes the curtains. "Before you know it, you'll be well enough to get discharged. Now, how does that sound?" She smiles expectantly at Kermit, who simply nods blankly. "Good. I'll tell your husband he can come in now." On her way out to fetch Augustus, the worker attaches Kermit's medical chart to the hook on the round metal bed frame and disappears through the curtain.

Minutes pass before an ashen Augustus peeks around the curtain, holding his bark-brown felt fedora. "How are you feeling?" he asks, his voice quiet and strained with tension. He moves closer to her bedside, then leans in for a soft kiss. Combing his fingers through her ruffled black hair, his eyes trace the tube running from her arm to the intravenous bag.

"Oh, Gus," Kermit cries as her eyes start watering. "I want to go home."

"I know, baby, but don't cry," Augustus says, wiping the tears streaming down onto her pillow. Placing his hat on her blanket, he snatches two tissues from the box on the bedside table and dries his wife's tear-stained face. Squeezing her free hand, he bends over and kisses her again. "I love you, and I don't want you to be in here either. But listen, baby, you need to get better first."

"Please, Gus, I don't want to be here," Kermit begs, her brown eyes wide with fear. "I want to go home with you and Hugh."

Augustus strokes Kermit's hair before responding, "You know you really scared me. When they told me you'd fainted and been taken to the hospital, I was so afraid I'd lose you." He kisses the back of his wife's hand and rubs her shoulder. "You've lost too much weight, and you know you've got to eat for yourself and the baby."

"I know, honey. I just haven't been able to. The same thing happened with Hugh, remember? After the first few months, I got my appetite back."

Augustus shakes his head and says, "This time's different. You didn't get this bad before. You need to stay so they can figure out what's going on."

On the other side of the curtain, her roommate's bed creaks repeatedly, and her sheets rustle as she adjusts positions, groaning. After settling down, she starts snoring softly.

"What about Hugh? Momma only takes him during the day. Who's going to take care of him at night if I'm stuck in here?" Grabbing the crumpled-up tissues in her lap, she dabs her eyes and nose.

"What about me? I can handle Hugh, with your mother's help, of course," Augustus chuckles. "He's getting to be a big boy now – almost a year old already."

Kermit sniffs, "So, you don't need me now, huh?"

"Come on, honey, you know I'm not saying that," he chuckles. "Just saying, your mother and I can hold down the fort until you get better."

Kermit fidgets with her wedding ring, silently twisting the band around her pale finger. "I'm afraid, Gus," she whispers, fresh tears rolling down the sides of her face. "What if they can't figure out what's wrong with me and I end up dying in here?" She covers her face and starts bawling uncontrollably.

"Oh, honey, don't say that," Gus says, embracing his wife. "You're not going to die in here. The doctors and nurses are going to get you better so you can come home." He holds her until her crying subsides, then pulls more tissues to wipe her tears. "Please, you know I can't take you crying. You'll get through this. I need you, and so does Hugh, and your mother. We all do, including that baby inside you." Augustus holds Kermit tightly.

"I'm okay," Kermit sniffs as she presses the tissues against her nose and lashes. Trying to fight off more tears, she closes her eyes and feels exhaustion washing over her as she sinks into the pillow. "I'm too tired to argue right now," she concedes. "But these doctors better get me out of here fast. And you better bring my baby in here tomorrow. I don't know how I'm going to sleep tonight without seeing him."

"Okay, I promise," Augustus says, kissing her lips. "I'm going to get out of here now so you can get some sleep. I love you and will see you in the morning."

"I love you, too," Kermit replies. "And don't forget to bring Hugh tomorrow."

The following weeks blur together in a routine of medical examinations, tests, and visits from family and friends. From her hospital bed, Kermit watches outside her window as a vibrant mosaic of orange, red, and brown autumn leaves transitions into stark, bare branches. She enlists a small army of family, friends, and neighbors to assist Augustus with babysitting, cooking, and cleaning in her absence. Her dearest friend, Geraldine, takes the lead, regularly bringing over home-cooked dishes, taking Hugh to play with her son, and keeping Kermit's spirits up during hospital visits.

To Kermit's dismay, she remains hospitalized on November 6th when Hugh turns one. With Geraldine's help, she improvises a birthday party in her hospital room for an impromptu celebration. During her stay, she develops brief friendships with her roommates, but one by one, they are all discharged while she remains. Despite frequent visits from church members, coworkers, and friends, Kermit grows weary of the poking and prodding from incessant medical tests that provide no conclusive results, except for confirming her pregnancy.

On the Wednesday before Thanksgiving, a despondent Kermit lies on her side, facing away from the door as a new doctor arrives. His hospital-embroidered white calf-length coat hangs loosely over his white shirt and pants, accented with a maroon tie. He retrieves Kermit's medical chart from the bed frame, flips through the pages, and adds notations to the record.

"Good afternoon, Mrs. Hill," he begins. "How are you feeling today?"

Not moving from her position, Kermit mumbles, "About the same."

"I see. Well, is your husband here?" The doctor moves to the other side of the bed to face Kermit.

"No," she sighs. "He won't be here until after work." Kermit pulls her blanket over her shoulder and stares out the window, avoiding eye contact.

"Well, I have some news about your condition."

Finally turning to meet his gaze, Kermit asks, "What is it? Is it serious?" The physician appears to be in his mid-forties, with a thin black mustache against his mocha complexion.

"Let's go over it," the doctor states, patting her shoulder. "I'd prefer Mr. Hill was here to discuss your diagnosis, but I'll have one of our nurses go over it with him this evening." Reviewing her chart, he continues, "While you've been with us, we've performed multiple tests and monitored your vital signs. Over the past six weeks, your blood pressure has remained elevated, which is causing swelling in your arms and legs."

Kermit presses on the taut tan skin straining against her bloated forearm, then glances at the thicker silhouette of her legs under the blanket. "When admitted," he continues, "you were extremely underweight and dehydrated due to persistent nausea and vomiting. Left untreated, any one of these conditions can cause organ breakdown and complications with your pregnancy. Based on your lab tests, you have been diagnosed with hyperemesis gravidarum, commonly called severe morning sickness. Your high blood pressure and blurred vision symptoms also suggest preeclampsia."

After a brief silence, Kermit asks, "Can they be treated?" She anxiously wrings her hands in her lap, trying to anticipate his response.

"Yes," the physician replies. "We started administering medications to treat your condition last week with marked success. We believe that if you continue this prescription regimen at home and stay in bed until the baby comes, you should continue to improve."

Relieved, Kermit recites a silent prayer as the physician continues speaking. Afraid she has misunderstood his last sentence, she asks, "Did you say I'd have to be in bed... until the baby comes?"

"Yes, I'm afraid so," the doctor states. "It's best not to take any chances that might risk the health of your unborn child. Of course, you can get up to use the bathroom or take a bath. But for the most part, you'll be confined to your bed or sofa. I advise you eat there too."

Kermit places a hand on the barely noticeable bump on her abdomen. "But how long will that be?"

"It's hard to tell at this early stage," he says while brushing a speck of lint off his starched jacket sleeve. "But I'd say around five, maybe six months."

The idea of being confined to her bed until spring seems unimaginable to Kermit. Not only will she be unable to return to work, but she will also miss Christmas, New Year's, and possibly even Easter celebrations. Her job already placed her on unpaid maternity leave two weeks ago when she exhausted her accumulated sick and annual leave. Since then, their growing family has been solely dependent on Augustus' post office salary. Now their household income will continue to be drastically cut in half until the baby arrives.

Suddenly, Kermit realizes something else the doctor has said. "Wait, are you saying I can go home now?" She straightens up in bed, leaning closer to him.

"We are preparing a discharge plan for you, so you should be able to go home in a few days. Probably sometime this weekend." He pauses to jot a note in the chart before adding, "But if you're not feeling any better in a couple of weeks, you need to come back here immediately. Otherwise, follow up with your physician in a couple of months."

"Thank you, doctor," Kermit says, her eyes widening with new hope. "I will."

True to his word, the doctor discharges Kermit that Saturday morning, sending her home with strict instructions for complete bed rest and a regimen of medications. The transition from hospital to home brings both relief and new challenges as she adjusts to her confinement while managing household duties and a growing toddler's needs from her sofa.

One month later, three inches of snow pile on top of the two already covering the ground from the previous day. Christmas cards display on the maple phonograph console, tuned to a holiday music station. With temperatures hovering in the twenties, Kermit drapes a beige cable blanket over her swollen legs as they stretch across the burnt orange sofa. Her protruding stomach pushes against her forest green maternity top as she adjusts to a more comfortable position. While wrapping a wooden spinning toy in red foil paper, she keeps a watchful eye on Hugh, who busily crawls across the hardwood floor. Dressed in blue overalls and brown hard-soled shoes, he grabs onto the coffee table and pulls himself up into a standing position, gurgling happily.

"Will you look at my big boy," Kermit muses. "I see you." She outstretches her arms. "Come to mommy. Let's see if you can walk to me."

Hugh smiles, his body bouncing as his legs wobble to keep him upright. Cautiously, he takes a step toward his mother, who claps and leans closer to him.

"That's it," Kermit encourages. Holding onto the coffee table for support, Hugh takes another shaky step. "You're doing it!"

12-25-1948 Hugh Hill

He squeals in excitement, jamming his index finger and thumb into his drooling mouth. Stepping closer to his mother, Hugh loses his balance and plops down into a seated position, then crawls the rest of the way.

Kermit carefully lifts her son into her lap and hugs him. "I'm so proud of my big boy." He fusses and squirms, then wiggles out of her arms and slides onto the floor to crawl away.

"Oh well," Kermit sighs. "I guess you're not mommy's little baby anymore."

The basement stairs creak as Augustus arrives on the landing, clutching a rocking horse. "Oh, you finished it," Kermit exclaims. "Just in time, too."

Hugh crawls to catch up with his father as Augustus crosses the living room. "What do you think?" Kermit admires the two-foot-tall wooden toy, running a hand against the oak seat and rockers. She grasps the metal handles flanking either side of the horse head and yanks at the attached tan leather strap.

"I like it," Kermit says, ringing the metal bell that hangs around the horse's neck. "Was it hard to put together?"

"Not too bad," Augustus says, pulling on the legs to check for sturdiness. "I think Hugh will like it."

"I guess it's kind of hard to wrap," Kermit says, examining the toy from all sides. Picking up a red ribbon from the sofa, she loops it around the rocking horse's neck and ties it into a bow. "There. That'll make it look a little festive."

Reaching down, Augustus lifts his son. "Are you excited to see what Santa's going to bring you tomorrow?" he asks, tickling his stomach.

Hugh giggles and writhes in his arms, trying to escape. Chuckling, Augustus carefully puts his son on his feet. The toddler stretches out his arms to steady himself, then takes a hesitant step. As he is about to fall, Augustus catches his hand and helps him walk across the floor. When they return to Kermit, he releases his son's hand.

"He's growing up so fast," Kermit says. She hands the rocking horse and the wrapped present to Augustus. "Could you take these to the tree for me, honey?"

"Sure," Augustus says, first stashing the gift under his arm, then taking the bulky toy from her. "Who's coming to dinner tomorrow?"

"Besides Momma, I only invited Geraldine and her family since I'm still on the mend," Kermit replies, wrapping another present in her lap.

"How are you feeling?" he asks, cupping her face in his free hand to examine her. "Do you need anything?"

"I'm better," she replies. "My legs are still swollen, so I'm keeping them elevated like the doctor said."

"Take your medicine today?"

"Not yet. But I will after I eat a little something."

"Well, don't forget." He crosses the hardwood floor to place the rocking horse and gift under the balsam fir tree, its evergreen branches festively decorated with a string of white Christmas bulbs and silver tinsel.

Hugh trails behind Augustus again, scooting across the floor onto the white throw rug in front of the tree. As he reaches for the silver tinsel strewn across the Douglas fir branch, Kermit cautions, "No, Hugh! Don't touch that!" He looks back at his mother, then starts sucking his finger and thumb. When he tries to grab the diamond-shaped green and yellow ornament, Augustus picks him up and returns him to the sofa.

"I hope our decorations make it to Christmas with Hugh around," Kermit says, laughing. "Last Christmas, he was still a baby." Placing him on her lap, she turns so they face the window. "Look at the snow," she points. "Isn't it pretty?" Hugh bangs on the windowpane, trying to catch the snowflakes as they float by.

Augustus whistles, assessing their snow-covered yard. "Boy, it's really coming down out there."

"Sure is! Looks like we're definitely getting a white Christmas this year," Kermit chuckles. "Maybe you can take Hugh out to play in the snow tomorrow."

"Hmm. I guess I can bring him with me when I shovel in the morning."

"I bet he'll like that," she says. "I'll dress him in his snowsuit, so he won't catch cold."

Opening the closet, Augustus removes the snow shovel and leans it against the door frame. "You going to bed anytime soon?"

"In a minute," Kermit answers. "I have a few more presents to wrap for the Williams." Patting the cushion pillow next to her, she adds, "Come sit with me and Hugh for a while."

Augustus joins her on the sofa. He places her legs on his lap and begins softly massaging her feet.

"Aww, thank you. That feels nice," Kermit says, resting her head on the couch's deep buttoned tufting. Hugh babbles, crawling between his parents before finally settling against his mother and drifting off to sleep.

While snowflakes pile up against the frosted windows, Kermit marvels at the blessings surrounding her. Just two months ago, she feared she might not survive her hospital stay, yet here she is, celebrating Christmas Eve at home with her growing family. Her physician's orders restricting her to bed rest force her to relax her fierce independence and graciously accept help from others. As 1949 approaches, she looks forward to the new year with renewed hope.

Downtown Drama

May 19, 1949

Early Thursday morning, a chorus of birds chirps merrily from the bright green trees lining Newstead Avenue. Light rain showers the neighborhood while muted sunlight filters through the windows onto Kermit, who prepares breakfast for her husband. At the kitchen table, Augustus, dressed in a starched white Oxford shirt, maroon tie, and tan trousers, sips his coffee while scanning the St. Louis Post-Dispatch.

Kermit arranges a bowl of oatmeal, boiled egg, and toast beside the newspaper spread across the table. "Here you go," she says, her teal housecoat clinging to the perspiration glistening on her almond-toned skin.

"Thanks," Augustus replies, folding the newspaper back along its creases. As Kermit disappears through the doorway, he tosses the paper onto the nearby beige highchair decorated with cartoon images of a rabbit and bear.

Kermit pushes open their sons' bedroom door and peers at six-week-old Augustus Jr., still fast asleep in the bassinet his older brother outgrew a year earlier. A few feet away, eighteen-month-old Hugh yawns and rubs his eyes before sliding out of bed. Kermit places a finger to her lips, signaling quiet, then leads her oldest son to the bathroom.

After Hugh's bath, she returns to his room with his cocoa-brown body wrapped in a towel. As Kermit struggles to dress him, he begins to fuss, resisting her efforts. Hugh's complaints wake Augustus Jr., and soon both boys are crying.

"Now look what you've done," Kermit sighs. "If I didn't know any better, I'd swear you two were in cahoots."

Leaving Hugh on the bed in his shirt and diaper, Kermit crosses the floor to retrieve her infant. Augustus Jr.'s wheat-colored fists punch the air as he cries, his feet kicking off the blanket. As Kermit cradles her baby, she gently pats his back and shushes him until he quiets. While his mother tends to the infant, Hugh darts into the kitchen where Augustus is finishing his breakfast.

"Well, hello," Augustus chuckles. "Where are your pants?"

Hugh giggles and hurries to his father, who catches him and balances him on his lap. Augustus drains the rest of his coffee, holding the cup out of reach of his son's grasp. As he feeds Hugh the last spoonful of his oatmeal, he says, "Your mommy will make you some more, but I've got to get to the post office." He lifts his toddler in the air before placing him in the oak highchair. Hugh strains against the locking tray, knocking the newspaper to the floor. While Augustus gathers the scattered pages, Hugh whines and reaches for his father when the tray will not budge.

"Mommy's coming," Augustus reassures him, patting his son's tuft of black curls. He turns to call in a louder voice, "Right, mommy?"

"Yes, coming," Kermit replies, swaddling her infant in a pale blue blanket. "Almost finished."

With Augustus Jr. on her shoulder, she scoops up Hugh's discarded shorts as she leaves the room. Kermit enters the kitchen just as Augustus sets his dishes on the counter next to the sink. At the sight of her, Hugh extends his arms and fusses.

"I'm off to work," Augustus says, pecking Kermit on the lips. Retrieving his tan suit jacket from the back of his chair, he slips it on as he rushes down the hall.

"Okay," Kermit says. "Have a good day."

Augustus pulls on his black raincoat and felt hat before heading out the door. "See you this afternoon," he calls.

After settling Augustus Jr. in his bassinet, Kermit prepares a bottle of milk, warming it in a pot of heated water. She tests the temperature on her wrist before handing the bottle to Hugh. As he drinks, Kermit pulls his pants over his chubby legs, which dangle from his highchair. Meanwhile, as the water in the pot begins to boil, Kermit sprinkles oatmeal flakes from the cylinder container featuring a smiling Quaker man wearing a navy hat. As she stirs the hot cereal, Arvolin taps on the back door.

"What are my grandsons up to today?" her mother asks, crossing the threshold. She gives Hugh a kiss on the forehead before continuing to the living room to see Augustus Jr.

"I was thinking about going downtown," Kermit says, retrieving a plastic bowl from the dish rack. Patting her stomach, she chuckles, "I need new work clothes because I can't fit any of the ones in my closet after the baby."

"You're going back to work already?" Arvolin asks, crossing her arms.

"What do you mean, 'already'?" Kermit huffs. "I haven't worked in seven months!"

"Really? Doesn't seem like it's been that long," Arvolin says. "When are you supposed to go back?"

"In a week," Kermit replies, sprinkling sugar into the oatmeal. "I start back next Friday, and I don't have a decent thing that fits." After spooning the hot cereal into a bowl, she pulls a chair next to Hugh's highchair and begins feeding him.

"Do you need me to watch the babies?" Arvolin asks, joining them at the kitchen table.

"Why don't you come with us?" Kermit suggests. "You might want to get something for yourself, and you can help me keep up with them while I'm looking."

"What about the baby?" Arvolin questions. "Isn't he still too young to be out and about?"

"The doctor said to wait a month," Kermit answers, glancing at the mountain scene calendar on the wall. "Today's two weeks past his one-month birthday, so he should be fine by now."

"Hmm," Arvolin grunts. She begins playing peek-a-boo with Hugh, covering and uncovering her eyes with her hands. Hugh laughs, spraying chunks of oatmeal onto his mother and making him giggle harder.

"Momma!" Kermit cries, startled. Wiping her face, she shoots her mother a look.

"Uh-oh," Arvolin chuckles, covering her mouth. "Sorry about that." She hands her daughter a napkin from the table. "Where are you thinking about going shopping?"

"Well, they're still protesting at Stix, Baer & Fuller because they won't serve Negroes at the cafeteria," Kermit says. "They're holding sit-ins at the lunch counters, and I don't feel it would be safe bringing the boys around all that commotion."

"I don't blame you," Arvolin nods, leaning over to wipe the oatmeal Hugh has smeared on his face.

"They want our money at the store, but don't want us sitting next to them to eat," Kermit says, wiping Hugh's hands and mouth with the napkin.

"That's right," Arvolin agrees. "And you never know. Some fool might start shooting or something."

Collecting Hugh's empty bowl and bottle, Kermit sets them on the counter next to Augustus' dishes. "I don't want to take that chance." After rinsing the dirty dishes, she fills the sink with hot water. "So, I'm thinking about going to Famous-Barr. They're not much better, but at least there isn't all that chaos there."

Taking a small knife, Kermit shaves pieces from a bar of Ivory soap into the sink, then vigorously whips the water into suds. She places dishes in the water and begins washing them.

"Okay, I'll come along," Arvolin says as she releases Hugh from the highchair.

Later that afternoon, Kermit strolls through the swing doors of the department store, located in the Railway Exchange Building at the corner of Olive and North 6th Streets. Wearing a buttercup short-sleeved dress, black peep-toe shoes, and a yellow straw hat with silk flowers, she navigates a black folding coach with large, white-spoked wheels that holds Augustus Jr. Beside her, Arvolin, sporting a belted, olive-and-white striped dress, keeps a firm grasp on Hugh, who strains to investigate every candy and jewelry aisle they pass. Both women wear white gloves, pearls, and matching earrings as they browse the expansive retail floor.

Salespersons greet customers from behind round glass display counters that encircle grand white columns stretching toward the high ceilings. The constant hum of bustling shoppers is occasionally pierced by the ringing of cash registers and chimes from sales managers' call bells.

Ignoring the occasional stares and whispers from white customers, Kermit leads her family through the maze of cosmetics, handbags, and lingerie. A trace of tobacco hangs in the air as they pass the Men's Furnishings and Smoke Shop. They arrive at a bank of elevators against the rear wall, each adorned with a copper semi-circular dial mounted above the door. An arrow rotates along the half-moon's arc, indicating the current location of each elevator car, from "B" for Basement to ten.

Kermit and her family walk past seven elevators until they reach the one marked "Negroes Only." They wait, watching empty elevators reserved for white customers sit idle. When their crowded, segregated car finally arrives, Kermit greets the departing passengers with a nod before guiding her family inside.

"Women's department, please," Kermit asks the elevator operator, whose skin is the shade of soda crackers. She repositions the baby carriage in the tight quarters, making room for other passengers squeezing into the car.

After stops on the second and third floors, the operator announces, "Fourth floor. Junior Shop, Town and Country, Bridal Shop, Women's World."

"Thank you," Kermit says as she exits the elevator with her family.

Upon reaching the Women's section, she maneuvers the carriage around a colorful rack of spring dresses and suits. Searching for professional outfits to fit her new size, she is abruptly blocked by a white man in a gray pinstripe suit. Kermit smiles. "Excuse me," she says, continuing around him.

Selecting a striped red and white dress, Kermit drapes it over the carriage's extended canopy. The man crosses the floor and snatches it away. "Are you trying to steal that by sneaking it in with the baby?"

"No, I intend to buy it," Kermit objects.

"I'll take it to the cashier," he says, grabbing the dress from her. "If you actually want to purchase it, ask for it there." Turning his back to Kermit, he crosses the floor and hands the clothing to the saleswoman at the register.

Shaking her head, Kermit says to her mother, "Told you Famous-Barr wasn't any better." Glancing around, she adds, "There's not much of a selection here anyway. I'll look for a couple more things, then we can go."

"Don't let them run you off," Arvolin advises. "Take as much time as you want." A moment later, she feels Hugh slip from her grasp and dart away.

"Hugh! Come back here," Kermit calls. "Momma, stay here with the baby," she directs before chasing after her toddler.

Rushing through the store, Kermit catches Hugh on his tiptoes, reaching for a glass vase of ceramic flowers displayed on the counter. "No!" she yells, yanking his hand away. Outfitted in a pinstripe cobalt shorts suit and white Stride Rite shoes, Hugh erupts into a tantrum, screaming, kicking, and sliding to the floor. Squatting beside him, Kermit hisses, "Hugh!" As nearby white customers and clerks gather to watch the spectacle, her face flushes with embarrassment. When he will not stop, Kermit stands and calmly walks away, leaving him to cry in front of the onlookers. She rejoins her mother, keeping a watchful eye on Hugh from a distance.

A few minutes later, Hugh opens his eyes to find himself surrounded by a swarm of unfamiliar faces. Pushing himself up, he scans the aisles for his mother, spotting her a short distance away. Rubbing his eyes, Hugh scurries over, sucking his thumb and finger. Kermit crouches next to her son and whispers, "Hugh Allen Hill, you wait till we get home." Squeezing his hand, she selects a pink suit from the rack and brings it to the cashier.

Hoping to escape the humiliating scene, Kermit writes out her check and presents it to the cashier, along with her driver's license. After scrutinizing the check and identification, the saleswoman rings the bell to summon the store manager for approval. Twenty agonizing minutes later, Kermit is finally able to leave, her purchases nestled in a tan Famous-Barr shopping bag. Despite her son's embarrassing outburst, she exits the store with her head held high.

Back in Yak

August 29, 1949 – Yakima, Washington

The last time Kermit visits her in-laws in Yakima, Washington, is December 1945. Augustus has just returned from his two-year military stint overseas, and his mother insists on seeing him right away. They make the cross-country journey from New Jersey for a week-long visit with Augustus' parents. During the couple's entire trip to the Pacific Northwest, temperatures stay below freezing, and over a foot of snow covers the ground.

Now that Della's only son's namesake is born, she demands to see Augustus Jr. and her other grandson. She believes it is only fair for Kermit and Augustus to visit Yakima since she traveled to St. Louis last year to see Hugh. After an exhausting three-day journey with an infant and toddler in tow, Kermit and Augustus return to Yakima. This time, temperatures near a scorching one hundred degrees, but the dry heat offers a welcome change from the muggy St. Louis summers.

Shortly after arriving at her in-laws' one-story home on the corner of South 17th and Rainier Streets, Kermit helps Della prepare dinner in the L-shaped kitchen. While brushing the dirt off potatoes, she keeps an eye on Augustus Jr., who lies on a gray blanket spread across the living room floor. Outside in the backyard, Augustus and his stepfather, Elmer, chat on the porch while Hugh plays in the flower garden.

"So, Gus told me you're Vice President of the Colored Women's Club here," Kermit remarks, slicing the brown skin off the potatoes with a paring knife. She vows to work harder to get along with her mother-in-law on this trip.

"To God be the glory," Della replies, raising her hand in praise. "But it's not just here, it's over the whole state. I'm just His humble servant. We're the

Washington State Federation of Colored Women's Clubs." Reaching under the sink, she removes three beets, their bright green stems still attached.

"Well, that's wonderful," Kermit agrees. "It's quite a blessing."

"We held our convention up in Seattle in June," Della continues. "It was in the papers and everything." As Della scrubs and trims the beets, their reddish-purple juices stain her pale hands.

"You don't say," Kermit comments, collecting the potato peelings in her hands. As she carries them to the trash, Hugh storms into the kitchen, the screen door slamming behind him.

"Mommy," he squeals, squeezing her legs. While playing in the yard, Hugh has managed to keep his shorts set white, but specks of beige dirt dust his black shoes and white socks.

Reaching down to hug him, Kermit gently guides Hugh away from Della, afraid the beet juice on her hands will stain his outfit. "How are you doing?" Kermit chuckles. "You having fun?"

"Yes!" Hugh opens his hands, revealing a red wooden toy car in each palm. "Car!"

"I see," Kermit chuckles. Hugh darts into the living room to see his brother, with Kermit following closely behind. "Be careful with the baby," she cautions, placing her hands on Hugh's shoulders. Augustus Jr. grins at his older brother, who returns the smile. Hugh tosses one of his cars onto the blanket before running back outside.

"He sure loves his baby brother," Della remarks as she cuts the beets into thin slices.

Returning to the kitchen, Kermit rinses the potatoes in the sink and starts dicing them. The two women's sharp chops resonate throughout the kitchen.

"You know all these vegetables are from my garden," Della says, holding a sliced beet between her stained fingers. "You should start a garden in St. Louis. It'll save you and Augustus a lot of money."

"Hmm. That's a good idea," Kermit nods. Finishing with the potatoes, she searches the cabinets until she finds a suitable pot. After filling it with water, she adds the potato cubes with a plop. "Anything else I can help with, Momma Woods?" Kermit asks. As she washes her hands, Augustus Jr. begins to fuss.

"You can set the table," Della says, gesturing toward the red oak dining set along the kitchen wall.

"Okay," Kermit replies, drying her hands on her floral apron smock. She then crosses into the next room to retrieve her crying son. "I'll be right back," she calls, transferring him to the makeshift guest bedroom. After securing Augustus Jr. between two pillows on the bed, Kermit steps around Della's walnut sewing machine cabinet and reaches for her luggage. She snaps open her black suitcase and rummages through the neatly folded items until she finds a cloth diaper and a teal barbell toy. After changing her son, Kermit sits on the sewing stool and cuddles him. Enjoying the brief respite, she closes her eyes and nurses him while quietly singing, "Hush little baby."

Once Kermit finishes attending to her four-month-old, she returns to the living room and carefully places Augustus Jr. on his stomach on the blanket. She shakes the barbell in front of him, its rattling sound catching his attention. When he reaches for the rattle, she says, "Here you go," and places it in his grasp. Kermit then joins Della in the kitchen, collecting plates and glasses from the shelf.

"It warms my heart that Augustus has a son named after him—and one named after his daddy," Della says. "You know, it's important to pass down family names from one generation to the next. It keeps our legacy alive." She removes a pot from the cabinet, stacks the beet slices inside, and covers them with water.

Her mention of Augustus' father catches Kermit off guard. Della almost never speaks of him. Kermit considers pressing while the door is briefly open, but the moment slips away before she can act.

"I'm praying y'all name the next one Elmer, in honor of Augustus' stepdaddy."

Kermit raises her eyebrows. "The next one?"

"Yes, that's right," Della replies. "Do you know your Bible? The good Lord says in Genesis 1:28 to be fruitful and multiply."

Kermit catches herself before pointing out that Della only had one child. Instead, she simply says, "Hmm," while trying to recall how old her mother-in-law was when she married Elmer. *Let me see*, she thinks. *Gus is thirty-two now, and he was about seven when they married. Thirty-two minus seven equals twenty-five, so that's how long they've been married.*

Pursing her lips, she circles the table, setting out the dishes, napkins, and silverware as she works through the math. *Della just turned fifty this month, so she was just twenty-five when she married Elmer. So why didn't they 'be fruitful and multiply'?* Kermit realizes that while she was lost in thought, she missed most of what Della said. She offers a vague, "Uh-huh," to cover her silence.

"Let's get some fresh air out back while dinner's cooking," Della says, grabbing her straw hat hanging by the door. "I can show you the garden to give you some ideas."

"Alrighty," Kermit says. Before heading outside, she places Augustus Jr., still clutching his rattle, in his bassinet. She slips Hugh's toy car into her dress pocket and deposits the bassinet on the back porch. As she walks down the steps, Kermit waves to Elmer and her husband, who are surveying the property along the woven wire fence. "Hey there," she calls.

"Hey," they respond in unison. When the men wave, Kermit notices the sweat stains on the armpits of Augustus' white cotton shirt and Elmer's ribbed polo.

A variety of garden tools lies along the home's white-painted wooden siding. Hugh closely observes his grandmother as she selects a green hand rake and pruning shears from an old coffee can nailed to the back wall.

"Come on, Kermit," Della calls as she walks through the grass to the garden. "Get one of the tools, and I'll show you how to garden."

Kermit glances at her marigold polka-dot dress peeking out from beneath her apron. "Well, I'm not quite dressed for gardening," she chuckles, "but I'll watch you for now." She picks up the red trowel and joins her mother-in-law. As Kermit approaches the garden patch, the heels of her peep-toe sandals sink deeper into the moist soil.

"Look-a-here," Della says as she kneels beside a row of sprouting leaves. "These are my carrots." She loosens the dirt surrounding the plants with the rake. "You need to keep the soil moist and give it some air, like this." Mimicking his grandmother, Hugh squats and begins digging with his toy car. Augustus and Elmer join them to observe.

"You trying to make a farm girl out of Kermit?" Augustus chuckles, grinning at his wife. "You know she's a city girl, true and true?"

"Oh, hush," Kermit says, blushing. "Momma had a garden in Little Rock. I know a little something."

"Well, it's time she learns," Della adds. "I told her it would save y'all a lot of money. Especially with your growing family."

"That's true," Augustus agrees. "I guess we have enough space out back to start a little garden. Looks like Hugh can help out, too." He crouches beside his son and ruffles his tight curls. "Isn't that right?"

"Yes!" Hugh says, holding up his dirt-covered toy.

As Della leans on her hands to steady herself, Augustus rushes to hold her arm and helps her stand. She removes her hat to wipe the sweat from her brow before leading them to the next row of plants. Crossing the path, Della strides to the flower garden. "I have some carnations—some pink, white, and red. Black-eyed Susans over here." She removes the clippers from her pocket and snips a variety of colorful flowers. "We can dress up the table tonight with these." She hands them to Kermit. "Find a vase in the kitchen and put them in water."

"They're beautiful," Kermit says, holding them by the stems. "You've given me some good ideas to get started."

Della claps her hands together to brush the dirt off. "I guess the food should be ready by now. Let's go eat."

***

After four consecutive days hovering around 96 degrees, Yakima's temperatures finally break 100 by September 1st. While the rest of the household prepares for the day, Della grabs her hat and heads out back as the sun peeks over the horizon. She guides the reel mower over the lawn, sending bright green grass flying from the spiraling blades like confetti. After mowing, Della unwinds the garden hose and begins watering the plants. By the time she finishes her yard work, the morning sunshine shimmers across the yard.

Inside, Kermit irons her taupe blouse while she waits for her father-in-law to come out of the home's only bathroom. Augustus lights a cigarette as he sits on the edge of the bed in his white sleeveless undershirt and boxers. Still wearing his navy-footed pajamas, Hugh sleeps on the pillows along the headboard while Augustus Jr. coos in his bassinet.

"What time do you think Vernessa will get here?" Kermit asks, pressing the hot cast iron along the blouse collar.

"I think her train's due in around lunchtime," Augustus replies. After taking a drag, he flicks the cigarette ashes into the metal bowl on the bedside table. "She's bringing her boy up, but her husband had to work."

"What's her husband's name again?"

Augustus chuckles. "I don't remember. Something with an E." He blows the smoke from his mouth. "But she just calls him by his last name—Bennett."

"Well, they just got married last year," Kermit says, laughing. "Maybe she doesn't remember his name either."

"Could be," Augustus says, standing to glance out the open window onto Rainier Street. "But she did that with her first husband, too, remember? Always called him McGhee."

"I know. I was just kidding," Kermit says. "Don't tell her I said that, though. She may not appreciate it."

The bathroom door opens, and Elmer shuffles down the hall to his bedroom. Augustus swiftly crosses the floor. "Let me get in real quick before you and the boys take over."

"Gus," Kermit laughs, shaking her head.

"I'll be in and out before you know it," he winks, a trail of smoke following him through the door. "Promise."

That afternoon, Augustus and Della pick up Vernessa and her son, Taledo, from the train station. When they park in front of the house, Hugh yelps and scurries to the front door. A thin adolescent, dressed in a long-sleeved white shirt, brown tie, and slacks, opens the rear car door and extends his hand. Vernessa steps out, wearing an elegant sea green sleeveless dress accented with an alligator-skinned purse and matching slingback pumps. Both mother and son share similar features of beige skin and thick, black hair.

"Welcome, welcome," Kermit greets, hoisting Augustus Jr. on her hip to face them. She descends the steps to greet them, closing the gate behind her. Hugh, unable to keep up with his mother, starts to whine when he finds himself trapped in the fenced yard.

"I'm so glad you could come up to visit," Kermit says, hugging Vernessa and kissing her cheek.

"Me too! This weekend's perfect timing," Vernessa says. "On Monday, the dress shop's already closed for Labor Day. So, I just told my boss I might as well take the whole weekend off to see my cousins."

Kermit chuckles. "You are too much." Turning to examine Taledo, she marvels, "And will you look at this young man! How old are you now?"

"Sixteen," Taledo mumbles, distracted by the violent clanging of metal fencing as Hugh shakes it against the poles.

"Talley! You better speak up when your cousin speaks to you," Vernessa scolds, frowning at him over her black cat-eyeglasses accented with diamond embellishments on the tips. "Now go give her a hug while I take this handsome little man." She grabs Augustus Jr. and bounces him in her arms.

After Kermit hugs Vernessa's son, she asks, "You mean you're already in high school?"

"Yes, ma'am," Taledo replies.

"He's almost as tall as I am," Augustus interjects, opening the car trunk.

"Well, that's not saying much," Vernessa quips. "I'm taller than you are."

"Only in heels," he says, laughing.

"You two act more like siblings than cousins," Kermit chuckles.

"They sure do," Della agrees, standing beside the car in the shade. "Those two were thick as thieves growing up together in Conway. Always off playing somewhere when it was time for chores."

When Kermit turns to open the gate, Hugh tries to run to his father, but she catches him by the collar. "Hold on, there. Say hello to your cousins. Tell Cousin Vernessa 'Thank you' for the nice sailor suit she sent you."

Hugh clings to his mother's A-line gold skirt, noisily sucking his index finger and thumb.

"Now I know you're not quiet after all that racket I just heard you making," Vernessa says. After handing Augustus Jr. to Kermit, she takes a step closer to Hugh and outstretches her arms. "Come give your cousin a hug."

Reluctantly, Hugh steps closer, and Vernessa tightly wraps her arms around him.

"Talley, go help your cousin with those suitcases," Vernessa directs. "Let's get out of this heat." She loops an arm around Kermit and leads her into the house. "In fact, let me go freshen up a bit. I'll be back." Vernessa disappears into the bathroom.

Della enters the house, with Hugh straining against her firm grip on his hand. Augustus and Taledo trail behind, carrying the luggage. After storing the suitcases, Taledo stays in the room, while Augustus joins Kermit in the living room.

"Vernessa said she and Talley want to see the sights," Augustus whispers to Kermit.

Overhearing her son, Della says, "We need to wait for Elmer to get back from work first." Hugh finally pulls away from his grandmother to go to his father, who picks him up.

"Fine by me," Kermit smiles, wiping the sweat beading on her husband's brow. "You alright?"

"I'm okay," Augustus replies. "Can you see if there's something to drink?"

"Sure." Kermit crosses into the kitchen. "I think everyone could use something cool to drink about now." She removes a pitcher of sweet tea from the refrigerator and pours five glasses. When Vernessa returns to the living room, freshly made up, Kermit offers, "Have some tea, Vernessa."

Holding a glass in each hand, Kermit attempts to give one to her mother-in-law, but Della blocks the offer. "Give it to Augustus," she protests. "You're supposed to serve your husband first."

Vernessa sucks her teeth as Kermit hands the glass to Augustus, who shares it with Hugh. She gives the other glass to Della before retrieving another for Vernessa.

As Kermit carries the fourth glass to Taledo in his room, his mother calls out, "Talley! Come in the kitchen to drink that. Aunt Della and Uncle Elmer don't want you drinking all over their nice house." Taledo follows Kermit into the kitchen, then leans against the door frame to drink.

Picking up the last sweet tea, Kermit joins the rest of the family, who are now seated in the living room. "Sorry your husband couldn't make it," she says, sitting next to Vernessa on the sofa.

"Me too! He would've loved to see y'all," Vernessa says. She turns to Augustus and adds, "Bennett could give Gus a free haircut, too."

Subconsciously smoothing his black hair from his side part, Augustus chuckles. "What? Do I need a haircut?"

"It is a little long," Vernessa chuckles. "But he can do all the latest styles and have you looking sharp for Kermit."

"I'd like to see that," Kermit chuckles. "Maybe next time we visit y'all in Bakersfield, we'll have him give Gus a haircut, and maybe the boys, too."

"Good idea," Vernessa agrees. "I'm still hoping you two will come on over to California to stay. The weather's warm all year and there're still plenty of good jobs too."

"I'm about to apply for a promotion at the post office," Augustus says. He strokes Hugh's back, who is asleep on his lap. "Now that we've started a family, I want Kermit to be home to raise the boys."

Della interjects, "It's the mother's responsibility to train up a child in the way he should go, Proverbs 22:6, and when he is old, he will not depart from it."

"Oh, Aunt Della," Vernessa moans. "You're always quoting the Bible." She glances at Kermit, who avoids eye contact and silently sips her tea.

"You need to know your Bible," Della replies.

Just then, Elmer comes in the front door, dressed in denim overalls and a gray work shirt. Around his waist hangs a canvas tool belt holding a wrench, pliers, and pipe cutter. "Hello," he greets, removing a cloth from his back pocket to wipe the sweat off his face. After kissing Della, Elmer crosses the floor to kiss Vernessa on her cheek, then waves to her son. "Hey, Taledo. You seem to grow every time I see you."

"Hi, Uncle Elmer," Vernessa says. "You're looking well."

"Why, thank you. You too, as always," Elmer replies. "Where have you been off to lately?"

"Well, I just got back from seeing the Queen in London," Vernessa says.

"Oh, Vernessa," Kermit gushes. "One day I'm going to travel like you."

"You should. You'd love it," Vernessa says. Turning to her son in the kitchen, she directs, "Talley! Go find my photographs in my bag."

As Taledo leaves to retrieve the photos, Della rises. "Elmer, you need to hurry up and change. Vernessa and them want to have a look around town before dinner."

While Della leaves to help Elmer get ready, Vernessa shares the pictures from her trip to the United Kingdom.

"Here's when I visited Buckingham Palace," Vernessa chuckles. "As hard as I tried, the guard never broke a smile. He stayed serious."

1949 Vernessa Bennett, Buckingham Palace in London, England

"He looks just like they do in the movies," Kermit remarks. "Got that fur hat and red jacket and everything. It must be hot in that getup."

"Yes, you could see him sweating, but they couldn't move a muscle," Vernessa comments.

Vernessa flips to the next photograph. "Here I am in front of Westminster Abbey."

"Wait. Doesn't that sign say, 'No photography' behind you?" Kermit asks, leaning closer to get a better look.

"Girl, I pretended I didn't speak English," Vernessa chuckles. "I just took the picture and moved on."

"Vernessa, you're a mess," Kermit teases.

"You need to drag this one to Europe," Vernessa nudges Augustus. "He needs to see the world."

"I would love to," Kermit grins.

"I've seen plenty," Augustus counters. "Y'all must've forgot the Army dragged me halfway across the world and back."

When Elmer and Della return, the group gathers around the black De Lux Ford to figure out seating. Elmer slides behind the wheel, and Della claims the passenger seat, with Taledo awkwardly squeezed between them. In the back, Vernessa settles behind Elmer, Kermit slides in the middle with Augustus Jr., while Hugh sits in his father's lap.

As Elmer steers the car through Yakima, Della peppers them with interesting facts about the various landmarks. She occasionally recites a Bible verse that seems relevant at that moment. When they pass the state fairgrounds, Della points. "Over there's where the Central Washington Fair will be next month. Too bad y'all can't stay longer. Your boys would love it."

Elmer pulls in front of a church and shuts off the engine. As he walks around the car to open Della's door, Vernessa asks, "What's this?"

"This here's Elmer's new flock," Della replies as she exits the car. "Come on and take a look. It's Morning Star Church of Christ Holiness."

"Aunt Della, we didn't come up here to see a church," Vernessa quips.

"I heard you going on about that church you visited in London. So, you can see your uncle's church too," Della counters.

"That's different. It was a famous landmark," Vernessa says, but Della and Elmer are already ascending the church stairs.

As they tour the sanctuary, Kermit pulls Vernessa aside as they lag behind the group. Ensuring the others are out of earshot, she whispers, "I've been wondering, do you know anything about Gus' real daddy?"

Vernessa slows her pace, diverting them away from the tour. "Gus never told you?" she asks quietly.

Kermit shakes her head.

"Well, I heard Aunt Della and Gus' daddy were really in love," she begins softly. "Her daddy and older brothers, including my father, were really protective of her since she was the youngest of the family. They didn't like Hugh, it's crazy to think about now, but it was mostly because they thought he was too dark for her."

"No!" Kermit says, pausing to examine Vernessa's face for confirmation.

"That's all it was. Aunt Della refused to stop seeing him, so they ran him out of town with a shotgun. I don't think she ever saw him again. Gus either, far as I know."

"That's awful," Kermit says, checking over her shoulder for anyone coming behind them.

"Funny thing is, Aunt Della isn't like that, though," she chuckles. "You see, she got herself another dark-skinned man in Uncle Elmer."

"I guess you're right about that," Kermit says. "I didn't realize Gus never met his father."

Vernessa shakes her head. "I guess he named your son Hugh as a kind of tribute to his real daddy's memory."

Voices of the other family members grow louder as they are joined by the rest of the group. The family returns to the Woods' home for dinner.

Over the next few days of persistent ninety-degree temperatures, they reminisce about their days living in Arkansas. Kermit chuckles as Augustus and Vernessa exchange old stories of their amusing childhood adventures on the Conway farm. Della shares stories from white-passing cousins only she can visit because her pale skin will not reveal her race. Shortly after midnight on Saturday, the Hill family departs Yakima, promising their next family reunion will be soon. Kermit leaves with new knowledge about her husband's birth father and the colorism steeped in Della's family. Following an exhaustive three-day journey, the couple makes it back in time to report to work in St. Louis by Tuesday morning.

WORK HOME BALANCE

November 30, 1949 – St. Louis, Missouri

S ix months after returning to the office from maternity leave, Kermit maintains an efficient routine to manage her family and work responsibilities. She realized in high school that laying out her clothes and bathing before bed saves precious morning time. Kermit also discovers she needs less sleep than most, allowing her to rise and dress by five o'clock in the morning. Now that she juggles a full-time work schedule with two young sons, she feels equal to the challenge.

During weekdays, Kermit prepares sack lunches for herself and her husband the night before. She lays out the family's clothes, puts Augustus Jr. down for the evening, then bathes Hugh. Augustus bathes while she tucks Hugh into bed, and her bath comes last. Up before dawn's first light, she makes breakfast, then dresses and feeds her boys before her mother arrives to babysit. After work, Kermit rushes home to prepare dinner while spending time with her sons. On weekends, she completes household chores and accompanies the family to church on Sunday. Her non-stop adrenaline sustains her, and she finds the multiple roles of wife, mother, and employee rewarding.

The previous month, Kermit received a reassignment to a military allotment clerk, though her duties and pay grade remain largely unchanged from her previous fiscal accounting clerk position. Her current salary stands $200 higher than when she returned in May, but still $300 less than the $3,397 she earned as a claims examiner the year before. She frequently checks with her supervisor and the Personnel Officer about higher-paying opportunities to better support her family.

On this crisp November afternoon, Kermit grips the leather strap as the streetcar rumbles through the city after work. Her mind buzzes with

Christmas preparations, determined to make the holiday special for her sons. As the car turns onto Newstead Avenue, pewter clouds gather behind bare oak branches. Approaching her stop, Kermit tightens her forest green scarf against the biting wind.

Stepping onto her stoop, Kermit knocks four times in rapid succession, announcing the game she often plays with her sons. Peeking through the door, she sings the opening line of the 1947 Louis Jordan hit, "Open the door, Richard." Hugh races to meet her, giggling and singing along, "Richard, why don't you open that door?" Grinning, Augustus Jr. bounces playfully on the braided rug.

"How was your day?" Arvolin calls from the living room, crocheting in a mahogany rocking chair. She wears a long-sleeved burgundy dress with a wool blanket draped across her lap. Her arthritic fingers move more slowly in a practiced rhythm, expertly forming a loop with the scarlet yarn before inserting the silver hook.

Kermit hugs a giggling Hugh. "Good," she answers. Bending down, she lifts Augustus Jr. and tickles his stomach. "Since tomorrow is December, I was thinking about getting the Christmas tree this weekend." Augustus Jr. snatches off her pearl clip-on earring. "Hey!" she cries, prying it from his tight grip. "Oh no, you don't. Mommy needs that." Placing her seven-month-old back on the floor, she hangs up her coat and scarf.

"Christmas will arrive before you know it," Arvolin remarks, counting the row of stitches with her finger. Her loose silver curls frame her almond-toned features, mirroring her daughter's complexion.

"Only three and a half weeks," Kermit concurs, stepping into the kitchen. "Christmastime feels more festive with children around. This will be Augustus Jr.'s first Christmas, and Hugh knows a lot more now." At the sound of his name, Hugh runs to his mother's side. "Are you ready for Christmas, Hugh?"

"Yes," he replies with enthusiasm.

Kermit ties an apron over her cream-colored sweater and gray slacks and says, "I was sick last year and didn't get to do much for the holidays." She retrieves a Dutch oven from the cabinet and fills it with water. After lighting the gas burner, she sets the pot over the blue flame and sprinkles salt into the water. From the pantry, Kermit selects a box of egg noodles, two cans of tuna, canned peas, and cream of mushroom soup. "This time

I want to get them something special and do it up right." She arranges the cans along the counter, then removes a can opener and metal box grater from the utensil drawer.

"That sounds fine," Arvolin says. "You know, Christmas falls on Sunday this year. Maybe you can get them something dressy to wear to church."

Kermit pours the noodles into the bubbling water, then lights the oven and retrieves a ceramic casserole dish. She mixes in each ingredient to create a colorful combination of emerald peas, pale tuna, and golden spiral noodles. Before placing the casserole in the oven, she grates orange cheddar cheese on top.

Glancing toward the back door, Kermit walks Hugh back into the living room and begins speaking in hushed tones. "Momma, I don't know what to do. Gus keeps saying he wants me to quit my job, but I honestly don't know how we will make it on just his salary." She picks up Augustus Jr., who struggles to crawl away from the oak radio console.

Arvolin lays her hands in her lap, keeping her fingers in their crocheting position. "He told me he wants you to be home with the kids," she says, adding, "You know how much I love watching my grandsons, though."

"I know," Kermit replies. "But I think the real reason he wants me to quit is because..." She stops to glance over her shoulder again, then whispers. "Momma, you can't say anything about this, but you're the only one I can talk to about it."

Arvolin stops rocking and furrows her brow. "What is it, baby?" she asks. "You know I won't tell anyone."

"Well, I think it bothers him because I make more money."

"Hmm. Much more?" she whispers.

Kermit shakes her head. "Not much. It comes to about $600 more a year. But I can tell it bothers him."

"Well, you know how men are," Arvolin says, returning to her rocking and crocheting. "They don't feel like they're taking care of their families if their wives are the ones bringing home more money."

"But how are we going to raise a family on his..."

Before Kermit can finish her sentence, Augustus enters through the back door. She quickly places Augustus Jr. next to his brother and greets her husband.

"Hi," Augustus calls, removing his black fedora and leather gloves. After kissing Kermit, he unbuttons his gray wool overcoat while crossing into the living room. "How's everybody doing?"

Hugh scampers to his father. "Daddy!" he yells, raising his arms to be lifted.

Augustus tosses his hat and gloves on the burgundy sofa before scooping up Hugh into his arms. When Augustus Jr. scoots over to his father's feet, Augustus bends down to grab his infant son as well. "Ugh," he grunts. "You two are getting heavy." After placing them back on the floor, he carries his outerwear to the front closet, revealing a chestnut pinstriped suit, mahogany striped tie, and crisp white shirt underneath.

"Hey, Augustus. What's going on at the post office?" Arvolin asks, briefly glancing up as her fingers work the crochet hook through the yarn.

Reaching into his shirt pocket, Augustus removes a box of cigarettes with a matchbook tucked inside the cellophane wrapping. "Nothing much," he says. In one fluid motion, he shakes out a cigarette, holds it between his lips, and lights it with a match. Noticing Arvolin's blanket, Augustus asks, "You cold?" Walking behind her chair, he holds his hand over the cast-iron radiator to test the heat output.

"I'm alright. I got my blanket," Arvolin says, tucking it underneath her legs.

Augustus leans over to reach the radiator valve and turns it counter-clockwise. The radiator hisses as it releases a burst of steam. "There, that should feel better," he says, waving his hand above the heater. As he inhales, the tip of his cigarette glows bright orange.

"Thanks," Arvolin says.

He nods, crossing into the hallway. "I'm going to wash up for dinner."

"Okay," Kermit replies. She cracks open the oven door to peek at the casserole. "Dinner will be ready soon."

Later that evening, Kermit enters the bedroom in her cream full-length nightgown. Making her way to bed, she pauses at the dresser to retrieve a black silk turban containing a comb, bobby pins, and a round tin of hair gel. Beneath the soft glow of a brass lamp, Augustus sits on the edge of the bed in his cotton undershirt and steel blue pajama pants. Papers, a notepad, fountain pen, and a glass ashtray litter the nightstand as he sorts through monthly bills.

Kermit sighs as she settles on the opposite side of the bed. "What're you working on?" she asks, parting her jet-black hair into four sections.

Augustus slides his finger under the mortgage envelope and removes the statement. "Going over these here bills," he answers, fanning the envelopes across the nightstand. "Tomorrow starts a new month, and all these come due. I'm taking them with me to mail at the post office in the morning."

"I see," Kermit says, applying hair gel onto her scalp. "Christmas is coming next month, too, so I want to start decorating the house this weekend. Maybe after church, we could take the boys to look for a tree."

Augustus opens another envelope and scribbles on the pad. He repeats the action until he finishes calculating the total amount due for the month. After writing out the checks, he places them in envelopes, licks the stamps, and seals each flap. "I can bring up the decorations from the basement when I get home Saturday," he says, stacking the envelopes. "And we can look for a small tree Sunday."

"Sounds good," Kermit wraps a strand of hair around her finger and secures it with a bobby pin. "Hugh and 'Gustus Jr. will get a kick out of seeing all the Christmas trees in the lot." She finishes pin-curling her hair and wraps it in the turban.

"But lookee here," he states, "Come January, I need you home with the boys full time."

Kermit sputters, "Gus! You can't really think we can afford to do that."

"Of course we can," Augustus insists. "We just need to reduce spending and stick to a budget."

"But with the boys getting bigger... and Momma.... plus, your mother asking for money all the time..."

"I know all that," Augustus snaps. "But I want my sons raised right. Now's when they need their mother the most – when they're young. You can't be working and raising them, too."

"But Gus," Kermit protests, her eyes welling with tears. "I *am* raising them now!"

Augustus shakes his head, "Not all the time. Your job keeps you away from them for most of the day and most of the week, too. Your mother can't keep up with those boys, running wild all over the house. They need you here."

Kermit stares silently at her husband in disbelief. She wipes her eyes with the back of her hand, shaking her head. "Maybe I can find something part-time?" she suggests weakly. "I can ask down at the Personnel office."

"Kermit," Augustus says firmly. "Your job is being home, taking care of our sons." He reaches across the bed and holds her hand. "We always talked about having a large family, too. We said we were going to have six children. Remember? Don't you still want that?"

A dog's ferocious barks echo from the darkness outside, momentarily breaking the silence. As the barks subside, Kermit stammers, "I do. Eventually." She turns and rummages through the nightstand drawer for a handkerchief, then wipes her eyes and nose. "But my work helps soldiers just like you who fought for our country."

"Well, they can find someone else to do that. Our sons can't find another mother." Augustus yanks the chain on the lamp, plunging the bedroom into darkness. With a mumbled, "Good night," he rolls away from Kermit and slides under the covers.

The frigid wind rattles the windowpane. Kermit, arms crossed against the chill, sits up past midnight. Her mind races, searching for ways to convince Augustus that she can balance work and family. While she understands his wounded pride prevents him from seeing reason, she must admit she enjoys working and having her own money. After a restless night, sleep finally comes just thirty minutes before her alarm sounds.

Nine days before Christmas, the Hills' home fills with the woodsy fragrance of the balsam fir tree positioned by the front window. Draped with silver tinsel, crimson ornaments, and strings of popcorn, the tree displays a gold star at its peak. A collection of Christmas cards scatters across every surface, while colorfully wrapped presents sit on high counters, beyond the reach of little hands.

Dressed in her black wool suit, Kermit fidgets with the jeweled brooch on her jacket while waiting outside the Personnel Office of the Army Finance Center. When called inside, she informs the Director of her decision to resign in three weeks. They go back and forth, with him trying to convince her to stay and her tearfully resisting his pleas. Reluctantly, he hands Kermit a Civilian Personnel Action Request form to complete. Reality strikes when she reaches the question: "I hereby resign for the following reasons." Feeling her stomach churn, Kermit holds her breath and writes, "To care for my family."

In the first week of 1950, St. Louis temperatures plummet from a balmy sixty degrees to a bone-chilling twenty. By Friday, January 6th, over an inch of snow blankets the ground as Kermit walks out of the Correspondence Branch in the Class E Allotment Building for the last time. In her arms, she carries a collection of framed photographs and personal belongings, gathered from her moves from Washington, D.C., to Newark, New Jersey, and finally to the St. Louis Administration Center. Hugging her colleagues goodbye, 30-year-old Kermit struggles to envision her life without the work that has defined her for over seven years.

House Guests

September 18, 1950

The afternoon sun defies the crisp autumn weather, driving temperatures into the high eighties for the first time this month. Augustus blows smoke out the window of the family's Tawnee Buff Oldsmobile as he navigates through a neighborhood lined with lush green trees. Beside him, Augustus Jr. attempts to climb over the seat to join his older brother and grandparents in the back. Kermit snatches him back onto her lap by his sweater as a soothing breeze sweeps over her flushed face. This morning, she woke with a scratchy throat and clammy forehead and immediately gargled with salt water to ward off a possible cold. Now, as she feels a chill spread beneath her ruffled pink dress, she knows she is getting sick.

Behind them, Hugh sits on Arvolin's lap while she chats with Augustus' mother and stepfather, who are visiting from Yakima, Washington. Della tilts the brim of her black hat, trying to catch Augustus' eye in the rearview mirror. "I sometimes don't understand why my Lord and Savior suffers me to be apart from my only child," she laments to her son. "I do wish I could see you and my precious grandsons face-to-face more often."

Kermit glances at her husband, who stares straight ahead without commenting. As she starts to respond, a sneeze interrupts her.

"Bless you," Arvolin says.

"Bless you, Mommy," Hugh echoes, sparking laughter around the car.

"Why, thank you," Kermit chuckles, gently repositioning her youngest son on her lap. She rummages through her pink leather bag until she finds her handkerchief. Wiping her nose, she continues, "Well, we're so happy you and Mr. Woods are here now."

"We sure are," Arvolin adds. "It's so nice seeing y'all whenever you visit."

Augustus clears his throat and exhales another stream of smoke out the window. "Uh-huh. We'll plan a visit to Yakima soon." As he turns south onto Kingshighway Boulevard, Kermit tightens her grip on her younger son to keep him in place.

"The sooner the better," Elmer interjects.

"Amen to that," Della agrees, "because being away from my own child grieves me deep inside my heart."

Steering the car into the Forest Park entrance, Augustus announces, "We're here." He slows down in front of a majestic water fountain surrounded by bald cypress trees and cattails.

"Very pretty," Arvolin comments, then directs her grandson to look out the window at the spraying water jets forming the shape of a blooming flower. "See the water, Hugh?"

Kermit turns to address her in-laws in the back. "Forest Park is one of the biggest city parks in America."

Augustus slows his pace, allowing his passengers to admire the park's array of crystal-blue lakes, colorful gardens, and evergreen trees. Following the road, he enters a roundabout circling an island adorned with a white marble structure. The round bandstand features concrete columns, bronze rails, and a copper roof.

"This is a pagoda, where they have concerts," Kermit explains, pointing between the trees that encircle it. "I read a storm blew it away twenty years ago, and they had to rebuild it." Before Augustus can exit the circle, she instructs, "Go around again, Gus, so they can see the Muny on the other side." When he cruises toward the back of the pagoda, she continues, "This is the Muny—an outdoor theater. The Rodgers and Hammerstein Musical Festival opened here last month."

Augustus circles back past a river flowing through colorful wildflowers and pale green lily pads dotting the surface. "Okay, let's get out here for a bit," he says, pulling into a parking lot. After opening Kermit's door, he lifts Augustus Jr. from her lap and offers her a hand to help her out of the car. He then opens the door for Arvolin while Hugh jumps out. While Elmer assists his wife out of the back seat, Augustus retrieves his camera from the trunk.

With Hugh running ahead, they follow the path leading to a large, Mediterranean-style open-air pavilion. A prominent terracotta roof tops the rectangular façade, with seven stone archways on each side. The building is flanked by two square towers constructed of the same material with open arched windows on the top level.

Continuing her tour, Kermit says, "This here's the World's Fair Pavilion."

Hugh wraps his arms around one of the decorative stone balls placed at the base of the pavilion and attempts to lift it. When he tries to mount it, Kermit grabs his hand and waits for the rest of the family to join them.

"Was this where they had the St. Louis World's Fair?" Arvolin asks, her white floral dress fluttering in the wind.

"Well, it was held around this area of the park, but the pavilion wasn't built yet," Kermit says, guiding her son through the center archway. Shaded underneath the red-tiled ceiling, she gestures around the open columns. "They constructed all this with the money they got from the 1904 World's Fair."

The group wanders through the open breezeway, reaching out to touch the cool stucco walls. As they emerge into the sunlight on the other side of the pavilion, they find themselves on a circular plaza overlooking a vast, grassy field. Below the manicured lawn, a magnificent multi-tiered fountain cascades down stone steps, creating a waterfall that flows into a rectangular pool. A flock of mallard ducks splashes merrily in the water.

"Oh, will you look at that," Arvolin says as she gazes over the horizon. "This is beautiful."

"It's such a nice park," Kermit agrees, standing between her mother and husband. "There's so much to see here."

When Elmer joins them, he lets out a low whistle. "Imagine having to mow that lawn," he laughs. "I wonder how many men it takes to maintain this place. Must take them all day, seven days a week to keep it looking like this."

"You better believe it," Augustus agrees. He sets Augustus Jr. on his feet and leads him around the perimeter of the patio.

Kermit descends the gravel path that cuts diagonally across the lawn. She releases Hugh's hand and watches him dash into the field toward another toddler. Glancing back at Augustus, she says, "Let 'Gustus Jr. go play with them a while." The brothers cheer as they race toward the fountain, scaring away the ducks. "Don't get in the water," Kermit calls after them.

As Elmer and Augustus follow the boys to the fountain, the women rest on the concrete bench along the path. Della brushes gray dust off her black and white saddle shoes, then examines Kermit's slingbacks and Arvolin's wingtip oxfords.

"Y'all should get that dust off your shoes before it's too late," Della cautions. "Them black shoes are harder to clean." The women comply as she continues, "I invited Augusta's cousin, Hazel, from Kansas City, to come visit while we're in town."

Kermit tries to clear her scratchy throat, then croaks, "You did?"

"Yes. She told me Kansas City is right up the road from St. Louis. So she wants to see me and Augusta, too," Della says. "Her husband may even come along with her."

Kermit swiftly retrieves her handkerchief and covers her nose before sneezing. "When are they supposed to come?"

"Saturday," Della says. "I'm trying to get Babe to come up from Arkansas, too."

"Aunt Babe?" Kermit asks, fanning herself with the handkerchief.

"Uh-huh, my sister. I figured they could stay in those apartments upstairs."

"With me?" Arvolin questions.

"No," Della continues. "I'm talking about the empty rooms I saw up there the last time I was here."

"We have lodgers in those rooms now," Kermit says. "Lillie's in one and Ann's in the other. Plus, Mr. and Mrs. Bowles are in the third room." She places the back of her hand on her forehead to check for a fever.

"Hmm," Della says. "Well, I'm sure y'all will make a way for family."

Sweat dripping from their brows, Augustus and Elmer return with Hugh and Augustus Jr. in tow. Elmer fans himself with his white cap while Augustus' pale blue shirt clings damply to his undershirt.

"The boys keeping you busy?" Arvolin asks.

"Yes indeed," Elmer chuckles. "My grandsons are full of energy."

"You ready to go?" Augustus asks.

"Let's take some pictures first," Della says, rising. "Kermit, take me and Augusta." She removes her hat, revealing straight salt-and-pepper hair parted in the center. Glancing down at her canary polka-dot dress, she adjusts her black belt and smooths away wrinkles.

Kermit takes the camera from Augustus as he joins his mother in front of the bench. Looking through the viewfinder, she adjusts the lens until they come into focus. "Okay, I see you two. I'm about to take it now." Kermit snaps the shutter. "That should be a good one."

"Augusta, make sure to send that photograph to me as soon as you get it developed," Della says.

Kermit points to Elmer, who is sharing a bench with her sons. "How about one with your stepdaddy?"

"Yes, and let's get my grandsons in the picture too," Elmer agrees. Augustus picks up his youngest son and sits next to Elmer.

Peering through the viewfinder, Kermit calls out, "Look over here at Mommy!" Waving to get their attention, she snaps the photo just as Hugh darts out of the frame to join her. "Hugh!" she cries in surprise.

"That's all right," Elmer chuckles. "At least I have one grandson in my photograph."

Kermit leads Hugh back to the bench and hands the camera to Augustus.

"You and Augustus should get a photograph together, too," Arvolin says, standing. "Sit here and I'll take all four of you."

"Do you remember how to use it?" Augustus asks.

"I think so," Arvolin says. "Just show me which button to push."

"This one," he points to the shutter, then rotates the lens. "Turn this until we look clear and in focus."

While Augustus and Kermit chat, Arvolin steps a few paces away, squints through the viewfinder, and snaps the photo. When she returns the camera, Augustus asks, "You already took it?"

"Yes. Nothing to it," Arvolin says.

"But we weren't ready, Momma," Kermit protests. "Next time, you have to let us know."

"Oh well. You didn't say that," Arvolin says with a shrug.

As they return to the car, Kermit sidles up next to Augustus out of earshot of the others. "Your mother said Hazel, her husband, and possibly Aunt Babe are all visiting this weekend," she whispers, glancing over her shoulder. "Did you know?"

"Last thing I heard, Momma was going to try and see Hazel and Aunt Babe while she was in town," Augustus begins. "But I didn't know they were definitely coming."

"Well, apparently all three are coming on Saturday," Kermit says. "I love seeing your family, but it would've been nice to know ahead of time. Where are we going to put all these house guests?"

Augustus sighs. "I don't know. Let me think about it."

***

By Saturday, Kermit's scratchy throat has developed into a full-blown cold, which she unfortunately passes on to Augustus. Despite being sick, they have a house full of company to host for the weekend. Before leaving for work, Augustus borrows sleeping cots from the Scotts next door. He then sets them up in the basement, where he, Kermit, and Augustus Jr. will sleep that night. Now they can accommodate Hazel and her husband in their bedroom. Elmer moves to the sofa to make space for Babe, who will stay with her sister in the boys' room. Finally, Hugh will sleep upstairs with Arvolin.

After lunch, Della, Elmer, and Arvolin chat at the kitchen table while their grandsons build cabins with Lincoln Logs in the living room. In the afternoon sunlight, Kermit collects the freshly laundered linens flapping on the clothesline out back. She busily moves from room to room, making beds and laying out towels for their arriving guests. Catching her haggard reflection in the bathroom mirror, Kermit soaks a washcloth in cold water and presses it against her flushed cheeks. Just as she is about to take the empty laundry basket down to the basement, a knock at the door interrupts her. Dropping the basket in the hall closet, she hurries to answer the door.

"Kermit, it's so good to see you," Hazel exclaims. Her brown eyes sparkle behind wide-rimmed glasses as a smile spreads across her fair complexion. After their embrace, Hazel lightly touches the arm of the man standing stiffly beside her. His short black hair is brushed away from his mocha-toned face, which matches the rich color of his glasses. "You remember Anderson?"

"Of course I do," Kermit croaks. She clears her throat, but her voice remains hoarse. "So glad you made it here safely. Come on in." As they enter the foyer, Kermit covers her hacking cough with a handkerchief.

"You don't sound too good," Hazel says, studying her ashen face.

"Fighting this cold. I'll be all right," Kermit reassures her, wiping her nose. "How's your sister?"

"Hilma's good," Hazel says. "Momma too. They're sorry they couldn't make it, but they send their best."

"That's good," Kermit says, leading them into the living room. "There are some people in here you may know."

"Aunt Della," Hazel cries, rushing to embrace her. "I've missed you so much." She squeezes her tightly.

"Me too, baby," Della says. She takes a step back to examine her niece, then rubs her hands along the sleeves of Hazel's black and white striped dress. "Looking the spitting image of my brother, may the Lord bless his soul. We may soon be reunited together, never to part."

"Oh, Aunt Della, don't talk like that," Hazel says softly. "We all miss Daddy, but we pray you'll be around for a long time."

Kermit joins them. "This is my mother, Arvolin Bland. Momma, this is Gus' cousin Hazel."

Arvolin offers her hand. "Nice to finally meet you. I've heard so much about you."

"I hope it was good," Hazel quips. "It's nice to meet you, too, Mrs. Bland." She walks around the table to greet Elmer. "How are you, Uncle Elmer?"

Elmer steadies himself on the table as he stands to embrace her. "I'm fine. Good to see you."

"This is Anderson." Hazel glances back, spotting her husband crouching beside the boys. "How did I just walk right past these two?" she asks. "Are these your fine sons, Kermit?"

"Yes. This is Hugh Allen—he'll be three in November," Kermit motions to her eldest son. "And this is 'Gustus Jr., who's one." As Kermit starts to laugh, she triggers another coughing spasm.

"Well, hello," Hazel kneels and gently pinches their cheeks. "I'm your cousin, Hazel, and this is your cousin Anderson."

"Say hello," Kermit prompts her sons.

After introductions with the rest of the family, Hazel scans the room. "Where's Gus?"

"He had to work a half day at the post office, but he'll be home soon," Kermit says. "Where are your bags?"

"They're in the trunk. I'll go get them," Anderson says, heading out the door.

Hazel pulls Kermit aside, whispering, "Where's the little girls' room? Anderson doesn't like to stop once we get going on the road. You never know if it's going to be safe, or if they'll even let us use the restroom."

"Oh, don't I know it. This way," Kermit says, leading her down the hall. When Anderson returns with their luggage, she directs him to their bedroom. Once they return to the living room, Kermit asks, "Are you hungry? Do you want something to drink?"

"Show me around your lovely home first," Hazel says, locking elbows with her.

Starting on the second level, Kermit guides her guests through the house, her toddlers trailing behind. While introducing them to their tenants, Hazel and Anderson peer curiously inside their chambers. They explore the shared bathroom and kitchenette upstairs before descending to the first floor.

"We're going to replace these old windows and floors," Kermit explains when they arrive in the living room. "Gus will install the new ones once they get delivered."

"Augusta didn't tell me y'all were getting new windows," Della interrupts. "How much is that going to cost?"

Trying to mask her irritation, Kermit says, "I'm not sure. He ordered them himself." She then swiftly ushers her visitors downstairs, concluding the tour in the basement. Back upstairs, Kermit leads them to the porch, where they observe the neighborhood activity. As the afternoon sun wanes, Augustus pulls up in his car, honking his horn.

"Gus," Hazel waves. "I've been wondering when you'd show up."

Augustus ascends the steps as Hugh and Augustus Jr. dash to cling to their father's pants. "Good to see you," he says, embracing Hazel. After shaking hands with Anderson, he kisses Kermit, then starts coughing.

"Don't tell me you're sick too?" Hazel asks.

Grinning, Augustus tilts his head toward his wife. "Guess who I got it from?"

"Oh no," Hazel laughs. "I wish I had known before we came. I hate to put you two out while you're not feeling well."

"Don't worry about it," Kermit says. "We're just glad to have you."

After returning inside, Kermit begins preparing dinner, perspiring over the hot stove. She tries to position herself next to the oscillating fan, but it fails to dissipate the thick, humid air around the kitchen. While the food cooks, Kermit plays hostess, offering her guests refreshments and snacks. Augustus plays music on the radio and shares his collection of photographs of visits with relatives. Another knock at the door announces the arrival of Babe, a slightly taller and slimmer version of her sister, Della. Following another round of introductions, hugs, and warm greetings, they gather around the table for the evening meal.

In response to another one of Augustus' coughing spells, Della remarks, "You need to be careful, Augusta. This is pneumonia weather with it being cold one minute and hot the next."

Augustus wipes his mouth with his napkin. "Yes, Momma. I will."

"You also need to wear plenty of warm clothes, eat wholesome food, and keep dry feet," she continues. "And above all, serve the Lord Jesus Christ out of a pure heart and shun all evil doings."

"Della, let him eat," her older sister interjects. "He knows all that. Plus, Kermit takes good care of him and these boys."

"He is my own one child," Della stammers, wiping her eyes. "I am the beginning of Augusta H. Hill Sr."

"It's all right, Aunt Babe. It's all right, Momma," Augustus says. "Let's just enjoy this nice meal together."

Kermit picks up the serving dish of creamed corn and passes it around the table. "Help yourself, everyone. Make sure you get enough to eat."

Hazel takes a sip of lemonade. "Kermit, you outdid yourself with this delicious dinner," she gushes. "We so appreciate you going to all this trouble for us, and you not being well on top of it." The other guests voice their approval.

"Thanks, Hazel, it's no trouble at all," Kermit smiles.

Hazel wraps her arm around her husband and continues, "We would love to have you and your whole family come to K.C. just any time."

"We'd be glad to," Kermit says.

After the last bite of dessert disappears, the family gathers around photo albums as they relive cherished memories of the Conway farm. At sunrise, the flurry of activities starts with church, followed by Sunday dinner, and a whirlwind tour of St. Louis sights. When the final guests drive away, twilight has painted the sky a deep purple, studded with a few twinkling stars. Exhausted but content, Kermit and Augustus tuck in their sons and retreat to their own bed, grateful for the time with family.

PART IV

Neighborhood Children

February 13, 1951

After relenting to her husband's wishes, Kermit quit her job and spent the past year caring for their toddlers full-time. Initially, they offset the lost income by renting out the three unused rooms on the second floor. However, their family finances suffer a significant blow when all their lodgers move away at the end of November. Without rental income, they now depend solely on Augustus' earnings.

Over the holidays, Kermit devises a plan to stay home with their sons while earning extra money. She proposes babysitting the children of working mothers on the first floor, with her family relocating to the vacant rooms upstairs. Unable to find any other solutions, Augustus agrees to this arrangement, stipulating that it cannot interfere with her primary responsibilities of caring for their sons and managing household duties.

Kermit eagerly launches into her new project, seeking referrals and suggestions from neighbors, church members, and former coworkers. Rummaging through the bins at the F.W. Woolworth Co. store, she finds small blocks, crayons, and dolls to supplement her sons' toy collection. At her induction into the Athenian Literary Club, she consults fellow members about nurturing reading in preschoolers. By the first week of February, she successfully recruits four neighborhood children for her home day care program.

On the morning of her opening, Kermit wakes up an hour before her 5:15 a.m. alarm, unable to stop thinking about the endless tasks she needs to complete. With outside temperatures hovering around thirty degrees, she wraps herself tightly in a housecoat to protect against the morning chill. Quietly leaving her sleeping husband and sons upstairs, she begins preparing her home for the arrival of young guests.

Once downstairs, the air feels even colder, so she cranks up the radiator before starting a pot of coffee. Steam hisses from the valve as she tidies the living room, removing fragile glass ashtrays and ceramic figurines. In her old bedroom, she pushes chairs and nightstands against the walls to create a spacious play area. Meanwhile, toys scattered around the first floor are gathered and tucked neatly into a basket in the new playroom. Between sips of coffee, Kermit slices oranges and apples into bite-sized pieces and stores them in the icebox. Next, she pulls blankets and sheets from the linen closet to dress the cribs in her sons' former bedroom. Pillows are covered with sheets to provide extra bedding on the floor. Finally, before heading back upstairs, she prepares oatmeal and toast for breakfast.

As she lands on the second floor, Augustus pokes his head out of the bathroom. His almond-toned face is covered with a thick layer of white shaving cream, and a hand towel hangs over his bare shoulder. "What are you doing up so early?" he asks.

"Couldn't sleep," Kermit replies. "Decided to get ready for the little ones."

"Looks like we got some freezing rain last night," Augustus observes. "I'll put some salt down out front, so they won't slip and fall."

"Thanks, honey," she says, caressing his shoulder. "That's a good idea."

As Kermit heads toward their sons' bedroom, he teases, "What? No kiss?"

Grinning, she gently pulls his head closer and kisses his forehead, careful to avoid the mound of foam on his cheeks. "There," she chuckles.

Once Augustus departs for work, Kermit draws open the Venetian blinds, ushering morning sunlight into the living room. Her fingertips sting as she wipes away the frost from the windowpane, leaving streaks in the condensation. While her sons finish breakfast, she washes the dishes and sweeps the floor. Kermit then unties Augustus Jr.'s bib, then cleans the oatmeal off both boys' faces and hands. Lifting her younger son out of the highchair, Kermit dresses him in a maroon sweater and black wool pants, matching his brother's attire.

Before leaving the kitchen, Kermit sternly looks at her sons while firmly clasping their hands. "Remember those children I told you about?" she asks. "They'll be here in a few minutes, and I don't want any trouble out of either of you. That means no fighting or arguing. Do you understand?"

Hugh replies, "Yes, Mommy," and his younger brother mimics him seconds later.

While Kermit waits for the parents, she anxiously paces around the foyer, repeatedly checking her hair, makeup, and steel-blue suit in the hall mirror. The first to arrive is a mother dragging her four-year-old son, dressed in a knitted snowflake-themed cardigan and black pants. After he kisses his mother goodbye, Kermit ushers the little boy into the new playroom, where her sons rush up to greet him. Next comes a one-year-old girl in a plaid flannel pleated skirt and white blouse, clinging tightly to her mother's coat. Kermit quickly offers the girl a baby doll from the toy basket, coaxing her to join the boys. Finally, Lulu from next door drops off her three-year-old twins: Elizabeth, wearing a forest green wool jumper, and Milton in a red checkered shirt and gray corduroy shorts.

In the playroom, Kermit arranges the children in a circle, then joins them on the floor. After placing the youngest girl in her lap, she says, "Okay, boys and girls, we're going to begin by getting to know one another. I want each of you to tell us your name and how old you are." Pointing to her oldest son, she grins, "Why don't we start with you, young man?"

Kermit's sons and the twins from next door erupt in laughter, exchanging playful nudges. "You know who I am, Mommy," Hugh protests.

"That's your mommy?" the four-year-old boy asks skeptically.

"Yes, I am," Kermit answers, then addresses her son. "You're right. I do already know you, but this nice boy and girl don't. So, go ahead and tell them your name and age."

Hugh introduces himself, followed by Elizabeth, her brother Milton, and four-year-old Michael. Kermit then helps one-year-olds Augustus Jr. and Sydney use their fingers to indicate their ages after sharing their names. She concludes the icebreaker by introducing herself as Mrs. Hill.

"You forgot to say how old you are, Mommy," Hugh says.

"Well, it's impolite to ask a woman her age," Kermit says. Then she leans closer, cupping her mouth conspiratorially. "But just this once, I'll tell you a secret. I'm thirty-one." The toddlers murmur in disbelief as she chuckles. "How about we start off the day with a song?" she continues. "Who knows 'Patty Cake'?" Acknowledging a few raised hands, she launches into the first verse, clapping rhythmically. As Kermit begins her third nursery rhyme, her mother meanders down the staircase wearing a blue striped dress with a square collar.

Hugh and Augustus Jr. leave the circle to hug Arvolin, calling out, "Grandma!" The others stop singing to inspect the new person joining them. First, Elizabeth and Milton, then the remainder of the preschoolers, follow suit, affectionately wrapping their arms around her.

"How sweet. Aren't they little darlings?" Arvolin gushes, patting them gently. Settling into a rocking chair by the window, she asks her daughter, "How's it going?"

"It's good," Kermit says, then quickly redirects the children. "Let's get back into our circle." Once they return, she leads them through another round of nursery rhymes before serving the morning snack. As she distributes orange slices, Augustus Jr. starts hitting Sydney with a block. Before Kermit can intervene, her mother swiftly snatches his hand and removes the wooden object.

"Stop that," Kermit snaps, rushing to comfort the crying girl.

"That's mine," her younger son whines.

"You know better than that," Kermit says. "These toys are for everyone, and you're supposed to behave like a little gentleman." She returns the block to the basket and moves it to the shelf out of reach.

After a lunch of bologna sandwiches, apples, and milk, Kermit puts the toddlers down for a nap on the makeshift beds. The boys nap on the floor pillows while the girls sleep in the cribs. As the children doze off, Kermit shares a quiet cup of coffee with her mother. The brief silence is shattered by one-year-old Sydney's wailing cries.

"What's wrong?" Kermit asks. "Did you have a bad dream?" As she lifts the toddler, Kermit feels the girl's skirt and tights are wet. A quick check of the sheet reveals the bedding is soaked through to the mattress. Discreetly carrying the girl to the bathroom, Kermit cleans her in the bathtub and wraps her in a towel. After washing the soiled clothes in the sink, she realizes Sydney has nothing else to wear.

When Kermit returns, she finds Arvolin removing the wet linens and scrubbing the mattress. "Thanks for doing that, Momma," Kermit whispers. "Listen, can you go upstairs and get some pants from either Hugh or Gustus Jr. that I can put on her?"

Arvolin nods, returning with a pair of gray trousers. As Kermit attempts to slip them on Sydney, she protests, "Those are for boys."

"I know, sweetie," Kermit chuckles. "You only need to wear them a little while."

Once Sydney is dressed, Kermit wakes up the other children and makes sure everyone uses the bathroom. Returning them to a circle, she teaches them how to play Duck, Duck, Goose. Leaving Arvolin to supervise the game, Kermit warms milk on the stove, then stirs in hot cocoa powder. Retrieving small Dixie cups from the pantry, she pours in hot chocolate and lets it cool before serving the children.

"Okay, boys and girls," Kermit calls from the kitchen. "I want you to walk, not run, to have some cocoa." Despite her instruction, the eager pre-schoolers rush to her side, hands outstretched and cheering. "I said walk," Kermit repeats. She waits for the children to calm down before handing each of them a cup. "Take small sips and stay right here until you're finished."

Before Kermit can react, Michael tilts his cup too quickly and misses his mouth.

"No," Kermit cries, startling him and causing the drink to spill down his sweater. She grabs a hand towel, runs it under the sink, and dabs at the spreading chocolate stain.

"Let me," Arvolin offers, taking the four-year-old's hand. "I'll work on getting that out." She leads the boy to the bathroom while Kermit cleans the brown drops splattered across the table, chair, and floor.

"Thanks, Momma," Kermit sighs, pursing her lips. "It all happened so fast." Gathering them in a circle, she watches closely as they finish their drinks. When they return to the room, she retrieves the toy basket and kneels on the floor. "It's time for free play. You can take one toy each. Or, if you can play nicely together, you can share a toy." While the toddlers make their selections, Michael returns wearing a snug gray shirt with the sleeves falling above his wrists.

"See," Arvolin smiles, holding up the damp sweater. "I was able to get the stain out. I found him something to wear until it dries."

"Thanks again," Kermit says. "You've been a big help today."

Before the five o'clock pick-up time, Kermit checks the laundered clothing and finds that only the sweater is dry enough to wear. While Arvolin puts the sweater on Michael, Kermit packs Sydney's damp clothes into a paper bag. As the outdoor temperatures drop with the setting sun, she bundles the children in their snowsuits, hats, and gloves as they wait for their parents.

When Michael's mother arrives, Kermit apologizes, explaining that her son's sweater had been soiled. Although they managed to clean it, she asks her to provide a change of clothes in case of future accidents. Kermit reiterates her request to her next-door neighbor when she picks up her children. As she escorts the Scotts out, the last mother slides past her.

"Mommy!" Sydney exclaims, rushing toward her. Then, pointing at Kermit, she pouts, "That lady made me put on these boys' pants."

"What happened?" the mother asks, examining her daughter's attire.

"Well," Kermit chuckles nervously, "we had a little accident at nap time. I'm afraid we didn't get to the bathroom in time."

"Oh, okay," the mother replies sheepishly. "We're still working on getting Sydney potty-trained." She glances at her daughter, patting her head gently.

Kermit passes her the bag with her daughter's clothes. "I washed her tights and skirt, but they didn't dry completely. I didn't want her going out in wet clothes and catch pneumonia in this cold weather."

"Thank you," the mother replies.

"I'm asking all the parents to bring in a spare outfit that I can keep here in case of emergencies," Kermit says. "I'll see you in the morning." Turning to Sydney, she adds, "And you too, young lady."

After they leave, sudden quiet blankets the house. Hugh and Augustus Jr. linger in the foyer before climbing onto the sofa to peek out at Newstead Avenue. The faint yellow glow of streetlamps flickers on the passing evening traffic as sleet taps a staccato rhythm on the windowpane.

"Get off the sofa," Kermit reprimands, glancing at her watch. Whining, the boys obey as she closes the blinds and tidies up the living room. Crossing into the kitchen, she ties an apron over her dress and starts preparing dinner.

"Well," Arvolin starts. "Not too bad for your first day, don't you think?"

"Huh. It could've gone smoother," Kermit chuckles. Unwrapping pork chops from butcher paper, she seasons both sides with salt and pepper. "You're staying for dinner, aren't you?"

Before Arvolin can respond, Augustus enters with traces of melting sleet on his black fedora. A gray wool scarf wrapped around the upturned collar of his coat obscures his face, while the brim of his hat covers his forehead.

"How's everybody?" he asks. "Let me tell you something; it's cold out there."

"I bet," Kermit says, kissing him. She places the pork chops in the pan over the gas flame, where they begin to sizzle. Grabbing a can from the pantry, she opens it and pours spinach into a pot on the adjacent burner.

"Guess what, daddy?" Hugh asks, trailing his father down the hall. "We had a lot of kids here today."

"Really?" Augustus feigns surprise as he hangs his coat in the closet. "How was it?"

"Fun," Hugh responds.

"Busy," Kermit adds. She grabs a spatula, flips the pork chops, and waves away the faint smoke rising from the crackling pan. "We had a couple of spills and bathroom accidents, so I asked the parents to bring in a change of clothes." She dumps the sliced vegetables into the frying pan, then turns down the heat. "I was thinking it would be good to have a place for the children to put their things."

"Uh-huh," Augustus says, eyeing her. "You mean you want *me* to come up with something?"

"Well," Kermit grins. "You're so good at that kind of thing. Maybe you can make little shelves from some of those boards laying around the basement." She combines the leftover oranges and apples in a bowl, then slices a banana and sprinkles confectioner's sugar to make fruit salad.

"Uh-huh," Augustus repeats. "I'll see what I can do."

"Thanks, honey," Kermit says, kissing his forehead. "I appreciate it."

Over the following days, Kermit quickly develops a strong bond with the youngsters, who look forward to spending time at her home. As the cold spell continues through the rest of the week, Kermit asks Augustus to bring down extra blankets from the attic, which they drape over chairs to create a warm, makeshift fort. When temperatures climb to an unseasonal 65 degrees, Kermit moves playtime to the backyard, allowing the children to run around in the fresh, warm air.

In the second week of March, St. Louis receives six inches of snow as temperatures plunge below freezing. That evening, a mother is late picking up her child, and no one answers the phone at her home or workplace. After twenty-five minutes, Kermit starts preparing dinner while anxiously peering at traffic crawling along the snowy streets. Augustus arrives after thirty minutes, but there is still no sign of the mother. An hour later, the mother finally shows up, apologizing and explaining that her car engine froze in the cold. After this incident, Kermit now asks each family to give at least two more emergency contacts who can pick up their child.

By the first day of spring, Kermit's babysitting service runs more smoothly than ever. When Augustus returns home from work, her face brightens as she recounts the day's childcare activities. The more she shares her vision, the more he recognizes the potential to turn it into a full-time business.

"If we're going to do this, we need to do it right," Augustus says, his willingness to join her mission evident in his voice.

Kermit studies him, momentarily caught off guard. He once resisted the idea of her working. Now he is making plans beside her, demonstrating his commitment to helping her succeed.

"I agree," she says, her voice rising with new enthusiasm. "We'll need new equipment and a strong early education program to convince parents this is where they want to bring their kids."

Together, they transform the first floor into a vibrant, child-friendly environment. Augustus installs pint-sized shelving and cabinets in the playroom to hold supplies and extra clothing. They brighten the walls with preschoolers' artwork—drawings and cutouts of nursery characters made from colorful construction paper. The once-formal living spaces now pulse with primary colors and small furniture scaled for toddlers.

As Kermit interacts with the preschoolers, she witnesses firsthand how her work positively impacts their early development and self-confidence. She watches shy children find their voices during circle time, sees toddlers master new skills with patient encouragement, and observes how structure and care create safe spaces for growth. For the first time since leaving her previous job, she feels a sense of purpose return—and with it, a quiet momentum that promises to carry her forward.

The Tiny Tot Day Nursery

April 8, 1951

Drenching rain tears white blossoms from the dogwood branches, scattering them across the slick sidewalk along Page Boulevard. Dense, gray clouds blanket the sky as rumbling thunder rattles the tall stained-glass windows of Church of Christ Holiness. Congregation members, hurrying to escape the storm, shake rain from their umbrellas, hats, and boots as they dash through the entrance. Inside, a damp musty scent permeates the building as rain pounds on the roof.

In the vestibule, Kermit chats with Geraldine while their husbands locate seats in the sanctuary. A silk pillbox hat sits securely atop Kermit's freshly pressed hair as she nods a greeting to fellow members rushing past. She tugs at the waistband of her snug mint-green suit skirt as they wait for the Sunday School teacher to dismiss their children.

"I still can't believe Bishop Mitchell is gone," Geraldine sighs, her glistening eyes hidden behind the veil of her silver hat.

"I know, it's such a shame," Kermit says. "Hard to believe someone his age would have a stroke. How's Sister Mitchell doing?"

"She's holding up," Geraldine replies. "Momma visited her last week. Says she's about as well as can be expected under the circumstances."

"I can't imagine what she must be going through," Kermit croaks, clearing her throat. "It's only been a couple months since he passed. It's going to take some time to mourn." She shifts her weight to relieve the discomfort building in her ankles and feet. "Have you heard anything about them appointing a new pastor?"

"Not a word," Geraldine says. She removes a handkerchief from the sleeve of her steel-blue dress and dabs away tears. "You remember it was because of Bishop Mitchell that we became friends?"

"Yes. I'm still sorry I ever believed that silly gossip," Kermit says. "I should've known you wouldn't cheat in that baby contest. Bishop set me straight and made sure we hugged afterwards."

"I'm so glad he did," Geraldine says as the two embrace.

The bustle of activity nearby grows as members prepare for the morning church service. The choir, outfitted in maroon robes, assembles into soprano, alto, tenor, and bass sections before filing into the sanctuary. Ushers position themselves at the doors, clasping stacks of bulletins in their right gloved hands while placing their left hands behind their backs. Women in all white dresses, shoes, and stockings line up and promenade down the aisle to take their seats on the front pew reserved for nurses.

"How is your babysitting service going?" Geraldine asks.

"I'm really enjoying it," Kermit beams. "In fact, I've convinced Gus to let me bring in more children."

"No kidding," Geraldine chuckles. "Has he finally stopped trying to keep you from working?"

"Well, he's at least warming up to the idea," Kermit says. "A couple of my parents told their friends how much they like it, and now they want to bring their children too. I'm putting together some flyers to pass out. The deacon board said I could put some up here at church. Maybe make an announcement too."

"That's great. I'm here to help you with whatever you need."

"Thanks, Geraldine. I'm so grateful for you," Kermit says.

"I mean it too."

"Why don't you bring Ronald and DeWayne over to visit sometime?" Kermit suggests. "You can see the nursery for yourself and let me know what you think."

"That would be nice," Geraldine agrees. "I know they'll enjoy playing with all those kids."

Children laugh and squeal as they file out of Sunday School classrooms, but are immediately shushed by waiting parents. Kermit and Geraldine spot their sons and move to quiet them as they approach.

"Look, Mommy!" Augustus Jr. exclaims, opening his hand to reveal crinkled gold cellophane. "My teacher gave me some candy for my birthday."

"Where's the candy?" Kermit chuckles. "All I see is a wrapper."

"I eat it already," her son giggles.

"Ate," Kermit corrects him. "You ate it already."

"Happy Birthday, young man," Geraldine says. "Our family has a present for you."

"Really?" Augustus Jr. asks, his eyes widening. "Where is it?"

"You'll have to wait until after church. We'll bring it to your birthday party this afternoon."

"Yay!" he shouts.

"Shh. Remember you're still in church," Kermit whispers.

The women clasp their sons' hands and lead them to the line waiting to enter the sanctuary. When they reach the doorway, an usher presents them with a program and escorts them to the pew where their husbands are seated. As the assistant pastor signals the congregation to stand, organ music swells. Kermit glances at the bulletin, then flips through the hymnal to find the opening song. Throughout the sermon, she alternates between quieting her sons and nudging her husband to stay awake.

Over the next few days, Kermit's mind races with ideas to attract more children to her program. After dinner, she calls referrals from relatives, friends, and current parents, seeking new clients. She scrutinizes each portion of the first floor of their home with Augustus, asking him for suggestions on how to make the space more appealing to both parents and children. Late into the night, Kermit sits at the kitchen table, brainstorming ways to incorporate festive holiday celebrations into the activity schedule.

When Kermit finally crawls into bed, Augustus sits up in his underwear, reading the St. Louis Post-Dispatch. The brass lamp on his nightstand casts a soft glow, while cool night air drifts in through the slightly open window. After pulling the blanket over her pink lace nightgown, she glances at him. "You're not cold?"

Augustus shakes his head. "No, but I guess you are," he chuckles. He rises, closes the window, then returns to bed. Wrapping his arm around her shoulder, he begins to rub away the goosebumps rising on her bare arm.

"Thanks," Kermit says with a kiss. She retrieves his discarded sections of the newspaper and begins scanning the articles. As she tears out a story about a toddler fashion show, she asks, "What do you think I should call my nursery?"

Augustus scratches his stubble, thinking. "Huh. I just thought you'd call it Hill's Nursery or Hill's Babysitting."

"I thought about that too," Kermit replies. "But it doesn't sound... very creative. I wanted something with a bit more oomph to it. More professional." She grabs the notepad off the nightstand. "Tell me what you think about these." After flipping through the pages, she starts. "How about Jack and Jill Nursery School?"

"Isn't that the story where Jack falls and cracks open his head?" Augustus chuckles. "I don't know if I would bring my child to a place like that."

"Humph," Kermit says. "I guess you have a point." She glances back at her notes. "Then what about Mother Goose?"

"That's better. I can't think of anything bad that Mother Goose did." He rubs his chin before continuing. "Any other names?"

"The last one is Tiny Tot," Kermit says, placing the notepad in her lap. "That's also the name of a diaper service in the county. But I didn't see it for a nursery. Which one do you like best?"

"Tiny Tot. It's got a good ring to it. Sounds like a nice place for kids."

Kermit smiles. "Good," she nods. "I like it too." She circles the name on her pad. "Now that I have a name, I can finish up those flyers. Maybe put a small ad in the paper."

On Saturday, a spring heatwave pushes temperatures thirty degrees higher than the day before, reaching seventy-four degrees by the afternoon. Sunlight gleams through the windows of the Van-Del Café as Kermit weaves through the restaurant in a tan floral dress, white gloves, and beige peep-toe shoes. She greets the lunch crowd, reciting a prepared speech about Tiny Tot before dropping a flyer on each table. Hugh and Augustus Jr. wait by the door, dressed in matching navy jackets and shorts typically reserved for church. As Kermit approaches the final customer, the strong scent of Chinese food overpowers her, forcing a quick retreat to the sidewalk for some fresh air.

"Aren't we going to eat there, mommy?" Hugh asks as he follows his mother outside.

"Yeah, I'm hungry," Augustus Jr. whines.

Kermit shakes her head, covering her mouth as cold sweat chills her body. She takes a few deep breaths and wipes her brow, leaving traces of tawny makeup on her gloves. "Mommy has a few more stops to make first," she finally says, rubbing the stain on her glove. She glances both ways down

North Vandeventer Street. "There's a park in the next block. We can rest there a bit, and you can eat these sandwiches I brought."

"But I want their food," Hugh whines, pointing to the restaurant.

"Me too," Augustus Jr. agrees.

Kermit frowns at them while biting her bottom lip. She tugs her sons' hands. "Let's go," she sighs, leading them across the street to the park. She removes their jackets and lets them play on the rocking horse and swings. While resting on the bench, she slips off her shoes and massages her feet and ankles. After her sons finish eating, Kermit stops by the hair salon and grocery store to distribute more flyers. Spotting a sidewalk sign advertising a children's photo contest, she drops in at the Rogers Photography Studio.

"Good afternoon, young lady," the photographer greets. A maroon pin-stripe suit hangs loosely off his slender frame, and his mahogany-toned face crinkles with a smile. "I'm Mr. Rogers. Are you entering these handsome twins in our photo contest?"

"Good afternoon. My name is Mrs. Augustus Hill," Kermit says as they shake hands. She turns her toddlers' shoulders to face him. "They're not twins, though. Hugh Allen here is three, and Gustus Jr. just turned two last week."

Mr. Rogers lets out a soft groan as he crouches down. "Well, hello there, young men," he says, shaking their hands. "You both look very sharp in those blue suits." Standing up, he turns on four studio lights, revealing a wooden table draped with a white cloth. He adjusts a metal box camera mounted on a tripod, aiming it at the illuminated area. "Let's set them up over here."

"Oh, hold on," Kermit starts. "I just stopped in to get some information. You see, I'm opening up enrollment for my childcare on Newstead." She reaches inside her bag and presents him with a flyer. "I thought we might be able to help each other out. I could encourage the parents from my nursery to enter their children in your contest. In exchange, you could tell your customers about my nursery."

"I see," Mr. Rogers says, studying the flyer. "How many children do you have? I mean... how many are in your nursery?"

"Seven, including my two," Kermit says. "But at least three more families are starting next month. Maybe you can put the flyer in your window or hang it on the wall?"

"So, you aren't entering your sons in the contest?" Mr. Rogers asks.

"I'll need to talk to my husband first," Kermit says. "We do need to have a family portrait done, though, so we'll see what he says."

The front door creaks open as a woman with cinnamon-toned features enters, cradling a sleeping infant. A man carrying a small boy follows, their skin the color of lightly toasted bread. The family, dressed in a pale blue palette, glances expectantly at the gathering.

"Welcome, welcome! I'll be right with you," Mr. Rogers says with a wave. "Why don't you come over here, and I'll get you set up after I finish with these nice people." He gestures to the table, then turns his attention to Kermit. "Mrs. Hill, you talk a good game," he says. "Our children's photo contest runs every year. I think this will work out for both of us."

"Thank you so much, Mr. Rogers," Kermit says, placing another flyer on the counter. Before leaving with her sons, she hands the mother a flyer and recites her pitch for Tiny Tot.

The next day, Kermit and her family attend Antioch Church at the invitation of a fellow Athenian Literary Club member. After the service, Kermit's friend introduces her to the church members who staff Antioch's daycare program. While Hugh and Augustus Jr. play on the equipment, the staff shares their joys and challenges of caring for young children. Kermit and Augustus tour the facility, gathering more inspiration for updating Tiny Tot. That evening, Kermit fills three more notebooks with ideas to expand enrollment and improve her childcare service.

On Friday, Geraldine arrives with her two toddlers to visit the day care program. In the playroom, Kermit captivates the preschoolers gathered around her with a lively portrayal of Curious George's adventures. Meanwhile, Arvolin and Geraldine prepare more flyers at the kitchen table while sipping sweetened iced tea.

A loud thud against the porch door initially startles the women, but they soon catch a glimpse of the paperboy cycling away. "It's here!" Geraldine calls out, hurrying to the door. She steps into the shimmering sunlight and retrieves the tossed newspaper. After closing the door behind her, she hands it to Kermit. "Here you go. Fresh off the presses." Arvolin joins them in the playroom and settles into a nearby chair.

As Kermit takes the paper, she closes the book in her lap. "We're going to finish reading a little later," she tells the children, who whine at the news.

"We'll start playtime a little early, so you can go pick out a toy." The toddlers cheer and scamper to the toybox. With Geraldine and Arvolin peering over her shoulder, Kermit unfolds the St. Louis Argus and starts to trace her finger along the pale green newsprint.

As Kermit searches the fourth page, Arvolin asks, "You sure it's supposed to be in there today?"

"That's what they told me, Momma," Kermit replies. "The Argus only comes out on Fridays, so it has to be in here." When she reaches the top of the sixth page, she exclaims, "I found it!"

All three women lean closer to the paper as Kermit reads the post aloud. "Attention Mothers - Announcing Opening of The Tiny Tot Day Nursery. Qualified Directress." Kermit chuckles at this. She playfully blows on her knuckles, then pretends to polish a medal on her chest. As the women laugh along, she continues. "Reasonable Rates. 3212 N. Newstead. Goodfellow 4866 – Mrs. A. H. Hill. All modern facilities."

"You made it in the paper!" Geraldine exclaims. "That's really something."

"I'm so proud of you, baby," Arvolin beams. "It's a good advertisement too. Are you going to cut it out?"

"I will, but I want to show Gus when he gets home first," Kermit says. "I'll also show the parents when they come pick up their children. Oh, and I'll ask the Scotts if they can save me their copy of today's Argus."

"You can have ours too," Geraldine offers. "I'll bring it to church on Sunday."

"Thanks," Kermit says. "I hope a lot of people see the ad and it encourages them to bring their children here."

"I'm sure they will," Geraldine says. "How can they miss it with 'The Tiny Tot Day Nursery' in those big letters?"

"Oh, look, it's right above this huge wristwatch ad," Kermit says as she scans the page. "And this one for a diaper service should attract parents."

"Uh oh, Kermit. Look," Arvolin says, pointing to the bottom of the paper.

"What? How could they put me on the same page as Canadian whiskey?" Kermit exclaims. "That's not a good place to advertise my nursery." She sighs and refolds the paper so the ad faces front.

"It'll be alright," Geraldine says, patting her friend's shoulder. "You never know. People who drink Canadian whiskey could turn out to be your best customers." The women laugh as Kermit deposits the newspaper on the foyer table. As she directs the children to wash up for Graham Cracker snacks, the telephone rings.

Kermit crosses into the kitchen and picks up the receiver. "Hello?" Following a pause, she grins and waves her hand to catch Geraldine and Arvolin's attention. "Yes. This is The Tiny Tot Day Nursery."

Open House Disaster

August 23, 1951

Kermit's gown clings to the perspiration sliding down her protruding abdomen as she paces the linoleum floor. Her heels click rhythmically against white tiles while she weaves between the porcelain sink, gleaming medical equipment, and examination table draped in starched bedding. Sunlight streams through the six-pane window, illuminating paint chips scattered across the weathered sill. Kermit lingers before the rotating fan, allowing the mechanical breeze to cool her elevated body temperature. When her thoughts drift to next month's open house, she purses her lips and resumes her winding path around the cramped room. The thought of the open house sends a knot tightening in her stomach. So much to do, so little time. This doctor's appointment, an irritating interruption, is a luxury she cannot afford. She resumes her winding path, counting the days in her head.

She stops abruptly as her doctor bursts through the door with a lit cigarette dangling from his lips.

"Good afternoon, Mrs. Hill," he says as faint smoke trails behind him. "How are you feeling today?"

"I'm alright, Dr. Robinson," Kermit responds. She smooths the back of her gown as she prepares to position herself onto the metal chair.

"Wait. Don't sit yet," he says, moving to the standing scale against the wall. "I'll need to get your weight first."

Kermit removes her tan sling-back sandals and deposits her cloth handbag in the chair. "Can I take off my watch and earrings too?" she jokes.

The sliding bar clinks against the metal frame as her doctor helps her onto the scale platform. As he slides the weights along the bar, she closes her eyes, resting her hands on her extended belly. When the clinking stops, she peeks with one eye as the pointer slowly tilts up and down. Once the bar balances, she groans and steps off the rubber mat.

"Don't get too fat now," Dr. Robinson warns, patting her stomach. After noting the chart, he steers her onto the examination table. "You shouldn't gain more than fifteen pounds while pregnant, twenty at the most."

"I'm trying," Kermit sighs. "I've just been so busy running around with my nursery."

Suddenly, the concentrated smell of antiseptics mingling with stale smoke triggers her nausea. Unable to swallow it down, she asks, "May I have some water, please?"

Retrieving a glass from the sink, he fills it and hands it to her. "Maybe now's not the best time to be starting up a nursery," he says. "With two youngsters already at home and a third on the way..."

"It's too late for that now," Kermit snaps. "I'd already started it before I got pregnant." She inhales deeply, attempting to calm herself, then takes a sip from her drink.

"Well, remember what happened with your last pregnancy? You don't want to end up in the hospital again."

Kermit nods as she wipes the sweat from her hairline. After draining her glass, she sets it on the table.

Dr. Robinson lifts the stethoscope from around his neck. "Lie back," he instructs while guiding her shoulder. He inserts the instrument's tips in his ears, then warms the metal bell in his palm. "This may feel a bit cold," he warns, placing it on Kermit's chest.

After listening to her heart, he moves the bell around her abdomen to examine the fetus. As he gently squeezes her calves, he asks, "Are you having any cramping or swelling in your ankles?"

"Sometimes, but isn't that normal?" Kermit asks. "I had it with my other pregnancies."

"Well, your legs shouldn't get so swollen that you have difficulty walking," Dr. Robinson replies. "How about trouble sleeping?"

Kermit feels her baby move inside her as she starts to respond. "Oh! Somebody just woke up," she laughs, rubbing her stomach. "Some nights I do have a hard time getting comfortable now that this little one is getting bigger."

Dr. Robinson nods as he flicks cigarette ashes into an ashtray. He pulls a flexible cloth tape from the front pocket of his white coat and measures the height of her womb. "Okay, Mrs. Hill, I've finished your exam," he says, moving her purse before settling in the chair. While finishing his notes, the doctor takes long drags of his cigarette and then extinguishes it.

Kermit props up on her elbows before transferring to a sitting position on the table's edge. She reaches for the glass but stops when she remembers it is empty.

After referencing a thick medical book, Dr. Robinson says, "You're on track to deliver within ten to twelve weeks."

"Really?" Kermit exclaims, pausing to count aloud the months on her fingers. "September, October, November – That's around the same time my oldest son was born. Wouldn't that be something if they shared the same birthday?"

"Uh-huh," Dr. Robinson nods. "I really think you should put off doing this childcare stuff, or at least, find some help. As I said, you don't want to go to the hospital until it's time to deliver that baby."

"Alright, I will," Kermit promises.

Dr. Robinson rises and heads to the door. "Call the office if you're feeling worse or experience any pain."

***

As an orange glow stretches across the horizon the following evening, Kermit welcomes a group of women into her home. She wears her gray skirt and striped pleated top, the fabric accommodating her growing frame. In the kitchen, Arvolin and Geraldine arrange shortbread cookies and pound cake on serving platters as the rich aroma of brewing coffee fills the air. Kermit serves her guests refreshments on ivory china accented with delicate floral patterns.

"Thank you so much for coming out tonight," Kermit says, circling the room. "I'm so grateful to you for helping me with my open house next month."

"When is it?" Geraldine asks. She clears empty dishes from the dining room, placing them on the counter for Arvolin to wash.

"It's next Sunday, September second," Kermit replies, loud enough for all to hear. "That only leaves us a little over a week."

As the women finish eating, Kermit retrieves a large paper bag from the hall closet and empties its contents onto the dining room table. She presents a box of stationery to the group and continues. "Here are the invitations I had printed. I think it would be faster if we set up an assembly line of sorts. The first group addresses the envelopes, then passes them to the second group to stuff them."

Kermit holds up a small tan sea sponge in a metal dish. "Gus was able to get me two of these moistening sponges from the post office. The last group can use them to apply the stamps and seal the envelopes." She places a coil roll of three-cent purple stamps next to the sponges. "How does that sound?"

When the women nod and murmur in agreement, Kermit passes out the supplies and makes assignments to those seated at the table. Once they settle into their tasks, she opens the cabinet and retrieves two rolls each of pink and blue crepe paper.

Turning to the remaining volunteers in the living room, she says, "Now, I would like you ladies to twist these pink and blue rolls together to make streamers. I have tape and scissors over there," she gestures toward the table. "Drape them across the doorways and walls, but make sure they're high enough so the little ones can't reach and pull them down."

As they dive into their tasks, Augustus comes up the basement steps holding a one-by-two-foot wooden sign with a saw blade edge. "Tiny Tot Nursery" is carved in the center, with profile images of three-foot-tall children depicted holding the sign on either side. Trailing behind him are Hugh, Augustus Jr., and Geraldine's sons, Ronald and Dewayne. The toddlers explore the room, peeking at the activities as the women pause their work to greet them.

Augustus searches for Kermit, then approaches her in the living room. "What do you think?" he asks, presenting his handiwork.

"My, you're a really talented artist!" Kermit exclaims. "Excuse me, ladies," she announces. "I think most of you know Gus. If not, this is my husband, Augustus Hill." She places a hand on his arm as he smiles and acknowledges their greetings. "Look! This is the sign he made for the open house."

Kermit shows the carved panel to the gathering, who applaud and express their admiration. Addressing her husband, she asks, "Is it ready to paint?"

"I still need to sand it first," Augustus says, tracing the splintered edges with his fingers. "I bought pink and blue paint, and there's some white left-over downstairs I could use. Should I paint the whole thing?"

She studies the sign before responding. "Well, maybe just paint the girl's dress pink and the boy's shorts blue," she states, pointing to the figures. "Mix it up a little by adding a pink stripe to his hat and a blue ribbon for the girl's hair. If you have enough white, use it for the letters, then paint the background blue so the name will stand out."

"Got it," Augustus says, nodding. As he turns to leave, Kermit grabs his arm.

"And please take your little helpers with you," Kermit chuckles. "They are holding up our progress up here."

***

One week later, temperatures soar to a summer high of 98 degrees on the last day of August. Kermit adjusts her position on the avocado cushions lining the patio furniture as eleven toddlers play in the shade behind her home. Seeking relief from the stifling humidity, she removes a washcloth from a bowl of melting ice water, wrings out the excess liquid, and cools her face.

"Line up, boys and girls," she calls, returning the towel to the ice bowl.

After the children form a ragged line, Kermit wipes their flushed faces with the cold cloth. "Okay, you can go back and play."

Once the children resume their game, the back door slams as Arvolin steps onto the porch in a white collared tan dress. "*The Argus* came," she announces, shading her eyes from the afternoon sun.

Grasping the railing to help pull herself up, Kermit laboriously climbs the white wooden steps. Reaching the landing, she steps out of the sun beneath the blue and white striped metal awning. "Thanks, Momma," she says, tugging the hem of her yellow smock over her bulging stomach. "I guess you're not coming outside?"

"Naw, you won't catch me out there in this heat," Arvolin says, handing her daughter the newspaper. She waits as Kermit removes the rubber band and starts scanning the pages.

"Here it is," Kermit says. "Tiny Tot Nursery School invites you to Open House." Arvolin steps closer as Kermit folds the paper in half before continuing. "Sunday, September second, five o'clock to seven o'clock p.m., 3212... Wait!" Kermit gasps, pausing mid-sentence.

"What is it?" Arvolin asks, following her daughter's gaze.

"They put the wrong street," Kermit shrieks. "Look! It has 3212 North Whittier instead of Newstead! Where did they get Whittier from?" Her heart pounds in her ears. *Whittier? Whittier? How could they make such a mistake?* All of the work, the planning, the hours her friends have spent addressing invitations—it all feels wasted. It is not just a typo; it is a disaster. A single, small mistake could be the end of everything. Tears well up, hot and heavy, blurring the headline on the page.

"I don't know, baby," Arvolin replies, gently patting her daughter's shoulder.

"And there's no telephone number," Kermit adds, feeling overwhelmed. "There's no way they can call to get the right address." She frantically flips through the remaining pages, pursing her lips. "Maybe they reprinted the ad with the right address somewhere else."

After reaching the last page, she starts over, meticulously scrutinizing each section again. "Oh, Momma, what am I going to do? The open house is in two days," she sniffs as her face flushes with growing irritation.

"We'll figure something out," Arvolin says.

Kermit wipes her eyes with the back of her hand. "I need to call Gus," she says. "I need to call *The Argus,* too. I wonder what time they close?" she adds, checking her watch.

Turning towards the backyard, she shouts, "Time to come inside. Line up!"

A few preschoolers groan as some gradually stop their games. "You said we had more time," Hugh whines, tossing a ball to his brother.

"It's time to line up," Kermit repeats, tucking the newspaper under her arm. She carefully descends the stairs, wrings out the washcloth, and tosses the ice water onto the grass. "Hurry up," she snaps as she climbs back to the porch, the children trailing behind her.

Arvolin takes the bowl from her daughter and guides the children into the house. As they cross the threshold, she wipes their faces and hands. "Is Whittier even a real street?" she asks.

"I remember seeing it somewhere, but not sure where," Kermit replies. She turns to the page with *The Argus*' masthead and locates their phone number. Crossing into the kitchen, she removes the telephone receiver and dials. "I just can't believe this," she moans as fresh tears form.

***

Dark gray clouds threaten rain the following afternoon, driving temperatures ten degrees cooler. From her metal porch chair, Kermit anxiously peers down Newstead Avenue while Arvolin watches her sons inside. When Augustus' car pulls to the curb, she grips the chair's arms and rises to her feet. After smoothing the wrinkles from her rose-colored skirt, she pulls on her white gloves and grabs her beige purse and tote bag from the table.

"He's here," Kermit calls through the doorway.

Hugh and Augustus Jr. rush to her, and she kisses each boy's forehead. "I'll see you all later," she adds, closing the front door as Augustus arrives at the porch. Swinging her purse onto her forearm, she hands him the tote as he helps her down the steps.

After guiding Kermit into the passenger seat, Augustus climbs behind the wheel and asks, "You ready?"

"Uh-huh," Kermit responds. She retrieves a street map from the glovebox and opens it. "You know where you're going?"

"I think so," Augustus says as he pulls away from the curb. At the end of the block, he turns right, slowly cruising down Ashland Avenue. As he approaches an intersection, he pauses to read the street sign before crossing to the next tree-lined block of brick homes. "Vine Grove, Clarence, Marnice..." he recites as Kermit traces her finger along the map.

"Right," Kermit concurs. "After Lambdin here, you should have about five more blocks to go."

"Okay," Augustus says, maintaining his measured pace. After crossing into the next block, he slows to a stop as they approach a group of white children playing baseball in the street. He sighs and pauses, waiting to see if they will yield to the car. When the children continue their game, Augustus taps lightly on the horn. None of them move, merely turning their heads to assess the car's passengers.

"Be careful, Gus," Kermit whispers, her voice tense. She glances nervously at the houses lining the street and protectively strokes her stomach. "You don't want to rile them up or have their parents come out here."

"I know," Augustus replies, briefly checking his rearview mirror for an escape route.

After a few more seconds, the children scatter onto the sidewalk, clearing the way. Augustus drives past slowly while they peer inside the car. Kermit watches intently from the corner of her eye for any sudden movements, but the children simply rush back to their positions and resume their game.

Kermit glances through the back window to ensure no one follows them. "Thank God," she exhales, turning back to the map. They cross an alley, then pass a string of red brick homes with one painted white.

"Alright, it should be coming up next after Rolla."

As Augustus is about to turn, he suddenly slams on the brakes and extends his arm in front of Kermit to prevent her from lunging forward. "Sorry, didn't realize this is a one-way street," he says, steering the car back into the lane. "I'll need to go to the next road and come around."

Augustus circles the block, turning onto Fair Avenue, then Labadie. "Whittier, finally," he says as he makes a right turn. He parks behind a car and glances at the houses on either side of the street. "The even numbers are on the right side," he says, pointing through the windshield.

"Okay, I'll check the addresses as we go up the street," Kermit says, refolding the map and returning it to the glovebox.

As they cruise by red brick duplexes and single-family homes, a light shower begins to fall. Girls playing hopscotch squeal and dash into the rain. Enjoying the cool September day, some residents tend to their yards while others relax on their porch under metal awnings. A few pause their Saturday activities to watch Kermit and Augustus pass by.

"I didn't realize Whittier was in a white neighborhood," Kermit says. "I don't see any of us out here."

"Uh-huh," Augustus agrees. "Are you still checking the house numbers?"

"Yes. We haven't gotten to 3212 yet," she replies. "This one's 3124."

"Huh," Augustus says, checking the house numbers on the left. "We're almost back on Ashland Avenue." He turns on the windshield wipers to clear the spray of raindrops off the car window.

"We're coming up on the last house on the right side," Kermit says, pointing. When the car drives past the front of the house, she adds, "It's 3134." She turns to read the remaining addresses on the left side as Augustus parks in front of the last house on the block.

"So, there is no 3212 North Whittier," Augustus says. "This is the last house, and it's 3147." He glances at Kermit, who stares back blankly.

"There's no 3212," she finally repeats. "I thought I could convince who-ever lived here to post a flyer on their door in case people come here for the open house." Kermit removes a handful of flyers from her tote bag. She flips through them, then places them on the seat. "But there is no such address. Of course, I didn't realize they would be white people living here. They probably wouldn't agree to do it anyway." She sighs and leans back in her seat. "*The Argus* really put me under a barrel with this."

"I'm sorry," Augustus says, rubbing his wife's shoulder. "Look, maybe we can get someone to be here tomorrow. If anyone comes looking for 3212 Whittier, they could let them know the paper printed the wrong address."

"Who would do something like that?" Kermit asks. "I need all the people helping out at the open house."

"Let me find someone," Augustus says. "Let's get back home."

***

Once communion is served on Sunday morning, the deacon opens the floor for announcements from the congregation. Kermit makes her way to the front of the sanctuary and shares the details of Tiny Tot's Open House. Following the service, she greets members outside the church, where late summer temperatures linger around seventy degrees. While Augustus takes their sons to the car, Kermit spends time answering questions and distrib-uting flyers before heading home to prepare for the event.

An hour before the opening, Kermit slips into a sapphire seersucker dress that flows over her pregnant frame. Augustus stands before the bathroom mirror in his royal blue suit, wrapping a blue paisley tie around the starched collar of his white dress shirt. Hugh and Augustus Jr., dressed identically in newsboy caps, blue and white striped vests, navy collared shirts, and velvet pants, watch their father intently.

Augustus wraps the leather camera strap around his neck and carries the wooden Tiny Tot Nursery sign outside as his sons hurry to keep up. He places the sign at the bottom of the steps and positions his boys on either side.

"Stay here while I take your picture," Augustus instructs. Taking a few steps back, he focuses the lens and waves at his sons. "Hey, Hugh and 'Gustus Jr., look at Daddy."

As he snaps the shutter, Augustus Jr. turns to watch Geraldine pull up with her husband Leonard and their two sons. After exchanging greetings, Geraldine shepherds all four boys inside. Augustus speaks with Leonard, who departs for Whittier Avenue to redirect any visitors misled by *The Argus'* misprint. Just as Augustus heads back inside, Lulu appears from next door with her three-year-old twins.

9-2-1951 Augustus Jr. and Hugh Hill at Tiny Tot Nursery

Kermit hugs the women at the door, a nametag and pink carnation affixed to the shoulder of her dress. "Thank you so much for helping out," she says, distributing badges and corsages to her volunteers. "Your children can go into the playroom," she says, gesturing to the doorway adorned with pink and blue crepe paper streamers. "The parents will be able to see our new play equipment in action," she chuckles. "Lulu, since Elizabeth and Milton have been with us from the start, I've assigned you in here so you can answer questions and supervise the children."

"Sounds good," Lulu replies, ushering the six toddlers into the playroom. "Come on, children."

Kermit escorts Geraldine into the main room, decorated with crepe paper streamers and a "Tiny Tot Nursery Open House" banner strung across the wall. A floral centerpiece sits atop a white lace tablecloth, its aroma filling the air.

"You'll be in here," Kermit says. "I'll need you to help serve the guests and make sure the refreshments are refilled."

"My usual," Geraldine chuckles. After searching the kitchen, she asks, "Where's my helper?"

"Momma's upstairs resting up," Kermit laughs. "She's been busy helping us get ready all afternoon, so I told her to take a break." She starts to leave, then adds, "Make sure to tell Leonard thanks for being our lookout on Whittier. I'm still so mad at the paper, I could spit."

"Don't worry about it, he's happy to help," Geraldine says. "Put it out of your mind and just focus on your open house."

As the clock ticks past five o'clock, a solemn hush settles over the nursery. A glass cylinder on the foyer table fills with scrolled registration forms, each secured with a pink or blue ribbon. In the playroom, preschoolers color quietly at child-sized tables as Lulu praises their artwork. From her rocking chair, Arvolin peers through the front window, watching for pedestrians approaching the house. Geraldine restraightens the napkins, cups, and plates lining the refreshment table, then ladles punch into the crystal bowl.

In the hall, Kermit adjusts Augustus' white boutonniere and pocket square. "You ready?" she asks.

"Uh-huh," he replies. "How are you feeling?"

"Nervous," Kermit whispers. "What if nobody shows?"

"They will," Augustus says, squeezing her hand reassuringly. "Stop worrying."

Twenty minutes later, a hesitant knock interrupts the quiet anticipation. A young family peeks through the Venetian blinds covering the door's glass panel. Kermit welcomes the first visitors to the open house, introducing herself as Tiny Tot's Director and identifying Augustus as the owner. After presenting her friends and the other preschoolers, she leads the guests on a tour of the nursery. She invites the couple's children to play with toys while showing the parents the cots, lockers, and lunchroom.

When she reaches the kitchen, two more families arrive. Augustus guides the second group around the facility, following the same routine as Kermit.

Before long, more than forty prospective parents, toddlers, grandparents, and older siblings fill the nursery. Kermit emphasizes Tiny Tot's warm and engaging environment for young children, while Augustus showcases the new equipment and furniture. As the playroom becomes increasingly crowded with children, Lulu enlists Geraldine's help to manage the chaos, leaving Arvolin to take over the refreshments.

As the nursery opening event winds down, preschoolers weave through their parents, who gather around the refreshment table. Kermit collects enrollment forms and payments at the kitchen table, finally succumbing to her aching legs. As the sun dips into the lavender horizon, Leonard returns from Whittier Avenue and joins the fathers smoking in the backyard.

By that evening, Tiny Tot enrolls fifteen new children for the upcoming fall school year.

BLIZZARD

November 5, 1951

Powdery snow swirls from dense gray clouds on Monday afternoon, blanketing St. Louis in white. Blizzard conditions intensify throughout the day as temperatures hover below freezing. Pedestrians, bundled in thick winter attire, tackle icy sidewalks while automobiles skid across slick roads. As the storm rages into the evening, an inch of snow accumulates over the midwestern region.

In the Central West End neighborhood, snow-capped evergreens create a picturesque winter scene in the 1,300-acre Forest Park. Across the street, whipping winds whistle through Kermit's window at St. Louis Maternity Hospital. A nurse taps on the open door before wheeling in a crib carrying a newborn, his writhing almond-toned limbs visible through the white slats.

"Good evening, Mrs. Hill." The nurse's voice carries warmth despite the cold pressing against the windows. "It's someone's dinner time." She tenderly lifts the baby from the mattress into Kermit's outstretched arms.

"Well, hello there." Kermit coos as she cradles her son. "How's mommy's baby boy?" She glances back at the nurse. "Weren't you in the delivery room with me yesterday?"

"Yes, that's right. I'm Grace."

"Nice to meet you again."

"Baby Hill appears to be doing well." Grace smooths the newborn's wispy black curls. "Have you and your husband decided on a name?"

Kermit glances at the door before whispering, "My mother-in-law wants us to name him after her husband, Elmer. I'm not crazy about the name, though."

"So that's your husband's father?"

315

"Stepfather." Kermit shifts the baby's weight. "His mother married him when Gus was seven or eight, so he's really the only daddy Gus knows."

Grace wiggles the infant's hand playfully. "Hey there. What do you think, little one? Would you like to be called Elmer?" The two women laugh as Kermit begins to nurse her newborn. The nurse crosses the room to draw the curtains against the swirling snow.

"It's really coming down out there. I hope Gus makes it here in all that snow."

Grace returns to Kermit's bedside and tucks the blanket under the mattress. "I'm sure he'll be okay. Where's he coming from?"

"Downtown, at the post office." Kermit glances back at the door. "He should've been here a half-hour ago."

The nurse places a stethoscope in her ears and buckles a blood pressure cuff around Kermit's upper arm. She squeezes the rubber bulb until the cuff inflates, then places the stethoscope bell under the strap. While listening to Kermit's pulse, she slowly deflates the cuff.

"Your blood pressure's still a little high, but it's improved from yesterday." Grace charts the reading, then inserts a thermometer inside Kermit's mouth.

Augustus enters with melting snow collected on the brim of his navy fedora and shoulders of his tweed coat. "I'm here." He removes his hat and brushes snow from his coat.

"Oh, Gus, I've been so worried," Kermit mumbles around the thermometer.

"Mrs. Hill, you need to keep your mouth closed until I get your temperature."

After draping his coat and hat on the chair, Augustus crosses to Kermit, his boots squeaking across the tiled floor. "The roads are really getting bad." He kisses her cheek and combs through her hair with his fingers. "It's supposed to keep snowing into tomorrow." Kermit nods, obediently waiting until the nurse finishes taking her temperature. He glances at his youngest son. "How's he doing?"

"He's doing well," Grace responds before Kermit gets a chance. After checking her watch, she removes the thermometer. "Okay, you can go ahead and talk now. I'll leave you two alone for a while." She refills the water cup before slipping into the hall.

Kermit glances at their infant as the baby snuggles closer. "He doesn't seem to be hungry." She gently nudges him to nurse. "I guess he's just sleepy." She lifts the newborn to her husband. "Maybe he wants his daddy."

"Are you sure it's okay?" Augustus asks, gingerly cradling their son.

"Yes. Just be careful." Kermit caresses their infant's head while he squirms in his father's arms.

"I spoke to Momma today." Augustus begins. When their son starts to fuss, he tries gently rocking the baby while pacing around the room. "She's asking if we've decided on a name."

Kermit sighs as she leans back in her bed. "Well, I guess I'm okay naming him after your stepdaddy. I also like the name DeWayne, like Geraldine's son."

"Uh-huh. DeWayne's nice too. How about Elmer DeWayne?" When the infant's wails intensify, Augustus returns him to Kermit's arms.

"Elmer DeWayne." She repeats the name, shushing their newborn until he eventually quiets.

As snow flurries float past the window, Kermit and Augustus take turns cradling their son while discussing their day. When Grace announces that visiting hours have ended, Augustus leaves to find an additional two inches of snow covering his car in the hospital parking lot.

The massive storm continues to rage through the following day, grinding the city to a halt. Snow drifts bury abandoned cars while accumulating on windowsills and rooftops. Overburdened tree limbs snap under the weight of heavy snow, downing electrical wires and plunging the city into darkness. With roads becoming impassable, schools, businesses, and public transportation shut down.

Nervously glancing at the intensifying snowstorm outside her window, Kermit sits up in bed and dials the operator. When her mother answers, she greets, "Hi, Momma. How are y'all doing in all this snow?"

"It's just crazy out here. Never seen so much snow in my life!"

"That's for sure. I don't know how we're going to ever dig out of it." She shivers and covers her shoulders with the blanket.

"Augustus took the boys out in the yard yesterday before it got so bad."

"Are they behaving?"

"You know how they are." Arvolin chuckles. "How's my newest grandson?"

"Good. They just took him back to the nursery a few minutes ago. Listen, put the boys on the telephone before I let you go." She hears her mother calling her sons to the phone, the sound of their approaching footsteps growing louder.

"Hi, Mommy!" Her sons shout in unison.

"Hello." Kermit chuckles. "Are you two behaving for Grandma?"

"Yes," they drag out the word in a singsong voice.

"Happy birthday, Hugh. Sorry Mommy couldn't be there for your fourth birthday."

"That's okay. Am I getting a gift?"

"Yes." Kermit laughs, wiping away a tear. "Both you and 'Gustus Jr. are getting a present when I come home in a few days. I'm bringing you a new little brother." Kermit listens for her sons' response, but only hears static on the line.

"They're gone," Arvolin chuckles, breaking the silence. "Back to playing with their toys."

"Oh well. I guess they'll meet Elmer DeWayne when we get home. Who knows when that'll be. This snow's showing no signs of stopping." She strains to view the street through her window, then relaxes on her pillow. "People are driving too fast on Kingshighway and crashing into each other. I told Augustus not to come by tonight because it's too dangerous, although I'm so lonesome here by myself."

"I know, baby, but it's probably for the best. A lot of cars are getting stuck in all this snow along Newstead."

"Uh-huh, it's like that out here, too. Guess it's a good thing the baby came when he did because no one can get to Tiny Tot now anyway."

"Yes, it turned out to be a blessing. You don't need to worry about the nursery being closed because practically everything's shut down now. No one can even get to work, so they're not trying to get here. Take it easy and just focus on that new baby boy."

"Okay, I will. Take care, and hopefully I'll see you soon."

As night falls, over ten inches of snow accumulate during the second day of the blizzard. Most businesses close for the week as they begin the slow process of recovering from the record-breaking storm. On Thursday, daytime temperatures rise above freezing, enabling the city to plow the melting snow. By Saturday, temperatures reach the sixties as patches of grass emerge through dwindling snowbanks.

As dusk settles over Newstead Avenue, Augustus brings Kermit and Elmer DeWayne home to the delight of Arvolin and their older sons. Arvolin rushes to hold the baby, while Hugh and Augustus Jr. crowd around for a glimpse. That first night back, Kermit lies awake with Elmer DeWayne tucked against her chest, listening to a lone cricket chirping somewhere in the quiet house. Beside her, Augustus snores softly, one hand resting on the blanket near her arm. She strokes the baby's back, watching the slow rise and fall of his breath.

Over the weekend, Kermit adjusts to caring for a newborn and two active toddlers while recovering from childbirth. She contacts Tiny Tot parents, informing them that the nursery will reopen on Monday. Additionally, Kermit arranges for a rotating schedule of aides to help with the preschoolers until she can get back on her feet.

Monday morning, steady rain washes away the residual traces of last week's snowstorm as parents drop off their children at Tiny Tot. Cradling Elmer DeWayne, Kermit greets the families at the door while Arvolin directs the preschoolers into the classroom. At lunchtime, Kermit puts her infant down for a nap in the back room. As she turns to leave, he starts gurgling and fussing. She waits by the door, hoping he will quiet himself.

"Shh." Kermit soothes, creeping back to the crib. When Elmer DeWayne begins coughing, she places him on her shoulder. "What's wrong, baby?" She gently pats his back while softly bouncing him. Once he calms down, Kermit carefully returns him to the cradle. Quietly, she steps backward, keeping a watchful eye on her son.

When she reaches the doorway, Elmer DeWayne starts crying and hiccupping between gasps. Hesitating once more to see if he will stop, she eventually gives in to his cries. She swaddles him in a blanket and carries him into the next room.

When Arvolin spots them, she asks, "What happened? I thought you were letting my grandson take a nap."

"I don't know what's going on. He's been fussy and crying a lot lately. He only stops when I pick him up."

"My grandson's got you wrapped around his little finger already." Arvolin chuckles, stroking his back. "Don't spoil him now."

"I won't." Kermit settles into a chair, gently rocking him until he falls asleep.

The following day, Kermit and Augustus struggle to comfort their nine-day-old son. Although Elmer DeWayne appears content while being held or sitting upright, he grows increasingly agitated whenever he lies down to sleep. They try various strategies—propping him up on pillows, adding and removing blankets, and moving his crib into different rooms—but nothing stops his persistent cries. Exhausted, Kermit ultimately resorts to sitting up in bed, attempting to sleep while cradling her newborn.

On Wednesday, Kermit lifts her wailing infant from the cradle in their bedroom and notices an unusual bluish undertone to his typically light-beige face. She pushes up his sleeves and discovers his hands and feet have the same discoloration. As she examines him more closely, his skin color gradually returns to normal.

After soothing Elmer DeWayne, Kermit attempts to return him to his crib. Her concern deepens as she watches his fussing resume and his skin once again take on a bluish hue. "Momma... Gus!" She shouts, rushing into the hallway of their second-floor residence. "Come here! He's turning blue."

Augustus bolts out of the bathroom. "What'd you say?"

"What's going on?" Arvolin asks, joining them from her bedroom.

"Look!" Kermit lifts Elmer DeWayne's arm. As tears well up in her eyes, she repeats, "He's turning blue!"

All three examine Elmer DeWayne, taking turns stroking the newborn's arms, legs, and face.

"Where?" Augustus asks. "I don't see it."

"It happens whenever he lies down." Kermit leads them into their bedroom. "Look." She gently returns their newborn to the cradle, with her husband and mother leaning in for a better look. After a brief silence, Elmer DeWayne starts to fuss. When he begins sobbing, Kermit shouts, "See? Look at his skin." She retrieves their crying son and holds out his hands.

"He *is* turning blue." Augustus strokes Elmer DeWayne's cheeks.

"Something's wrong with him!" Kermit cries, tears flowing down her cheeks. "I knew something's not right."

"It'll be alright." Augustus comforts his wife while holding back his own tears. "I'll call the doctor." He hurries down the hall to use the kitchen phone.

"His color is returning." Her mother rubs his arms and kisses the baby's forehead.

The women follow Augustus into the kitchen, listening as he speaks with the doctor. When he hangs up, Kermit asks, "What did he say?"

"He wants us to bring the baby to St. Louis Children's Hospital in the morning. It's next to the maternity hospital on South Kingshighway. I'll call the post office and let them know I'm taking tomorrow off." Unable to sleep, Kermit and Augustus keep a vigilant watch over Elmer DeWayne, who spends a fitful night in his mother's arms.

Five days after being discharged from the maternity hospital, the anxious parents return to the Washington University Medical Center's children's hospital at daybreak. The medical staff immediately rush their inconsolable son to intensive care, leaving Kermit and Augustus frantic in the waiting room. Following the physician's orders, a nurse carefully places an agitated Elmer DeWayne in a white crib enclosed by a transparent plastic tent. When she switches on the oxygen tank, its loud hum startles the infant, who immediately begins to wail. She attempts to soothe his muffled cries, but her words drown in the machine's persistent drone.

As night falls without any news, a hysterical Kermit sobs in Augustus' arms. Two hours later, a gray-haired man in a white coat enters the waiting room. "Mr. and Mrs. Hill? I'm Dr. Goldring. I've been attending to your son, Elmer."

"How's he doing?" Kermit asks, wiping her nose with a handkerchief.

"He's stable at the moment. We believe Elmer's suffering from cyanosis, a severe congenital heart defect that prevents oxygen from reaching his bloodstream. It's commonly referred to as Blue Baby Syndrome, which is why you observed a bluish tint in his skin color."

"Can it be treated?" Augustus asks, glancing at his wife as he grips her shoulder.

"He's in an oxygen tank now that helps him breathe. We've administered an EKG, which examines his heart." The doctor flips through the chart before continuing. "We're consulting with a pediatric surgeon at Johns Hopkins..."

"Surgeon? But he's only eleven days old!"

"Yes, that is one of our concerns, too. The surgeon at Johns Hopkins successfully operated on an 18-month-old with Blue Baby Syndrome. The little girl has survived for seven years now, but so far, no one has performed the surgery on an infant Elmer's age."

"Can he live without the operation?"

"Unfortunately, we cannot definitively predict his chances of survival with or without an operation. We are administering various medications and will carefully monitor his response. Given his young age, his prognosis remains uncertain."

Kermit cries out, burying her face in Augustus' shoulder as he comforts her. He pulls his wife closer, then dabs the tears falling down his cheeks.

"I'm so sorry. I wish I had better news. We'll continue to monitor Elmer's progress over the next few days and consult with other pediatric specialists for possible treatments."

A cry builds in Augustus' throat, but he chokes it back. "Thank you," he manages. "Can we see him?"

"Yes, of course. Come this way."

Dr. Goldring leads Kermit and Augustus to the intensive care unit on the second floor of the hospital. As they navigate through the facility, piercing sounds of children in distress overwhelm them. Rows of cribs, encased in transparent plastic tents, line the room. Catching sight of their sobbing newborn, sealed within a plastic bubble, sends fresh tears streaming down the parents' faces.

Kermit gasps and brings a hand to her mouth. "Can I hold him?" she asks, her voice muffled behind her fingers.

"I'm afraid not right now. He needs to remain isolated for the first 24 hours to prevent potential infections while he receives oxygen. You can speak to him; it might comfort him to hear familiar voices. Speak loudly so he can hear you over the medical equipment."

Kermit and Augustus approach their son's crib gingerly, peering through the plastic opening. A nurse enters the unit and quietly consults with Dr. Goldring before he departs. She smiles encouragingly at the parents as the rhythmic clanking of oxygen respirators reverberates off the walls. The teary-eyed parents exchange glances before Kermit steps closer to the crib.

"How's my baby boy?" Kermit calls out, her voice raised to be heard over the medical equipment. "Don't cry. Mommy and Daddy are here." She nods at her husband to speak.

"Hi, Elmer DeWayne. It's Daddy. Be a big boy for me now."

They watch their son intently, who appears unresponsive to their words. At the nurse's prompting, Kermit and Augustus take turns consoling their son. Eventually, Elmer DeWayne drifts into a restless sleep while his parents keep vigil. When visiting hours end, the nurse escorts the exhausted couple out of the intensive care unit at midnight.

The following morning, the bleary-eyed parents hurry to their car as fresh snow flurries drift onto the streets and sidewalks of Newstead Avenue. In silence, they drive through The Ville neighborhood, both unable to voice their fears about their son's condition. Kermit blankly stares at the passing houses as Augustus cruises along the snow-covered Kingshighway Boulevard. He pulls into the hospital's circular driveway and gets out to open Kermit's passenger door.

"Call me at the post office if anything changes." Augustus helps Kermit out of the car. She nods as they kiss, and he watches as she disappears into the hospital.

Kermit spends the day at Elmer DeWayne's bedside, praying for the doctors to save his life. Despite her comforting words, her son's irritability continues to worsen, his piercing cries unrelenting. Growing increasingly despondent, she finds the nurses have no guidance to offer regarding his condition. That afternoon, Kermit observes a physician making rounds in the intensive care unit, wearing a white face mask and latex gloves. As he approaches her infant's crib, she recognizes him as Dr. Goldring.

"Is there any news on my son?" Kermit asks, rubbing her bloodshot eyes.

"I'm about to examine him now." Dr. Goldring removes the oxygen tent, causing Elmer DeWayne's cries to intensify. The pediatrician lifts the child's arms and legs, observing as they fall limply onto the mattress. When he drags a metal instrument along the soles of Elmer DeWayne's feet, the infant shows no response. Finally, the physician turns the infant on his stomach to take his temperature.

As Dr. Goldring starts to replace the oxygen tent, Kermit asks, "Can I hold him now?"

After briefly considering her request, he says, "Just for a moment." He removes a white gown and a pair of latex gloves from the medical cabinet and hands them to her. "Put these on first. Nurse, please drape this over Mrs. Hill."

"Thank you, doctor." She quickly pulls on the gloves and raises her arms as the nurse wraps her in a medical gown. Tears slide down her cheeks as she gingerly holds Elmer DeWayne while shushing him. "Don't cry. Mommy's here. Mommy's here." As Kermit rubs her newborn's back, her eyes widen and her voice strains. "He's so warm... and his body is stiff."

"Yes, that's enough now. He needs to get back on oxygen therapy."

Reluctantly, Kermit releases her son to the pediatrician, who places the crying newborn under the plastic tent. "He... he doesn't seem to be getting better."

"We're doing everything we can. He's at one of the best children's hospitals in the country, for whites and Coloreds."

Kermit nods, but his words only deepen her suspicion of inferior treatment. She stiffens, wondering if their baby's prognosis would be different if their skin were a different color. She locks eyes with the doctor, willing him to fight for her son as if he were his own.

"Then why isn't he getting any better?" Kermit stares at her son.

"Well, little Elmer is very sick for such a young child. In addition to his Blue Baby Syndrome, he also appears to be suffering from an infection called E. coli Meningitis. We're administering antibiotics to treat his fever and stiffness. We hope this will help him, but it's too soon to tell. He may need to have heart surgery, but he's not strong enough now."

"No." Kermit cries, shaking her head. "How could this happen? Did he get an infection from the cold and the snow?"

"No, it has nothing to do with the weather. Some babies are just born with birth defects."

"Then was it something I did when I was pregnant?"

"Not at all. As I said, some babies are just born with these complications. Don't blame yourself for this."

Kermit stares through the plastic layer at her weeping son, his limbs thrashing violently. "Okay. Thank you, doctor. I need to call my husband." With the nurse's help, she removes her gown and mask, then leaves to find a phone.

The next day, freezing temperatures turn the snow-covered roads into sheets of ice as Kermit and Augustus make their way to the hospital. Upon arrival, A nurse rushes toward them.

"It's Elmer," she says quietly. "He's taken a turn for the worse."

Panic-stricken, the parents rush to the intensive care floor, only to be directed to the waiting room.

Hours pass without a word. Kermit and Augustus alternate between praying for their youngest son's survival, weeping uncontrollably, and pacing anxiously.

"I can't bear this waiting." Kermit stares at the clock. "It's almost noon, and nobody's told us what's going on."

"I know, baby. The doctors must still be working on him. We just need to be a little more patient."

"I'm afraid, Gus. I've been hearing crickets since we brought him home."

Augustus studies his wife before responding, "You can't think like that." He shudders and pulls her closer.

"But they say if you hear crickets chirping, it means death's coming. I'm afraid it means Elmer DeWayne—" Unable to continue, she collapses into Augustus' arms, sobbing.

Half an hour later, an unfamiliar physician approaches. "Mr. and Mrs. Hill? I'm Dr. Shermon."

"Where's our son?" Augustus asks, his voice tight. "Where's Elmer DeWayne?"

Dr. Shermon shakes his head. "I'm so sorry. Your son suffered a seizure earlier this morning. We performed emergency surgery, but despite our best efforts, we were unable to resuscitate him."

Kermit gasps. "Oh no. No! Please, God, no!" She collapses into a chair as Augustus catches her, wrapping his arms around her. Their sobs break the silence of the waiting room, the sound thick with anguish.

"Again, I'm so sorry," Dr. Shermon says gently. "Baby Elmer passed away at 12:18 p.m."

"No. Not my precious baby," Kermit cries. "There has to be something else you can do."

"I'm afraid we've done all we can," the doctor replies. "I'm deeply sorry for your loss." He rests a hand on Kermit's shoulder. "When you're ready, a nurse will take you to see him. I've also contacted the hospital chaplain, should you wish to have final rites performed."

Tears streak down Augustus' face as he holds his wife close. Wordlessly, he nods at Dr. Shermon, who steps away, leaving them in their grief.

When the chaplain arrives, he leads the couple in a prayer for acceptance of God's will in taking their youngest son. In the days that follow, Kermit and Augustus undertake the heartbreaking task of informing family and friends of their loss, receiving telegrams of condolence in return.

Overwhelmed by grief, they close Tiny Tot for the week while they prepare for their 13-day-old infant's burial. They meet with their neighbor, Mr. Baker, who operates the WJ Baker & Son Funeral Home across the street. Three days after Elmer DeWayne's death, the Hill family, surrounded by family and friends, lays their youngest son to rest at Saint Peter's Cemetery on the Tuesday before Thanksgiving.

The sky stays gray the day they bury Elmer DeWayne. Wind cuts through their coats as the small white casket is lowered into the frozen ground. Kermit clutches Augustus' arm, her gloved hand trembling. Hugh and Augustus Jr. stand on either side of Arvolin, too young to grasp why everyone is crying but quiet all the same. As the pastor's voice carries over the cemetery, Kermit closes her eyes. She can still feel Elmer's warmth in her arms.

First Fashion Show

April 8, 1952

A classroom full of toddlers cheerfully sings "Happy Birthday" as Kermit enters carrying a coconut cake decorated with three flickering candles. She carefully places the round dessert before a grinning Augustus Jr., whose silver, cone-shaped party hat bobs to the song. Four-year-old Hugh sits beside his brother, matching his attire in a gray Oxford shirt and pants. Colorful balloons tied with ribbons adorn the child-sized chairs, and blue streamers spiral from the ceiling. Once they finish singing, the group erupts in applause, eagerly awaiting the sweet treat.

"Happy Birthday, 'Gustus Jr.," Kermit says, kissing her youngest son's forehead. "Make a wish and blow out your candles."

"I wish for the biggest piece of cake," Augustus Jr. announces, rising to his feet. As he takes a deep breath, the boy across the table blows out the candles before he gets a chance. "Hey," he protests. "I'm supposed to do that."

"It's okay," Kermit assures him while patting his shoulder. "You'll still get the biggest piece, birthday boy." She cuts the cake into slices and distributes them to the excited children. As the celebration winds down, tears well up in Kermit's eyes, and she quietly slips out of the room before anyone notices.

In the four months since losing Elmer DeWayne, Kermit finds special occasions the most emotionally draining. Thanksgiving passes in a blur—she remains numb from burying their newborn two days prior. Finding joy during Christmas proves equally difficult in a home filled with memories of their loss. Though she tries to put on a brave face, her mind inevitably wonders what their family would be like if their baby had survived. When she attempts to discuss these feelings with her husband, Augustus typically withdraws, overwhelmed by his own grief. Compounding her stress, Kermit is pregnant again, intensifying her fears of losing another child.

Mercifully, Tiny Tot provides a much-needed distraction, and Kermit immerses herself in it with passion. She schedules weekly meetings with other childcare directors to gather tips and explore fundraising opportunities. After integrating early childhood education into the curriculum, eager parents respond, doubling enrollment to nearly twenty preschoolers.

Later that afternoon, a woman with mahogany skin enters the nursery, her buttercup topper coat swaying gracefully over a tan print dress. She approaches a teacher who diligently coordinates the steady stream of parents arriving to collect their children.

"Good afternoon," the visitor says. "I'm here to see Mrs. Augustus Hill."

"Just one moment, I'll take you to her," the teacher, Mary Smith, responds. Mary is the sister of Kermit's classmate at Dunbar, Elsie May Whitlow, now married to their friend Elihu Moore. Elihu and Kermit met while participating in choir and pep squad together. After buttoning a girl's jacket, Mary waves as the child leaves with her father. "See you tomorrow," she calls out warmly. Turning to the guest, she adds, "Okay, follow me."

The two women walk through a playroom filled with toddlers and their parents until they find Kermit and her sons in the kitchen, which doubles as an office. Augustus Jr., still sporting his birthday hat, and his brother toss balloons in the air.

"Hi, Virginia," Kermit greets, standing to shake her guest's hand while stepping into her beige pumps from under the table. "I'm so glad you could stop by." As the teacher turns to leave, Kermit calls, "Thank you, Mary. I'll see you Wednesday." After introducing her sons, they quickly scamper off to the front playroom.

"You have such a lovely setup," Virginia says, removing her coat and gloves.

"Thanks. I was so impressed with Pyramid Nursery Institute when I visited last month. And seeing those adorable boys and girls model at your fashion show was absolutely precious."

"Well, that's why I'm here," Virginia says. "After we met, our Mother's Club wanted to invite Tiny Tot to participate this year."

"Really? That's wonderful," Kermit exclaims. "Our parents will love seeing their children in a fashion show."

"It's going to be at the Phyllis Wheatley YWCA on Locust Street. The date's set for Sunday, the twenty-seventh, at four in the afternoon."

"This month?" Kermit asks, flipping to the date on her desk calendar. "That's... just a little over two weeks."

"I know it's fairly soon, but the kids just have to walk across the stage as the MC describes their clothes."

"Okay, that sounds doable," Kermit agrees, jotting down the information in her calendar.

"After our Mother's Club finishes ironing out the details, I'll give you a call next week with what type of outfits your children will be modeling."

"This will be so much fun."

The women rise as Virginia slips into her coat. Kermit guides her guest back through the playroom, now empty, except for her sons. After the two women embrace, Kermit opens the door and feels the cool evening air prickle her skin.

***

On a chilly Good Friday afternoon, gray overcast skies mute the afternoon sun as preschoolers hunt for Easter eggs in Tiny Tot's backyard. Bundled in heavy coats and wool mittens, the children struggle to gather the eggs into wicker baskets in the unseasonably forty-degree temperature. When raindrops begin to splatter across the yard, their teacher, Mary, gathers them to retreat indoors.

Once the children finish eating their collected eggs, Kermit arrives to prepare the toddlers for their modeling performance. "Hello, boys and girls," she begins. "Is everyone ready for the Easter Bunny on Sunday?"

The class roars, their high-pitched squeals reverberating against the walls. "Inside voices," Mary commands, placing a finger to her lips.

"I have some exciting news for you today," Kermit continues. "You'll be modeling in a fashion show! We're going to practice in the afternoons to get ready." With the teacher's help, she lines the boys up on one side of the room and the girls on the other. "Hugh and Elizabeth, I want you to go first. Everyone else sits cross-legged on the floor."

While the rest of the class watches, Elizabeth approaches tentatively as Hugh arrives, sucking his index finger and thumb. "Stop sucking those fingers," his mother directs, removing them from his mouth. She crosses the room, demonstrating how to walk tall. Pairs of children practice with Kermit as M.C., introducing them and describing their outfits.

Every afternoon, Kermit practices with the children, setting up the runway outside whenever the weather permits. When Virginia calls to say the children will dance too, Kermit adjusts, improvising steps from her dancing days at the Savoy. The busy schedule helps to keep her mind occupied, but her grief still lingers, thwarting the joy in her eyes. At the end of their final practice, Kermit grabs the camera to capture the dancers posed in their positions.

***

On the day of the performance, Kermit and her family pile into their Chevrolet as temperatures soar to eighty degrees. As Augustus maneuvers through the neighborhood, Kermit rolls down the window to ward off the carsickness brought on by her pregnancy. When they arrive on Locust Street, Augustus parks beside a three-story red brick building with a U-shaped design. Joining the stream of other visitors, the family climbs the concrete stairway to the entrance. They pass between stone columns and continue through the red doorway, which is adorned with a broken scroll.

At the registration table, Kermit spots Virginia, welcoming visitors and participants as they arrive.

"We're so glad you included Tiny Tot," Kermit says. She turns and waves her family over. "Virginia Gilbert, this is my husband, Augustus Hill, and my mother, Arvolin Bland. You met Hugh and 'Gustus Jr. when you came by the nursery school."

After Virginia distributes the programs, she directs them down the hall to the auditorium.

Kermit says, glancing at her bulletin. "Tiny Tot Fashion Show? It's named after us?"

"I knew you'd ask that," Virginia chuckles. "It's just a happy coincidence that Tiny Tot is the name of your nursery school. But in this case, 'tiny tot' refers to the little ones in our fashion show."

"Oh, I see," Kermit chuckles, moving to the auditorium.

At four-fifteen in the afternoon, Virginia introduces the radio personality to the packed audience. Kicking off the show with an early morning scene, two Beaumont High School students take turns describing toddlers waking up in their stylish pajamas. Kermit watches in amazement as Virginia expertly directs forty preschoolers in a fashion production. Once the children modeling street clothes exit the stage, Janet Dailey, the KSTL radio personality, sets the scene for the next act by sharing a story about school days.

When Virginia calls for the play clothes models, Kermit gathers her eight Tiny Tot preschoolers. She inspects their appearance, straightening bow ties and repositioning hats while giving last-minute instructions. "Remember to dance just like we practiced at Tiny Tot. Instead of me, the two nice teenage girls by the stage will tell everyone about your beautiful clothes. Make sure to smile at your parents in the audience."

When Virginia calls for Tiny Tot, Kermit leads her young performers to the platform steps, whispering last-minute instructions as they stroll across the wooden floor in pairs. As the amplified record player's needle crackles through the speakers, she quietly takes her place next to her husband and mother in the audience.

The girls twist in their pastel ruffled dresses, their black patent-leather shoes tapping to the beat. Boys twirl their dance partners in graceful circles, performing synchronized step-tap movements. At the song's conclusion, the young models take their bows and excitedly parade off the stage. A proud Kermit leads the audience in a standing ovation, celebrating Tiny Tot Nursery's first public performance.

Baby Girl

October 14, 1952

Kermit screams as agonizing pain grips her body. Her jet-black hair, soaked with perspiration, clings to her almond-toned face, and her moss green hospital gown adheres to her protruding stomach. She struggles to find a more comfortable position on the thin mattress, but the straps holding her legs in the stirrups prevent movement. When the pain subsides, she pants in relief, but before she can catch her breath, another, more intense wave engulfs her.

"Oh Lord, please make it stop!" Kermit's repeated pleas echo off the stark white tiles surrounding her.

"You're doing great, Mrs. Hill," the nurse encourages, dabbing Kermit's forehead with a washcloth, leaving traces of taupe makeup on the white cloth.

"Noooo. It wasn't this bad before," Kermit moans, tears streaming down her face. "Why did Gus get me pregnant again?"

As the physician extracts the newborn's head with forceps, Kermit yells from the overwhelming pressure gripping her abdomen. "Stop! That hurts! I'm not ready yet!"

"Almost there," the physician says, gently guiding the emerging body. "Give me another big push."

"Ouch! Why did you do that?" Kermit yells at the doctor. "I told you I wasn't ready!" Despite her protests, her body takes over as a surge of energy provides the final effort of release. The piercing cry of her baby instantly redirects her thoughts.

"Congratulations, Mrs. Hill," the physician says. "You have a little girl."

"Is she okay?" Kermit asks desperately. "Does she look... blue?"

"Just a minute," he responds over the wailing infant.

A harsh clank resonates through the delivery room as he drops the forceps into the white metal bowl at his feet. He clamps and cuts the umbilical cord, separating the shivering infant from her mother. The physician and nurse work together to clean the newborn and clear her airways.

"I'm checking her vital signs now," he says, swaddling the baby in a blanket.

The physician gently places the newborn on the sterile sheet covering the warming table to conduct a thorough Apgar assessment. First, he watches closely as the baby's pale bluish-purple complexion gradually transitions to a healthier light beige. With his stethoscope lightly pressed against her delicate chest, he listens to the baby's heartbeat, checking the rhythm against his watch's second hand. Satisfied, the doctor moves on to the respiratory exam, observing the rise and fall of her chest between every sputtering cry. Finally, he prods the infant's flailing limbs, checking their reflexes and muscle tone.

While the physician evaluates the baby, the nurse releases Kermit's aching legs from the restraints. She cranks the metal wheel at the head of the delivery bed, slowly elevating Kermit's upper body from the reclined birthing position. From her new vantage point, she finally catches a glimpse of her newborn across the room. Holding her breath, Kermit props herself up on her elbows to conduct her own visual assessment of her crying child.

After another agonizing sixty seconds, the doctor gently slides the newborn into Kermit's outstretched arms. "Here you go, Mrs. Hill. Your baby appears healthy. We'll conduct follow-up Apgar tests every five minutes to ensure her condition remains stable."

"Thank you, doctor," Kermit exhales, cradling her baby to her chest.

"I'll let your husband know you have a new baby girl," the nurse says as she wheels Kermit out on her bed.

***

After a three-day stretch in the eighties, daytime temperatures plunge into the low forties for the first time in over a week. A brisk afternoon breeze carries colorfully painted leaves past Tiny Tot's rectangular windows. In the classroom, chattering toddlers fidget at round tables, trying to guess the lunch menu by the aromas. Mary and Louise, the part-time aide Kermit hired during her last trimester, move around the tables, scooping fruit cocktail and peas onto every plate. Sitting at the kitchen table, Kermit pours milk from a glass jug into a row of paper cups.

Running footsteps stomp on the porch as Hugh, Elizabeth, and her twin brother, Milton, burst through the front door, sending a cool gust of wind into the foyer. Following closely behind, the twins' mother steps in and quickly shuts the door. Excited to see his older brother, Augustus Jr. jumps up from his table to greet them.

"Thanks, Lulu," Kermit waves to her neighbor, then addresses the new arrivals. "How was kindergarten?"

The three grin at each other, then chant in unison, "Good."

"You know I want to hear more than that," Kermit smirks. "But right now, go and wash your hands and find a seat."

She finishes pouring while Lulu helps the kindergarteners hang up their jackets and wash up. Augustus Jr. trails behind them, then nudges another student out of her seat so he can sit next to his brother. Elizabeth and Milton find seats at the next table.

"I'll be back to pick you two up later," Lulu says, kissing her children goodbye.

After rinsing the empty milk jugs, Kermit quickly steps outside to leave them on the porch for the milkman. Another burst of cold air escapes inside as Kermit closes the door. She approaches Mary, who cuts tuna fish sandwiches diagonally. "Remember, we're going over the early childhood materials today," she says.

"Okay," Mary replies as she distributes sandwich halves onto the youngsters' gray plastic plates. Once everyone is served, she leads them in grace. "God is good..."

"God is great," the children join in with a sing-song tone. "Let us thank Him for our food. By His hands, we must be fed. Give us, Lord, our daily bread. Amen."

As they begin eating, a piercing, rhythmic cry fills the room. Kermit hurries to a white wicker bassinet trimmed in pink and blue ribbons.

"Shush," Kermit soothes, picking up her fourteen-day-old infant. "Mommy's here." After wrapping her daughter in a pink wool blanket, she positions her on her shoulder and returns to Mary. "I'll be back down at nap time." She gingerly climbs the wooden stairway to her family's living quarters upstairs.

In her bedroom, Kermit fluffs the pillows before carefully propping herself against the headboard. After giving birth to three sons, she is overjoyed to finally have a little girl to doll up in dresses and ribbons. Having allowed Augustus to name their three boys, she insists it is her turn to choose their next child's name. During a spring trip to Chicago to visit her cousin, Cora Mae, they discover they are both expecting. They agree that if they have girls, they will each name their daughter Patrice.

In July, Cora Mae delivers the first Patrice in the family, and two weeks ago, Kermit delivered the second. For her middle name, she chooses to honor her mother with Arvolin, though the birth certificate arrives with it misspelled as Arvolyn.

As she nurses her infant, her thoughts inevitably return to the loss of their son, Elmer DeWayne, who died at just thirteen days old. Though Patrice shows no signs of illness, Kermit remains vigilant over her daughter, fighting the urge to become overprotective. Each night, she falls to her knees, praising God for blessing her family with three healthy children.

Kermit returns downstairs as the children settle in for their nap. She pulls the Venetian blinds' lift cord, casting shadows across the room. After delicately lowering her sleeping daughter into the bassinet, she picks it up by the wooden handles and navigates through the maze of cots. She instructs the aide to watch the napping children, then signals Mary to follow her to the kitchen.

"I'll be right there," Mary whispers. "Let me get something to write with first." She retrieves a notepad and pen from her bag in the closet. As Kermit places the bassinet on a nearby table, Mary takes a seat.

Kermit joins Mary, grabbing a folder with a sketch of children on the cover. Speaking quietly, she starts, "I'm so glad Virginia Gilbert told me about this Conference on Nursery School Education." She removes colorful flyers and brochures from the folder and spreads them across the table. "You remember Virginia from Pyramid Nursery?" Kermit says, setting out the flyers. "She invited us to that Easter fashion show last spring."

"Of course," Mary replies, glancing at the materials. "They're hosting the Halloween party this week."

"Oh, right, that reminds me," Kermit says. "Make sure to tell the parents to bring their children's costumes on Friday." She shuffles through the pamphlets, searching for the syllabus. "The conference was held on the Maryville College campus. I'd say about two hundred nursery school workers attended in all. Virginia brought some of her staff there, and I hope to bring you next year."

Throughout the nap period, Kermit reviews the conference materials while Mary takes notes. When they finish, she returns the items to the folder and hands it to the teacher.

"Let me know if you have any questions, and we can schedule another session whenever you like."

***

In the glow of Friday afternoon sunlight, preschoolers decked out in Halloween attire pile into two cars in front of Tiny Tot. Mary takes the wheel of one car while Louise holds Patrice in the passenger seat of the other. In their mother's back seat, Hugh and Augustus Jr. sport red felt cowboy hats with leather whipstitching around the brim. They squint through black Lone Ranger masks secured with elastic bands around their closely cropped hair. Next to them sits Elizabeth, her mahogany face covered with a painted mask of a blonde, white princess wearing a crown and red lipstick. Milton wears a white clown costume with a large, frilled red collar, and an exaggerated frown painted in lipstick circles his mouth.

The toddlers' excited squeals raise the volume inside both vehicles as they drive down Newstead Avenue for the mile-and-a-half trip. As Kermit crosses Enright Avenue, she gestures past the aide with one hand while keeping the other on the wheel. "Gus and I used to live on this block before we had to leave," she chuckles, pointing toward the passenger window. "Before we moved in, our landlord told us from the jump he didn't allow any children. Then I got pregnant, and we had to quickly find a new place before he found out."

"No kidding," Louise replies with a laugh.

At the next street, Kermit turns left onto Delmar Boulevard and parks in front of Pyramid Nursery Institute, with Mary pulling up behind her. Stepping out into the humidity of the seventy-degree weather, Kermit instructs the teachers to leave the children's jackets in the cars, so their costumes are fully visible. Cradling her daughter, she quickly counts the toddlers gathered along the sidewalk sprinkled with gold fallen leaves. Laughter and chatter grow louder as they ascend the stairs of the brick structure with its wide, white-trimmed arched window. A handwritten note taped to the door's glass pane reads "Welcome to the Festival of Pomona. Door is unlocked." Kermit twists the brass knob, pushing through the entrance to lead them inside.

Pint-sized witches, skeletons, bandits, and ghosts scurry about the packed room, guided by a handful of adults. A sweet aroma of gingerbread mingles with candy corn, filling the air, while soft music plays from a vinyl record on a mahogany phonograph. Wearing a red dress and floral wreath atop her black hair, Virginia Gilbert approaches Kermit.

"Welcome, Tiny Tot," she greets, kissing Kermit's cheek. "Oh, will you look at that precious baby."

"Thanks," Kermit replies. "I love your costume. But tell me, what is the festival of Pomona about?"

"Pomona's the Roman goddess of fruit," Virginia gestures to a poster depicting a similarly dressed woman, picking an apple from a tree. "It's rumored she started the Halloween tradition of bobbing for apples."

"Huh," Kermit says. "You learn something new every day."

Virginia chuckles. "Go ahead and let your little ones enjoy the party and get something to eat. We're going to parade around the block in about a half hour."

"That's a nice idea," Kermit says. "They can show off their costumes." She directs the teachers to divide up and take the preschoolers around. Mary leads her group to the station with a metal tub of red and green apples floating in water, while the others pin the tail on the donkey. Once they finish playing the games, they enjoy hot dogs, applesauce, and hot chocolate.

Half an hour later, Virginia claps loudly as she spins around from the center of the room. "Attention, attention," she commands. "Everyone, line up in twos for the Halloween parade. Make sure you get a bag for your tricks and treats."

Screams bounce off the walls as the children scamper to the door. Pyramid staff distribute brown paper bags to each child lined up along the wall.

Kermit guides her Tiny Tot students into formation with the others. "Settle down, boys and girls," she instructs. Approaching the teachers, she adds, "I'm going to stay here with Patrice, but make sure you keep up with all our Tiny Tot children." She finds her sons in line and says firmly, "You two better behave and stay with the group."

"Yes, Mommy," they respond.

As Kermit rocks her infant in a porch chair, the costumed assembly of sixty children and parents strolls down the stairs in pairs. Motorists beep their horns and neighbors wave as the trick-or-treaters promenade down the street. In her Pomona costume, Virginia leads the parade through two square blocks, guiding them along Pendleton, Washington, and North Taylor Avenues. As the sun sinks toward the horizon, they return to find Kermit pacing anxiously on the sidewalk, frantically scanning both directions of Delmar.

"Thank goodness," Kermit sighs in relief as she spots the parade approaching. She quickly counts her Tiny Tot youngsters to ensure all have returned safely.

Her preschoolers swarm around her, exclaiming, "Mrs. Hill, look!" as they proudly show their bags filled with treats received from the surrounding neighbors.

"That's wonderful," Kermit smiles, trailing them up the stairs.

Inside Pyramid Nursery, a parent threads the 8mm film through the Kodak Instamatic projector, while a teacher removes the poster from the makeshift screen wall. Children sit cross-legged on the floor, snacking on moist gingerbread squares and cups of warm apple cider. The room gradually settles into hushed anticipation as the lights dim and the projector beam cuts through the darkness. Both big and small guests watch entranced as the magical world of "Snow White and the Seven Dwarfs" flickers before them. As the festivities conclude, Kermit vows to host her own Halloween party at Tiny Tot the following year.

FASHION REVUE

March 12, 1953

Following a morning of scattered showers, patches of blue sky break through the passing gray clouds. Raindrops cling to Tiny Tot's windows, filtering sunlight that shimmers across the hardwood floor. Rising humidity stifles the air throughout the first floor. Kermit switches on the black cast-iron fan, its swirling contour blades secured within a steel wire cage. The hem of her emerald swing skirt ruffles in the gentle sweep of the oscillating breeze.

Mary cleans sticky juice and spilled milk off tabletops as the toddlers finish their afternoon snack. The teacher retrieves rectangular tin boxes from the shelf and places them at the center of each table. She pulls off the lids, revealing crayons with worn-down points and frayed paper wrappings labeled Prussian Blue, Flesh, Indian Red, Maize, and Spring Green.

"Today is Mr. Hill's birthday," Kermit announces while passing out coloring paper to the class. "So, we're making him cards wishing him happy birthday."

"Are we going to have cake and ice cream?" Augustus Jr. asks his mother, prompting enthusiastic "oohs" from the children.

Kermit chuckles, gesturing at the leftover orange slices on the counter. "You all just ate."

"Please, Mommy!" her son begs as the others chime in.

"Well, if you do a good job on Mr. Hill's birthday cards," Kermit offers, "I'll see if I can find some vanilla cups in the icebox."

The children erupt in cheers. Kermit enters the adjoining room; shadows cast by drawn curtains. She tiptoes across the burgundy rug to check on her five-month-old daughter, asleep in a white wooden crib. Patrice snores softly on her stomach, her pink and green blanket kicked aside by twitching feet.

Kermit carefully replaces the wool cover without disturbing the napping infant. She gazes longingly at her daughter's wisps of thin black strands, wondering if Patrice will ever grow enough hair to tie up with all the ribbons she bought after finally having a girl.

A knock at the front door prompts Kermit to slip out of the room, easing the door shut behind her. Victoria Chapman peers through the glass frame, water dotting her olive trench coat and plastic hair bonnet.

"Come in out of the rain." Kermit gestures toward the foyer. "I'll take your coat, and you can—"

"Mommy!" Sharon squeals when she spots her mother. "Look, we're making birthday cards." Her three-year-old daughter rushes to hug her and present her drawing.

"Very nice, honey," Victoria responds. "Now go back and finish up while Mommy meets with Mrs. Hill." She gives her daughter a quick embrace and nudges her into the classroom.

While Victoria removes her coat, more parents arrive. "You get the door, Kermit. I know where to hang up my coat."

A light mist sprays the neighborhood as Delores Roberts and Lulu Scott arrive, sheltered beneath black umbrellas.

Kermit greets them, then waves them inside. "I'll take your things. Say hello to your children and meet us in the back." She deposits their rain gear in the hall closet and heads to the makeshift office behind the playroom.

Once the mothers settle, Kermit pours freshly brewed coffee from a polished aluminum electric percolator, its strong aroma filling the room. "I'm so happy you all agreed to join Tiny Tot's Parents' Club." After filling their cups, she serves slices of cinnamon crumb cake on matching plates encrusted with a thin blue band.

"Thank you for inviting us," Lulu replies, as the others express their agreement. "I think this is a great idea." She wipes her mouth with a napkin before cautiously sipping her steaming coffee.

"I can't believe it's already been two years since Tiny Tot opened," Kermit observes. "Now that we're growing, it's a good time to get the moms and dads involved." After pouring her own cup, she sinks into the empty chair between Victoria and Delores.

The Parents' Club's first order of business involves electing officers. As the newly elected president, Victoria calls the meeting to order while

Delores, the recording secretary, takes notes. They assign members to committees focusing on early childhood curriculum, fundraising, and school programs.

"Sharon really enjoyed modeling in the Pyramid Nursery's fashion show last year," Victoria says.

"Elizabeth did too," Lulu agrees. "I think even the boys got a kick out of it."

"Why don't we do our own show this year?" Victoria suggests. "Wasn't it around Easter last time?"

"That's right," Kermit interjects. She rises to remove the wall calendar, then flips to the following month. "Easter is April fifth this year, but I don't want to compete with Virginia's event. How about the following Sunday, the twelfth?"

"Sounds good," Delores says as the others agree. "Maybe we could even reciprocate and invite some of Pyramid's children to model in our show."

"I like that idea," Kermit says. "Virginia has been such a help with getting Tiny Tot started."

Following a spirited debate, the committee decides to use the fashion show as a fundraiser to purchase musical instruments for Tiny Tot. Lulu, their new Treasurer, will prepare a budget detailing expenses and ticket costs for their next meeting. After considering various program themes, they settle on the classic nursery rhyme, "There Was an Old Woman Who Lived in a Shoe." To cut down on costs, the treasurer suggests they only choose clothing options that most preschoolers already have in their possession.

Members agree to encourage all parents to sell tickets within their church, social club, and neighborhood networks to promote the event. Additionally, Kermit will place an ad in the St. Louis Argus newspaper two weeks prior to the production. When the Parents' Club meeting adjourns, Tiny Tot's first Fashion Revue is scheduled for the following month.

Augustus climbs the stairs to their second-floor residence as daylight fades into the horizon. Hugh and Augustus Jr. rush to meet their father at the landing with an assortment of birthday cards spilling from their arms.

"Daddy, look," his oldest son says as he awkwardly tries to contain the array of crayon renderings in his grasp.

"Daddy, look," Augustus Jr. parrots. He thrusts the papers in the direction of his father as they float to the floor.

"These are all for me?" Augustus asks, crouching down to help his youngest son collect the scattered drawings. "Thank you."

Kermit joins them, holding their baby on her shoulder. She turns Patrice toward Augustus. "Say, 'Happy Birthday, Daddy.'"

Augustus chuckles, shaking their daughter's hand.

"I see you got your birthday cards from the Tiny Tot children," Kermit nods at the papers.

"I did," Augustus says. "What a nice surprise." He kisses his wife, then carries his collection to the table.

After putting away his things, he returns to examine his birthday greetings, reacting to each child's unique designs.

"How does it feel to be thirty-six?" Kermit asks, patting his shoulder. "You feeling Ol' Father Time catching up with you?"

"Ha! Don't worry, you'll be here in a couple of years," Augustus teases, wrapping his arm around her waist. "But I can feel I'm not as young as I used to be."

"Isn't that the truth," Kermit chuckles.

Arvolin emerges from her bedroom, her silver hair neatly parted into braids. "Happy Birthday, Augustus," she says as she crosses to the kitchen counter, her white floral dress swaying with each step.

"Thank you, Momma Bland," he replies.

Lifting the circular metal cover, Arvolin presents a chocolate cake to her son-in-law. "I made you a special dessert for your birthday."

"That's so nice. I can't wait to try it," Augustus says in delight.

Over Augustus' celebratory dinner, Kermit shares the news about Tiny Tot's Parents' Club meeting and their plans for a fashion show next month. Once the children are bathed and tucked into bed, she and Augustus retire to their bedroom, continuing the discussion about the nursery school.

"I'm seeing more preschool programs sprouting up," Kermit says, slipping a white embroidered nightgown over her head. "At that nursery education conference, they said more parents want to give their children a head start on kindergarten—and they're willing to pay extra for it." She removes her clip pearl earrings and gold braided watch, then crawls into bed, leaning against the headboard. "We could fill another classroom if we had it."

"Huh," Augustus grunts, stepping out of his pinstriped gray pants and hanging them up. After putting away his clothes, he joins her in bed, the mattress squealing under the added weight. "Are you thinking about bringing in more children?"

"I really think there's a need," Kermit says, twirling sections of her black strands into curlers. "I get more and more calls asking if we have openings. But if we do, we'll need more teachers—and maybe a bigger space."

Augustus lights a cigarette and inhales deeply, surrounded by swirling gray smoke. As he exhales, the air grows stale with the stench of smoldering tobacco. "Let's make sure we're not losing money first," he says, flicking specks of white ash into the glass dish on the nightstand. "You should start keeping track of what we collect and spend on Tiny Tot to see if we're actually turning a profit."

"That makes sense," Kermit says. "The fashion show is a fundraiser, and we could plan more benefit events, too. We might even be able to raise tuition next school year." She opens the nightstand drawer and pulls out a memo pad and pen to jot down notes.

"I can check with the credit union at the post office about applying for a business loan," Augustus says, taking another drag. "If we can show a profit, we might be able to get enough to build a larger space."

"Great," Kermit says. "Let's remember to talk to Mr. Thomas about it when he does our taxes on Saturday."

Over the next four weeks, Kermit works with volunteers recruited by the Parents' Club to prepare for Tiny Tot's Fashion Revue. After an artistic parent designs the background set for the show, the children spend mornings coloring and decorating it with tissue paper. In the afternoons, the youngsters rehearse their skit, practicing their roles as the old woman and her many children who live in a shoe. When the Parents' Club learns that the Phyllis Wheatley YWCA has recently renovated its gym, they secure the location to host their production.

On the Friday before the event, Kermit grabs her jacket when she spots the paper boy leaving the Scott's porch. She steps out onto the stoop and rubs her arms to warm up in the chilly April breeze. He tilts his cap as he reaches her walkway, and she responds with a quick wave. He adjusts the beige sack swung around his neck before retrieving the rolled-up weekly publication.

"Thanks," Kermit says, replacing the paper in his hand with coins for payment.

Back inside, she hangs up her jacket and then takes *The St. Louis Argus* to her desk. Scanning the pages, she locates the ad at the bottom of the "Activities in the Women's World" section. Below is an article about featured soloist Frankie Weathers, and next to a photo of a couple's spring wedding, the same announcement printed in last week's edition reads:

Don't Miss
The Tiny Tot's Fashion Revue
Sun., April 12
From 1 to 2
New Gym Phyllis
Wheatley YWCA
2709 Locust

Kermit scrutinizes the text for errors, still reeling from the fiasco two years ago when the paper mistakenly printed the wrong address for Tiny Tot's open house. Once she confirms the ad's accuracy, she calls the committee members to share the news.

Starting alphabetically, Kermit searches through the Southwestern Bell St. Louis directory until she locates the Chapman family's phone number. She spins the dial of the rotary eight times, then listens to the series of clicks and static while the line connects.

"Hi Victoria," Kermit says when the club president picks up. "Have you seen the ad in the Argus today?"

"No, not yet," she replies, her words echoing in the receiver. "How does it look?"

"Pretty good," Kermit says, glancing back at the paper. "It's on page eight again, in the Women's World section. It's close to the front, so I hope it brings more people on Sunday."

"I'm sure it will," Victoria says. "I stopped by the YWCA last weekend to see their new gym. They've really improved the space since we were there last year with Pyramid's fashion show."

"Yes! Gus and I dropped by after church on Sunday," Kermit says. "Are we ready with everything else?"

"Last I heard, we're on track," Victoria says. "I'll see you then."

Leaving the crisp, earthy air beneath overcast skies, Kermit carries Patrice into the Phyllis Wheatley YWCA, where the distinct scents of fresh varnish and paint greet them. Hugh and Augustus Jr. rush ahead into the bustling hall, while Augustus assists Arvolin up the stairs, gently holding her hand as she steadies herself with the black iron railing.

In the entryway, Kermit greets the nursery school's children and their parents roaming in the foyer. They dote on her newborn, outfitted in a pink wool pant set trimmed with white piping and blue embroidered butterflies. She catches up with their boys at the reception table, where Lulu collects and sells tickets to Tiny Tot Nursery's premiere performance. She guides their sons away from the reception table with her free hand while nodding hello to her neighbor.

Augustus and Arvolin join them, and Kermit leads her family into the renovated gymnasium. Toddlers dart across the stage against the backdrop of an enormous shoe-shaped house in a flower garden made of colorful tissue paper. Delores ushers her son, Michael, and the other wayward children off the stage with the teacher's assistance. The statuesque Victoria towers over parents in the committee as she reviews the afternoon's schedule. Kermit crosses to greet the women, her beige high heels rhythmically clicking on the new hardwood floor.

"You're back," Victoria says, her eyes briefly flicking to her clipboard. "I think we've checked off almost everything on your list while you were out."

"Good," Kermit says. "We can start lining up the children."

She moves through the crowd, personally thanking friends, former co-workers, and social club members for their support. As more people fill the gym, she joins Mary and the Parents' Club committee to lead the young performers backstage. When the lights dim, a hush falls over the audience as excited family members settle into their folded chairs.

Out of the darkness, a girl's high-pitched voice breaks through the quiet hall. "There was an old woman who lived in a shoe." A brilliant spotlight illuminates the life-size nursery rhyme scene. Center stage stands five-year-old Elizabeth, who introduced the show, her cherubic, bronzed face framed by the stiff brim of a beige poke bonnet. While she clutches a doll on her shoulder, she chases shrieking toddlers around the gold-buckled shoe house.

As the audience laughs, Kermit transfers her daughter to her mother's arms before slipping behind the podium. "She had so many children, she didn't know what to do," she chuckles, pausing as the preschoolers return to their opening positions. "Thank you for coming to Tiny Tot Nursery's Fashion Revue." Waves of applause sweep through the patrons as the youngsters grin and clap along.

Glancing over her shoulder to confirm the first model, Kermit begins, "Making his fashion debut is Milton Scott Jr." From the sidelines, Mary coaxes him to step forward. "Young Master Scott commands the runway in a white and green striped collared shirt. His stylish lime suspenders cross in the back and button to his shorts. Completing his fashionable look are black leather slip-ons, accented with gold buckles." After Kermit describes the last model's outfit, the preschoolers stroll off the stage to the sounds of applause.

Furniture scrapes across the platform as Augustus arranges oak chairs around a small round table for the second act. Mary sets the table while the next group of models scrambles around to find an empty seat. Once everyone settles, Kermit continues, "She gave them some broth and a big slice of bread."

Spurts of laughter spread around the table as Hugh and Augustus Jr. join their classmates in loudly slurping empty bowls and smacking on plastic rolls. After Kermit describes their outfits, the giggling children exit the stage as her husband replaces the dinner props with sleeping cots.

Preschoolers donning footed pajamas and clutching teddy bears drag blankets across the stage. They climb into bed, then yawn with an exaggerated stretch before snuggling under the covers.

"Then kissed them all soundly and sent them to bed," Kermit says.

"MWAH," pantomimes Sharon, the third girl portraying the Old Woman, as she playfully touches each sleeping child's head.

The gymnasium echoes with laughter as the audience rises to their feet in enthusiastic applause. Beaming in the glow of the spotlight, all the performers pile on stage to enjoy their encores. Kermit recognizes her family, the teachers, and members of the Parents' Club for their dedication to pulling off a successful event.

As the fashion revue concludes, elated moms and dads swarm Kermit, eager for a repeat performance of their preschoolers. Others express interest in joining the Parents' Club to plan the next fundraiser for Tiny Tot. Following a brief onsite meeting of the committee, Lulu delivers the proceeds from the event to Kermit. Later that evening, she reviews the event's balance sheet with Augustus, who deposits the funds in the nursery's recently opened Post Office Credit Union account the next day.

Tom Thumb Wedding

October 23, 1953

Burnt-yellow, rust, and olive-green leaves cling to tree branches as a crisp autumn breeze swirls through the Ville neighborhood. Faint traces of golden sunlight sink below the horizon, causing temperatures to drop below fifty on this early Friday evening. Dressed in a jade pillbox hat, tweed swing jacket, and white gloves, Kermit parks on Goode Avenue while her three children play in the front seat beside her. She slips her arm through her purse handle, positions her one-year-old daughter, Patrice, on her hip, then grasps four-year-old Augustus Jr.'s hand. Hugh, two weeks away from his sixth birthday, exits from the passenger side and hurries to catch up with his mother.

Kermit guides her children up the cement stairs of a three-story, red brick home, where three-paneled windows and the doorway are framed with crescent archways. The setting sun casts long shadows on the building's façade while the glass panes reflect the fading amber light. As they arrive on the landing, the distant notes of a classical piano piece float through the black wrought iron security door. Kermit rings the doorbell, momentarily interrupting the music before a woman's voice echoes from within.

"Don't stop," she directs, followed by, "Coming," as the playing resumes.

Following a series of metallic clicks from unlocking the deadbolt, sliding the chain, and turning the handle, a petite woman in a black knit dress and white belt appears, her white-rimmed cat eyeglasses a stark contrast to her dark chocolate features. A hint of lemon wood polish escapes through the entrance, its distinct scent lingering in the cool evening air.

"You must be Kermit," she greets, unlocking the security door and pushing it open.

"Who's that, Mommy?" Augustus Jr. shouts loud enough to be heard above the music swelling louder onto the stoop.

"I'm Alleda Ward Wells," she says with a warm smile, extending her hand to him, who tentatively offers his own. "And these must be your children."

"Yes. So nice to finally meet you," Kermit responds, ushering her boys inside and repositioning her daughter onto her other hip.

Alleda leads them through the dimly lit foyer into the front room, completely absent of typical living room furniture. Instead, three baby grand pianos of mahogany, high-gloss ebony, and white nestle together like puzzle pieces, while an upright oak piano sits against the front wall. At the black piano sits a young man in a navy suit, his warm brown fingers gracefully gliding across the piano keys while his feet expertly shift between the three floor pedals. He flickers them a welcoming smile, his glance lingering briefly before returning his focus to his craft. The elegant melody swells beneath his touch, piano keys simultaneously striking lower bass and upper treble strings, creating symphonic chords. The young pianist's supple wrists move with precise control, his mastery of the challenging composition evident in his flawless classical rendition.

"Mommy?" Augustus Jr. shouts, tugging at his mother's hand.

"Shh," Kermit hisses, quickly pressing a finger against her lips and offering the musician an apologetic look. She points to the upright piano's rectangular bench, directing her sons to sit on its wooden surface. After stashing her gloves in her purse, she props her daughter in a nearby chair. "Watch your sister," she whispers, before stepping closer to admire the inside mechanics of the instrument. While the dynamic piece echoes off the enclosed area, felt-covered hammer heads strike thick gold steel strings, and cushioned damper pads lift above them in perfect harmony. At the end of the musical selection, she applauds, and her children join in, their sporadic claps flat against their tiny palms.

"That was lovely. You are so talented."

"Thank you," the tone of his maturing voice rising and falling like an off-key melody. His hands hover instinctively above middle C on the keyboard, fingers curved in a position of readiness. His brown eyes dart curiously between the three children, his music teacher, and Kermit, assessing the unexpected audience members of his recital.

"This young prodigy is Dingwald Fleary," Alleda beams, her posture straightening with pride. "He's only thirteen years old but can play both the organ and piano like a pro."

Dingwald grins as he stands to shake Kermit's hand, then quickly waves at her children behind her.

"I can already see—I mean *hear*—you're quite good," Kermit says, approaching the teen. "One of my nursery school parents is a member of your father's Seventh Day Adventist church. When she heard I was looking for a pianist for our Tom Thumb wedding, she said I had to hear you play."

"I've been to one of those," Dingwald says with a grin, pushing his glasses up the bridge of his nose. "It's when little kids pretend like they're getting married."

"That's right," Kermit says. "It's our first time doing it, but we're thinking you could be the pianist for the ceremony. We'd start off with some relaxing background music as guests arrive." Holding out her index finger, she starts counting off the songs, extending another finger with each item. "Then the 'Here Comes the Bride' song as the brides—we're having a double ceremony by the way—march down the aisle. During the service, you would accompany the soloists on two songs, and finally, you'd play the Wedding March when the bride and groom leave the sanctuary." Glancing at all five fingers now splayed before her, she laughs softly. "That's five. Now that I say it out loud, it does seem like a lot."

"I think I can handle it," Dingwald says confidently, though his croaking voice appears to contradict him. "I'm familiar with the wedding songs already, but I'll have to check with my parents. They'll be here in a few minutes to pick me up."

"Dingwald's a quick study. I know he'll do an excellent job," Alleda says, patting his shoulder affectionately. "He's the lead pianist in my eight-piano recitals."

"Eight pianos?" Kermit gasps, glancing around at the pianos filling the room, trying to imagine twice this number. "How do you keep track of eight pianos at once?"

"Well, it's actually eight students—two play on each piano," Alleda explains, her voice melodious and warm.

"That sounds like quite a show," Kermit says. "I've got to make sure Gus and I come to your next recital."

"The music festival's held every first Sunday in June like clockwork," she replies, glancing at Kermit's children who fidget on the smooth wooden bench. "Have you thought about signing them up for piano lessons? Your boys are the perfect age to start learning how to play, and your daughter won't be far behind."

"Really? I thought they were too young," Kermit says, picturing her rambunctious sons sitting still long enough to perform at the piano festival.

"Not at all. I open up my studio to new students in the fall, so they can start lessons next September."

The music teacher invites Hugh and Augustus Jr. to turn around on the bench to face the piano, familiarizing them with the ebony and ivory keys and their various sounds. A few minutes later, Reverend and Mrs. Fleary arrive, and Alleda makes the introductions. Kermit expresses admiration for Dingwald's musical talent and requests their permission for him to provide the musical entertainment at Tiny Tot's event.

In the melodic rhythm of his Grenadian, British West Indies accent, his father reminds him, "You already have a lot on your plate, son. This Tom Thumb wedding can't interfere with your high school studies at Sumner, playing at choir rehearsals and church, or keeping up with your piano lessons with Mrs. Wells."

Once Dingwald assures him that none of his responsibilities will suffer, his parents readily agree, exchanging proud glances at their talented son. Working within his busy schedule, Kermit arranges for Dingwald to rehearse with Tiny Tot twice a week for the upcoming month before the November event.

***

Low-hanging gray clouds release intermittent showers for the fifth consecutive day. Rain-soaked brown leaves scatter across the ground, leaving the wet pavement slick in the cooler late November temperatures. While clearing the dinner dishes after church, Kermit glances through the rain-splattered kitchen window, hoping the overcast skies will pass before the afternoon Tom Thumb wedding. At the dining room table, Augustus finishes his coffee in his starched white shirt and blue suit pants, smoke swirling from the lit Camel cigarette between his fingers. Stripped down to their underwear, their boys compete for his attention, voices tumbling over one another about their Sunday School class while their sister babbles, imitating sounds from her brothers.

After quickly cleaning the kitchen, Kermit checks her watch and announces, "Time to go," then drags her two youngest children away from the table as they whine in protest. "Hugh, come on and put your church clothes back on for now. You're changing into a tuxedo at the church." Turning to her husband, she adds, "Gus, we need to leave in twenty minutes."

"Okay," he replies, extinguishing his cigarette in the metal ashtray beside his cup and saucer. "I'll put the things in the car and be waiting out front."

As Kermit hurries down the hall, Augustus stops by the bathroom to check his appearance. He smooths his thin mustache, then brushes the black, wavy curls of his promenade hairstyle framing his copper-toned face. Before heading down the steps, he slips into the bedroom to put on his navy striped tie and suit jacket.

Once the family is dressed, Kermit meets Augustus in the car, holding their daughter in her lap while their sons climb into the back. Moist humidity hangs in the air as Augustus navigates the slippery streets in the midtown Piety Hill neighborhood. Drizzling rain sprays the windshield as he pulls into a parking spot on Garrison Avenue and begins unloading the car. Kermit gathers their children under an umbrella, and they dash toward an imposing stone church with symmetrical gabled entrances. Beneath pointed archways framing vibrant stained-glass windows, they enter through Metropolitan AME Zion Church's crimson double doors, followed by Augustus hauling child-size wedding attire, floral accessories, and other decorations.

Inside the foyer, afternoon sunlight filters through the stained glass, painting faded rainbows across the wall-to-wall red carpet. Three-light brass wall sconces brighten the corridor where they meet the head deacon of the hospitality committee. With his charming baritone voice, he welcomes them into his church home with a broad smile, revealing a gold filling glinting beside his tobacco-stained teeth. With one hand positioned behind his black suit jacket, he directs the family past the sanctuary to the Fellowship Hall, constructed of beige cinder block walls and black tile flooring. A middle aisle stretches from the doorway, separating ten rows of twenty tubular metal folding chairs on either side and leading to a standing speaker, an upright oak piano, and a folding table at the front.

"Here you go. The bathrooms are down the hall," he gestures behind them, his booming voice echoing across the massive space. "Feel free to use any of these rooms on the side. I'll be in the choir room near the entrance until you're ready for me."

"Where should I put these?" Augustus asks, grunting slightly as he deposits the boxes at his feet.

"We can use this room for the girls' dressing room and this one for the boys," Kermit says, pointing to opposite sides of the hall. Following her direction, Augustus places the bouquets and two bridal gowns in the larger room and the boutonnieres and three tuxedos in the other.

As Kermit rummages through the decoration box, Victoria Chapman, Tiny Tot Parents' Club president, arrives with her four-year-old daughter, Sharon, her black hair freshly pressed into tight curls. Victoria removes her black raincoat, revealing a navy dress with a scoop neckline.

"I see you brought some members of the bridal party," she says with a smile. Leaning closer to Hugh, she asks, "Are you ready to act as father of the bride and escort Sharon down the aisle?"

Augustus Jr. giggles, covering his mouth as he points at his older brother gleefully. Hugh glances at Sharon, who hides behind the flowing skirt of her mother's dress. "I think so," he grins. Nervously, he jams his thumb and index finger into his mouth and sucks them, a soothing habit his mother continuously tries to break.

"Well, I'm counting on you to be nice to my little girl," Victoria teases, gently patting Sharon's shoulder. Turning to Kermit, she asks, "What do you need me to do?"

"We're putting the girls in here," she replies, gesturing to the room beside her, gowns neatly hung on clothing racks and floral arrangements spilling out of boxes. "Get Sharon into her dress and veil first, then you can help the other girls get ready as they arrive. Once the ceremony starts, just get them down the aisle."

As Victoria takes her daughter to get dressed, Kermit crosses to the opposite room and turns to her husband. "Gus, take the boys into this room so you can get Hugh into his tux." She nudges their sons toward him before adding, "Some of the fathers are coming to help with the other boys, too."

Their daughter begins playfully drumming the table with her hands, the sound falling flat against the metal surface. Kermit swoops down and grabs the toddler as her pudgy arms and legs fling wildly.

"Stop it," she snaps, firmly restraining her daughter's limbs in her grasp. "I'll take Patrice with me while I set up for the wedding."

She retrieves a roll of white ribbon and scissors from the box of supplies, then heads to the front of the hall, Patrice balanced on her hip.

Anxious parents, excited nursery school students, and their guests begin to fill the hall, their voices creating a growing buzz of anticipation. As they arrive, Kermit directs the pint-sized wedding party to the dressing rooms to prepare for their debut and assigns decorating tasks to members of the Parents' Club. After placing her daughter in a chair, she ties the ribbon into a bow and attaches it to the back of the first seat. Continuing down the aisle, she twists the ribbon until it reaches the next chair, blocking entrance into the row from the center aisle. She repeats this process on both sides of the aisle, reserving the front five rows for participants.

Half an hour before the ceremony, guests occupy all four hundred seats in the Fellowship Hall as the overflow crowd jockeys for position outside the doorway. Kermit stops by the dressing rooms to help Delores Roberts and the other parents' club members zip up toddlers' dresses, buckle shoe straps, and clip on bow ties. She spots her husband struggling to pin a white carnation on their oldest son's tuxedo lapel while he twists and spins around.

"My, you look handsome," she says, straightening the tilting corsage as Hugh grins shyly.

"Are you ready for the floor runner?" Augustus asks, retrieving another boutonniere from the florist's box.

"Not yet. It doesn't roll out until the bride's about to come down the aisle," she replies, checking her watch. "I'm really worried about Dingwald, though. He should've been here by now."

A young man's apologetic voice behind her croaks, "Sorry I'm late, but I'm here now!"

Kermit turns to find the young pianist, flanked by his parents and Alleda Ward Wells directly behind her, all decked out in formal wedding attire. "Well, there you are," she says, her cheeks flushing warmly. "So glad you made it. I was getting worried."

After a quick embrace, she guides them into the hall. "Dingwald, you can go straight to the piano and start playing the reception music we rehearsed." As the teenager hurries to set up his sheet music on the piano rack and push back the key cover, she addresses the others, "I've roped off the front for Tiny Tot, but you three can sit anywhere behind these rows."

A few introductory chords lead into the classical piano notes of "Ave Maria," which hush the noisy conversations and blanket the audience with a serene calm. Kermit takes her place behind the podium in a sleeveless white, beige, and brown color-blocked dress, cinched at the waist with a black sash fashioned into a bow. She welcomes the packed auditorium to Tiny Tot's first Tom Thumb Wedding, thanking the parents' club members for sponsoring the special occasion. As the music plays softly in the background, her subtle nod signals Delores to start the ceremony.

Kermit introduces Gerald Reeves, the wedding usher sporting a navy suit, polished leather shoes, and a white corsage. While Kermit reads off the young wedding guests' names, he escorts Stephanie Powell and Elizabeth Scott to their seats on the bride's side, then Martha Matthews and Milton Scott Jr. on the groom's. To audience applause and gasps of wonder, Kermit announces the four sets of groomsmen in matching black suits as they escort bridesmaids in baby pink taffeta gowns down the aisle. When the couples reach the table, now made up to resemble an altar, they part ways, separating into groomsmen and bridesmaids.

Standing in the position of pastor, the church's deacon reappears, guiding the two four-year-old grooms, Andrew Richmon and Terrell Moss, to the altar in black tuxedos with tails loosely flowing from their jackets. Starting at the hall's entrance, Augustus rolls the white cloth runner down the aisle to the altar, blanketing the linoleum tiles. Kermit nods at Dingwald, who begins the opening notes of the Bridal Chorus, its familiar tune signaling the audience to stand, creating sounds of chairs scraping against the tiles and quiet murmurs across the area.

As Kermit makes her way to the top of the aisle, the young bride-to-be, Sharon, prepares to make her grand entrance, stunning in a white satin wedding gown cinched with a satin bow and puff sleeves. A white tulle veil flows from her perfectly coiffed hair, draping softly behind her. She clasps a bouquet of white flowers with white elbow-length fingerless gloves as her mother watches breathlessly from her bird's-eye view along the aisle.

Gently holding Sharon's right arm is Hugh, portraying the reassuring father of the bride. His black tuxedo and tails are topped by a white bowtie, wing-collared, white buttoned shirt with French cuffs, and his black leather shoes reflecting the ceiling lights.

Standing behind the young father and bride, Kermit whispers in their ears. "You two ready?"

When they give a slight nod, she gently guides them forward, quietly prompting, "Okay, go ahead. Remember to walk slowly on the runner."

The couple takes measured steps down the aisle, following Dingwald's melodic tempo while Kermit watches, nervously clasping her hands. When they reach the altar, Hugh presents Sharon to her intended, Andrew, who takes her arm while Hugh returns to repeat the process.

Dingwald transitions into a new musical key, performing another version of the Bridal Chorus as Hugh arrives to escort the second bride, Sidney Sprull, to her soon-to-be husband, Terrell. Once the brides, grooms, and wedding parties are in position at the altar, the deacon officiates over the mock double wedding. Dingwald's instrumental piece kicks off the ceremony, followed by the best man, Augustus Jr.'s solo, "I Love You Truly." Bridesmaids Carol Ellis, Connie Harris, and Yolanda Powell join in a trio performance of "At Dawning," with Dingwald as accompanist.

11-22-53 Tom Thumb Wedding Hugh Hill, Sharon Chapman, Kermit Hill

The highlight of the ceremony arrives as the deacon announces the couples pretend husbands and wives, replacing the usual kissing of the bride with shaking hands. The uplifting strains of the Wedding March resound through the hall as the audience cheers and applauds the joyous occasion. The newly married couples and their wedding parties ascend the aisle as wedding guests throw rice in celebration.

Augustus emerges from the crowd gathered outside the hall. He slips an arm around his wife's waist, embracing her. "Great job. It was a lovely wedding," he whispers in her ear. "I just have one question. Who's going to clean up all this rice?"

They both laugh as they scan the floor tiles sprinkled with grains of tan rice.

"Live and learn," Kermit says, smiling. "Next time, no rice."

Sweet Birthdays

February 14, 1954

A cloudless cobalt sky allows the winter sun to push temperatures to seventy-four degrees on Valentine's Day, enticing St. Louis residents outside into the unseasonably warm Sunday afternoon. Neighbors lounge on front porches and steps, watching children jump rope and ride bikes along Newstead Avenue. Tiny Tot Nursery, normally closed on weekends, bustles with activity as a steady stream of families flows from the sidewalk, up the pathway, and through the welcoming door to join the festivities.

At the entrance, Kermit warmly greets her guests, her gold jewelry gleaming against the warm almond tones of her skin. Her attire, carefully chosen for the romantic holiday, features a white carnation pinned to her vibrant red and white striped dress. She shifts her weight as she stands, feeling her red shoes tighten around her swollen feet. Next in the receiving line, Augustus stands distinguished in his black pinstriped suit and white boutonniere, a crimson paisley tie, and matching pocket square, adding touches of color. Each visiting family receives a colorful Tiny Tot Nursery birthday card outlining the daycare services, age groups, staff training, and essential contact information for referrals.

Inside the cheerful facility, Tiny Tot's teachers and parents' club members wear red carnations as they chat with families while their children explore the array of shiny toys on display in each room. Walls brightened with hearts colored by the nursery's preschoolers, interspersed with red and white balloons and playfully twirling crepe paper streamers. A white banner draped prominently across the playroom wall announces "Happy Birthday Tiny Tot" in bold red block letters.

As the program begins, Kermit moves to the front of the crowded room, thanking Athenian Club members, Geraldine Williams, and parents for their support. She pauses in front of the birthday banner, welcoming the visitors to Tiny Tot's second birthday celebration, then acknowledges the staff, parents' club officers, and her family members for making this day possible.

"This is actually Tiny Tot's third birthday," Kermit muses, as whispered remarks ripple across the room. "In 1951, I started babysitting four neighborhood children along with my two young sons, and that's how the nursery school was born." A few individual claps turn into a wave of applause that builds across the room, sparking a warm glow of appreciation on Kermit's face. When the ovation subsides, she continues. "Today we're going to celebrate our anniversary with a royal coronation that's even grander than the one held last year for Queen Elizabeth the Second. We will crown the first king and queen of Tiny Tot." While another round of exuberant cheers and applause swells among the audience, Kermit whispers to her husband to start the music.

Augustus removes the black vinyl *Pomp and Circumstance* record from its square cardboard jacket, blowing dust off the surface before fitting its center hole onto the turntable's spindle. He sets the speed to thirty-three and a third rpm, its circular grooves becoming a dizzying pattern in the light as it spins clockwise. In one smooth motion, he cleans the needle with his index finger while carefully lowering the arm onto the outer edge of the rotating album.

Following the crackle of the album's static feedback, the measured beats of the royal march fill the room. The crowd parts down the middle, forming an open path for the upcoming majestic processional. As the music crescendos, a parade of toddlers strolls down the aisle, each boy and girl paired and walking arm-in-arm. Boys in formal black suits escort their partners in white lace dresses, their practiced steps matching the song's deliberate rhythm.

With the teachers' assistance, the couples line up against the front wall, divided into boy and girl rows. The children and audience turn to face the back of the room, anticipating a more elegant appearance. The chords of the royal march swell across the school as Augustus raises the volume. Cloaked in violet blankets that trail majestically behind them, Pamela Campbell and Charles Richard emerge, their tiny heads tilted skyward, indicating their imperial status. The paired preschoolers make their grand entrance, acknowledging their adoring subjects with a royal wave as they promenade down the aisle. When they reach Kermit, she greets them with a demure curtsy, and they both respond with a grand bow. Delores joins Kermit at the front of the room, carrying one pink and one blue paper crown, each covered in glitter that sparkles in the light.

Initiating the monarch recognition portion of the ceremony, Kermit unfurls a beige parchment scroll rolled between two wooden toy drumsticks. "Hear ye, hear ye!" she announces in an authoritative voice that reaches the visitors crowded into the back room. "I hereby present unto you Queen Pamela, your undoubted Queen of Tiny Tot Nursery. Wherefore all of you who have come this day to show your loyalty and service. God save the Queen!" Delores turns over the pink crown to Kermit, who gently lays it on top of Pamela's brown curls, depositing a few shiny specs of glitter in her hair. The first Tiny Tot queen spins on her heels and bows to the crowd, who enthusiastically chant, "God save the Queen!"

As the chants for the first ruler subside, Kermit repeats the proclamation for the king, declaring, "I hereby present unto you King Charles, your undoubted King of Tiny Tot Nursery. Wherefore all of you who have come this day to show your loyalty and service. God save the King!" Taking the blue crown from Delores, Kermit places it on the monarch's tight black curls, pushing it down to secure it in place. He turns to address the spectators as they respond in kind, "God save the King!" bowing at the waist while cautiously holding his crown to prevent it from falling.

The coronation party poses as Augustus photographs the royal court, while amused parents jockey for better positions to see their performing toddlers. After the participants' procession, Kermit awards prizes and certificates to Tiny Tot's longest-enrolled families, youngest and oldest students, and parents' club officers. The recipients graciously accept their gift-wrapped boxes with red ribbons, offering grateful embraces in return.

At the end of the royal ceremony, Augustus rolls out a one-layer rectangular birthday cake on a utility cart, the flames of three candles flickering in the center of the icing decorations. Pupils, parents, and visitors begin a spontaneous round of *Happy Birthday*, with *Tiny Tot* replacing a person's name in the song.

As the guests leave the celebration, Kermit, with her clean-up committee, readies the facility, reveling in the success of the nursery school's anniversary party. She reviews the lessons learned from the day's event, proposing improvements for Tiny Tot's Fashion Review scheduled for April.

As she and Augustus prepare their little ones for bed, they feel confident that the daycare has potential for future success.

***

On the fifth day of Spring, March's brisk temperatures hover around the mid-forties, leaving beads of moisture on the dark green lawn as the sun sinks below the surrounding homes. In the hallway of the Hill's second-floor residence, steam hisses from the cast-iron radiator air vent, releasing waves of heat throughout the home. After dinner, Kermit and Augustus linger at the kitchen table, while Arvolin spends time with her grandchildren before their bedtime. Augustus examines the St. Louis Post-Dispatch newspaper while Kermit reviews the plans for Tiny Tot's fashion review scheduled for next month.

"How's the new job going?" Kermit asks, momentarily setting aside her spiral notepad. "Are you getting more responsibilities with your promotion?"

Augustus folds the headline news section of the newspaper into quarters, then drops it on the floor beside his chair. "It's going okay," he sighs, opening the paper's Editorial section. "I'd hoped to get more assignments with the mail clerk promotion, but it's not the same for Coloreds. At least I got paid more."

"That's something," Kermit says, scratching her scalp with the back of her pen. "Now we finally have enough money to take the kids on vacation this summer. I'm looking forward to it and the kids are too."

"That's good," he agrees, then nods at her notepad. "How's the fashion review coming along?"

"Pretty good," she sighs. "I'm going over the budget from the parents' club. They want to make sure we outdo the one from last year."

"I'm sure you do too," Augustus chuckles, retrieving a pack of Camel cigarettes from his pale blue shirt pocket. After shaking out a cigarette, he holds it between his lips while striking a match to light it, then extinguishes the flame with a flick of his wrist.

"Well, you got me there," Kermit laughs. "We have more children now, so that means we can put on a bigger production." She returns to her task, flipping the pages of her pad. "Oh, did you see the letter from your mother?" she asks, rising to retrieve it from the oak mail holder hanging by the door.

Watching her move across the tile floor, he shakes his head and says, "Uh-uh." She places the envelope in his outstretched hand, and he thanks her. The envelope displays eight purple three-cent stamps across the top and two lime green one-cent stamps on the left. On the top right, below the stamps, "Air Mail Special" is handwritten in pencil, and at the bottom, beneath his name and address, is the scribbled prayer: "Lord Jesus take care of this letter I pray, A-man."

While Augustus reads through four pages of Della's spidery handwriting, Kermit observes him with cautious glances, attempting to interpret the expressions crossing his face. She continues jotting down notes, pretending not to notice her husband's furrowed brow, soft grunts, and sighs as he massages his temples. She suspects her mother-in-law's correspondence contains numerous complaints laced with Biblical scriptures. She also expects Della's letter to include spiteful comments about her—someone who will never be good enough for her only son, even after nearly thirteen years of marriage. Feeling a heated anger rising from her chest up her neck, Kermit's grip on the pen tightens. She sets it down, slow and deliberate, then stands.

"I'm going to put the kids to bed," she says, rising from the table. After tucking her pen behind her ear, she secures her notepad under her arm and leaves the kitchen.

"Okay," Augustus mumbles as he pores over the pencil-written cursive on white and yellow stationery.

After bathing their daughter and putting her down for the evening, Kermit checks on their sons washing up in a shared bathtub. Condensation droplets cover the foggy surfaces of the mirror and window as she scrubs behind their ears in the steamy bathroom. Once they are in their pajamas, she kneels beside them at the bedside and leads them in their nightly prayer.

Kermit enters the dimly lit bedroom with the faint scent of Ivory soap lingering on her moist skin. She finds her husband perched on the edge of the bed in his white sleeveless ribbed undershirt and boxers, his limbs now a lighter shade of beige from months out of the sun. The bedside brass lamp casts a soft glow over the envelope and pages of his mother's letter spread across the nightstand.

As Kermit sinks onto the bed beside him, Augustus folds the letter, slides it into the envelope, and tucks it into the drawer. She leans against the headboard, pulling her legs beneath the yellow top sheet and cotton blanket. After a brief silence, she glances at her husband, unable to hold her tongue.

"Well?" she sighs, crossing her arms. "What did your mother say?"

Augustus glances over his shoulder at his wife and lets out a low, humorless chuckle. He retrieves the envelope, removing the letter and straightening the folded creases. Augustus grunts as he shifts his weight to sit beside her, slipping under the covers while the bed linens rustle around his legs. Organizing the pages, he clears his throat before summarizing her writings. "Well, Momma's saying here how I forgot to send her the ten dollars she'd asked for my birthday."

"*Your* birthday?" Kermit asks, sucking her teeth. "You're supposed to send *her* money on *your* birthday?"

Augustus exhales hard through his nose and rubs the back of his neck. "I told her I'd send it by Tax Day," he mutters. "That was last Monday. I also forgot to send my stepdaddy's gift for his birthday last month."

Kermit shakes her head and sighs, "Does she say when she's coming to town?"

Augustus turns to the next page, scanning the contents. "She wants me to send for her before our vacation. So, I guess she's coming sometime this summer."

"'Send for her' as in pay for her trip?" Kermit asks, glaring at her husband. "Never mind. What else?" She pulls the blanket up to her chin, hiding her twiddling thumbs underneath.

"I didn't understand what she wrote about a 'fleshy heart' and having an operation while we're on vacation. Do you know what that means?" he asks, flipping through the pages.

"A fleshy heart?" Kermit scoffs. "That's what church folks call being kindhearted. That doesn't need an operation. Let me see." Removing the covers from her top half, she offers him her hand. Augustus hesitates briefly, glancing at the sheets of paper, before handing them over.

Kermit turns to the first page, deciphering the cursive and occasional misspellings. "Oh, honey," she says, covering her mouth in stunned surprise. "How could she say these things about you after all you do for her?"

"Don't," Augustus says, looking at his hands. "That's just how she talks. She doesn't mean it."

"What?" Kermit begins reading portions from the letter, mimicking her mother-in-law's southern drawl while struggling through grammatical errors. "'I slaved too hard for my son, for my only son to have such little care and be so little concern about his only mother dear... You makes my heart bleeds the way you are doing your mother dear. Where are you motherly love'?" She glances at Augustus, pausing to see if he will offer an explanation. When he remains silent, she continues quoting Della's letter, returning to her own voice. "She has the nerve to say, 'You won't even help your mother'? After all the scrimping and saving we do to send her all that money, gifts, and train tickets every year? And she claims to have a kind heart?" Turning to her husband, Kermit finds him avoiding her gaze. The letter falls into her lap as she pulls him into a tight hug, tears now rolling down her cheeks. "I'm sorry, honey. I'm so sorry," she soothes, her voice becoming tight and hoarse with emotion. "You don't deserve to be treated like this."

"It's just her way," Augustus says softly, embracing his wife. "Deep down, I know she doesn't mean anything by it."

Kermit releases her embrace, returning the letter to her husband as she wipes away tears. "Look, I know she's your mother and you love her. I guess this is how she... I don't know. I know she loves you, too."

He nods, folding the letter into the envelope and placing it in the nightstand drawer. "Let's just go to bed. We'll talk about it another time."

Augustus kisses Kermit, and they turn off their nightstand lamps, plunging the bedroom into darkness. For the next hour, the bouncing, creaking mattress and rustling sheets from her husband's constant tossing prevent Kermit from falling asleep. As she lies awake, she contemplates how to help her husband cope with such a demanding mother. She sees now what Augustus rarely states aloud—that his mother's love is entangled with judgment, and her approval, for both her son and his wife, remains just out of reach. Kermit cannot shield him from the weight of his mother's words, but she can offer support and a deeper understanding of his quiet burden.

By half past midnight, a weary Kermit shifts her focus to the ambient sounds of the night—the ticking clock on the dresser, the occasional passing car, a distant barking dog. Eventually, Augustus' movements subside, allowing them both to drift into a fitful sleep.

GRADS AND DADS

June 20, 1954

Father's Day arrives amid record heat across the St. Louis community. Stagnant humidity and daytime temperatures hover above ninety degrees for the tenth consecutive day. Heat radiates from cement sidewalks and brick buildings, making each day feel more oppressive than the last. Air quality deteriorates, driving residents indoors to escape the suffocating conditions.

Augustus rises early, uncomfortable in the muggy bedroom. He travels from the sweltering attic to the damp basement, adjusting each fan to its highest speed. When he returns to the bedroom, their two sons and daughter rush to greet him. Pajamas cling to three small sweaty bodies as bare feet patter across the hardwood floor. Each child waves a hand-drawn Father's Day card in his direction while Kermit presents him with a rectangular gift-wrapped box.

"Happy Father's Day, Daddy," they cheer, surrounding him as he crosses the threshold. Small beads of perspiration dot their foreheads as they encircle him, thrusting their cards into his hands.

Augustus squats to embrace all three in a bear hug. "Thank you, thank you," he says as he accepts each child's present.

"Happy Father's Day, Daddy," Kermit chuckles, using her hand as a fan. "You're 'King for a Day!' Here's your special gift." She kisses him and hands him the present, then gestures toward the gold crushed velvet and walnut-framed chair by the window. "Have a seat at your throne and open your presents."

Their three children trail behind him, squirming and shoving on his lap in a competition for the best spot. Kermit watches from the edge of the bed, amused by their battle for their father's attention. Once the children settle, he starts with their twenty-month-old daughter's card. He admires her artwork scribbled in blue, green, and red crayons, then smiles at the toddler peacefully sucking her fingers.

"Is this for me?" Augustus asks, presenting the drawing before her. When she only shrugs and giggles, he says, "Well, thank you. It's very nice."

"My turn," five-year-old Augustus Jr. insists. He points to his crayon illustration of a man outside a house; the boy's squiggly signature runs along the side.

"Very nice," Augustus muses, examining the drawing. "So, this is me standing in front of our house?"

"Uh-huh," their youngest son beams, teasingly sticking his tongue out at his brother.

Patrice loses interest and slides off her father's lap. She climbs onto her parents' bed, lying down for a nap. Augustus reads their six-year-old's card, commenting on his improving handwriting. Finally, he unties the red ribbon to open the box, revealing a tan Oxford shirt and tie with a brown, white, and red swirl pattern.

"Thank you," Augustus says, holding the clothing to his neck. "I can't wait to wear them." He wipes his brow with the back of his hand, then kisses the children's clammy foreheads.

"Do you really like them?" Kermit asks, rising to assess the clothing more closely. "We can always have them exchanged for something else."

"No, I really do," Augustus assures her. "In fact, I'm going to wear them today to church."

"Good," Kermit replies. She stands, moving around the room to corral their children. "We need to get ready too, so we can be on time for the special Father's Day service."

***

The following day, the heat wave continues with no sign of relief as temperatures remain in the nineties. Tiny Tot schedules abbreviated recesses, limiting outside activity in the oppressive humidity. Children amuse themselves by chasing the white, fluffy tufts from poplar trees, watching the seeds glide lazily around the backyard. Once inside, the sweaty toddlers enjoy a refreshing cooling station stocked with ice-cold water, ice cream cups, and chilled face towels.

Kermit meets with the officers of Tiny Tot's Parents' Club in the school's makeshift office, finalizing plans for Sunday's graduation ceremony. She serves sponge cake with raspberry jam filling while her guests sip refreshing glasses of sweet tea. Kermit sticks with black coffee. Harsh afternoon sunlight spears through the window, intensifying the stagnant heat and humidity in the uncomfortable space. A gray Westinghouse fan whirs noisily on the tiled linoleum floor, its spinning tri-blades circulating the thick air around the kitchen. In the nearby classroom, cheerful voices sing nursery rhymes, accompanied by their off-beat cymbals, triangles, tambourines, and drums.

Raising her voice to be heard over the musical instruments, Delores asks, "How many Tiny Totters are graduating this year?" She pushes up the long sleeves of her yellow floral dress, then dries her moist forearms and brow with a handkerchief. Clasping a black pen above her notebook, she prepares to jot down the meeting's minutes.

"I know Kermit's youngest son, Augustus Jr., and my daughter, Sharon." Victoria pauses, then glances across the table at Kermit. "How many more?"

"Four in total are being promoted to kindergarten. We're also letting the four-year-olds participate in the ceremony since they move up to the five-year-old class," Kermit says. "This is our second go round, so we're giving the children a full graduation experience this year." She leans closer, her infectious excitement radiating across her almond-toned face framed with black loose curls. "We've already rented four child-size caps and gowns to be picked up on Friday. But this year, the five-year-olds' teacher, Mary Smith, has selected the top two students in the class to be the valedictorian and salutatorian."

Victoria gulps down her tea, placing her glass on a coaster with a slight thud. "Really?" she asks anxiously, wiping her mouth with a napkin. "Who are they?"

Kermit winks at her with a sly smile, breaking off a piece of cake with her fork. "We won't announce them until Sunday, but they've already been practicing their speeches. You'll have to wait and see like everybody else." She slips the piece in her mouth, then rinses it down with her coffee.

Victoria groans, resuming drinking her tea. "Well, I know Sharon would've told me if it was her."

"She wouldn't know," Kermit grins. "Since there are only four graduates, Mary has them all practicing the speeches. So, none of them know."

"All right then, I guess I'll have to wait," Victoria sighs, smiling at Kermit. "Next on the agenda, will we have a commencement speaker?"

"Yes. Virginia Sanders from Pyramid Nursery Institute has agreed to do it," Kermit says. "I asked her to prepare a motivational speech that would be interesting to both children and parents. She'll also be in line with me, Mary, and Gus as the Tiny Tot owner to present the diplomas."

"Oh, that's wonderful," Delores chuckles, turning to the third page as she continues writing. "Three speeches, caps and gowns... what about music? Is Dingwald still available to play?"

"Yes, last I heard. I'll call him tonight to confirm," Kermit says, writing a reminder to herself on the desk calendar. "He's been so busy performing concerts around town. He's really making a name for himself, so I hope he can still come."

"Okay, that should do it," Victoria says. "Unless anyone has any other news?" She pauses to inspect the women's faces around the table expectantly. "Then, meeting adjourned."

***

Tiny Tot Nursery School's 1954 graduation marks the third consecutive day of scorching temperatures soaring above one hundred degrees during the city's unrelenting heat wave. Hugh and Rodney, the son of the five-year-olds' teacher, act as ushers. In their matching tan suits, the school-age boys greet the graduation guests, directing them to their seats and distributing graduation programs. Proud parents and relatives bravely endure the blazing outdoor air, squirming on burning metal folding chairs arranged across the steamy concrete playground. Using their paper commencement programs as fans, women in stylish dresses, hats, and gloves, and men in suits, find little relief in the stagnant courtyard. Despite the oppressive conditions, both spectators and preschoolers await the commencement festivities, excitedly glancing at the back door for someone to appear.

Inside the humid nursery school, Kermit oversees last-minute preparations in a crisp white belted dress, accented with pearl clip earrings and necklace. Moving quickly through the facility, she straightens preschoolers' white graduation attire before instructing the teachers to lead their classrooms to the reserved second row seats outside. Their entrance sparks a smattering of applause from the anxious audience.

Sweating through his pinstriped black suit and steel gray tie, Augustus clips a chrome microphone onto a thin stand, its tilted, rounded, rectangular head accented with horizontal grill lines. To avoid a tripping hazard, he untangles the black cord running up the stairs, past the door, and into the hall outlet plug. His assistant and six-year-old son, Hugh, trails behind his father, securing the cord in place with strips of masking tape.

Kermit leads the two teachers of the graduating classes and the commencement speaker to their seats on the concrete dais. Dingwald begins playing Pomp and Circumstance on the oak standing piano propped against the red brick wall. The audience rises in an energetic standing ovation as they recognize the graduation procession: four girls in white ruffled dresses march forward, followed by four preschoolers who balance white mortarboard caps atop their heads while their white ceremonial gowns flow to their ankles.

Once the graduates are in place, Kermit welcomes the audience to Tiny Tot Nursery's second graduation ceremony. When Sharon Chapman approaches the microphone to present her Valedictorian speech, her mother, Victoria, gasps in surprise. The Parents' Club president tears up as her five-year-old daughter shares the lessons she learned throughout her years at Tiny Tot. Following a thunderous round of applause, Augustus Jr., the Salutatorian, gives his speech, also warmly received by those in attendance, including his misty-eyed parents.

When Virginia takes the stand for the keynote address, she inspires the audience, predicting a brighter future for the Tiny Tot Nursery School graduates as they continue their education. She cites last month's landmark ruling by the Supreme Court declaring racial segregation in public schools unconstitutional. The spectators cheer as the speaker credits the Brown v. The Board of Education decision with leading to greater opportunities for the Tiny Tot class of 1954.

At the end of Virginia's commencement address, she joins the receiving line with Kermit, Augustus, and the teachers as Dingwald resumes his performance of Pomp and Circumstance. Beginning with the four girls promoted to the five-year-old class, Kermit announces each name while the audience applauds. As they practiced over the past month, she presents their rolled diploma secured with a silver ribbon with her left hand, while crossing her wrists to shake their right. After receiving their diploma, the students continue down the line, shaking hands with the other members on stage as their parents take photos of the memorable occasion.

The four preschoolers promoted to kindergarten rise to receive their conferral of degrees. Sharon and Augustus Jr. lead their class to accept their diplomas as Kermit recites their full names and the kindergarten school where they will enroll in the fall. Once the four newly graduated classmates return to their seats, diplomas in hand, they participate in the traditional turning of the tassel ceremony. Still standing, they move the white tassels on their mortarboard caps to the left side of their faces in unison, sparking enthusiastic cheers from the gathering. Despite the unbearable sweltering conditions, Tiny Tot's second graduation concludes in glowing success.

6-27-1954 Tiny Tot Graduation

ALICE IN HER
WONDERLAND OF FASHIONS

April 12, 1955

S cattered showers break the rising humidity on the Tuesday after Easter, leaving slick sidewalks and moist lawns for the third consecutive day. Three to five-year-old Tiny Tot students wake drowsily from their afternoon nap and munch on their snack of apple slices and orange juice. Muted sunlight creates soft rectangular shapes on the hardwood floor as teachers raise the white vertical blinds on the front windows, the metal chains clinking softly against the window frames. The aides clear child-sized furniture from the center of the room to rehearse for the upcoming fashion show this weekend.

Kermit passes through the five-year-olds' classroom wearing a vibrant turquoise taffeta dress, the empire bodice threaded with a black velvet ribbon. She feels a ping of yearning as she scans the cherub faces without seeing her two sons, now enrolled in elementary school. The students' teacher approaches her, carrying a handwritten schedule of the fashion show program.

"The children are almost finished eating," Mary Smith says, her voice lifting in the same Little Rock accent she shares with Kermit. "I'll have them get into their costumes and we'll be ready for rehearsal in fifteen minutes."

"Sounds good," Kermit says, moving to the younger children's rooms. When she spots her young daughter struggling to keep pace with the three-year-olds, she squats next to her to encourage her progress. Although Patrice is only two and a half, her mother placed her in Tiny Tot's youngest group, hoping to give her a jump start when she reaches kindergarten. Once Kermit completes her rounds, she returns to her office to collect the props for the production.

As the combined classrooms gather, the playroom fills with the lively sounds of children's voices and scraping furniture. When Helen Williams, the new president of the Parents' Club, arrives, her five-year-old son, Theodore, rushes to greet her wearing a giant top hat. They embrace, knocking his hat to the floor, their shared laughter revealing a clear family resemblance.

"Glad you could make it," Kermit says, lugging a box of accessories into the foyer. She sets it down and pulls out the typed news release she's prepared for the fashion show, listing the children's names and their characters. Handing it to Helen, she adds, "Look this over to make sure it's okay. I'm going to submit it to the St. Louis Argus to go with a picture from the photographer I hired. He's stopping by this afternoon to take pictures of the children during rehearsal."

"Okay, will do," Helen says, reviewing the document.

"Teddy, help your mother find someplace to sit so she can watch the rehearsal."

Helen's son leads her into the classroom where she delicately positions her petite frame into a child-sized chair, crossing her ankles gracefully to the side.

To kick off rehearsal, Kermit calls Carol Ellis to the chair positioned in the center of the room to perform her role as Alice, her natural waves extending gracefully from her white headband. The teacher begins reading the opening lines of the children's book, *Alice in Wonderland*, then describes the outfits worn by the characters in the first act. Kermit straightens five-year-old Gary Michael Burnley's large White Rabbit ears, then hands him a large pocket watch. The children burst into spirited laughter when he hops across the floor, shouting, "I'm late," while checking his watch.

Carol meets The Mad Hatter, portrayed by Teddy. Helen chuckles as her son hosts the tea party, holding the cup and saucer supplied by Kermit.

A knock at the door prompts the three-year-olds' teacher to admit a white man with glasses and cropped black hair. He enters carrying a boxy camera by the handle and a rattling metal equipment bag flung over his shoulder.

Kermit greets the photographer in the doorway. He grins at the elaborate children's dress rehearsal unfolding behind her.

"Welcome to Tiny Tot," she says. "You must be Mr. Bulkin."

"Yes," he replies, scanning the scene. "I see you've got quite a production here."

"Thank you," Kermit says, motioning for Helen to join them. "This is Mrs. Williams, the president of our Parents' Club, who is sponsoring the event."

"Nice to meet you," Helen says as they shake hands. "The fashion show is also a fundraiser for Tiny Tot supplies." She hands him the release. "Here's a print up of the program."

Kermit continues introducing him to the teachers while the children peek from behind costume racks, staring curiously at the white man in their midst.

"And these are the stars of the show—our Tiny Tot children. Boys and girls, say hello to Mr. Bulkin."

The children stumble over the pronunciation of his name, laughing at the variations.

"That's close enough," he chuckles. "Let me just set up my camera, and I'll be out of your way."

He removes a tripod from his bag, extends its telescoping legs, and locks the camera into place. With practiced ease, he attaches the flash and checks the film before extending the accordion-style lens.

"Ready. Who's first?"

Kermit arranges Carol between Gary Michael and Teddy. The photographer focuses on the trio and calls out, "Look here, children." They blink and rub their eyes as the flash bursts across the room, then giggle.

With help from the teachers, Kermit rotates character combinations for more pictures. Once finished, Mr. Bulkin disassembles his gear and slips the news release into his bag.

"I'll stop by tomorrow morning with your photographs," he says, clutching his camera. "That'll give you plenty of time to get them to the *Argus* for Friday's edition. Thank you, and good luck with your fashion show."

***

Partly sunny skies keep temperatures at a comfortable seventy-seven degrees on Sunday afternoon. The scent of floor polish mixes with fresh paint in the Phyllis Wheatley Gym at 2711 Locust Street, while the warm spring air carries hints of blooming magnolia through the open doors. Helen Williams joins her team of Tiny Tot Parents' Club officers, collecting the thirty-five-cent admission at the door, the coins clanking in the metal money box. The familiar hum of excited conversation spills through the gymnasium doors, punctuated by the occasional shriek of delight from young voices.

Families stream inside the expansive space, donning their best church attire. Voices reverberate off the painted concrete walls and arched steel trusses of the ceiling. Hugh and Augustus Jr. help their father arrange painted cardboard trees, depicting the opening act where Alice starts her adventure. Dingwald takes his place at the upright piano positioned beside the stage, his fingers dancing across the keys in a whimsical melody that creates a fantasy atmosphere.

Backstage, costumed children fidget with their props. Teachers line up the four-year-olds behind Carol, whose full-lace skirt billows as she twirls. Moving through her students, Kermit shares words of encouragement and compliments on their appearance. Shortly after five o'clock, she adjusts her white gloves and checks her wristwatch before gracefully strolling to the podium. Dingwald concludes his piece as Kermit stands poised at the microphone in a fitted aqua jacket and skirt.

"Welcome, ladies and gentlemen, to *Alice in Her Wonderland of Fashions*—a fantastical journey through story and style, presented by the Tiny Tot Nursery School!" She pauses for applause, smiling at the enthusiastic response. Before introducing Mary Smith, she acknowledges the Parents' Club, who stand and wave from their seats.

Mary Smith joins her, clipboard in hand, and signals Dingwald to begin. The first group of children ascends the stage.

Carol steps forward, black patent leather shoes glinting under the lights. "I'm Alice," she declares, "and I've fallen down a rabbit hole into a wonderful world of beautiful fashions!"

The five-year-olds' teacher begins her narration, blending story with spring fashion descriptions. Wiggling the cotton tail pinned to his trousers, Gary Michael hops across the stage, his oversized rabbit ears flopping with every movement. "Oh my ears and whiskers, I'm late! I'm late!" he exclaims, pulling an oversized pocket watch from his jacket. The audience erupts in delighted laughter as he freezes mid-hop, spotting Alice, who follows him in curious pursuit.

In Act Two, Carol encounters the Cheshire Cat, who disappears and re-appears on stage. Teddy greets her with a dramatic bow, the brim of his Mad Hatter hat shading his twinkling eyes. Dressed in an oversized patchwork blazer, paisley scarf, and clashing plaid trousers, he sips from his teacup. "Tea party, anyone?" he asks with a flourish, before joining the table of storybook characters.

The fashion show unfolds like a living storybook. Dingwald's piano accompaniment weaves through the performance, his melodies shifting from playful to dramatic as the story demands. Parents crane for glimpses of their children, some dabbing their eyes with handkerchiefs.

Scene after scene showcases themed outfits loosely inspired by Wonderland moments. Patrice tumbles through "Tulgey Wood" with the three-year-olds. In the "March of the Cards," five-year-old boys parade across the stage wearing sandwich boards decorated front and back with hearts, spades, diamonds, and clubs. Beneath the painted trees of *Through the Looking-Glass*, two boys dressed in identical striped shirts and black pants portray Tweedledee and Tweedledum. Mary Smith narrates each scene, describing the coordinated miniature ensembles.

As the final model bows, Carol returns to center stage, surrounded by all the students. "And that's how Alice discovered that Wonderland has the most wonderful fashions of all," she says, arms spread as the others join her for the finale. The audience rises, some calling out their children's names, while others snap pictures. The young performers beam under the lights, adrenaline flushing their faces with a tinge of color.

Kermit returns to the microphone. "The children outdid themselves," she says, sparking another round of applause. "Please join us in June for the Tiny Tot graduation and our Tom Thumb Wedding in December."

She mingles through the gym, embracing children and thanking teachers and parents. As the space empties, Helen brings the final tally—the fundraiser exceeds their goal, allowing them to purchase an even larger collection of books for their growing enrollment. After ensuring the gym is restored to order, Kermit leaves with her family, grateful for another successful showcase of her Tiny Tot children.

Winter Wedding

December 4, 1955

A winter chill settles over St. Louis as the sun rises on a clear December morning, the temperature hovering below freezing. An hour into the Church of Christ Holiness' Sunday service, the Hill and Williams families sit in their usual pew along the middle aisle. Their collection of four boys fidget, occasionally flipping through the hymnals stashed in the pew rack. In the drafty sanctuary, Patrice naps on Arvolin's lap, a wool coat covering her bare shoulders. Despite Kermit's objections, the obstinate three-year-old insists on wearing her gold ruffled maid of honor dress to church.

Well past twelve-thirty, Reverend Matthews steps to the pulpit to begin his sermon. Kermit checks her watch, lips pursed, calculating how long the sermon and communion will take. She must cross town to Antioch Baptist Church to prepare for the Tom Thumb Wedding's five o'clock start time. She prays she can spare herself the embarrassment of tipping out of church early with three noisy children in tow.

She redirects her attention to the pastor, who shares news of racial conflict brewing in Montgomery, Alabama. It began last Thursday when a Colored woman was arrested for refusing to surrender her seat in the bus' segregated section to a white passenger. Although an unreasonable practice, Reverend Matthews reminds the congregation that Jim Crow laws require Negroes to stand when all white-reserved seats are occupied. Whispered murmurs drift through the congregation as tension thickens the sanctuary air.

"I heard she was just tired from working all day," Geraldine whispers. "Wasn't trying to cause trouble or anything."

Kermit shakes her head. "That's a shame. Just when you think we're making some progress."

"Ministers down South and around the country are rallying together to decide how to handle this injustice," Reverend Matthews continues, his voice rising with conviction. "We don't have many details at this hour, but we know the woman's name is Rosa Parks. In the coming days, I will speak with other clergy and inform you of any changes as they occur. Amen?"

The church responds with a somber chorus of "Amens" as the pastor launches into his prepared message. Following the sermon, ushers serve communion comprised of Welch's grape juice and Nabisco saltine crackers, broken into bite-sized pieces. All baptized members participate as the trays pass among the pews.

Before the pastor signals the congregation to stand, Kermit's three children are already buttoned into winter coats, hats secured under their chins. She slips on her fur coat the moment the benediction concludes, then quickly ushers her sons into the biting cold. Augustus escorts Arvolin from the sanctuary while carrying their daughter.

Their car crawls through the Ville neighborhood, delayed by leisurely after-church traffic. During the drive, Augustus notices his wife's pursed lips as she alternately checks her watch and grips the door handle.

"Don't worry, we're almost there," he says, reaching past their daughter to pat Kermit's hand. "Only a few more blocks to go."

Kermit smiles at his reassuring touch, feeling the tension in her neck ease. Minutes later, he parks on North Market Street near the corner of Goode Avenue, where the imposing Antioch Baptist Church stands. Built thirty-four years prior, the red brick structure displays Victorian Gothic design, featuring buttressed corners and arched windows. A square corner tower anchors the building, framed by pointed arches and tall windows.

Driven by frosty wind whipping through the street, the family hurries past heavy red doors adorned with festive green Christmas wreaths. Inside, radiators hiss while they remove their outer layers. Kermit leads them to the Educational Building, completed just months earlier. She and the Parents'

Club officers spent the previous night transforming the space into an elaborate nuptial setting rivaling any adult ceremony. Flowers, pastel streamers, and palms line the aisle. White ribbons mark the bride's path to the child-sized altar.

Mary Smith and other Tiny Tot teachers arrive first, bundled in their finest winter coats, followed shortly by Parents' Club committee members. Teachers establish dressing areas while club members prepare admissions. Kermit coordinates between groups, her experience from the first Tom Thumb wedding evident in her efficient directions.

When groomsmen, Teddy Williams Jr. and Gary Michael Burnley, arrive, the boys catch up with their friends, Hugh and Augustus Jr., to race around the perimeter.

With Theodore Sr.'s help, Augustus blocks their path. "Stop running," he commands. After the fathers corral the four boys in the doorway, Augustus says to Teddy's father, "Let's take them to get changed in the back." While they go to the dressing room, Arvolin explores the new educational wing with her granddaughter.

Mr. Bulkin enters with his photography equipment, ready to capture each moment of the miniature nuptials. As a special memento for parents, Kermit arranges for the photographer to take individual portraits of their children in formal wedding attire. In exchange for business referrals, Mr. Bulkin agrees to donate his usual fee to the Parents' Club. He sets up his makeshift studio in the room's corner, using the floral arrangement as an elegant backdrop.

Augustus emerges with their sons in black tuxedos—Hugh's white bow-tie marking his elevated status as officiant, while Augustus Jr.'s black one designates him as father escort.

"You two look so handsome," Kermit says, brushing specks of lint from their fresh haircuts. She ties Patrice's matching gold bonnet with a large bow made of netting, then adjusts her daughter's pearl necklace. "Gus, can you take them over to Mr. Bulkin so they can have their picture taken?"

"Let's go," Augustus says, leading their children to the photographer's workspace.

12-4-1955 Tom Thumb Wedding Hugh Hill, Patrice Hill and Augustus Hill Jr.

As families arrive, the well-rehearsed Parents' Club efficiently directs traffic to separate dressing rooms. Laughter and excitement float through the air, but conversations repeatedly return to the woman arrested in Alabama. Parents exchange worried glances over their children's heads, sensing the gravity of events unfolding hundreds of miles south.

Dingwald arrives with his parents and piano teacher, Alleda Ward Wells. The young musician has become a sought-after accompanist across the city's churches, his reputation having grown considerably since their first collaboration. After quickly placing his sheet music on the piano stand, he performs a classical piece, instantly establishing the musical backdrop for the matrimonial celebration. Parents and grandparents settle into chairs, faces reflecting both pride in their children and unease about the changing world outside these walls.

Ten minutes before showtime, the wedding party assembles with the confidence of experienced performers. Many children who participated in the 1953 mini-wedding ceremony were now older and more poised. Reprising his role as the officiating minister, Hugh clutches a Bible as his mother drapes a white stole around his neck. The twin grooms, Wayne Forby and Derek Novel, stand ready in matching tuxedos, while ushers prepare to guide the larger crowd to their seats.

The elaborate double ceremony unfolds with the precision of a well-rehearsed production. Dingwald's fingers dance across the keys as Johann Pachelbel's Baroque chamber music, Canon in D, fills the space. The joyful, serene melody creates an atmosphere of anticipation while late arrivals find their seats. In two opposite aisles, the groomsmen and bridesmaids make their entrance. When Teddy steps forward for "I Love You Truly," his voice carries the innocence of youth, unaware that the world around him teeters on the edge of monumental change.

"You may now kiss the bride," Hugh declares, prompting laughter from the audience.

The recessional begins as Dingwald plays a triumphant wedding march. The twin couples lead the procession back down the aisle, followed by their wedding party in reverse order. Throughout the room, guests rise to cheer their little ones and call out well-wishes.

After the ceremony, the wedding party and guests file into the adjoining dining room. Folding tables are covered in white cloths and decorated with lace-trimmed doilies and poinsettias. The air carries the scent of vanilla cake and lemon-lime frappe. As Bulkin's camera flashes, the brides and grooms cut the wedding cake side by side, surrounded by a sea of proud parents and beaming children.

As the celebration winds down, parents linger longer than usual, reluctant to return to a world where news from Montgomery grows more troubling each day. Children carefully carry pieces of wedding cake wrapped in napkins, chattering about their performances.

Outside, winter darkness falls early, streetlights casting long shadows across the church grounds. Another Tom Thumb wedding concludes, but the innocence it represents feels more precious now, more fragile against the backdrop of history unfolding.

The following day, Rosa Parks faces trial and conviction for disorderly conduct and violating Montgomery's segregation laws, resulting in a ten-dollar fine and four dollars in court fees. Her arrest ignites protests against the bus system's segregation policies, with a citywide campaign urging Negro residents to boycott public transportation. That evening, twenty-six-year-old Dr. Martin Luther King Jr. is elected president of the newly formed Montgomery Improvement Association.

By December sixteenth, when *The St. Louis Argus* publishes "Picturesque Tom Thumb Wedding," the same newspaper reports that nearly ninety percent of Montgomery's Negro bus passengers have abandoned public transportation. As young faces from Tiny Tots' double ceremony grace the weekly paper's pages, protest organizers coordinate carpools for boycott supporters. City officials scramble to address the budgetary crisis caused by losing forty-five percent of ridership.

On the same day, one Argus reporter celebrates the "pre-holiday season's most gala and colorful... nuptial setting," another declares that Montgomery's Negro community remains steadfast in its campaign to dismantle restrictive Jim Crow laws, undeterred by threats, intimidation, and violence. The juxtaposition captures a moment when childhood's protected sphere still exists alongside a world about to transform forever.

JACK AND JILL

April 8, 1956

Five years after founding Tiny Tot, Kermit has become a recognized figure in the North St. Louis community. Her reputation as a successful businesswoman grants her access to elite social circles once beyond reach. She participates actively in community service through her church and various civic organizations, volunteering at recitals hosted by renowned St. Louis musician, Alleda Ward Wells, where both her sons study piano.

Last fall, Delores Roberts, a former officer of the Tiny Tot Parents' Club, told Kermit about her involvement in Jack and Jill of America, Inc. This national organization of mothers dedicates itself to providing educational, recreational, social, and cultural enrichment for children. Delores invites Kermit and Augustus to a formal dance hosted by the St. Louis Chapter. While there, Kermit runs into Deborah Dupree, whose children, Arthur Jr. and Deborah Ann, also attended Tiny Tot with both of her sons and Delores' two boys. The two Jack and Jill mothers also include Hugh and Augustus Jr. as guests at their children's group holiday activity.

On this April evening, Kermit delivers her closing remarks at Tiny Tot's *The Pied Piper and His Show of Fashions*, held in the Educational Building of Pleasant Green Baptist Church. Through the auditorium windows, the sun settles low on the horizon, washing the sky in amber light. After a standing ovation, the audience gathers their belongings—many clutching souvenir programs from the school's fourth annual fashion show. Parents bundle up toddlers still dressed in costume, preparing to step into the chilly evening.

As Kermit reviews the fundraiser's final tally with members of the Parents' Club, Delores approaches her from the crowd.

"Thank you so much for coming," Kermit says as they embrace. "How's Michael doing?"

"He's good," Delores replies. "Hard to believe he'll be finishing third grade in a couple of months." She steers Kermit toward the hallway for a more private conversation. "Listen, Kermit, I've been meaning to talk to you about something. You do such a wonderful job with these children's programs."

"Thank you, Delores. I'm sure you remember putting these together when you were in the Parents' Club."

"Yes, and I miss it so much," she says with a smile. "But what I wanted to talk to you about is Jack and Jill."

"Jack and Jill?" Kermit echoes, surprised.

"That's right. I think you'd make a perfect candidate. What you've built with Tiny Tot over these five years is incredible. Your volunteer work in the community is just what we're looking for. Plus, it would be a great experience for your three children."

"You're too kind," Kermit says. "But I always thought of Jack and Jill as being more..." She hesitates, searching her friend's face, "I guess... *highfalutin*?"

"You mean *saditty*?" Delores laughs, tilting her nose in the air. "Is that how you see me?"

"Of course not," Kermit laughs along.

"I've heard those same stereotypes about Jack and Jill, too. It's just silly gossip by people who don't know us."

"I just never thought I'd fit in with those women. Don't get me wrong— I'd love to be a member. I just never imagined myself in that organization of doctors and lawyers."

"Well, you should—because you definitely belong," Delores replies. "Our chapter is accepting new members, and I can sponsor your application. Think it over. I'll check back with you in a week."

On the ride home, Kermit discusses Delores' proposal with Augustus while their three-year-old daughter naps between them. In the backseat, her mother chats with eight-year-old Hugh and Augustus Jr., who turns seven today. As Augustus navigates through the fading daylight, he wonders aloud if their modest income can support the group's financial demands.

"I thought about that too," Kermit says. "I'll ask Delores what other expenses are expected besides the annual dues."

"Why do you want to join Jack and Jill anyway? Don't you have enough to do?"

"Well, I've heard it's a good way to expose your children to different experiences they might never have. It gives them a sense of self—seeing other Negro families who've achieved more right here in St. Louis. We're always saying we want our kids to have a better life than we did. I think this is one way to do it."

"I agree," Arvolin interjects from the back. "I think it would be good for the boys, and Patrice too, once she's a little older." She leans forward, speaking softly so the boys cannot hear. "But I'm surprised Delores asked. I thought they only accepted light-skinned Negroes."

"Well, I'm certainly not light-skinned," Kermit chuckles, pushing up her coat sleeve to reveal her copper-toned forearm. "I guess we'll find out if they let me in."

That night after dinner, Kermit and Augustus continue weighing the pros and cons of joining Jack and Jill. Kermit follows up with Delores to better understand the expected costs, then reviews their finances with Augustus. Ultimately, the deciding factor becomes the possibilities the organization can offer their children. With cautious optimism, she completes the application—hopeful that inclusion marks a new chapter in their family's legacy.

On the first Tuesday of June, Kermit navigates through the affluent Central West End neighborhood, the fingers of her white gloves tapping nervously against the steering wheel. A chestnut brown fur stole drapes across the cap sleeves of her white chiffon gown, trimmed with a lace neckline. She turns onto Westminster Place, slowly cruising the block while scanning house numbers in the twilight. When she reaches the three-story, red brick mansion, the street ends, forcing her to make a U-turn.

After parking at the curb, Kermit pauses to admire the imposing structure silhouetted against the deepening sky. The intricate stone motifs, moldings, and window ornaments contrast with the red brick in elaborate detail that seems too sophisticated for a Negro establishment.

"So, this is the famous Vagabond House," she murmurs to herself. "I never would've dreamed we'd be in someplace so fancy."

Kermit checks her reflection in the rearview mirror, reapplying lipstick and powder. Grabbing her beaded clutch purse from the passenger seat, she exhales, then steps outside the car. She brushes the fabric of her skirt, then smooths the strands of her pearl necklace. As she walks beneath the shade of mature, towering oak trees, her heels click along the sidewalk and up the steps flanked by four black lion sculptures.

She rings the doorbell at an entrance framed by two colossal columns that support a classical pediment. A man with light-brown features opens the door. His black formal pants are topped with a royal purple blazer emblazoned with a prominent "RV" gold emblem and gold pocket square.

"Welcome to the Royal Vagabond Club House," he says, stepping aside to wave her in.

"Thank you," Kermit replies, entering a grand foyer where hardwood floors gleam beneath elaborate mahogany furnishings. The scent of pipe tobacco and leather mingles in the air. "I'm here for the Jack and Jill event."

"Right this way," he says, closing the door behind her with a soft thud. He leads her past a formal parlor adorned with luxurious gold molding against cream wallpaper. At the center of a rectangular panel, an ornate gold insignia crest sits prominently displayed, flanked by a latticework design. Soft light from the chandelier's frosted globe and wall-mounted candelabra-style sconces streams across deep burgundy upholstery with carved wooden frames. Men donning the same fraternal purple blazers smoke cigars and sip drinks in low conversation. As they notice her, they rise, nodding and greeting, "Good evening."

"Good evening," Kermit responds, offering a smile. She imagines Augustus joining these men in such luxurious surroundings.

They continue down the hall, past a magnificent mahogany-carved wooden staircase that curves and wraps around several levels. The balusters are turned spindles topped with a thick, continuous handrail. Rounding the corner, the hum of women's conversation grows louder until they enter an opulent room lined with striped wallpaper in muted gold and green. The ceiling boasts heavy plaster moldings, with an ornate chandelier suspended from a grand medallion. It hangs majestically over a long dining table dressed in a white lace runner and topped with a silver candelabra. Thick ivory drapery frames tall, double-hung sash windows.

The women, all dressed in elegant white formal attire, turn as Kermit enters, their smiles welcoming. Delores steps forward from the group and embraces her.

"Oh, Kermit," she says. "I'm so glad you're joining us."

"Thank you so much for sponsoring me," Kermit says. "I didn't realize how beautiful it is in here."

"Come on," Delores says, taking Kermit's arm. "Time for you to meet your fellow Jack and Jill mothers."

She takes Kermit around the gathering, introducing her to the members around the room. Each woman extends her hand with genuine warmth, welcoming Kermit into their sisterhood. Standing beside the table, they approach a woman with black bouffant-style curls framing her beige complexion.

"Kermit, I'd like to introduce you to Hortense Brooks, the founder of the St. Louis chapter of Jack and Jill," she states. "Hortense, this is Kermit Hill, one of the new members being inducted tonight."

"The founder? Oh, it's a pleasure to meet you, Mrs. Brooks," Kermit says breathlessly.

"Please call me Hortense," she says as the women shake hands. "It's my pleasure to welcome you to our chapter. And congratulations to you, Delores, for becoming an officer."

"Thank you so much," she says. "I'm looking forward to serving the chapter."

"I didn't realize you were being inducted tonight, too," Kermit says. "Congratulations on your new position."

As the social hour concludes, the chapter's founding member calls the group to order, opening the ceremony in prayer. The women arrange themselves in a semicircle around the dining table, where individual white tapered candles rest in silver holders beside the central candelabra.

"Tonight marks a special evening in our chapter's history," Hortense announces, her voice carrying practiced authority. "We gather not only to install our new officers but to welcome ten remarkable women into the Jack and Jill family. I implore each of you to do whatever you can to implement Jack and Jill's mission to provide constructive, educational, recreational, and cultural programs for children. We believe in a strong emphasis on child development, mothers' education, and community service."

She lifts the central candle from the candelabra, its flame casting dancing shadows across the ornate room. "This light represents the flame of service and sisterhood that has burned bright in Jack and Jill chapters across the nation since 1938. Tonight, we pass this flame to our incoming leadership."

One by one, she calls forward the nine new officers. Maxine Stark steps forward first, accepting the responsibility of chapter president as her candle lights from the central flame. Delores Roberts and the other new officers light their candles, adding to the growing circle of flickering light.

"And now," Hortense continues, her voice steady with emotion, "we welcome our newest members into this sacred circle."

Kermit's heart pounds as her name is called alongside the nine others. As she steps forward, she feels the flame's warmth on her face. Hortense lights her candle, the small flame flickering briefly before steadying.

"Kermit Hill, by this light, you pledge to promote and uphold the mission of Jack and Jill of America—to nurture future leaders, to strengthen our community, and to provide cultural enrichment for our children. Do you so pledge?"

"I do," Kermit states, her voice thick with pride.

As the ceremony concludes, the room fills with the soft radiance of nineteen candles, each flame representing a commitment to developing fully integrated children and helping mothers provide better opportunities for their families. Each new member receives a chapter handbook and a copy of Jack and Jill of America's local and national bylaws.

When the formal ceremony ends, champagne glasses appear, filled with sparkling cider. Toasts are offered to the new officers and members; laughter mingles with heartfelt congratulations, and Kermit finds herself surrounded by women who share her dreams for their children's futures.

That Sunday, the sun beats down mercilessly on the grounds of the Postal Employees Club in Black Jack, Missouri, as afternoon temperatures climb into the nineties. Following a twenty-five-minute drive from home, newly inducted Jack and Jill member Kermit arrives with her family at the chapter's year-end picnic. Before leaving the passenger seat, she places her white hat on top of her black curls, dressed in a blue and white polka dot dress. Augustus opens her car door, sporting a straw fedora with a tan striped band, matching brown striped shirt, and khaki trousers.

They survey the sprawling grounds dotted with families at picnic tables and children dashing across the grassy lawn. The breeze carries the scent of fresh-cut grass and blooming honeysuckle. Hugh and Augustus Jr. race ahead to join Michael and Steven Roberts, already engaged in a ball game near the pavilion. Their three-year-old daughter lingers behind, chatting with her grandmother, following along the pathway.

"Nice day for a picnic," Kermit comments, shading her eyes against the sunlight. "Although it's a little hot right about now."

Delores waves from beneath a pavilion where several mothers busily prepare for the picnic in the shade. "Kermit! Over here!"

As they approach, Kermit recognizes many faces from the candlelight ceremony five days earlier. The newly elected president, Maxine Stark, organizes the food table of covered dishes, while Hortense directs the mothers setting up games for the children. Delores directs Augustus to the other fathers congregating at picnic tables, while Kermit joins the other new members assigned to serving the feast. The aroma of fried chicken mingles with egg salad and fruit punch.

"It's nice to see so many families out here," Kermit says to Delores. "My boys haven't stopped talking about this picnic all week."

"Wait until they start getting into their activities," she says. "They get to explore so many new things they wouldn't have at school. In a couple of years, your daughter will too."

Following the meal, Kermit mingles with the chapter's membership, getting acquainted and sharing their experiences with the group. She introduces her boys to the mothers leading their age groups, then chats with various committee members about their objectives, helping to determine which ones she will serve in September.

"The kids seem to really be enjoying themselves," Kermit murmurs to Augustus as they reconnect at the pavilion.

He nods, watching their boys participate in a relay race organized by the picnic committee. "The fathers I spoke with were very nice. We had a good talk."

As families begin collecting tired children and saying their goodbyes, Hortense approaches with a smile. "How was your first official Jack and Jill event?"

She looks around at the families of various shades laughing together with a sense of community and support. "Everything was just lovely," Kermit replies, spotting her children playing with new friends. "Our whole family enjoyed it."

Walking back to their car, Arvolin falls into step beside her daughter. "I guess I was wrong about Jack and Jill. These are some nice folks out here. I think y'all will fit right in."

As they drive home through the gathering dusk, Kermit and Augustus agree that joining Jack and Jill was a good decision for their family. Their boys chat excitedly about their new friends and the activities ahead. The Jack and Jill chapter of her family's story begins.

FIFTH ANNIVERSARY CELEBRATION

October 20, 1956

Although Tiny Tot's official fifth anniversary falls in February, Kermit and the Parents' Club officers plan a special celebration for October to mark the milestone. What begins as a simple banquet evolves into an afternoon of dining and inspiration, featuring a panel of respected educators from the St. Louis area. The event focuses on topics designed to engage Tiny Tot's parents and teachers, while also welcoming interested members of the broader community.

To ensure strong attendance, the planning committee distributes invitations to members of early education associations, public and private childcare facilities, churches, and social clubs. As a newly inducted member of Jack and Jill, Kermit extends invitations to the mothers from her chapter. She now serves on the club's Gift Committee, actively preparing for their benefit dance and fall festival in November. This annual event at the Masonic Auditorium collects gifts for children afflicted with polio, identified by the March of Dimes charitable association. Her community service with the organization brings a heartwarming experience she never imagined, adding personal meaning to her already strong commitment to children.

After weeks of careful coordination, Tiny Tot's planning culminates in this Saturday afternoon gathering at Lane Tabernacle Church, located a straight shot down North Newstead Avenue from Tiny Tot. Inside the educational wing of the historic gray limestone building, Kermit leads a team of thirty volunteers, wearing a formal black dress with elbow-length sleeves, accented with pearls and a white pillbox hat.

Parents' Club president, Helen Williams, efficiently arranges the audience seating with fellow club members. Wearing a hunter green dress with a scoop neckline, her gold necklace catches the light as crisp white tablecloths billow over round wooden tables. The group busily arranges place settings and floral centerpieces at each table. Teachers prepare the dais, placing nameplates for the panelists and testing microphones, the electronic hum and occasional squeal piercing through muted conversations. The white carnation corsages and boutonnieres pinned to every host enhance the floral scent, punctuating the air.

From the kitchen, the aroma of baked chicken, green beans, and macaroni and cheese drifts through the air as Geraldine directs the food committee in assembling the meal. Outside, light rain begins to fall while Augustus unloads boxes of programs and decorations from the car with help from other Parents' Club fathers. Arvolin stays at home to babysit her grandchildren during this adult-only affair.

A record crowd fills the education hall, engaging in animated discussions as the panelists take their positions behind their nameplates. Kermit takes her place at the head table alongside Augustus, his white boutonniere contrasting against his black suit and tie. He smiles at her, gently patting her shoulder to acknowledge her hard work in amassing the impressive turnout. Five years of nurturing young minds at 3212 North Newstead Avenue brings them to this moment—a celebration that draws distinguished St. Louis educators and child development experts to share their wisdom with the Tiny Tot community.

Helen steps up to the microphone, tapping it gently before speaking.

"Welcome, parents, teachers, and friends, to Tiny Tot Nursery School's fifth anniversary celebration. We're so happy that so many of you are interested in hearing from our panel on 'Understanding Emotional Needs of the Young Child.'"

The audience applause swells, faces beaming excitedly in anticipation of the panelists' presentations.

"We will begin our program with the invocation. Please bow your head."

Following the prayer, the banquet begins with the steady rhythm of forks against china plates echoing against the walls. As the lemon pound cake is served, Helen returns to address the gathering as the sweet citrus aroma drifts through the room.

"Tonight, we gather not only to celebrate our school's milestone, but to deepen our understanding of the precious children in our care," she announces, her words carrying clearly through the hall. "Our panel moderator brings with her an expansive teaching background, specializing in the field of early childhood education. Let me introduce Miss Bessie Chandler."

The skilled educator steps forward to the podium as the audience applauds, her black-rimmed cat-eyeglasses reflecting the overhead lights. She introduces the distinguished panel members seated at the long table, outlining their impressive credentials for the audience.

"We are privileged to have with us experts who dedicate their lives to understanding and nurturing young minds," Bessie says, gesturing toward the panel members seated on either side of her on the dais.

Jennie Wahlert of Washington University's education department rises first. A black hat tops black loose curls framing delicate tan features. Her black Chanel blazer sags under the weight of her larger speaker's corsage, adorned with two carnations and white ribbons. She speaks in measured tones about early childhood education and its natural place in child development, drawing from years of work in the field. Parents lean forward in their chairs, absorbing her insights about the crucial foundation years that shape their children's futures.

Dr. Helen Nash, one of St. Louis' most outstanding pediatricians, follows with practical advice. Her petite stature and youthful appearance contrast with her extensive knowledge as she approaches, wearing a black dress trimmed with white piping at the Peter Pan collar and sleeves. She emphasizes the need for parents to guard against careless accidents that could permanently injure children. "The necessity of calling a doctor when a child is ill cannot be overstated," she tells the attentive audience, "rather than relying on ancient home remedies that may prove inadequate or harmful."

Child psychologist Richard Hands explains how adult reactions to problems often connect to early childhood experiences. His words resonate with parents who recognize patterns in their own responses to their children's behavior. The audience nods in understanding as he bridges the gap between professional psychology and practical parenting. As the only male panelist, his beige suit and black tie also set him apart from the other women at the table dressed in darker attire.

Uxenia Livingston, community organizer for the Missouri Social Hygiene Association, wears a black dress with a beaded appliqué neckline and a white crescent hat. Her specialized Christian education gives deeper meaning to her discussion of sexual education elements, a topic that requires delicate handling in polite society.

During the program's musical interludes, Jacqueline Norwood's rich contralto voice fills the hall with two carefully chosen selections. Aquilla Brown's skilled piano accompaniment flows from the upright instrument positioned at the front, providing sophisticated entertainment that elevates the educational focus.

Kermit listens to each speaker with the attention of an educator, always seeking to improve her methods. The panel's diverse perspectives reinforce her belief that Tiny Tot's motto, "Where Your Child is Taught with Care," encompasses their emotional, physical, and intellectual development. She exchanges glances with Augustus, recognizing the validation their work receives from these respected professionals.

As the presentation progresses, parents engage with the panel through questions that reveal their genuine concern for their children's well-being. Teachers take notes, recognizing valuable insights they can apply in their own classrooms. The informal discussion format encourages participation, creating an atmosphere of shared learning rather than formal lecturing.

Bessie guides the conversation with skill, ensuring each panel member has opportunities to share their expertise while keeping the discussion focused on practical applications. Her role as moderator requires balancing the educational content with the social aspects of the anniversary celebration.

The *St. Louis Argus* photographer navigates carefully through the hall, his camera flash briefly illuminating the plaster ceiling as he documents Tiny Tot's fifth anniversary banquet and panel for newspaper coverage. His presence underscores the event's significance within St. Louis educational circles, where Tiny Tot earns recognition for its innovative approach to early childhood education. Before the program concludes, he positions Tiny Tot's Parents' Club members and teachers around Kermit and Augustus to capture those responsible for producing the exceptional event. He then takes another photograph of Tiny Tot's owner and director standing at the head table with the seven panelists and staff.

As the panelists depart their positions at the table, conversations continue in smaller groups throughout the hall. Parents approach panel members with specific questions about their children's development, while teachers discuss implementation strategies for the insightful recommendations.

Participants approach Kermit, thanking her for providing a resource to exchange early childhood information. The educational building buzzes with animated discussions long after the planned program ends.

Kermit mingles among the guests, accepting congratulations on Tiny Tot's fifth anniversary while engaging in substantive conversations about child development practices. The anniversary event represents more than a celebration—it affirms the school's commitment to continuous learning and improvement in serving young children and their families.

As the last guests trickle out of the education hall, the soft murmur of lingering conversations fades beneath the high ceiling. Helen and Kermit stand near the dais, collecting discarded programs and surveying the room, now dotted with empty chairs and cleared tables.

"Can you believe this turnout?" Helen says, her voice low but animated. "We packed the entire hall! I saw the audience hanging on the panelists' every word."

Kermit nods, resting her hand briefly on the back of a chair as she slips off her heels.

"I know," she says softly. "It means so much to see everything come together like this. When we opened Tiny Tot five years ago, I envisioned reaching more people in the community—but this was so much more."

"Well, your hard work made today possible," Helen says, folding a program in half.

"You mean *our* hard work. None of this would've happened without you and your Parents' Club members."

"Thanks," Helen chuckles. "But you created a space where people actually come together to understand children—not just teach or discipline them."

Kermit looks toward the now-vacant head table where the panelists sat just hours before.

"That's exactly what I hoped for," she says. "Tonight reminded me why we do this. Their insights provide the ammunition we need to keep going—for the sake of our children."

"Agreed," Helen says as they walk toward the door. "This felt like a milestone. And I'm already thinking about our next fundraiser."

Once the educational hall is cleaned, Kermit and Helen join their husbands and step into the October twilight. The shadow from the church's corner bell tower and stone buttresses blankets their cars as they depart the 900 block of North Newstead Avenue. The success of the fifth anniversary dinner establishes a tradition of bringing together parents, educators, and child development experts in service of the youngest members of their community. The foundation is set for continued growth and excellence in early childhood education at Tiny Tot Nursery School.

Valentine's Serenade

February 15, 1957

Eight months after Kermit lights her induction candle in the circle with Jack and Jill mothers, the organization's demanding schedule quickly integrates into her family's already bustling life. Monthly meetings at members' homes, enriching children's cultural outings, and dedicated volunteer work now nestle alongside Tiny Tot, school, piano lessons, Cub Scouts, and church commitments. Tonight marks a special occasion: Kermit and Augustus attend their first Jack and Jill Valentine's party, an evening dedicated to dancing and entertainment in celebration of romance and love.

Augustus adjusts his black bow tie in the bedroom mirror while Kermit clips on her pearl earrings and necklace. She wears a gold and white polka dot silk dress with three-quarter sleeves, its fitted bodice accentuating her figure. A delicate gold and diamond brooch adorns her left shoulder, and her freshly pressed black curls frame her almond-toned face.

"How many people you think are coming tonight?" Augustus asks, his voice sounding strained.

"Oh, I don't know," Kermit replies, applying red lipstick in the mirror beside him. "We have about forty mothers in the chapter, so if everyone's husband comes---I'd say about eighty."

"Eighty! I, uh, didn't expect that many," he stammers, catching her eye in the mirror's reflection.

"Why?" she asks. Her brow furrows, the lipstick tube suspended in mid-air. "We've been to lots of events larger than that."

"I know." He releases their glance and starts brushing his hair. "Just surprised so many people would be there." He resumes checking his reflection, smoothing his mustache, then applying cologne.

"Well, I'm looking forward to it," she continues, finishing her lipstick. "I still remember how mad I got when you were at Prairie View and forgot to send me a Valentine's Card."

Augustus chuckles. "Oh, and you never let me forget it."

"Why should I? I was heartbroken. The most romantic day of the year, and my so-called boyfriend just forgets about me." Her voice rises with the memory.

"Well, I hope tonight will make up for it," Augustus says. He sits on the edge of the bed and slips into his black dress shoes. "You almost ready?"

"Yes. Just zip up this dress for me, and then I just need to put on my stockings and shoes, and I'll be ready."

They bid farewell to Arvolin and their children before bundling up for the sub-freezing temperatures. The February air carries a crisp bite as they drive through the winter evening, the pale beam of their headlights piercing the darkness. Red paper hearts decorate home windows along the route, still on display from yesterday's romantic holiday. Augustus taps nervously on the steering wheel as he navigates the path to Westminster Place. Kermit directs him to turn at the brick mansion's driveway that she missed on her first visit.

"Look at all those cars," Augustus observes as he pulls behind Vagabonds House, tapping the steering wheel again. Cadillacs and Buicks line the parking lot, their chrome bumpers gleaming under the lights.

"That's about what I expected," Kermit says, giving a final look at her makeup in her compact mirror. "Seems like everyone made it out tonight."

Augustus opens Kermit's car door to escort her from the car. She tightens her fur shawl as they walk arm in arm through the frigid evening. They follow the sounds of soft music mixing with laughter and conversation into a grand foyer adorned with red paper hearts suspended from the ceiling. White tapered candles flicker on every surface, and sequined outfits sparkle in the warm glow from the gold chandeliers. The flowery scent of perfume mingles with the savory aroma of hors d'oeuvres.

"Kermit! Augustus!" Delores calls out as they enter the opulent ballroom. She approaches wearing a black velvet dress with a white collar, her waves draping off her shoulders. "You both look absolutely wonderful."

"So do you," Kermit says as they embrace. "This place looks so romantic." She glances around the decorated space. Red roses in crystal vases adorn every table, their petals scattered artfully across white linen tablecloths.

Heart-shaped decorations hang from the ornate plaster moldings, and the chandelier dims to create an intimate atmosphere. "The Valentines committee did a bang-up job tonight."

"Did you see the flower decorations?" she gestures toward the center of the parlor, where admiring onlookers gather.

"No," the couple responds together.

Delores leads them to a large heart-shaped floral arrangement made of red carnations, nestled with baby's breath, quickly becoming the centerpiece of conversation.

"Oh my, it's beautiful," Kermit says, tugging on her husband's jacket sleeve.

"Now that is really something," he agrees. He leans closer to the floral display, marveling at the intricate design.

"You haven't seen anything yet," Delores says, turning toward the stage area by the fireplace. "Wait until the show begins."

"Oh, I see Arthur Dupree over there," Augustus says suddenly. "I'm going over to say hello." He kisses Kermit's cheek before disappearing into the crowd of elegantly dressed couples. Kermit watches him cross the room, surprised by how easily he engages with the small group of Jack and Jill husbands already speaking with Arthur.

"He's been acting strange all night," she observes.

"The men have been planning something special for tonight," Delores whispers conspiratorially. "They've been practicing for weeks, though none of them will admit it."

"Practicing for what?" Kermit asks, intrigued.

"You'll have to wait and see." Delores winks. "Come on, let's get something to eat. I'm starving." She steers her toward a table laden with gourmet hors d'oeuvres. Crystal glasses filled with champagne catch the candlelight, while silver platters display canapés, stuffed mushrooms, and delicate finger sandwiches.

They join the familiar faces of Jack and Jill members, sampling a variety of savory appetizers and bubbling champagne. Kermit mingles with the members, swept into the warm camaraderie of the couples. The wives she knows from chapter meetings introduce their husbands, creating a web of new connections. Augustus joins her, carrying two glasses of champagne, and hands one to her.

"How is it?" Kermit asks, nodding to the flute. Resisting the urge to question him about the fathers' mysterious plans, she slips her arm through his, now understanding his nervous behavior.

"Well, you know I don't usually drink this stuff, but when in Rome," he chuckles, tilting his glass to her and taking a sip.

Delores approaches them. "I want you to meet Wini Scott. She's our entertainment for the evening."

She leads them across the room to where a striking woman in a white satin gown stands surrounded by admiring couples. Her dark hair is styled in soft bouffant curls, and her smile radiates sophisticated grace.

"Wini, I'd like you to meet Mr. and Mrs. Augustus Hill," Delores says. "They own the Tiny Tot Nursery School. Both of my boys went there when they were little."

"Oh yes, I've heard of Tiny Tot," Wini says, her voice carrying the rich tones of a trained performer. "How nice to meet you."

"Nice to meet you, too," Kermit replies modestly.

"I'm looking forward to hearing you sing tonight," Augustus says, shaking her hand.

The room dims, signaling the start of the evening's festivities. Kermit and Augustus locate their assigned table, sharing it with Deborah and Arthur Dupree, and Maxine and Frederick Stark. A pink crystal vase holding six red roses and delicate white baby's breath rests on the white tablecloth, adding a romantic touch. Following greetings exchanged around the table, Maxine rises from her seat and moves to the microphone positioned next to the dance floor.

"Ladies and gentlemen," she announces, her voice carrying easily across the gathering. "For those of you who may not know me, I'm Maxine Stark, president of the St. Louis chapter of Jack and Jill of America." Applause fills the room as couples murmur in conversation. "I'm delighted so many of you came out on this cold night to celebrate our Valentine's Day party. It's especially nice to see so many of our handsome Jack and Jill dads joining us." The audience erupts in more applause, the women beaming at their husbands or patting their backs affectionately. "Now," she continues with a broad grin, "it's time for our featured entertainment. Ladies and gentlemen, please welcome the incomparable Wini Scott!"

The room erupts in applause as Wini takes center stage near the fireplace. Her gold jewelry catches the firelight as she begins her first number—a sultry, original composition about love found and lost. Her voice fills the ornate room with rich, professional tones that hold every couple spellbound, drawing them closer to one another. She performs three original pieces, each showcasing her range from playful to passionate. Between songs, she engages the audience with witty commentary about romance and marriage that has everyone laughing.

"And now," Wini announces after her final number, "I understand some very brave gentlemen have prepared a special surprise for their lovely wives."

Some of the wives exchange puzzled glances as their husbands begin moving toward the center of the room. Augustus squeezes Kermit's hand before joining the gathering group of men, arranged in a semicircle. Their wives applaud cautiously, not sure what to expect.

Arthur steps to the microphone. "Ladies," he announces, his bass voice adding theatrical flair, "we, your loving husbands, have prepared this special presentation as a small token of our appreciation for the wonderful women who make our lives complete."

The wives giggle as their husbands clear their throats nervously. Augustus stands near the back in the second row, fidgeting with his tie while furtively glancing at the men beside him. Kermit recognizes his nervous tic, brushing his cheek with the back of his hand. Whatever is about to happen, he feels out of his element.

Arthur raises his hand like a conductor, and the men begin harmonizing in barbershop quartet fashion. Their voices blend surprisingly well as they perform "Let Me Call You Sweetheart," followed by "You Made Me Love You." Some of the men are clearly more comfortable than Augustus, but their earnest effort and obvious affection for their wives create a touching moment.

Kermit feels tears pricking her eyes watching her husband's performance. She has never seen him sing in public before, even in high school, so his willingness to participate in this romantic gesture touches her deeply.

The performance concludes with "My Wild Irish Rose," during which each husband steps forward to present his wife with a single red carnation from the heart-shaped arrangement. The flowers have been fashioned into wrist corsages with white ribbon, and each wife receives hers with a kiss from her husband.

Augustus approaches with her corsage, his eyes shining with pride and affection. "Happy Valentine's Day, sweetheart," he says, slipping the flower around her wrist. He leans closer to whisper in her ear. "And I hope this makes up for that time I forgot your Valentine's Day card."

"Oh, yes, it does," Kermit chuckles, rising to embrace him. "Thank you so much." She kisses his cheek, then wipes off her smudge of lipstick. "You did so well out there, you really surprised me. I'm so proud of you."

The room fills with applause and laughter as couples embrace and admire their corsages.

"Well done, gentlemen!" Wini Scott calls out, leading another round of applause. "I've performed in many venues, but I've never seen such a romantic gesture."

Maxine returns to the microphone, announcing, "If I could have all the Jack and Jill wives meet me in the parlor down the hall. We have a photographer ready to take our picture for the *Argus* newspaper."

Kermit and Deborah join the Jack and Jill wives as they leave their seats, all admiring their matching corsages and laughing about their husbands' singing performance.

"Did you know Arthur was organizing this?" Deborah asks.

"No idea," she replies. "They really know how to put on a show, though. I could not believe Gus was up there singing." She smiles, looking back at Augustus talking with the other men, their shoulders relaxed after their presentation.

Maxine and Delores join the other Jack and Jill officers on the sofa and chairs in front, while Kermit stands alongside other members on the two levels of risers behind them.

"Ladies, if I could have you look this way," the photographer pleads with the women, caught up in animated chatter. When they turn their attention his way, the camera flashes on the smiles of forty Jack and Jill wives delighting in the memory of their husbands' romantic serenade.

The women return to their husbands, dancing and socializing as the hi-fi music resumes. The heart-shaped arrangement, now depleted of its flowers, becomes a backdrop for couples to pose for photographs.

As the evening winds down near midnight, couples begin saying their goodbyes and collecting coats from the Royal Vagabond attendant. The February air is even colder than when they arrived as Kermit and Augustus return to their car.

"That was quite an evening," Kermit says, rubbing her hands together as they wait for the car to warm up. "I can't get over you singing tonight. I'm so impressed. I just loved it." She leans over and kisses him, caressing his cheek. "This is the best Valentine's Day gift ever."

"Thank you, baby. Arthur convinced us it would be romantic," he chuckles. "Though I'm not sure any of us believed we could actually pull it off. I was surprised myself how good we sounded."

As they return through the deserted streets, Kermit reflects on how Jack and Jill has opened their family to new experiences. She never could have imagined her husband performing in front of a large crowd before tonight. Their sons already attend so many places they never thought possible. Now, all three of their children will grow up seeing a community of Negro families achieving success as an everyday occurrence.

QUEEN VICTORIA THE FIRST

March 16, 1958

Along North Newstead Avenue, patches of snow cling to the ground from morning flurries, but inside Tiny Tot Nursery School, warmth radiates from every corner. The front playroom overflows with voices of visitors punctuated by the squeak of dress shoes against black-and-white checkered tiles. Parents press shoulder to shoulder along the room's edges, clutching younger children while gripping cameras and rolled programs. Afternoon sunlight filters through overcast skies, washing the crowded space in muted gray light. Intertwined streamers in pale pink and baby blue stretch overhead like a festive canopy. A wide aisle lined with crisp white paper cuts through the assembly toward the makeshift throne.

At the doorway, Kermit maintains her composure in a navy and white striped dress accented with pearls. For ten minutes, she guides three nervous flower girls down the aisle, her calm voice and steady hands keeping them focused on scattering rose petals cut from red construction paper. The paper petals flutter to the floor like crimson confetti. After the maid of honor completes her solo processional, four-year-old boys representing king's attendants and consorts escort their queen's counterparts with newfound confidence. Once the royal court takes position, Kermit steps aside for the queen's entrance.

Silence spreads through the room as Queen Vicki Chapman appears. At three years old, she commands attention despite her small stature, radiant in a crisp white petticoat dress with delicate lace cap sleeves. Her full skirt bounces with each step, catching overhead light as the white train fastened at her shoulders trails softly behind her. She grips a small bouquet of silk flowers in her gloved hands, each step deliberate—step, together,

step—matching the first and third beats of "Pomp and Circumstance" floating from the corner record player.

Parents lean forward, craning their necks for better views. Some smile
and whisper softly while others quiet squirming toddlers in their laps. Vicki's
black patent leather shoes catch the afternoon light, the ruffled cuffs of her
ankle socks bobbing with each careful stride. She lifts her chin slightly,
aware of the watching eyes, though her gaze darts across the crowd seeking
one familiar face.

Vicki spots eight-year-old sister Sharon near the front, seated between
their parents. Sharon graduated from Tiny Tot in 1954 with Augustus Jr.,
six months before Vicki's birth. Sharon beams at her little sister, raising her
hand in a tiny wave. Their parents, Willie and Victoria Chapman, flank
Sharon in their finest church clothes. Victoria dabs her eyes with a handkerchief while Willie adjusts his hat brim on his knee, his gaze locked proudly
on Vicki. The sight steadies her, and she takes the next step with growing
confidence.

At the aisle's end, retiring King Harvey Randall and Queen Kathy
Braxton occupy the "throne"—two classroom chairs wrapped in white cloth
beneath the web of pastel streamers. The royal court surrounds them: girls
in gleaming white dresses and boys in white jackets against the busy, checkered floor pattern. Girls fidget with their flowers while boys shift their
weight, the rustle of starched fabric audible over the music.

To the right, future King Boyce Conway waits stiffly in his mono-
grammed white jacket, black short pants, and knee socks that sag slightly
at his shins. At three years old, he appears both regal and anxious, flanked
by his Attendants and Consorts in matching white jackets. Boyce tugs at the
ties of the white train bunched at his feet and glances nervously at the crowd.

When Vicki reaches the throne, an attendant leans in to whisper a
prompt. Boyce straightens abruptly and extends his arm. Vicki accepts it
with steady hands, her gloved fingers resting at the corner of his elbow.
Together, they turn toward the retiring monarchs. Boyce bows with his
right hand in front and left behind, while Vicki dips into a graceful court
curtsey.

Harvey rises first, removing the scalloped-edged crown from his head
and placing it carefully on Boyce's closely cropped hair. Kathy follows,
lifting her sparkling paper crown and lowering it gently onto Vicki's head.

The crowd erupts in enthusiastic applause as some parents rise for better views. Kermit steps forward again, leading the applause and announcing, "I present to you, Tiny Tot's new King Boyce Conway and Queen Vicki Chapman!"

Vicki and Boyce, now crowned, climb carefully onto the cloth-draped chairs. Boyce's knees bump against his seat edge as he arranges the heavy train behind his chair while Vicki folds her gloved hands around her bouquet, the silk flowers compressed between her small fingers.

The photographer crouches low at the aisle's end, his camera flashing as he captures the moment. Each burst of light freezes the scene in stark contrast against the pastel decorations. He snaps the formal group photo of the entire royal court, then directs Vicki and Boyce to stand side by side for their official portrait—the ones that will appear in *The St. Louis Argus* days later. Parents approach the photographer, requesting personal pictures of their children to add to their collections. Victoria Chapman marks the occasion by procuring a photo of Sharon kneeling beside her younger sister, the newly crowned Queen of Tiny Tot.

3-16-1958 King Boyce Conway and Queen Vicki Chapman

As parents line up with their own cameras, Kermit makes her way through the crowd to the Chapmans. She greets the family with warm embraces, then turns her attention to Sharon.

"What do you think of your little sister?" she asks, nodding toward the throne where Vicki and Boyce continue posing for pictures.

"She looks so pretty in her white dress and crown," Sharon says excitedly. She spreads the skirts of her yellow checkered dress and curtsies, mimicking her sister. "Vicki was a really good queen."

"I agree," Kermit smiles. "Do you remember when you were on stage at Tiny Tot's fashion revues?"

"Uh-huh," Sharon nods, smiling. "That was a lot of fun."

Kermit thanks them for their support of Tiny Tot, adding how proud she feels of both their daughters. Willie nods, his voice low but full of pride, while Victoria clasps Kermit's hand in gratitude. For a moment, they watch together as the photographer calls, "Hold it right there!" Vicki's small shoulders square as she freezes in place, her crown tilting slightly to one side. The camera captures this instant, preserving the ceremony in black and white.

Unexpected Diagnosis

April 25, 1959

Beneath Saturday's stifling heat, the afternoon sun pushes temperatures past eighty degrees. A rhythmic squeak from the seesaw punctuates the humid air, drifting across the Hills' backyard where Hugh and Augustus Jr. balance on opposite ends of the wooden bench. Gravel crunches and shifts under their shoes each time the two boys push off, their laughter carrying on the still air. Funded through matching contributions from the Tiny Tot Parents' Club and the school's playground budget, last month's teeter-totter purchase proves a hit at recess.

While Augustus works his shift at the post office, Kermit persuades her mother to join her under the shaded back porch. At seventy, Arvolin's declining health and swollen legs limit her mobility, confining her mostly to their second-floor apartment. This afternoon, she relaxes in a metal patio chair, its seat creaking softly as her six-year-old granddaughter plays "beautician." Patrice's small fingers work through the silver strands, twisting her thinning hair into loose plaits.

Still in her pink cotton housecoat and terry cloth slippers, Kermit flips through a stack of newspapers on the patio table, catching up on the week's news. When she retrieves yesterday's *St. Louis Argus,* her irritation resurfaces. The editor had promised that Tiny Tot's Operetta would appear in last Friday's edition. Now, nearly three weeks later, she fears the delay will dampen the excitement generated by the April sixth event. She sighs, the sound heavy with frustration, and scans the pages for coverage of the annual fashion show.

Suddenly, Kermit perks up, her eyes widening with excitement. She recognizes the faces of the forty smiling children on the top of page five.

"Here it is," she exclaims, her voice rising with surprise.

"You found it?" Arvolin asks, turning to glance at her daughter.

"Grandma!" Patrice protests as one of the twisted plaits unravels. "You have to stay still."

"Oh, I'm sorry, baby," Arvolin chuckles. "Let me look at the photograph and then I'll let you finish."

Kermit folds the paper and hands it to her mother, who squints at the image through eyes clouded with age.

"Oh, that's a nice one. Look, Patrice—do you see yourself? And there're your brothers too."

The six-year-old glances at the paper and shrugs. "You said I could finish your hair."

"Okay," Arvolin says, returning her head to its original position. "Tell me what it says."

Kermit clears her throat and begins reading:

"'Tiny Tot Nursery School presented their annual Spring Operetta and Fashion Show, "The Selfish Giant," Sunday at Turner Branch School.' Then it just lists the children's names in the photo," she mutters, her frustration flaring again. "What about the rest of the coverage?"

The paper rustles sharply in her hands, trembling in her clenched grip. "I practically wrote the article myself! I typed up the story of "The Selfish Giant," building a fence around his garden to keep out the children. Plus, I included the names of the children playing the characters. I even listed all the adults involved in the program. And this is all they wrote?" She stomps on a stray ant crawling from a crack in the concrete, then wipes the sole against the rough ground.

"I'm sorry, baby," Arvolin soothes. "But don't get yourself so worked up."

Kermit hastily flips through the remaining pages, the paper crackling with each turn. "I just can't believe..." She pauses when she spots another piece in the same *Trade Maker* section. "Oh, wait. They did write more—on page nine." She flips between the two pages. "But there's nothing here to say it's continued on another page. How would anyone know?"

"Well, it's still good there's more about the show," her mother says gently. "Let me hear some of that part."

Kermit scans the text and begins again:

"'A welcome was extended to the audience by the school's king and queen, Darryl James and Celeste Ann Walker. The part of "The Selfish

Giant" was played by Darryl James, and Robert Streator was the Friend Giant.' Then it goes on: 'Children adorned in colorful costumes represented various flowers—roses, buttercups, violets, pansies...'" She stops when she spots her ten- and eleven-year-olds leap off the seesaw, their feet hitting the ground with solid thumps, kicking up clouds of gravel dust in their path.

"I'm faster!" Augustus Jr. yells as they thunder up the back stairs, the wooden steps groaning under their weight, slipping past the women and disappearing into the house.

"Slow down," Kermit snaps as the screen door slams with a metallic clatter. Clamoring sounds from the kitchen rise—cabinet doors banging, dishes clattering—as the boys search for something to eat. "Make sure you clean up after yourselves!" she calls through the screen.

Sighing heavily, she returns to the newspaper and resumes reading. "'Other children represented Wind Children and Snow Children. The Nursery modeled the elegant fashions for Spring for bedtime, sport, church, and party.' It ends with the names of the pianist, M.C., Parents' Club, and me as the Director."

"The Argus came through after all," Arvolin says brightly

Kermit leans back in her chair and crosses her ankles. "Uh-huh."

Stiffly holding her head still, Arvolin eyes her daughter from the corner of her vision. "What's wrong, honey? You don't seem like yourself these days."

She turns to her mother. "I don't know. Everything's been getting on my nerves lately."

"I can tell something's up. You're usually gone somewhere by now. It's way past noon, and you're not even dressed."

"That's another thing," Kermit sighs, glancing down at her housecoat. "Momma, I'm getting so fat. Most of my clothes don't even fit anymore."

"Maybe you're going through the change," Arvolin whispers, checking to see if her granddaughter is listening.

"What? At thirty-nine?" Kermit shrieks. "Momma! Now you're making me even madder." She hastily gathers the newspapers, their pages rustling loudly, and drops them by the door with a soft thud. "Maybe it's just this heat. Let's get inside and out of this hot weather."

She helps her mother from the chair, supporting her elbow as Arvolin rises stiffly. They walk indoors, the cool air of the house washing over them. Patrice collects the scattered rubber bands and comb, then follows them inside.

When Augustus returns home, dusk's shadows fill the bedroom. He finds Kermit still in her housecoat, asleep in the waning light that filters through the curtains. He follows the voices of their children arguing—their words sharp and overlapping. The sounds lead him to Arvolin's room, where she dozes in a rocking chair while his sons fight over a toy.

"Hey! What's going on?" he shouts, his booming voice startling his mother-in-law awake. "Sorry I woke you, Momma Bland."

"He won't give me my car," Augustus Jr. whines.

"They won't let me play," Patrice adds.

"Go wash up and set the table," Augustus says, gesturing toward the bathroom.

"Yes, Daddy," the children chorus as they leave the room, their footsteps pattering down the hall.

"Why's Kermit in bed?" he asks. "Is she okay?"

"I don't think so," Arvolin says, straightening in her chair with a soft grunt. "I've been kind of worried about her—something feels off. About an hour ago, she was tired and went to bed."

Augustus scratches his chin, his fingernails making a soft rasping sound against stubble. "Now that you mention it, I've noticed things too." He nods. "Thanks. I'll check on her."

He walks down the hall, the floorboards creaking beneath his footsteps. The lamp switch clicks as he turns it on, casting a soft beige glow across the room.

"Kermit. You feeling okay?" he asks, sitting on the edge of the bed, the mattress dipping under his weight.

She groans softly, stirring from a deep sleep. "Hmm?"

"How are you feeling?" he repeats.

"I'm just tired," she mumbles, turning toward him with her eyes still closed. "What time is it?" She squints against the light, her face scrunching as he helps her sit up.

"You've been tired a lot lately," he says, wrapping an arm around her shoulders. "It's not like you to nap this time of day."

"I know," Kermit murmurs, resting her head against his chest. "I'm afraid something else is wrong, but I've been avoiding it." She clutches his hand, her fingers intertwining with his calloused fingers. "I know I've been quick-tempered with you and the kids." Pinching the soft flesh of her stomach, she adds, "I'm mad I can't get this weight off and just keep thinking you're going to leave me."

"You know that's not going to happen," Augustus replies gently, smiling.

"Momma thinks I might be going through the change," she adds softly.

"Well, I don't know what's going on, but I think it's time to see your doctor," he says. "You need to call first thing Monday morning to get an appointment."

On the Friday after Mother's Day, temperatures drop from Sunday's high of eighty-three degrees to a chilly fifty-seven. After not following up with her physician for a full week, Augustus and Arvolin convince Kermit to make the appointment for today.

Cold air rushes through the openings of her pale green hospital gown, raising goosebumps along her exposed back. The sharp antiseptic smell fills her nostrils while fluorescent lights hum faintly overhead. With her slightest movement, the paper covering the examination table crinkles beneath her. Following a series of questions about her symptoms and health history, her doctor leaves to take a phone call in his office. As she waits, her legs dangling over the table's edge, she closes her eyes and clasps her hands together, her fingers pressed tightly in prayer. *Dear God, thank you for your blessings of Gus, Momma, and our three children. If it is Your will, please let—*

A rapid knock interrupts Kermit's prayer as her doctor swings open the door, bringing with him the musky scent of aftershave. He wears a blue suit and tie, his cropped dark brown hair in stark contrast to his ruddy complexion. "Sorry for the interruption. Barnes Hospital needed me for a consultation."

"I understand," Kermit responds, clasping her hands tighter and pursing her lips.

The physician glances at his clipboard, tracing his notes with his index finger. He checks her vital signs, then balances the floor scale to record her weight. When she returns to the examination table, he gently guides her shoulder and says, "Please lie back." The doctor's fingers probe her abdomen, pressing in circular motions across the sides, front, and bottom.

Kermit watches him curiously, squirming briefly when his fingers land on her sensitive side, a brief smile easing her nervous tension.

"Does that hurt?" Dr. Eastman asks, glancing up from his exam.

"No, no," Kermit says lightly. "Just tickles a little."

He resumes the examination, then helps her sit up. The rubber hammer taps against her knee, testing reflexes, then traces along her spine. Completing his notation, his bushy eyebrows knot together tightly as he jots down notes. The silence fills with the quiet scratch of his pen against the clipboard.

"I found a tumor in your abdomen," he states flatly, his eyes still scanning the page. "We'll need to remove it before it grows any bigger." His gaze shifts to her, searching her face for a reaction.

The words hit Kermit with devastating force, the air seeming to leave the room. His lips continue moving, but she struggles to process the sounds. "Wait," she stammers, her mouth suddenly dry. She cradles her stomach protectively, asking, "A tumor? How?"

"It could be due to any number of factors—heredity, diet, environment. What matters is that we caught it in time. But we need to move quickly." The physician crosses to his hospital schedule by the doorway, his shoes squeaking on the linoleum. "I can do the operation—"

"An operation?" Her throat tightens, her voice thin.

"Yes—to remove it. This tumor could be cancerous, Mrs. Hill." Dr. Eastman flips through his medical datebook, pages rustling as he checks his availability. "If we leave it, it might grow and jeopardize your other organs. You wouldn't survive that. You're 39, correct?"

Kermit nods, her eyes fixed on the calendar, the dates blurring together.

"We need to schedule it right away, preferably before the end of the month."

Kermit wants to cry but feels only numb, disconnected from her surroundings. As she changes back into her clothes, her fingers fumble with the buttons on her black-and-white striped dress. On her way out, she assures the office nurse that she will call to confirm the surgery date once she clears her schedule. In the fading afternoon light, she wanders the medical building's parking lot, trying to remember where she parked. When she finally slips behind the wheel, hot tears sting her cheeks. With trembling hands, she rummages through her handbag and finds her cotton handkerchief. She waits in the car, watching the blur of coming and going vehicles, until she feels strong enough to drive back to Tiny Tot.

Mrs. Oliver greets Kermit at the door with her tan coat buttoned and navy purse draped around her arm. "How'd it go?" she asks as the two embrace.

"Okay," Kermit responds, not ready to rehash the diagnosis. She hears her children's raised voices in the back of the school, their banter animated.

"Good," the teacher says. She retrieves a manila envelope protruding from her purse. "Here's the tuition I collected today. Most everyone paid, a few said they would bring it next week."

"Thanks so much for staying late," Kermit says. She takes the envelope, then holds the door for her. "See you next week."

The clicks of Kermit's heels echo along the empty classrooms, bouncing off the walls as she straightens child-sized furniture and checks locked doors around the nursery school. Patrice follows closely behind her, chattering constantly, her voice a bright counterpoint to her mother's silence.

"I finished my homework already, but I need you to sign it. Augustus Jr. said my hair was ugly because my ponytail came loose."

Kermit barely nods, climbing the stairs to their living quarters while her sons run past them in heavy footsteps.

"Stop running," Kermit calls after them. "I want to see your homework after dinner."

When Kermit reaches the top of the stairs, she sees her mother waiting expectantly, leaning on her wooden cane for support.

"What did the doctor say?"

Instead of answering, Kermit embraces her. She breathes in the familiar scent of rose soap as tears begin to fall again. She cries not only for the upcoming surgery, but for how deeply she values her mother's steady presence through these difficult times. The two women hold each other, swaying gently.

"Aww, I love you too," Arvolin replies, swiping away tears with the back of her hand.

"Let's wait until Augustus gets home and the kids are in bed," Kermit says, glancing at her watch. "I better get dinner started." She helps her mother walk down the corridor to the kitchen.

At a quarter to ten, Augustus, Kermit, and Arvolin gather around the yellow and white Formica kitchen table, bathed in the warm glow of the overhead light. Kermit runs her palms over the smooth, cool surface as she repeats her doctor's words, holding back her tears. Her eyes glisten slightly as she recalls the line from the familiar bedtime prayer her children recited a few moments ago: *If I should die before I wake, I pray the Lord my soul to take.* The words hang in the air as her deepest fears begin to surface.

"What am I going to do? I don't want to have an operation, but what if I have cancer? Dr. Eastman said I could die if I don't take it out!"

Augustus and Arvolin reach for Kermit's hands at the same time, their touch warm and steady, offering comfort even as they grapple with the same terrifying thoughts. Augustus wraps his arm around Kermit's shoulders and pulls her close.

"You're not going to die, honey. We'll figure it out."

Arvolin squeezes her daughter's hand, her grip firm and sure. "You're in God's hands, baby. He will protect you."

Another week passes in a blur as Tiny Tot prepares for next month's graduation ceremony. The whirlwind of activity does little to distract Kermit, who continues to fret over her upcoming surgery.

On Saturday, May twenty-third, she drops her sons off at church in their khaki Boy Scout uniforms, the cotton fabric crisp with starch. The scent of worn papers and floor polish fills the fellowship hall as she escorts them to their troop meeting. Folding chairs scrape across the floor as the boys settle in.

On her way out, she spots Geraldine arriving with Ronald and Dewayne, and stops to chat with her friend. The two women slip into the empty sanctuary and settle into the last pew. Afternoon sunlight streams through the stained-glass windows, the only source of light in the otherwise darkened room. Kermit confides in Geraldine about her physician's diagnosis, her voice a soft whisper in the quiet space. Her friend's tears trigger her own, and they embrace, swept up in the gravity of the moment.

"What am I going to do?" Kermit asks, tearfully revealing her premonition on Geraldine's shoulder. "I have a terrible feeling that I'm going to die on the operation table."

"Oh, Kermit, don't say that," her friend says, gently rubbing Kermit's back in soothing circles. "Your family needs you. I need you too. You've got to be strong."

Geraldine retrieves a thin cardboard packet of tissues from her olive handbag, offering them to Kermit before taking one herself. They dry their tear stains, Kermit blowing her nose loudly, the sound echoing in the empty sanctuary.

"Look, Kermit, why don't you go to my doctor and see what he says?" Geraldine suggests taking another tissue from the pack. "Maybe he can treat your tumor without surgery."

A Boy Scout's mother swings open the sanctuary door, the creak of its hinges echoing off the vaulted ceiling. She stops short when she spots the women, the looks on their faces revealing the serious nature of their conversation. "Oh, I'm sorry," she whispers, backing out of the sanctuary.

Once the swinging door stills, Geraldine continues, "What do you think? Why don't you at least give him a try?" She searches her purse, the contents shifting with soft clicks and rustles, locating a pocket-sized leather-bound telephone book.

Considering her friend's suggestion, Kermit says, "You know I never even thought there may be another solution besides surgery."

"I'm not saying for sure, but it's at least worth a try." Geraldine retrieves a pen and hastily scribbles her doctor's information on the back of a receipt, the ink flowing dark blue across the paper. "Here," she says, placing it in her friend's palm.

"Thank you." Embracing Geraldine again, she says, "I guess it couldn't hurt."

After discussing it with her family, Kermit makes an appointment with Geraldine's doctor for the following week. With Dr. Eastman's June deadline approaching, she feels like time is slipping away.

On the last Wednesday of the month, scattered showers linger throughout the day, cooling the air to ten degrees below the previous day's eighty-seven-degree peak. Twelve days after her initial doctor's visit, Kermit sits on a different examination table, the paper beneath her rustling with each nervous shift. Following an initial consultation. Dr. Sampson conducts a complete physical exam, obtaining blood and urine samples. To Kermit's dismay, the doctor informs his anxious patient that the results will not be available until the following week in June. The timeline conflicts with Dr. Eastman's clear instruction that she should undergo surgery this month.

She drives home in distress, her hands gripping the steering wheel tightly. After dinner, she returns to the kitchen table and shares the latest development with her husband and mother, anxious over the dilemma she faces in addressing her growing tumor.

"Look-a-here," Augustus begins, settling beside her on the sofa. "You told this new doctor that Dr. Eastman wants to operate this month, right?"

"Yes," Kermit sniffs.

"Well, he must think you'll be okay if you hold off a week. He thinks it's important to get these tests back first."

"That's right, Kermit," Arvolin agrees from her chair. "If the surgery couldn't wait, this doctor would tell you. Plus, we're going to keep praying about it."

"Thanks. I guess you're right," she concedes, her head resting in her palm. She calls Geraldine to share the update, and the two discuss Kermit's predicament late into the evening.

On June 3rd, Kermit returns to Dr. Sampson's office, tightly gripping her husband's hand. Augustus has received approval to take the morning off so he can accompany her to the follow-up appointment. In the warm sunlight streaming through the physician's office, the couple waits in silence, anxious to learn whether the test results confirm that surgery is Kermit's only option. Twelve minutes stretch endlessly, each tick of the wall clock sounding like the countdown of a time bomb. When the physician finally taps on the door, Kermit draws in a sharp breath, bracing herself for the diagnosis.

Dr. Sampson introduces himself to Augustus, who rises as the two men shake hands. He greets Kermit before settling behind his desk. Augustus returns to his seat, wrapping his fingers tightly around his wife's.

The steady ticking of the clock grows louder in the silence as the physician opens the top medical chart and reviews the results. After studying her blood work and urinalysis, he looks up, smiling.

"I know you have been worried about the test results, so I will not make you wait any longer. It is good news!" His grin broadens. "There is no tumor at all," Dr. Sampson says, his smile widening. "Congratulations. You are expecting a baby."

For a moment, Kermit remains silent, the words failing to register. Her mind clings to the last two weeks—the diagnosis, the fear, the thought of leaving her children motherless.

She blinks at him. "I am... pregnant?"

Augustus squeezes her hand. "Yes, baby. It is not a tumor. It is a baby."

Her breath catches. "But... Dr. Eastman said it might be cancer."

Dr. Sampson nods. "I understand. It happens sometimes that we doctors get it wrong. We are not perfect. But your lab work confirms the pregnancy. That is a new life growing inside you."

Kermit presses her hand to her stomach, stunned. A sharp laugh breaks free—half sob, half relief. Tears roll down her cheeks as she leans into Augustus, the weight of weeks lifting from her chest.

She thinks back to her whispered prayer on the exam table, the words she never finished.

If it is Your will...

Maybe this is the answer.

A New Princess is Crowned

November 22, 1959

G olden autumn leaves drift across the Turner School parking lot on Billups Avenue as the Hill family arrives for the seventh annual coronation ceremony. The clear, crisp air of the late November evening drops the temperature to forty-five degrees, ten degrees lower than the daytime high. Against the cloudless sky, the school's Art Deco brick facade rises with geometric patterns, standing prominently in the Ville neighborhood. Originally designed for Stowe Teachers College, its clean modernist lines and decorative elements set it apart from other schools in the St. Louis community.

Augustus helps Kermit out of the passenger side, holding both hands as she steadies herself on the cold pavement. She sways slightly between her swollen feet, then releases his grip once she feels stable. She presses both hands against the small of her back to ease the persistent ache. She still thanks God for Geraldine's recommendation to seek a second opinion when her doctor misdiagnosed her pregnancy as a tumor. Chills run down her spine whenever she imagines what could have happened if she had followed his advice for surgery. After learning the seriousness of Dr. Eastman's near-fatal error, she never wants to see his face again. Since then, she has become Dr. Sampson's most faithful patient.

At forty, the physical toll is far greater than it was during her last pregnancy at thirty-three. She struggles to maintain her demanding routine as Tiny Tot leader, wife, and mother to three elementary school-aged children. At each check-up, she asks Dr. Sampson how much longer she has, always hoping for an earlier due date. His answer remains the same: the baby will come when ready. Desperate to move things along, Kermit eats spicy food, takes daily doses of castor oil, and climbs stairs repeatedly—all to no avail.

After the difficult start to her pregnancy and the heartbreak of losing Elmer DeWayne, all she wants now is a healthy baby for Christmas.

The family approaches the Turner School entrance, which rises several feet above the sidewalk. Red brick walls frame large windows that catch the last rays of sunlight filtering through bare branches. Twelve-year-old Hugh takes his mother's free hand while Kermit grips the cold metal handrail tightly to climb the steps. Her pace is noticeably slower than when they came for Tiny Tot's fashion show in April. Augustus Jr., now ten, and his seven-year-old sister race ahead to hold the door open, while Arvolin carefully alternates between her cane and son-in-law for support.

Inside the foyer, Kermit scans the space for a place to sit. Her legs tremble from the effort of climbing the steps. She enters the darkened auditorium, walking slowly toward the last row of wooden stadium seats. Augustus guides his mother-in-law to a seat beside her, then leads the children to the locker rooms to change into their costumes.

"How are you feeling, Momma?" Kermit asks as she slips off her fox shoulder wrap. She straightens the white Peter Pan collar of her navy A-line maternity dress, then smooths out the wrinkles with her palm. Stretching her legs forward, she rotates her ankles to reduce the swelling.

"Me? What about you? You sure you're not going to have that baby right here?" Arvolin chuckles. She leans her cane against the adjoining seat and unbuttons her emerald wool coat.

"That would be fine with me," Kermit says, shifting as the baby moves inside her womb. "I'm ready for this child to come."

A distinct click resonates through the beige and gray walls as the stage lights flicker on, bathing the thirty-foot stage in an amber glow. Kermit feels a familiar pre-event energy surge through her body, momentarily brushing aside the fog of pregnancy fatigue. A vibrant painted backdrop reveals the fairy tale world of "Star Land," with rolling meadows, distant castles, and royal courtyards. Decorative banners, flags, and floral arrangements line the stage, glowing under floor lamps with blue and purple gel filters. For the first time in seven years of Tiny Tot events, her pregnancy had kept her from helping with preparations the day before. This is her first glimpse of the finished set. The elaborate design, orchestrated by Maybelle Walker and the parents' club committee, renews Kermit's excitement.

"I need to get things ready," she says, energized by the anticipation of the children's performances. "Let me get you to the front row for a better view."

An hour later, more than a hundred attendees fill the venue, every seat offering a clear view of the elevated stage. Wearing red and white capes and hats, Heralds Hugh and Jacquelyn Walker appear first, unfurling scrolls to summon the members of the majestic court. Flower girls in white dresses scatter rose petals along the carpet runner that stretches from the entrance to the stage. Male attendants in tuxedos escort their maids of honor in flowing gowns, the couples gliding down the aisle with practiced grace.

A trumpet sounds, signaling the presentation of the royal golden crowns. Mary Smith's son, Rodney, and Emuel Long carry them on silk pillows. As the familiar strains of "Pomp and Circumstance" play, the newly appointed king and queen enter. King Kenneth Thurman Jr. wears a purple velvet robe trimmed with white ermine over his suit. Queen Rita Singleton's white gown features a fitted bodice and a full skirt that trails behind her.

From her chair in the stage wings, Kermit directs each act with quiet gestures and whispered cues. She signals Vicki Chapman, portraying Goldilocks, to begin her dance at the three bears' cottage; urges Rene Kirkland, dressed as Little Red Riding Hood, to flee from the Big Bad Wolf; and gently coaxes a hesitant Santa Claus to lead his pixies onto the stage before the finale. The coronation concludes with "In the Green Meadow," a Czechoslovakian scene featuring dancing children—including her two youngest.

At the end of the ceremony, Kermit steps forward with a warm smile, her voice full of gratitude as she thanks Tiny Tot's children, teachers, parents, and friends for helping create such an extravagant coronation. Her eyes sweep the crowd, glowing with pride. With a gentle wave, she calls her children from their story groups, motioning for them to join her at the front of the stage.

Shading her eyes from the glare of the spotlight, she scans the seated assembly. "Gus? Where are you?" she calls. "I need you to come up here, too, please."

The audience responds with polite applause, and a few rise in their seats, craning their necks in search of Augustus' whereabouts. Moments later, he steps out from behind the curtains, his brow slightly furrowed and his expression bemused, as if caught off guard. Kermit extends her arm toward him, her face softening. He steps forward, joining her and their children at center stage. A flicker of surprise crosses his face as he takes in the audience's attention. He glances at Kermit, then to the applauding crowd, the corners of his mouth lifting in an appreciative smile.

Taking his hand in hers, Kermit turns back to the crowd. "I want to introduce Mr. Augustus Hill to those who may not know him," she says, her voice rich with affection. "He's not only my husband of eighteen years and the father of our three children here, but he's also the owner of Tiny Tot Nursery School."

She pauses as the audience rises to their feet in a standing ovation. Augustus' eyes widen before he gives a modest nod. He gently squeezes Kermit's hand, visibly moved by her public recognition. When the applause quiets, she continues, her voice thick with emotion. "He's often working behind the scenes, like he was just now. But I want to make sure you know who he is and how much he does for Tiny Tot. Be sure to thank him if you see him around."

Another wave of applause ripples through the auditorium, warmer and more personal now. Augustus' twinkling eyes glisten as his smile deepens. He lifts a hand in a humble wave, touched by the crowd's acknowledgment.

Kermit shifts between her feet, her legs aching from the prolonged standing. She rests a hand on her protruding belly and brings her remarks to a close. "And as you may have noticed, we're expecting an addition to our Tiny Tot family any moment now."

Laughter spreads across the room, light and affectionate. On stage, the children giggle along with the audience, unsure why but caught in the moment.

"Thank you for coming out on the Sunday before Thanksgiving," she says, wrapping her arms around her family. "From our family to yours, have a wonderful and safe holiday."

Once the Turner School auditorium empties, Augustus makes a final walk-through to ensure everything is in order before the Hill family heads home. Kermit links arms with her mother, their steps slow and relaxed as Augustus pulls the car to the entrance. Their children pile into the front and back seats, voices tumbling over each other as they excitedly recount the night's performances. As Augustus and Kermit help Arvolin into the car, she lets out a familiar chuckle. "Well," she says with a playful grin, "I guess I'm not getting another grandchild tonight after all."

Following the excitement of Sunday's coronation, Tiny Tot remains open for three more days before closing for the remainder of the week in honor of Thanksgiving. Kermit welcomes the four-day break, secretly hoping the baby will arrive during this quiet window. Thursday brings unseasonably cold weather, with temperatures stuck below thirty-four degrees—one of the coldest Thanksgivings in recent memory. Overcast skies cast a silvery light through the fogged-up panes of the Hills' white-framed windows. Outside, frost clings to the front lawn and outlines the bare branches along North Newstead Avenue in shimmering white.

Thankfully, Lulu Scott graciously invites the Hills to join her family for Thanksgiving next door, sparing Kermit the exhausting task of preparing a full holiday meal while heavily pregnant. Though her neighbor urges her to bring nothing but her appetite, Kermit insists on contributing a dessert— something easy enough to prepare from the kitchen table.

That morning, with Arvolin calling out instructions from her chair, Kermit guides her children through the recipe. They take turns mixing the boiled sweet potatoes with butter, eggs, and evaporated milk, while sticky orange fingerprints and bursts of laughter fill the room. Kermit carefully rolls out the dough, sending a dusting of flour onto the floor. Once the pie is in the oven, the children scramble to clean up the mess—this time without complaining about the chore. As they dress for dinner, the comforting scents of cinnamon, nutmeg, and vanilla drift warmly through the house.

Even though the Scotts live just steps away, crossing the bitter cold requires coordination. With Arvolin's limited mobility and Kermit's slowed pace, Augustus takes charge. He assigns Patrice and Augustus Jr. to help their mother, while he assists his mother-in-law. He entrusts the sweet potato pie to twelve-year-old Hugh, who cradles it like a priceless treasure. Bundled tightly in coats, scarves, and gloves, the six of them brave the cold and manage the short walk in time for dinner.

Milton Sr. opens the door with a warm smile and welcoming "Happy Thanksgiving!"

The savory aromas of sage, roasted turkey, and simmering greens waft out into the cold. Lulu calls her greeting from the kitchen, and Kermit and Arvolin join her to lend a hand with any last-minute preparations.

Meanwhile, the Scotts' twelve-year-old twins, Elizabeth and Milton Jr., whisk their children off to the basement to play. The fathers retreat to the living room, settling into a conversation over cigarettes.

"Time to eat!" Lulu calls from the basement door, prompting the thunder of children's footsteps rushing up the stairs. The adults gather around the dining room table, exquisitely set with lace, china, and tall, flickering candles, while the children crowd around a nearby card table, already giggling among themselves.

From the head of the table, Milton Sr. rises and glances around at the smiling faces. "Let's bow our heads to thank the Lord for this day," he says, then offers a short, heartfelt prayer. Taking up the carving knife, he slices into the perfectly roasted golden-brown turkey.

The meal begins in earnest as steaming dishes are passed around—macaroni and cheese, candied yams, dressing, and collard greens. The children, classmates at the same school, dive into an animated exchange about playground gossip and who got in trouble last week. The adults, long-time neighbors and friends, settle into warm, easy banter, their conversations flowing effortlessly.

After dinner, they bring out the sweet potato pie, with its crimped edge of the crust baked to a perfect golden color.

"I made that," Augustus Jr. yells.

"No, we all made it," Patrice interjects. "Isn't that right, Mommy?"

"Yes," Kermit chuckles. "All three of you did a great job."

The three siblings sit taller, eager for their work to be tasted. As slices disappear from plates and compliments are exchanged, they proudly accept the praise, grinning at one another. Despite the bitter cold outside, the house glows with warmth, laughter, and the satisfaction of full stomachs. No one is in a hurry to leave, and the evening lingers comfortably into the night.

Later, back at home, the Hill household settles into a quiet calm. Coats are hung, shoes kicked off, and the children change into pajamas. Among themselves, they whisper about the lone sleeping cot in the basement where Milton Jr. says his father sleeps some nights. Augustus helps Arvolin to her room and then heads to the kitchen to make a pot of coffee, the familiar sound of the percolator beginning to bubble.

Kermit changes into her nightgown, then meets Augustus in the kitchen with a soft sigh, one hand resting on her belly. In that moment of silence, her thoughts drift to the months ahead. With her children in elementary school and her schedule already stretched thin by Tiny Tot's growing enrollment, the idea of starting over with an infant feels both joyful and daunting.

She gazes around the room, thinking about how her household will change once the newborn arrives, bringing sleepless nights, diapers, and constant feedings. On top of the added layer of responsibilities, she wonders how this little one's disposition will fit with her other children—all with unique personalities of their own.

As the percolator boils, Augustus returns with two steaming cups, the rich aroma of coffee filling the space between them. She smiles gently.

"Well, are you ready to start over with a new baby?" Kermit asks, her eyes searching his, unsure of her own reply.

He hands her the coffee and sits beside her. "We've done it before," he says, placing a hand over hers. "And we'll do it again—together."

A deeper sense of calm settles over her. She has done hard things before. With help from Augustus, her mother, and the community she has built, she knows she can find a new rhythm.

On Tuesday, December arrives under clear skies, creating a mild winter pattern with temperatures in the low fifties. Late Wednesday afternoon, cooler air drives temperatures into the thirties as the pale orange sun hangs over the horizon. Buttoned in his wool coat, a three-year-old boy plays blocks with Patrice while Kermit waits by the door for his mother to pick him up. The expectant mother wraps a crocheted blanket around her shoulders, her stocking feet propped on a child-sized chair. A chill creeps through her body, and she pulls the blanket tighter as she watches the clock.

Ten minutes later, the front door swings open, letting in a sharp gust of frigid air.

The child jumps up, abandoning his blocks, and runs into his mother's open arms.

"Hurry and close that door," Kermit calls, more sharply than intended. Then, softening her tone, she adds, "It's cold out there."

"Oh, okay," the mother says apologetically, turning to shut the door behind her. The glass rattles in the frame as it closes. "I'm so sorry for being late. I thought my husband was picking him up today." She rummages through her purse and pulls out cash for the late fee. "Here you go. It won't happen again."

"Thanks," Kermit says, rising to avoid another burst of cold air. "I understand. You two have a good night. See you tomorrow."

That evening, after dinner, Kermit retires early, her discomfort growing. Her body temperature swings between hot and cold, and she struggles to find a comfortable position in bed. She rises, pacing the hallway's hardwood floor in her bare feet, one hand on her belly. The baby's movements are stronger now, rhythmic and insistent.

Augustus helps pack a small suitcase, while Arvolin assists Kermit with getting dressed, pausing with her daughter through each deep breath and contraction. By ten o'clock, the unmistakable rhythm of labor contractions convinces her it is time to go to the hospital.

Arvolin stays behind to watch the sleeping children. At the doorway, she pulls Kermit close and whispers encouragement before letting her go. Augustus grips his wife's hand as they walk into the frigid evening. Under the amber glow of streetlights, he drives through deserted streets, one hand on the wheel and the other clasping hers.

Kermit braces herself against the car door during each contraction. Her face tightens with pain, a thin layer of perspiration forming across her brow.

"We're almost there, baby," Augustus says, squeezing her hand.

They enter the affluent, predominantly white, Central West End neighborhood, arriving at the medical complex on South Kingshighway Street in just under fourteen minutes. Without exchanging a word, the parents' shared grief resurfaces as they somberly recall the five days they spent on this very campus at Children's Hospital. On November 17th, almost eight years ago exactly, their thirteen-day-old son, Elmer DeWayne, passed just a few steps away. Both try not to look at the substantially larger building, but their eyes reflexively glance at the towering, renovated structure as they drive past.

Augustus turns into the parking lot of the imposing eight-story St. Louis Maternity Hospital, its brick and concrete façade looming against the night sky. He bypasses the brightly lit main entrance and pulls up at a smaller side door marked "Colored Patients." The wind howls between the buildings as he helps Kermit from the car, both bracing against the icy gusts.

Inside, the white receptionist, no older than twenty, directs them to a dim waiting room with faded wallpaper and worn furniture. Kermit shifts in a rigid wooden chair, gripping the armrests when the pain hits.

When Augustus eventually returns from the segregated parking lot, half a mile away, he panics seeing his wife still waiting to be admitted. He returns to the reception area, reminding the staff of the urgency of her condition. "My wife is in labor," he says calmly but firmly.

"I'll see what I can do, Augustus," intentionally addressing him with disrespectful familiarity. His throat tightens as he swallows his frustration, not wanting to risk his wife's medical care. He joins his wife, who shuffles along the ceramic tile floor, doing anything to quicken her delivery and end her agony.

Fifteen minutes pass before a nurse finally arrives at the doorway, glancing at the long list of names on her clipboard. "Kermit Hill?" When Augustus responds to her, she instructs, "Follow me."

He kisses Kermit and hands the nurse her suitcase. She accepts it with obvious reluctance. Kermit leans heavily on the railing as she follows the nurse down a narrow, dim staircase into the basement.

The maternity room holds six narrow beds separated by thin curtains, where several other women rest fitfully. The air carries the sharp antiseptic smell of disinfectant mixed with ammonia, and the once-white walls now appear a dingy gray. Kermit notices the small, high windows that let in only slivers of light from above, reminding her of the years she spent in the basement of the Colored Pulaski County Probation Office in Little Rock.

For the next hour, Kermit joins the unanswered chorus of mothers pleading for something to ease their labor pain. Due to the medical staff's false assumption that Negroes possess a higher pain tolerance, the nurses either ignore their patients or offer patronizing responses such as, "You'll be okay."

Shortly after midnight, a nurse wheels Kermit to the delivery room when her intense labor pains become continuous. The wheels of the gurney squeak against the floor as they move through the narrow corridors. At forty minutes past midnight on December 3rd, she gives birth to a healthy baby girl, weighing six pounds, eleven ounces.

The doctor gives the infant a quick examination, his cold hands efficient and impersonal. "Strong lungs," he announces. "Healthy color." He passes the baby to the waiting nurse.

When Kermit hears her daughter's first piercing cry echoing off the sterile walls, she exclaims, "Thank you, Jesus!" in relief.

The newborn's slick red hair surprises her, a vivid contrast against her translucent tan complexion. The nurse wraps the shivering infant in a hospital towel, giving her mother a brief glance before turning away.

"We need to get her cleaned up and to the nursery," the nurse says, already moving toward the door. "You can see her later today at feeding time."

The moment passes too quickly. Kermit watches the nurse carry her daughter away, her arms aching from the sudden emptiness.

Later, Augustus learns both mother and baby are healthy. He relaxes in a waiting room chair, his eyes heavy with exhaustion. When he is finally allowed in, he crouches beside Kermit's bed and kisses her damp forehead.

A nurse appears behind him, her voice sharp in the quiet room. "Sir, you'll need to leave now. Visiting hours are this afternoon from two fifteen to three thirty, and again at seven in the evening."

Augustus grips his wife's hand. "I'll be back as soon as they let me," he promises, his voice tight with frustration.

She watches him leave, then turns her face toward the small basement window where dawn begins to filter through the glass.

Outside, the December sky grows brighter as the temperature climbs toward fifty-eight degrees. The radiator hisses softly, sending bursts of dry heat through the corridor. Kermit lies in the narrow bed, listening to the sounds of the other mothers and their restless sleep—soft whimpers, the rustle of thin sheets, occasional footsteps in the hallway above.

She drifts into an uneasy sleep, dreaming of her baby daughter in a distant nursery, cared for by strangers rather than her motherly touch.

A few hours later, Kermit awakens to gentle nudging from the morning staff. When she opens her eyes, she sees her newborn's precious face and red hair in the arms of a smiling nurse.

"It's feeding time," the nurse says, her expression much kinder than the night staff. "Have you nursed before?"

"Yes," Kermit replies, reaching for her daughter with eager arms. "I nursed all three of my older children."

The nurse gently transfers the cooing infant into the anxious mother's outstretched arms. "Well, you're an old pro," she chuckles softly.

"Well, I don't know about a pro, but I feel a little old," Kermit quips, bringing her baby closer. She inhales deeply at the top of her head. "Oh, and there's nothing like that newborn smell."

"So true," the nurse replies warmly. "I'll leave you two alone to get acquainted. I'll be back in an hour. Don't forget to feed her."

Kermit opens her daughter's soft pink blanket, counting aloud as she checks ten perfect fingers and ten tiny toes. She rocks the infant gently, softly singing the same "Rock-A-Bye Baby" lullaby she once sang to her other children. Her voice is a quiet whisper, careful not to disturb the sleeping mothers nearby.

Eleven days after Tiny Tot's Royal Coronation ceremony, a new little princess is born into the Hill family by the name of Francene Mary Diane Hill.

FIRE SALE

June 16, 1963

Seven months after Tiny Tot's coronation last November, Kermit sits on an Iota Phi Lambda Business and Professional Women's panel celebrating One Hundred Years of Negro Businesses. The youngest of the family, red-haired Francene, stays close to her mother at Tiny Tot events, Jack and Jill meetings, and the school gatherings of her older siblings. Kermit often marvels at the twelve-year gap between Francene and their oldest, Hugh, who runs cross-country in his sophomore year at Sumner High School. She and Augustus balance the demands of raising four children across wide age ranges while he works full-time at the post office and supports their thriving childcare business.

On the third Sunday in June, Tiny Tot's graduating class of thirty-three breaks the school's record as the largest in its twelve-year history. Following the preschoolers' processional to Mendelssohn's *War March of the Priests*, Valedictorian Sharon Burnett and Salutatorian Karen Thomas address the audience. Each classmate joins in the commencement performances with songs, stories, and plays related to the theme, "A Good Beginning." Among the graduates stand Tiny Tot royalty—Queen Rhonda Williams and King Elvis Ballard—waiting to receive their diplomas. The class poses proudly on the front lawn in their white caps and gowns under overcast skies, the cool summer afternoon air carrying the scent of fresh-cut grass and approaching rain.

As Tiny Tot's summer program begins on Monday, their Irish neighbors next door mention they are preparing to move. Augustus and Kermit seize the opportunity, asking to tour the house and assess its potential as a childcare facility. The structure and layout practically mirror their own, promising minimal renovation.

That evening, a warm breeze flows through open windows while Augustus and Kermit meticulously evaluate Tiny Tot's budget. Dining room lamps cast pale yellow light across their work spread over the mahogany table. At one end, Augustus sorts through a cardboard box of bills, bank statements, and receipts, organizing them into neat piles. Sheets of yellow graph paper cover the table's surface—some tallying monthly income from tuition and fundraisers, others showing line items for salaries, insurance, supplies, and utilities. Kermit's fingers tap rhythmically on the numbered keys of a mechanical adding machine, metallic clicks punctuating the quiet evening as she verifies the school's expenditures in each category.

"I've double-checked the figures, and they all add up," Kermit says, tearing the curved white paper tape along the serrated edge of the machine. "We show a profit for the last year and a half."

Augustus nods, reviewing the list of repairs he compiled during the walkthrough. "Their house was built the same year as ours," he says, jotting down another item in his spiral notebook. "But they didn't keep up with the maintenance. We'll need to spend a lot more to bring it up to code for the nursery school license."

Kermit sinks into her chair with a groan. "So, in addition to the mortgage, we'll also need to factor in repair costs."

"Right. We can show steady income from my job and Tiny Tot's tuition. Plus, we've built up sixteen years of equity in this house."

"And the additional space will bring in more tuition..."

"And more expenses," Augustus interjects. "We need to cut some costs on all your weddings and coronations."

"What? We're already reusing most of the decorations and props," she begins, then catches herself. "But I suppose we can tighten our belts further."

Augustus pulls a cigarette from the pack in his shirt pocket, lighting it as he inhales the burning tobacco. Smoke streams from his mouth as he searches his wife's face. "So. Are we doing this?"

Kermit looks up from her papers, meeting his gaze. "We've been talking about finding a bigger space for some time now. Next door practically fell in our laps. I don't think we should pass this up."

He takes another drag from his cigarette, flicking ash into a small ceramic dish. "All right then." Standing to reach the top sheets of graph paper, he scans them to compare the totals. "You know, I'll be the first to admit, I wasn't completely on board when you started the nursery school. But there's no arguing with the success of the program. I think it's time for us to find a new place and have Tiny Tot take up both buildings."

Kermit grins, recognizing her husband's commitment to expanding Tiny Tot beyond its current reach. Their partnership in marriage and business aligns to provide quality childcare to the St. Louis community. When he notices her expression, a knowing smile spreads across his face. She stands and kisses him, wrapping him in a tight embrace.

"I'm so glad to hear you say that," she says, releasing a deep breath. "It's a big step, but I agree one hundred percent. The daycare business is really booming. If we can swing it, now is the right time to make a move."

"Okay, let's get started. Gather all the paperwork so we can type up a proposal. I'll make an appointment with Lindall Trust to see if they'll approve us for a mortgage, and hopefully a little extra to renovate the place. We need to meet with the real estate agent and our tax accountant, too."

The following day, the couple meets with their neighbors, expressing interest in purchasing the home. As they inspect the residence more carefully, Augustus points out malfunctioning items and provides estimated repair costs. Once the neighbors negotiate an acceptable offer, Augustus writes them a hundred-dollar check for the earnest money deposit. On a handshake agreement, they promise to hold the property for one month while the Hills secure financing.

Over the next few weeks, Kermit and Augustus begin the process of purchasing their neighbors' property while locating a new home for their family. They meet with real estate agents and business advisors to discuss financing, property taxes, and projected income. When they apply for the mortgage, supplying their extensive credit portfolio, the bank officer offers them two separate loans to cover the home purchases, but at a higher interest rate than the one advertised in the branch materials. Although the manager insists that their credit rating is to blame, they believe racial discrimination is the real culprit. Seeing no other viable options, they accept the loans and begin packing up their upstairs residence at 3212 North Newstead. They close on the property next door on the first Friday in July and purchase a new family home the following week.

On weekends and after work, Augustus throws himself into renovating the two-story building for its planned fall opening. He enlists his teenage sons to help with the project. An industrial-sized fan circulates humid July air while Augustus and his sons repair leaks in the roof, patch and paint drywall, and replace worn floorboards. Under the direction of his friend, Billy, a plumber, Augustus installs child-sized bathroom fixtures on both levels. After checking fire safety requirements with the St. Louis Fire Department downtown, he installs electric smoke detectors, emergency exit signs, and fire extinguishers throughout the facility.

While managing Tiny Tot's summer camp schedule of swimming, field trips, and picnics, Kermit focuses on recruiting more children to occupy the new site. Since the nursery currently offers after-school care, she includes enrollment of school-age children up to twelve. She notifies current Tiny Tot families of their expansion plans, then reaches out to families through neighborhood recreation centers and churches' Vacation Bible Schools.

By the first week of August, most renovations are complete, encouraging the couple that their September opening date remains achievable. As Augustus powers through remaining tasks with his sons, Kermit runs newspaper advertisements featuring a photograph of the new building annex alongside Tiny Tot's current facility. The caption lists the school's services while encouraging parents to enroll for the upcoming school year.

8-30-1963 Tiny Tot New Building Annex St. Louis Argus Newspaper Ad

The final requirement for the new facility's nursery school license is the fire safety inspection. After multiple failed attempts citing schedule conflicts, the Fire Marshal finally agrees to visit on Thursday, August 22nd—less than two weeks before the school year begins.

On the morning of the inspection, Kermit takes the beautiful weather as a good sign that the inspection will proceed smoothly. The sun blazes in the cloudless sky while a warm breeze keeps temperatures in the mid-eighties. Augustus takes the day off from the post office so he can personally escort the Fire Marshal through all the fire safety upgrades. He rises early, dresses in his gray pinstriped suit, then heads next door to conduct a final walkthrough before their eleven o'clock inspection. Selecting a lavender skirt suit, Kermit hurries their children through breakfast, dropping their daughters off at Tiny Tot before meeting her husband next door.

Posted above the doorway, a wooden sign identifies the annex as "Tiny Tot Nursery School" in bold, bright letters. Inside, a "Welcome" banner hangs across the foyer, accompanied by colorful brochures announcing the September opening. The scent of fresh paint and pine wood fills the area, and newly installed floors shine beneath overhead lights. Playrooms contain child-sized furniture, new toys, and books, while framed artwork depicting Mother Goose nursery rhymes lines the walls.

At the scheduled inspection time, they peer anxiously through the window, opening the front door to welcome his arrival. When no one arrives after fifteen minutes, Kermit paces in the foyer while Augustus stands on the sidewalk, scanning the street for their expected visitor.

Half an hour later, Kermit joins her husband outside beneath the harsh midday sun. "Do you think he got lost?"

"I don't know. I haven't seen a red car or anyone driving slowly." He shields his eyes as he continues to check both directions of the street.

"It was so hard to get him scheduled," Kermit sighs, furrowing her brow. "Should we call to see what happened?"

"Hold on, I think I see him," Augustus says. "From here, he doesn't look happy."

A red sedan cruises toward them with a flashing red beacon light rotating on the roof. Behind the wheel sits a white man with a thick, gray handlebar mustache visible through the windshield, his flushed facial expression radiating impatience and annoyance.

He parks at the curb, steps out, and places a white peaked cap with a black visor and gold badge over his salt-and-pepper hair. From the front seat, he retrieves a clipboard and a worn code handbook, its frayed cover and yellowing pages showing their age. His double-breasted navy jacket gleams with gold buttons, gold crossed bugles pinned to the collar, and his matching trousers bear a narrow red stripe down the seam.

He checks the house number, then begins up the stairs—looking straight through Augustus and Kermit, despite passing within feet of where they stand.

"Good morning!" Augustus calls, stepping toward him with Kermit by his side. "Are you here for the inspection at 3208 North Newstead?"

The man stops short, visibly startled. "That's right," he replies, his expression revealing that he had not noticed them until Augustus spoke.

"We're Mr. and Mrs. Hill. The owners." He extends his hand, which the inspector ignores.

The fire marshal's brow furrows. He glances at his clipboard, then at the house, then back at them with visible confusion. Finally, he mutters, "Well, I didn't expect y'all would be Negroes."

The couple exchanges glances before Augustus responds. "Let's show you around. It's all ready for you." He gestures toward the red brick structure, then waits for Kermit before following the inspector inside. "Do you want to start upstairs and work your way down?"

Without responding or introducing himself, the fire marshal pushes past them into the rooms, with the Hills following closely behind. When he stops to examine the fire extinguishers and exit signs, Augustus says, "Those are brand new. We made sure to get the ones they recommended downtown."

Kermit and Augustus exchange worried looks as the marshal continues his silent inspection. He opens the back door and glances outside, then moves to the kitchen. While he checks the stove fixtures, Kermit tries to engage him in conversation.

"We're looking forward to making this a welcoming place for our Tiny Tots," she starts. "Do you have any little ones at home?"

After a quick glance, he slams the oven door shut and heads for the staircase. "Augustus, let's take a look upstairs."

"Right this way," he responds, bristling briefly at the inspector's familiar use of his first name.

As Kermit starts to follow, the marshal blocks her path. "You stay here," he says, then continues after Augustus, leaving a confused Kermit behind.

When the two men reach the landing, she hears Augustus say, "Over here is the playroom." From her position at the bottom of the stairs, she listens as their footsteps grow softer, moving farther down the corridor in silence. When they stop, all she can make out are muffled voices; she cannot distinguish what is said. Cautiously, she places one foot on the first step and leans in, trying to catch more, but all she hears is the inspector's voice, deliberately hushed. She feels certain that whatever he is saying means bad news. After a few soft clicks of a ballpoint pen, she hears Augustus again. A few more whispers are exchanged, then the footsteps begin returning. She quickly steps back down and pretends to stack the brochures by the door.

The two men descend the stairs, the fire marshal in front, eyes set on the door.

"Everything okay?" she asks, intentionally lifting her tone to sound lighthearted, despite her feelings of dread.

He breezes by her without a word, the door slamming in his wake.

She turns to her husband as he steps into the foyer, his eyes burning with rage. "What happened? What's going on, Gus?"

"He wants money." Augustus' normally calm, measured voice comes out much louder than usual as he loosens his tie, removes his jacket, and drapes it over the banister knob.

"Money for what?" Kermit asks, fearing she already knows his response.

"Fifty dollars—under the table—to pass the inspection."

"Oh, I knew it," she spits. "He just looked racist from the start."

"He's mad we're over here making something for ourselves. Saw how we're ready to open up and wants to put a monkey wrench in it."

"What did you tell him?"

"Said I didn't have it, and he basically said it was the only way he was going to pass our inspection."

"Oh, Gus, he knows he has us over a barrel. We can't open without his say-so." Pursing her lips, she leans against the door frame, glancing around the new classroom, ready for children.

Augustus moves through the rooms, turning off lights and casting them into shadows, with faint afternoon sunlight streaming from the windows. "He's supposed to call back next week to see if I've 'come to my senses.' If we pay him the money, he's not going to stop. Just keep coming back year after year, asking for more. It'll be fifty dollars this time and a hundred the next."

"No wonder he didn't give us his name."

When he returns to the foyer and slips on his jacket, he says, "I'm going to see what I can find out from those people downtown. You call your nursery school contacts. See if they've ever run into something like this."

"Okay, but whatever we do, we need to act quickly." They lock the door behind them and return next door, ready to fight the obstacle in their path.

The following Monday, Augustus uses his lunch hour to meet with the St. Louis Health Department and review the regulations for a nursery school license. After the meeting, he calls Kermit to share the news.

"There's a loophole," he says, his voice quick with excitement. "I can't get into the details right now, but the health department gave us a way around that fire marshal."

Kermit returns the receiver to its cradle, her heart lifting at Augustus' possible solution. Unable to focus on next week's field trip plans, she drifts through the classrooms, watching the summer activities. Hugh and Augustus Jr., now promoted to junior counselors, lead a photography workshop for the older campers, which includes her ten-year-old daughter. She lingers in the nature study session, where her youngest, Francene, names outdoor plants with her classmates. The anxious wait gives her time to see exactly why the addition is worth the fight.

When Augustus arrives home, Kermit greets him at the door. "Tell me," she says. "I can't wait another second."

Augustus pulls a folded document from his pocket, lays it flat on the table. His finger taps the last paragraph.

Kermit leans over, reading. "...licensed plumber... plumbing code..." She looks up. "Not fire code?"

He shakes his head, a slow smile breaking through. "We don't need him to pass us. We just need to find a certified plumber to do the work, and we can get our license."

"How long will that take?"

"I'm not sure, but I called Billy and he's going to check if his company can install the sprinkler system for us. Hopefully, they can schedule it sometime this week."

"You're the best husband any woman could ask for." She kisses him and holds him in an embrace. "Oh, let's pray this all works out," she says breathlessly. "I'm hoping for a miracle."

The next day, Billy tells Augustus that he convinced his company to install the sprinkler system at a discount. However, they are unable to begin work until the following Tuesday after Labor Day. Although disappointed that the annex's planned opening will be delayed, they commission the plumbing company to complete the installation. Once City Hall approves the designs, major construction begins. The contractor runs piping through the ceiling and floors, adds sprinkler heads, and connects the system to the main water line. Roughly three weeks later, the fire suppression system is complete. They file the compliance documents with the Missouri Department of Health and receive their nursery school license at the end of September.

While the sprinkler system is installed, the Hill family of six moves into their new single-family home on Holly Place, just over a mile from Tiny Tot. The two-story brick structure has four bedrooms on the second floor, allowing the teenage sons to choose their own rooms while the three- and nine-year-old daughters share one. Built in 1921, the property features a butler's pantry between the kitchen and dining room and a screened patio overlooking O'Fallon Park across West Florissant Avenue. The move separates the sons' schooling for the first time, as the new district assigns Augustus Jr. to Beaumont High School instead of Sumner, where Hugh completes his junior and senior years.

On Sunday, October 6th, Tiny Tot opens its new annex to a line of smiling families stretching down the block in the unseasonably warm eighty-nine-degree weather. Kermit and Augustus welcome the eager visitors into the renovated nursery school facility. She sports a navy-blue, cap-sleeve dress, belted with a bow, while he dons his navy-blue suit, topped with a blue bow tie. Their three oldest children weave through the crowded space, handing out open house brochures updated to today's date. Left on her own, Francene scurries through the area with her friends from Tiny Tot, exploring the toys, books, and play equipment on both levels. Mary Smith and Cecile Oliver join the three new teachers in introducing parents and children to their modern classrooms. Parents' Club members circulate, recruiting new members to join their organization. Reporters from *The St. Louis Argus* capture the celebratory event, photographing Kermit, Augustus, the teachers, and Parents' Club members for their Friday edition. Over the hum of excited voices, Kermit and Augustus greet each guest—handshakes, warm smiles, the same words every time: "Welcome to Tiny Tot Nursery School." Outside, the line still grows, neighbors and friends eager to witness the Hills' nursery school dream fulfilled.

MR. AND MRS. AUGUSTUS H. HILL SR. owner and director, of Tiny Tot Nursery Schol, during Open House and Dedication Program, Sunday, October 6

10-18-1963 Tiny Tot Open House, Augustus Hill Sr. and Kermit Hill, St. Louis Argus Newspaper

Silver Anniversary

June 15, 1966

E arly Wednesday morning, Kermit stirs awake as the first slivers of sunlight sneak through a gap in the curtains. She slowly rolls over and squints at the clock. *Five-fifteen? Why didn't my alarm go off?* As she yanks off the covers to get out of bed, she stops and smiles at her sleeping husband. She crawls back into bed and kisses his cheek, his whiskers pricking her lips.

"Happy Anniversary," she whispers in his ear.

Augustus turns to face her, blinking himself awake. "Happy Anniversary to you, too." His voice remains groggy from sleep. He stifles a yawn as he props himself against the headboard, then kisses her lips. "Twenty-five years. It's hard to believe."

She sits up beside him, pulling the blanket over her legs. "Uh-huh. Twenty-five years and four kids."

"We were just kids ourselves back then." He holds her in an embrace. "But you still look as beautiful now as you did then."

"Aww, I don't know about that—especially right now." She chuckles, patting her head scarf concealing hair rollers. "But thank you just the same. And you're still my handsome husband whom I wouldn't trade for anything in the world." She adds the words with a kiss. "But I need to get going. Juanita and her husband are coming in tomorrow. I still need to clean their room and do laundry, so they'll have fresh linens." She turns on her lamp, then steps into her house shoes.

"Where are you putting them?"

"In Hugh's room. When he gets in from Dartmouth tomorrow, he can bunk with 'Gustus Jr. until the Monts leave." Kermit slips on her housecoat, then picks out clothes from the closet. "When does W.C. get in?"

"Friday, last I heard, but he's staying with relatives in town. You know W.C.—we probably won't see him until Saturday." He rises and draws back the two curtains. When he raises the windows, a warm, humid breeze flows into the bedroom.

"Well, tell him not to be late," she says, heading out the door. "We're not running on C.P. time."

***

Three days later, Saturday's first light filters through the open curtains, casting a warm glow across the neatly made bed in Kermit and Augustus' vacant bedroom. Their two daughters compete noisily for turns in the bathroom, while their sons sleep late in the adjacent room. The savory aroma of bacon drifts from the first floor where Kermit prepares breakfast for her house guests, Juanita and Mack Monts. Over coffee, the three friends from Little Rock reminisce about their hometown.

Outside, Augustus inspects the backyard decorated with yellow flowers arranged on white lattice panels. A walnut organ and bench sit propped against the brick wall, with extension cords running from the floor pedals to an outside outlet; yellow umbrellas with white fringe shade patio furniture positioned across the lawn. Crisp white tablecloths cover long serving tables set against the red brick walls of both house and garage. Inside the red wood carport, white wire bird cages filled with yellow flowers hang by the entrance, while white curtains and ribbons frame another serving area. He straightens the white stones circling the flowerbed and birdbath, then aligns folding chairs along the path to the back door.

After serving her guests, Kermit steps into the black-and-white tiled foyer at the foot of the stairs, still holding her metal spatula. "Hugh, 'Gustus Jr., Patrice, Francene—hurry up and come down for breakfast. We need to clear out of the kitchen before the caterers get here."

Upstairs, feet scramble across the hardwood and thump down the carpeted stairs.

Following a hurried breakfast and cleanup, Kermit directs everyone upstairs to get ready for the anniversary party. She instructs her thirteen-year-old daughter to help her younger sister get into her formal dress and leaves her husband in charge of their sons' attire. Juanita assists Kermit with her hair and makeup—just as she had twenty-five years earlier.

As the family dresses upstairs, Geraldine arrives, ready to lead the hostesses comprising Kermit's family and friends. In line with the party's color scheme, the thirteen women wear yellow corsages as they receive the steady arrival of guests. They display the anniversary gifts in the basement recreation room, most made of silver, recognizing the traditional symbol of strength, durability, and lasting beauty of a long-lasting marriage.

Dressed in white uniforms, the caterers commandeer the kitchen, unloading their serving plates and dishes onto every inch of the counters and table. Two men in white jackets, black bow ties, and trousers use toothpicks to expertly arrange cherry tomatoes, olives, and cheese into colorful crudité towers, while three women in white dresses assemble the three-tier anniversary cake.

As guests mingle and sample appetizers in the backyard, an intimate ceremony commences in the living room, witnessed by Geraldine, Cora Mae, Mack, and family. Irving Williamson positions himself behind the guests, ready to photograph Kermit and Augustus' silver anniversary celebration.

Still as uncomfortable in formal wear as he was on his wedding day, Augustus clasps his hands in front of the fireplace as his eyes dart across the room. A formal portrait of Francene and Patrice, both wearing matching dresses with black bodices, white skirts, and cinched with long red sashes, hangs above the mantel, the girls' painted eyes seeming to watch over the ceremony. Beside him, W.C. stands as best man, Reverend Guy officiates, and teenage Hugh and Augustus Jr., nearly their father's height, serve as groomsmen. All four wear white boutonnieres on their white tuxedo jackets, with black bow ties and trousers, while the minister wears a traditional black suit.

Francene enters first, red curls parted at the side, a yellow bow crowning her hair. She carries a bouquet bound with a yellow ribbon and lifts the hem of her yellow bridesmaid dress to keep from tripping. She walks toward her father, who beams at the sight of his youngest child. In a matching dress, her older sister follows in the wedding processional, her wrist-length white gloves clasping her bouquet. Juanita arrives next, wearing a yellow scoopneck dress, her white gloves stopping below the elbows.

As the assembly turns expectantly toward the foyer, Kermit appears at the entrance, the small gathering gasping at her sight. She wears a formal yellow gown with an open-back V-cut bodice, cinched at the waist by a wide, rhinestone-studded band, the embellishment glittering under the living room lights. A yellow netted veil tops her loose curls, and her pearl necklace and earrings complete her elegant ensemble.

She appears to glide down the makeshift aisle, smiling at the sight of her family. When she joins her husband, the wedding party turns to face Reverend Guy. With their maid of honor and best man in attendance, they recreate the wedding scene from twenty-five years earlier. The husband and wife repeat their original wedding vows, renewing their commitment to one another "until death do us part."

Reverend Guy concludes the ceremony, stating, "What therefore God hath joined together, let not man put asunder."

Before their children, friends, and family, Kermit and Augustus seal their renewed vows with a kiss as their children giggle, and the witnesses applaud.

Rushing outside, Geraldine signals the hostesses to distribute small yellow bags of rice to the guests and form a receiving line by the back door. Arm in arm, Kermit and Augustus burst through the back door, showered with rice as the organist performs Mendelssohn's "Wedding March." They cross the yard, now transformed into an elegant reception area, greeting guests under the warmth of the afternoon sun. As their friends and family look on, the honorees proudly pose for pictures with their children under an arched white trellis adorned with yellow flowers.

6-18-1966 Augustus Jr., Francene, Hugh, Kermit, Augustus Sr. Patrice Hill, 25th Wedding Anniversary Party

Crossing the lawn into the carport, the happy couple admires the towering wedding cake with white frosting, floral accents, decorative piping, and silver flakes. Each layer stacks carefully atop clear pillars, creating an elegant, graduated silhouette. The top tier bears a cake topper with two numbers forming twenty-five, marking their years of marriage.

The guests gather around the carport to catch a glimpse of the traditional wedding cake ceremony. The photographer captures Kermit and Augustus joining hands to hold the silver server, slicing a piece from the bottom layer of the dessert. Laughter and cheers erupt as Kermit feeds Augustus a piece of cake while more photographs preserve the moment.

Classical organ music provides the backdrop of the June celebration. Guests form a line to partake in the savory dishes presented on silver platters across the white linen tablecloths. Wearing their matching hostess corsages, Tiny Tot teachers, Mary Smith, Cecile Oliver, and Vernessa Bruce, replenish food trays and refill the punch bowls. The caterers circulate with platters of delicate sandwiches and slices of cake.

Francene, unwilling to wait in the long line, finds her mother talking with members of Jack and Jill, where Kermit serves as president. With her Tiny Tot classmates, William McKinney and Carol Elazier, she interrupts.

"Mommy, do I have to wait in line with all those people?" Francene points to the line stretching across the yard and along the walkway.

Kermit looks apologetically at her friends. "Say 'excuse me.'"

"Excuse me. But can't we just go get the food since it's our house?"

"No, that wouldn't be fair to all our guests," she says, turning her daughter toward the line. "You have to wait your turn like everyone else."

As Francene and her friends reluctantly join the end of the line, Augustus comes beside his wife, sharing the good wishes guests have offered. They look over the manicured lawn, where friends and family mingle.

"They've known each other since Tiny Tot," Augustus says, nodding toward their sons, joking with Deborah and Arthur Jr. Dupree by the carport.

Kermit spots their oldest daughter talking to Nancy Jones by the organist. "Them too. And now they'll be starting high school together at Lutheran North."

"Tiny Tot not only gives kids a head start in school, but it also helps them make lasting friends."

"Same for us," Kermit adds. "We've made so many friends through Tiny Tot. Just look around—parents and teachers here, celebrating with us."

Laughter punctuates lively conversation as old friends reconnect, sharing how they first met the Hills. The photographer moves discreetly through the gathering, even climbing to the second-floor balcony outside Hugh's bedroom for bird's-eye views of candid party moments.

Once guests have gone through the buffet, Augustus and Kermit invite friends to the serving table. The caterers weave through the crowd, popping bottles to fill coupe glasses for the anniversary toast. Surrounded by loved ones, they lift their glasses—not only to mark twenty-five years of marriage, but to honor everyone who has supported them.

As the sun begins its descent toward the horizon, the party takes on a golden quality under the spreading branches of the mature trees shading the backyard. As guests begin to leave, Kermit and Augustus thank them individually for joining in the celebration. Twenty-five years later, they finally enjoy the grand wedding they had delayed under the shadow of Augustus' military draft. Today's anniversary party represents the culmination of the life they have built together and the love that has sustained them through every challenge.

EPILOGUE

Augustus H. Hill Sr. Child Development Center
January 8, 1984

A crisp winter morning dawns over St. Louis, with temperatures hovering near thirty degrees. Frost glistens on grassy patches along the sidewalks and oak trees lining the Ville neighborhood. Inside the red brick building at 3201 North Newstead, the sounds of footsteps and moving furniture echo through the rooms. What began two years earlier as Augustus Hugh Hill Sr.'s vision finally becomes a reality. Tiny Tot School of St. Louis is now available to a younger generation of six-week-old infants to two-year-old toddlers who can receive the care and early education they deserve.

Kermit adjusts her corsage, a charming arrangement of red and white carnations, white baby's breath, and a red bow. As the Director of Tiny Tot School, she ensures her corsage is identical in size and detail to those of today's teen and adult hostesses, underscoring how much she values their contributions and wants them to feel appreciated. Her attention to detail is just one reason her childcare business is the gold standard of the St. Louis community, now celebrating over three decades of quality service. She has invested countless hours preparing for this moment, determined to fulfill the dream of her late husband. The ribbon-cutting ceremony and open house are scheduled to begin at three o'clock, followed by the dedication ceremony. Despite the January chill, she expects a full house for the opening of their newest facility, which spans both sides of the entire block.

Assisting their mother with the preparations are her three adult children: Dr. Augustus H. Hill Jr., Patrice Smith, and Francene Hill, who all hold officer titles on the Tiny Tot School Board. Their oldest brother and fellow board member, Hugh Hill, is unable to attend the celebration, as he is stranded in New York for work. Following in her mother's footsteps, Patrice operates the Florissant location of Tiny Tot School in St. Louis County.

"How are you doing, Mommy?" Francene asks. The youngest of the Hill children, she arrived seven years after her older siblings—an unexpected surprise that brought fresh joy to the family. "Are you ready?"

Kermit purses her lips, her composure wavering as memories of her husband threaten to overwhelm her. Following their five-year courtship and forty-two-year marriage, she spent most of her sixty-four years with Augustus by her side. They shared an intimate knowledge of each other that no one else in the world did. Now, less than three months after his sudden passing, the grandmother of five struggles to imagine leading their family and Tiny Tot without his steady presence.

"No," she chuckles, her black eyes sparkling with her ready smile. "But the show must go on." Sporting an elegant red and white outfit, Kermit smooths the wool fabric of her classic red suit and tightens the red bow around her white blouse. A fascinator hat adorned with white feathers and tulle sits atop her silver-gray curls. "I really wish Augustus could be here today. He worked so hard on getting this building ready." She blinks away tears threatening to fall on her almond-toned face, then dabs her nose with her handkerchief.

Originally built in the early 1900s, the transformation of the solid Victorian-style structure took months of planning and renovation. Surprisingly, the former funeral home proved ideal for conversion into a childcare facility. High ceilings maximize natural light from large windows, while the covered porch creates a homelike environment. The building's façade has been restored to its original grandeur. Fresh white paint highlights the trim against rich red brick, and a large sign stretches across the front porch announcing "The Augustus H. Hill, Senior Child Development Center. Infant Care Through Kindergarten."

As the appointed hour approaches, cars begin arriving along Newstead Avenue. The sound of car doors slamming echoes in the cold air as families bundled in winter coats emerge from vehicles. The scent of fresh paint mingles with the aroma of coffee and baked goods prepared for the reception. Brand-new cribs, colorful toys, and white cabinets fill rooms with newly installed sandy-brown tile floors that will withstand the daily activity of small children.

Francene moves through the gathering crowd, her 35mm camera capturing candid moments that honor her father's dream. She beams with pride, wearing a red carnation corsage pinned to her white sweater jacket, which tops her light blue plaid skirt. As she welcomes guests to the open house, she reunites with friends, classmates, and cousins she has not seen since attending graduate school at Penn State University.

The small mantle clock chimes three times as Elder Robert Pruitt calls the assembled crowd to order. Harsh winter sunlight provides little warmth for the sixty-plus attendees who huddle together to celebrate this milestone in the brisk forty-four-degree weather. The crowd includes current and former students, parents, members of the childcare community, city officials, and supporters of the Hill family's early education journey.

Geraldine Williams, Kermit's friend of thirty-six years, attends the grand opening with her daughter, Felece Brown, and grandson, Alonzo. He joins Patrice's daughters, Jerolyn and Jackie, as they run from room to room, exploring the newly installed features. As a testament to the bond between their families, Kermit is Felece's godmother, and Geraldine is Francene's. Additionally, Augustus Sr.'s cousins, Marion Evans and Preston Bosley, attend to honor the Hill family's milestone.

"Let us bow our heads in prayer," Elder Pruitt begins, his deep voice carrying easily through the crisp air. "Heavenly Father, we thank You for this day and for the vision of Augustus, which lives on through his family and continues to serve our community. Bless this building, bless the children who will learn within these walls, and bless the teachers and staff who will care for them. In Your holy name we pray, Amen."

The crowd responds with a unified "Amen" before Dannie Saines steps forward. At four years old, she embodies the confidence that comes from the school's nurturing environment.

"Welcome to the grand opening of the Augustus H. Hill Sr. Child Development Center," Dannie announces, her voice carrying clearly across the crowd. "We are proud to welcome our littlest children to our Tiny Tot family. Thank you all for coming to our special celebration."

Wallen Appleby, William McMath, and James Harrison offer brief remarks. The three men share their experiences working alongside Augustus Sr. in the construction and renovation process. When he passed last October, they were able to successfully carry on the mission, following the explicit vision he left behind. Each speaker emphasizes Augustus Sr.'s passion and explains how the facility embodies his dedication to the community.

The ceremony's highlight arrives when Augustus Jr. invites his mother and sisters forward for the ribbon-cutting. Dressed like the young surgeon he is, the Hill's second-oldest son wears a white boutonniere pinned to his gray wool jacket, layered over a cream sweater, olive tie, and black pants. Following the courteous training instilled by his father, Augustus Jr. assists his mother up the concrete stairs. Francene joins them in front of the building's entrance, followed by their sister Patrice, wearing the turquoise blue dress suit with a polka-dot blouse her mother purchased for the occasion.

1-8-1984 Augustus Hill Sr. Building Ribbon Cutting, Augustus Hill Jr., Kermit Hill, Francene Hill, Patrice Smith

Each sibling stands proudly beside their mother as they grip large scissors poised to cut the red and white ribbons stretched across the white porch columns.

"This new building represents our future," Augustus Jr. announces to the crowd, his features reflecting a younger version of his father. "We stand here today as a family, united in our father's vision and committed to carrying forward his legacy. The babies and toddlers who will soon fill these rooms represent hope for our community and promise for tomorrow."

A St. Louis Post-Dispatch reporter directs the guests to join the countdown to the final event. He aims his camera, clicking the shutter repeatedly to capture the exact moment Kermit and her three children cut through the silk ribbons. When the ribbons separate, a cheer erupts from the crowd. The Hill family embraces as applause echoes off the brick buildings lining the street. The ribbon pieces will be saved as mementos, framed and displayed in the school's office as a reminder of this historic day and the work that made it possible.

Following the ribbon cutting, Kermit's cousin, Bishop Carl Austin, offers the dedication prayer. His words are solemn and heartfelt, acknowledging both the joy of the moment and the tremendous responsibility that comes with caring for the community's youngest children. The winter air carries his voice as he asks for God's blessing on the building and all who will work and learn within its walls.

The formal ceremony concludes with closing remarks from Kermit, who has served as Director of Tiny Tot School for over three decades. Standing before the gathered crowd, she reflects on the journey that brought them to this moment.

"When I first proposed this idea to my husband back in 1951, he thought I was crazy," she says, her voice lifting with gentle humor as the crowd chuckles along. She continues, keeping her voice steady despite the emotion evident in her eyes. "Eventually, he came around, becoming my greatest supporter. Later, he retired from the post office to work at Tiny Tot full-time. I would not be here today without his continuous support—not only at the nursery school, but as a devoted husband and father."

She pauses, scanning the faces of former students, current parents, and community supporters. "Thirty-three years later, here we stand in our beautiful new facility, ready to welcome the youngest members of our community. Mr. Hill may not be with us in body, but his spirit lives on in every child who walks through these doors."

The crowd erupts in applause, many wiping away tears as they remember the man whose vision made this moment possible. Augustus and Kermit's three children exchange glances, their eyes glistening as they remember their father's steady presence that will no longer anchor their lives. Though he did not survive to see the ribbon cutting, his thoughtful guidance and gentle spirit will live forever in their hearts.

Following the dedication ceremony, guests stream inside for tours and refreshments. The open house allows prospective parents to explore every corner of the building, asking questions about curriculum, staff qualifications, and enrollment procedures. Tiny Tot alumni mingle with young students who roam the new building with wide-eyed wonder.

Visitors marvel at the nursery areas with their cushioned rocking chairs and pristine changing stations. The toddler rooms feature low tables perfect for art projects and snack time. Despite the cold, visiting children test the outdoor play area, their laughter ringing out as they try playground equipment secured within quality fencing.

"Where Your Child Is Taught With Care" has served as Tiny Tot School's motto since its founding in 1951. Every detail of the new facility reflects that commitment. Colorful artwork created by current Tiny Tot students brightens the walls, while educational materials fill every corner—books, puzzles, blocks, and toys carefully selected to stimulate young minds.

In the large playroom, a beautiful cake decorated with yellow, red, and green flowers and the words "Tiny Tot Nursery – Welcomes You" is served. The sweet aroma of vanilla and buttercream mingles with the scent of fresh coffee. Kermit cuts the first slice while amateur and professional photographers capture the moment. The Hill children share stories with guests about their childhood years in the early days of Tiny Tot, when the school operated from the first floor of their family home.

As the event winds down and guests begin to depart, Kermit walks through the empty rooms one final time. The late afternoon sunlight casts long shadows across the tile floors. The dream she and Augustus shared for so many years has finally become reality. As she turns off the lights and locks the door, Kermit allows herself to feel the tremendous void left by the loss of her soulmate. The Augustus H. Hill Sr. Child Development Center will serve as a living memorial to her husband's vision and dedication, ensuring that his commitment to educational excellence continues to benefit future generations.